The Information Systems Academic Discipline
IN AUSTRALIA

The Information Systems Academic Discipline
IN AUSTRALIA

Guy G. Gable, Shirley Gregor,
Roger Clarke, Gail Ridley,
Robert Smyth (Editors)

ANU
THE AUSTRALIAN NATIONAL UNIVERSITY

E PRESS

E PRESS

Published by ANU E Press
The Australian National University
Canberra ACT 0200, Australia
Email: anuepress@anu.edu.au
This title is also available online at: http://epress.anu.edu.au/info_systems_aus_citation.html

---

National Library of Australia
Cataloguing-in-Publication entry

Title: The information systems academic discipline in Australia /
                editors Guy G. Gable ... [et. al.].

ISBN: 9781921313936 (pbk.)
                9781921313943 (pdf)

Subjects: Information technology--Australia.
                Information technology--Study and teaching (Higher)
                    --Australia.
                Information storage and retrieval systems--Research.

Other Authors/Contributors:
                Gable, Guy G., 1954-

Dewey Number: 004.6

Cover design by ANU E Press

Cover ilustration by Jackson Gable

Table of Contents

Foreword

This book represents the second phase of a multi-method, multiple study of the 'information systems academic discipline in Australia'. In the first phase, conducted between 2005 and 2006 and drawing on Whitley's theory of scientific change, the study analysed the degree of 'professionalisation' of the information systems (IS) discipline, the overarching research question being, 'To what extent is IS a distinct and mature discipline in Australia?' Completion of the first phase of the study was marked by publication, in December 2006, of a special edition (vol. 14, no. 1) of the *Australasian Journal of Information Systems* (*AJIS*).

The second phase of the study, reported in this book, has sought to address several constraints and limitations in the first phase. To begin with, it was felt that the potential long-term significance of this first examination of the IS discipline across Australia warranted a more permanent documentation of its findings to complement the medium of the *AJIS* publication. A main aim of the study is to initiate a continuing, longitudinal evaluation of the state of the IS academic discipline in Australia. The study has, from the outset, been designed and executed with the expectation that it would be extended and repeated over time. A book offers an appropriate form to set down an initial long-term reference.

A book format also offered the opportunity to extend the work. A limitation of the first phase of the study was that—from necessity rather than choice—the theory framework continued to evolve in parallel with the progress of the individual research tasks. Hence, there is some variation among first-phase papers in relation to application of the theoretical framework. The second phase of the study allowed the researchers to further analyse the data in terms of the more complete theoretical framework described in Chapter 3.

In this second phase of the study, it was decided that the history of the progress of IS in the Australian states could be honoured through brief vignettes of a sample of the men and women who had made major contributions to the advancement of IS in those states.

The first phase of the study did not extend to a consolidated analysis across the completed individual sub-studies. In phase two, the editors undertook to examine the individual revised studies, with a view to arriving at an Australia-wide perspective. This analysis sought to evaluate collectively the data from the individual states in relation to the revised framework. The consolidated analysis also sought to highlight more striking Australian characteristics that emerged from the data but that could not be applied readily to the a priori theoretical framework.

All papers in the 'parent' *AJIS* special edition were subject to a rigorous three-tier peer review process: each paper was reviewed initially by the *AJIS* editors, feedback was provided to the authors and revisions were made. Each paper was then sent to one or more local IS experts; the results of this review were conveyed anonymously to the author of the paper for implementation of consequential revisions. Finally, all papers considered for the special edition were sent to two further IS experts for global review, with feedback from the reviewers again being forwarded to authors for revision of their papers.

The *AJIS* special issue was targeted conceptually at IS academics in Australia, being mainly a 'description' of the current state of things. This book—an extension and expansion of that material—includes further evidence, analysis and interpretation, and is crafted to be more accessible to IS and non-IS types within and outside Australia. It includes a glossary, which provides definitions of terms, expressions and acronyms used by chapter authors but warranting explanation for readers from outside Australian IS academia.

The book chapters were submitted to a review process similar to that for the earlier volume, including: editorial review, local reviews and global reviews. A full draft of the book was circulated widely within Australia in order to ensure balance and completeness of content. The full draft book was also circulated internationally to notable IS experts in the Australian diaspora, as well as to several past presidents of the Association for Information Systems (AIS), which sponsored the study and considered replication in other world regions.

The book chapters are structured around three main sections: a) the context of the study; b) the state case studies; and c) Australia-wide evidence and analysis. The book represents a 'check point'—a snapshot at a point in time. As the first in a hoped-for series of such snapshots, it includes a brief history of IS in Australia, bringing us up to the time of this report. As related more carefully in the 'Contextual framework' (Chapter 1), ideas and views represented herein are not intended to be definitive. Neither do views expressed in all chapters reflect the views of the editors. It is acknowledged that ideas presented are sometimes controversial (even among the editors).

The editorial team comprises: 1) Guy Gable, architect and leader; 2) Bob Smyth, project manager; 3) Shirley Gregor, sponsor, host and co-theoretician; 4) Roger Clarke, discipline memory; and 5) Gail Ridley, theoretician. The study—initiated, designed and led throughout by Professor Guy Gable—would not have been possible without the generous support of the IT Professional Services research program (ITPS), Faculty of Information Technology, Queensland University of Technology (QUT), mainly through Gable's extensive involvement and that of Dr Robert Smyth and Ms Karen Stark, Senior ITPS Research Associates.

While QUT has played the lead, The Australian National University (ANU) has been the main support, through the integral roles of Professors Shirley Gregor and Roger Clarke (thanks are due to the ANU E-Press for production of the final version of this book). Clarke has been involved in the IS discipline in Australia since its inception. His proclivity to hoard discipline-related artefacts and his provocative writing style made him the logical choice to craft the history chapter. The Clarke–Gable collaboration goes back to 1992 when they joined forces to turn Clarke's then Australasian IS faculty directory into an extended Asia-Pacific directory (sponsored by QUT, the ANU and the National University of Singapore), which after two hard-copy editions was combined with the European and Americas directories into the online directory at http://www.isfacdir.org/

Professor Shirley Gregor offered galvanising support for the project from early on, and served as invaluable theory sounding-board for Ridley. Gregor and the ANU hosted several key team workshops and, like all editors, Gregor has been involved closely in meta-analysis across the sub-studies. The ANU also contributed financial support for the copy-editing of the manuscript.

In seeking a theoretician on the evolution of the discipline of IS, Dr Gail Ridley was the obvious choice given her pioneering doctoral studies on IS as a discipline in an Australian context. Though the special issue and book were driven mainly by QUT, the ANU and the University of Tasmania, most universities in Australia have been instrumental in its production by contributing authors, interviewees, in vignettes or as reviewers. We acknowledge particularly the University of Tasmania through the extensive involvement of Ridley as architect of the theory framework chapter, the Tasmanian state case study and the meta-analysis chapter.

We take this opportunity to thank all who have contributed. Finally, we acknowledge seed funding from the AIS—International and from the Australian Computing Society (ACS), the two primary associations for IS academics in Australia (the AAIS being the Australasian chapter of AIS).

Contributors

Janice Burn

Janice Burn was appointed Foundation Chair of Information Systems (IS) at Edith Cowan University in Perth in 1997. She had previously held positions in Hong Kong, Canada and the United Kingdom. Her research interests centre on the strategic use of IS and its impact on organisational effectiveness in a wide variety of global contexts. She has published extensively in these areas and now enjoys a well-earned semi-retirement in the South of France, where she continues to supervise her doctoral students as a virtual professor.

Elsie S. K. Chan

Elsie Chan was born and brought up in the multicultural city of Hong Kong, so she was able to communicate and write fluently in English, Chinese and Putunghua. She started her career on her graduation from the Grantham College of Education, Hong Kong, in 1979 and has held various academic and administrative positions in a prestigious secondary school. She obtained her MSc degree in artificial intelligence at the University of Essex, United Kingdom, in 1989. Since then, she has been lecturing in various universities in Hong Kong, China and Macau, focusing on the development of the long-demanded open education in the region. Before her migration in 1994 to Melbourne, Australia, with her family, she registered as a PhD student at the Chinese University of Hong Kong but had to quit the research project due to her migration.

In Australia, she held various lecturing positions, mostly on a sessional basis, while continuing her research in information technology-related areas. Her achievements during the period were the establishment of closer links between international students and a building up of the relationship between Australian universities and universities in China. In early 2000, she was granted a PhD scholarship by Deakin University, Melbourne, so she decided to shift to a full-time mode of study. Her research focused mainly on e-commerce and education development and, during these years, she published a number of research papers. She also attended various conferences on e-commerce including the CollECTeR conference, which was a pioneer in the international e-commerce area. She completed her PhD degree in 2003 at Deakin University with the e-commerce and marketing integrated research topic of 'New Educational Service Products: Tertiary EC/EB Education—the Asia-Pacific Region'.

In early 2004, she was appointed as IS lecturer in the School of Business and Informatics (Vic), Australian Catholic University, where she dedicated her efforts to the improvement of IS teaching. Since 2006, she has been Course Coordinator of Business Programs at the Australian Catholic University. She is currently supervising IS, business Honours and PhD students. Her continuing research interest is in electronic commerce/electronic business and IS education, web design, service quality and marketing.

Elsie Chan is also committed to the children's section of an evangelical church in order to enhance religious education to youth in the community. As part of her continuous self-improvement effort, she is currently undertaking courses in Christian ministry training and a Graduate Certificate in Higher Education.

Roger Clarke

Roger Clarke is Principal of Xamax Consultancy Pty Ltd, Canberra. He is also a Visiting Professor in the E-Commerce Program at the University of Hong Kong, Visiting Professor in the Baker and McKenzie Cyberspace Law and Policy Centre at the University of New South Wales and Visiting Fellow in the Department of Computer Science at The Australian National University. He holds Honours and Masters degrees in information systems (IS) from the University of New South Wales and a doctorate in IS from the ANU. Since the late 1980s, his focus has been on strategic and policy aspects of e-business, information infrastructure and 'dataveillance' and privacy.

He has been active in the IS profession and discipline since 1971. This has included 12 years each as a professional in Sydney, London and Zürich, as a senior academic at the ANU, and as a consultant based in Canberra. He has been a substantial contributor to the professional and academic literature, including some 80 refereed papers. He has also been active on conference committees in Australia and internationally, on editorial advisory boards and as an editor of proceedings and special issues.

During his time as an academic, he made significant contributions to the development of the IS discipline. He established the first directory of IS academics in Australia in 1988 (which was upgraded in 1991, merged with Guy Gable's Asian directory in 1994 and absorbed into the world-wide online *IS Faculty Directory* in 1996). He was one of the founders of the ACIS Committee. He also established the ISWorld Australia page, and was Foundation AIS Councillor for the Asia-Pacific in 1994–95.

Using this breadth of experience, his personal archives and his knowledge of the people who have been active in IS, he was able to construct from scratch the first-ever history of the IS discipline in Australia.

Guy G. Gable

Guy Gable's career is characterised by movement back and forth between university and practice. His early industry experience as programmer, analyst and systems development manager—and later as a consultant—underpins his need to ground research in practice. His PhD is from the University of Bradford (ICIS'92 1st) and his MBA from Ivey Business School. Post-MBA, he was senior information systems (IS) consultant with Arthur Young in Canada. In 1983, Gable migrated to Sydney to join Price Waterhouse. From 1986 to 1994, as Senior Fellow with the National University of Singapore, Gable was much influenced by Gordon Davis (NUS Distinguished Shaw Professor, 1985–87) and worked closely with notable colleagues K. K. Wei, Chee-Sing Yap and K. S. Raman. In 1994, he joined the School of Information Systems at Queensland University of Technology (QUT), where he is now Professor and Chair of the IT Professional Services Research Program. Since 2002, Gable has spent one month each year at the University of Hong Kong as Visiting Professor. He is Senior Editor (Pacific Asia Region) for *JSIS*, Associate Editor of *MIS Quarterly* and on the editorial boards of the *Journal of the Association for Information Systems, Information Systems Frontiers* and *Australasian Journal of Information Systems*.

He has been at the forefront of Australian IS researchers via his continuing success with Australian Research Council (ARC) grants. He has been, since 1998, chief investigator on seven ARC collaborative grants (worth more than $3 million). He has published more than 100 refereed journal articles and conference papers and books. His research has involved mainly large, long-term projects in collaboration with practice—for example, National Computer Board (Singapore), Accenture (Australia and USA), SAP (Australia and corporate research), CUSC, Queensland Government and the Institute of Management Consultants. Key research interests include information technology (IT) professional services, IT research methods, enterprise systems and IT evaluation.

His successful collaboration with overseas head offices of large international corporations (for example, SAP, Accenture) has been notable. He brought to academia early recognition of the importance of package software and, in 1995, initiated one of the first programs of research and teaching in enterprise systems (ES/ERP). He cultured a collaborative relationship with SAP, which, under his direction, resulted in a contribution of more than $3 million from SAP, Digital and Sun Microsystems to establish at QUT the second international ES Application Hosting Centre. These early successes were undoubtedly influential in SAP's decision in 2001 to create in Brisbane only their fifth corporate research node world-wide.

Guy Gable has represented Australian IS in the region. In 1993, he conducted a comprehensive survey of IS academics in Pacific Asia, convincing Roger Clarke to merge his nascent Australasian directory to form the *Pacific Asia Directory of Information Systems Researchers*, which in 1998 merged with *ISWORLD Faculty Directory* (http://www.isfacdir.org/). In 1997, Gable brought the Pacific Asia Conference on Information Systems (PACIS) to Brisbane—its third running after Taiwan and Singapore—and initiated the first PACIS Doctoral Consortium. He was co-program chair of PACIS'97 and ACIS'00 with Ron Weber and Mike Vitale, co-doctoral consortium chair of PACIS'00 and PACIS'03 with Rutaro Manabe and K. K. Wei respectively, and has represented Australia to the PACIS executive since 1997. Championing this book and its related *Communications of the Association for Information Systems* (*CAIS*) and *AJIS* special issues has perhaps been among his largest contributions to the discipline in Australia and the region.

He has represented Australian IS internationally. He has been involved extensively in the Association for Information Systems (AIS), the main international IS body, including: 1) Nominations Committee, 1997; 2) National Secretary (Australia), 1996–97; 3) Bylaws Constitution Committee, 1997; 4) AIS Affiliated Organisations Committee, 1998; 5) AIS Region 3 Council Member, 1998; 6) Project Leader, 2003–06 AIS in Pacific Asia Region study; 7) *Journal of the Association for Information Systems* Editorial Board member, since 2002; 8) AIS Council nominee for AIS Presidency, 2006.

Shirley Gregor

Shirley Gregor has had a rather varied career, working across a number of different academic areas, in industry as well as academia, and in different geographical areas.

In her undergraduate science degree at the University of Queensland, she studied mathematics and psychology. On graduating, she had a change of direction and became a programmer-in-training (PIT) with the Australian government, based in Melbourne. The PIT scheme is quite famous in Australian information technology (IT) history and was a starting place for many IT professionals in the 1960s and 1970s. A not-quite facetious comment is that at that time the need for computing staff was so great that the government would take just about anybody! The government provided postgraduate training, which, for Shirley Gregor (née Eagles), was at the Bendigo College of Advanced Education. Stints working on the Brisbane City Council and then in IT positions in Glasgow and London followed. The consultancy firm of Datec Pty Ltd hired her in London in 1977 and paid for her to return to Australia to take up a position with its Brisbane office. This offer was a result of another period of shortages of IT staff in Australia, which meant overseas recruitment was in full swing. She benefited from a three-month bus trip across the Middle East and India as the passage home.

Another career change to motherhood followed, then a return to Rockhampton and the first step into academia as a part-time tutor—a position that could be combined with family duties. At this point, she began studying in earnest (for the first time really), and completed a Masters in Applied Science by research, and then a PhD in 1996 with Ron Weber as supervisor at the University of Queensland.

A number of her research interests grew out of her original interests in psychology and philosophy, which has led to work in artificial intelligence, knowledge-based systems and, more recently, the philosophy of technology. Her experience in industry has also led to a focus on the adoption and strategic use of IT in business. While in Rockhampton, she carried out a number of applied research projects with the beef industry and, since moving to Canberra, she has looked at IT in business more generally.

In 2001, she was appointed the Endowed Chair in Information Systems at The Australian National University, Canberra, where she heads the National Centre for Information Systems Research and is currently Head of the School of Accounting and Business Information Systems.

She has been successful in winning a number of Australian Research Council grants and other competitive grant income. Her publications include four edited books, 15 book chapters and more than 100 papers in conferences and journals such as *MIS Quarterly*, *Journal of the Association of Information Systems*, *International Journal of Electronic Commerce*, *International Journal of Human Computer Studies*, *European Journal of Information Systems* and *Information Technology & People*.

Shirley Gregor has contributed to the IT community in a number of ways, including as: inaugural President of the Australasian Association of Information Systems, 2002–03; Vice-President of the Australian Council of Professors and Heads of Information Systems; and, since 2007, Director of the Professional Standards Board, Australian Computer Society.

She was made an Officer of the Order of Australia in the Queen's Birthday Honour's list in June 2005. In 2005, she was also elected a Fellow of the Australian Computer Society.

Ernie Jordan

During his cadetship in industrial mathematics in the United Kingdom, Ernie Jordan gained his first experience of computing on a mainframe with 4 K of memory! On his graduation, the IBM/360 series beckoned and his career moved to commercial 'data processing' from mathematical and statistical applications. It was not long before the COBOL world palled and he returned to university (in Wales) for postgraduate statistics and then his first academic position, in Coventry (UK). Australia made the tragic mistake of accepting him as a migrant so he sailed into Sydney and took up a lecturing position in statistics in Central Queensland.

Four years later, he moved to Sydney to work as an accounts manager with a major computer services organisation that provided state-of-the-art application services to local, national and international companies. He then established his own business developing customised applications on mid-range systems for small and medium enterprises in the Hunter Valley region of New South Wales. He returned to the academic world as a lecturer in systems analysis and design in Newcastle, where he discovered that what he had regarded as the 'secret art' of systems analysis had been fashioned into theoretical frameworks and even textbooks.

A major career transition occurred when he took up a position with City University (then Polytechnic) of Hong Kong. He found an inspiring doctoral supervisor (Bob Tricker at the University of Hong Kong) for his thesis in information systems (IS) strategy. The rapidly expanding City University also threw up many opportunities for leadership in academic development within a new department of IS and the first degree in IS in Hong Kong.

At that time, he specialised in the area of strategic application of information technology (IT), which became concerned increasingly with electronic commerce. He developed and led Macquarie Graduate School of Management (MGSM) electronic commerce degree programs.

Some eight years ago, he carried out research that examined the reluctance of organisations in Australia to develop formal business continuity plans, which led to a more general concern about the risks that IT posed for organisations. For many organisations, that concern finds its way to senior management and board members under the heading of IT governance, which figured strongly in his recent book, *Beating IT risks*—now translated into Finnish and Mandarin.

During the past 10 years, he has had a significant presence within the MGSM, playing key roles in the development of the Doctor of Business Administration (DBA) degree and in the development of a strong research supervision practice within the school. He has supervised some 12 doctoral students to completion during this time. He recently moved from being Director of Higher Degrees Research (HDR) at MGSM to being Director of HDR Marketing and Development with Macquarie International, the international recruitment and partnering arm of Macquarie University.

Andy Koronios

Andy Koronios is the head of the School of Computer and Information Science, in the Division of Information Technology, Engineering and the Environment at the University of South Australia. Andy has degrees in electrical engineering, computing and education and a PhD from the University of Queensland.

Andy has extensive experience in commercial and academic environments and has interests in electronic commerce, information quality, computer security, strategic information management, multimedia systems as well as online learning technologies. He has worked as a consultant as well as a professional speaker on information technology (IT) issues in Australia and South-East Asia.

He has more than 20 years' experience in the academic environment and has received the University of Southern Queensland Award for Excellence in Teaching.

Andy Koronios has established two university research labs and a funded centre. He is currently research program leader of a federally funded centre for system integration in engineering asset management and has attracted more than $2 million in research funding.

He has published 10 books and several chapters as well as numerous research papers in diverse areas such as information security, data quality, electronic commerce, multimedia and online learning.

Edward Lewis

Edward Lewis was professionally educated as a behavioural scientist, with more than 20 years' experience in personnel and information systems (IS) planning. He served in the Australian Army as an infantry officer and as a psychologist, working in personnel research and information technology (IT) policy. Ed has also worked in the Australian Public Service, encouraging the use of IT by business, and as a marketing manager for a large international computer company (now defunct but not because of him).

He has carried out considerable research into the development of aids for decision making, resulting in the 'Select!Gain' and the 'Risk–Remedy' methods that have been adopted by many government agencies for tender evaluation. More recently, he has developed the 'Analysis of networks of Links' (AnnL) tool for systems planning, performance measurement and policy production.

He has presented more than 30 short courses about planning to national and international groups, primarily in the public sector. He has undertaken more than 40 consultancy projects for public and international private-sector organisations, including: ICT governance reviews; strategic planning; business cases; risk management; evaluation of more than 20 tenders; performance measurement; information management policies; and enterprise architecture.

Edward Lewis is the current chair of the IT-030 Committee preparing the Information and Communications Technology (ICT) Management and Governance Standards for Standards Australia.

Chad Lin

Chad Lin is a Research Fellow at Curtin University of Technology, Australia. In the past few years, he has conducted extensive research in the areas of: information systems (IS) and information technology (IT) investment evaluation and benefits realisation, IS/IT outsourcing, e-commerce, virtual teams, e-health, radio frequency identification technology (RFID) and strategic alliances. He has written and published almost 100 internationally refereed journal articles (for example, for *Information and Management, International Journal of Electronic Commerce, European Journal of Information Systems, Information Technology and People, Industrial Management and Data Systems, Lecture Notes in Computer Science* and *Journal of Research and Practice in IT*) and conference papers as well as book chapters. He has also served as a member of editorial review boards for several prestigious international journals.

Craig McDonald

Craig McDonald, PhD FACS, is Associate Professor of Information Systems (IS) at the University of Canberra. For nearly four decades, he has been developing, teaching, researching and consulting for projects for the creation of systems that embody data, information and knowledge. These systems have been effective in the public service, non-governmental organisations, private enterprise and in research organisations.

His continuing research work is in the foundations of the informatics field (especially semantics, modelling and ontologies, and information ethics) and in the responsible application of informatics to the domains of government, health, education and research.

Current research projects include the development of a pragmatic approach to concept analysis and its testing in a semantic analysis of drug intervention policies to reveal the conceptual structure of the illicit drug system (e-health), the incorporation of ethics into project management teaching (e-education), the nature of board-level IS (e-governance) and the human activity systems aspect of e-research. He holds external and internal research grants and has published widely in journals, conferences and books.

His academic experience includes four years at the University of Technology, Sydney, 11 years at Charles Sturt University and seven years at the University of Canberra. He has been visiting professor at the University of California at Los Angeles and twice a visiting fellow at The Australian National University. His teaching experience ranges from technology-based topics such as database and programming to the organisational impacts of systems and information ethics. He currently teaches research proposals and methods, project management and ethics. He supervises PhD and Masters candidates.

He had 16 years in industry before becoming an academic and has maintained a consultancy role. He spent most of the 1990s in technology-based knowledge representation and transfer with the Cooperative Research Centre for Viticulture in managing the development of the 'AusVit' system. He is active in university management and governance, holding the roles of Head of School, the elected academic on the University of Canberra Council, member of the academic board and member of various committees including Information Management and Systems and Academic Workloads.

Craig McDonald is Editor-in-Chief of the *Australasian Journal of Information Systems*, a member of the executive of the Australian Council of Professors and Heads of Information Systems (ACPHIS), an Australian Research Council 'expert of international standing' in IS and is head of the IS discipline at the University of Canberra.

Graham Pervan

Graham Pervan is Dean, Research and Development, at Curtin Business School, and has been a professor in information systems (IS) at Curtin University of Technology since 1996. Graham has a number of research and teaching interests including information technology (IT) adoption and management, IT and business process outsourcing and offshoring, measuring and realising the benefits of IT, the foundations of decision support systems, group support systems and other collaboration technologies. Graham has maintained links with practice as an IT consultant and facilitator.

He began his academic career in 1973 at the West Australian Institute of Technology in Perth. He has held a variety of senior roles, including five years as head of school. Graham has developed and taught programs at the undergraduate and postgraduate levels and in many IS topics, including research methods for Honours, Masters and PhD students in IS. He is also the external assessor for the Master of Information Management program at Victoria University of Wellington, New Zealand. He has successfully supervised eight PhD students to completion and currently has six PhD students.

He has been involved actively with the Australasian Conference on Information Systems (ACIS), having first presented a paper at ACIS in 1992. He was program chair of ACIS 1995 at Curtin University of Technology, Doctoral Consortium chair of ACIS 2003 and presented many papers and panel sessions in the years since, as well as serving on many doctoral consortia. He is a strong supporter of Australian IS/IT journals, having published 10 papers in the *Australian* (now *Australasian*) *Journal of Information Systems* and the *Australian Computer Journal* (now *Journal for Research and Practice in Information Technology*), and serving as a reviewer for both.

Graham Pervan completed a PhD in IS in 1993 and has since focused strongly on research. He is the Asia-Pacific Editor for the *Journal of Information Technology* and the IT Management Editor for the *Australian Journal of Management*. He has reviewed papers for most major journals and conferences. He has published the outcomes of his research in more than 150 refereed journal and conference papers in outlets including the *Journal of Information Technology, Information and Management, International Journal of Medical Informatics, Decision Support Systems, Journal of Computer Information Systems* and the *Journal of Group Decision and Negotiation*.

He has received more than $500,000 in research funding from the Australian Research Council and various industry and other sources. Since 2000, he has been the President of the Australian Council of Professors and Heads of Information Systems, the premier body for IS academics in Australia.

Carol E. Pollard

Equally at home in the southern and northern hemispheres, Carol Pollard has taught in three different countries on two continents in two hemispheres during her 14- year academic career. Her PhD and MBA are from the University of Pittsburgh, USA, where she was fortunate to be advised by William King, one of the founding fathers of the information systems (IS) discipline. In 1991, her first academic appointment took her 'north of the border' to Canada, where she was appointed to the IS department in the Faculty of Management at the University of Calgary, Calgary, Alberta, Canada. As she progressed from assistant professor to associate professor, her skills as a manager and an innovator were evident in her involvement with the development and inaugural delivery of a creative MBA degree that included team teaching, innovative industry projects and 'quick-hit' projects offered to small businesses in the area. In 1996, she relocated to the United States for a short stint at the University of Colorado, Boulder, where she lead the recruitment of IS majors in the Leeds College of Business by delivering the introductory IS course to as many as 500 undergraduates and directing 12–15 teaching assistants per semester.

She moved to Australia in January 2000 to take up a position in the School of Information Systems, University of Tasmania, at the Hobart campus. During her six years there, she served as Assistant Head of School for four years and Head of School for one—before her departure in December 2005. In addition, she worked hard to enhance the research culture of the School of Information Systems through her supervision of a large number of research students at the Honours, Masters and PhD levels, and as Postgraduate Research Coordinator and Masters Program Coordinator. In these roles, she was able to introduce a more positivist approach to the research program by teaching and using quantitative methods and mixed methodology research into the previously exclusively interpretivist, qualitative research culture. She also became heavily involved in the Australian IS community during her time at the University of Tasmania. She represented Australian IS regionally and nationally at conferences (PACIS, ACIS, AMCIS, GITMA) and, in December 2004, she organised the Australasian Conference on Information Systems (ACIS) in Hobart, Tasmania. She also served on the ACIS Executive Committee and has served as a member of the Australian Council of Professors and Heads of Information Systems (ACPHIS) since 2004.

Her research interests include business/information technology (IT) alignment, the impact of emerging information and communications technology (ICT) and technology transfer. Her current research focuses on small to medium-sized firms. She has published in *MIS Quarterly*, *Journal of Management Information Systems* and *Information and Management*. She has presented her research at numerous national and international conferences. Her global influence in the IS field extends from her involvement with the premier information systems conference, ICIS, as its Executive Secretary from 1995 to 1999 to her appointment in 2004 as an international expert assessor for the Australian Research Council. Since January 2006, she has been Associate Professor of Information Systems and Research Director, Center for Applied Research on Emerging Technologies (CARET), at the Appalachian State University, where she enjoys a close proximity to her two sons and their families. She is also Vice-President, International, of the Global Information Technology Association World Conference (GITMA); past chair, ACIS Executive Committee; and an Advisory Board member of Teradata University Network. Her continuing interest in the Australian IS community motivated her to be involved in this study project and she continues to be a loyal supporter of the Australian IS community.

Gail Ridley

Gail Ridley works as a Senior Lecturer at the School of Accounting and Corporate Governance within the Faculty of Business, at the University of Tasmania. Before working at this school, she was a staff member of the School of Information Systems at the same university.

Her first career was in teaching, where she worked in classroom and senior positions in teaching services within and outside Australia. Much of the classroom work was with students using English as a second language. After completing a Graduate Diploma in Science (Information Technology) at the School of Information Systems at the University of Tasmania in Hobart, she started work as an academic. In 2000, she completed a PhD at the same school, looking at the development of the information systems (IS) discipline in Australia and the use of different research methods. Her involvement in the current volume came about as a result of the topic of her doctoral thesis.

Most of her approximately 30 refereed journal and conference papers have examined research methods, information technology (IT) governance and IT control. She was one of the first academics to see the potential of the 'Control Objectives for Information and related Technology' (COBIT) framework for helping organisations to use IT to achieve their business goals. Having been 'COBITised' some years ago, much of her more recent research interests have had a link to COBIT. The IT control and COBIT journey has been a fascinating one, providing her with research settings that have ranged from IT audit in government audit offices to counter-terrorism in the Department of Defence. The background in IT control and IT audit gave her the opportunity to move to her present school.

An interest in textual analysis has led her to use different forms of the content-analysis method in her research. Content analysis has also been used in her contribution to this volume.

Gail Ridley's first career in teaching has manifested itself in the university environment in the rewards she has gained from working with students, and particularly her involvement in supervision of research students. She has been privileged to work with a series of highly able and motivated research students, most notably international students from countries including China and Thailand.

Graeme Shanks

Graeme Shanks is a Professorial Fellow in the Department of Information Systems at the University of Melbourne. Until recently, he was Associate Dean of Research and Professor in the School of Business Systems in the Faculty of Information Technology at Monash University, Australia. Before becoming an academic, he worked for a number of years as a programmer, programmer-analyst and project leader in several large organisations. He has a number of research and teaching interests, including conceptual modelling, data quality, identity management and the implementation and impact of enterprise systems and inter-organisational systems.

He began his academic career in 1982 at the Chisholm Institute of Technology in Melbourne. He was course leader for graduate programs in information technology (IT) and helped to develop the first Australian course-work Masters degree in IT in the mid-1980s. Many years later, he led the restructuring of the Master of Information Systems program at the University of Melbourne. For many years, he has developed subjects in the areas of data management, systems analysis, conceptual modelling, enterprise systems and data warehousing. He has published several papers on curriculum development in these areas. He has successfully supervised eight PhD students to completion.

He has been involved actively with the Australian Conference on Information Systems (ACIS), having presented a paper at the first ACIS in 1990; he was Program Chair of ACIS 1994, at Monash University, and has presented many papers and panel sessions in the years since. At the 1994 conference—together with others including David Arnott, Graham Pervan, Bernie Glasson and Rudi Hirschheim—he helped to devise the 'Evolving Charter' for ACIS, which defines the governance and operation of the conference series. He was Executive Officer of ACIS for several years, helping to ensure the successful operation of the ACIS conference series. He has been an active member of the Australian Computer Society for many years and was elected a Fellow in 1999. He also served on the Committee of the Data Management Association. He has been a member of the Australian Council of Professors and Heads of Information Systems (ACPHIS) for many years.

Graeme Shanks completed a PhD in information systems (IS) in 1997 and has since focused strongly on research. He is a member of several editorial boards, including *Asia Pacific Management Review* (Regional Editor), *Journal of Knowledge Management Theory and Practice, Data Warehousing Journal, International Journal of Data Warehousing and Mining, Journal of Database Management* and the *New Zealand Journal of Applied Computing and Information Technology*. He has published the outcomes of his research in more than 120 refereed journal and conference papers in outlets including *Information Systems Journal, Journal of Information Technology, Journal of Strategic Information Systems, Communications of the ACM* and the International Conference on Information Systems.

He has received more than $1 million in research funding from the Australian Research Council (ARC), including Discovery grants and industry linkage grants. He was a member of the ARC College of Experts from 2004 to 2005, representing the IS community. He has presented seminars on ARC grant schemes throughout Australia and at the annual ACPHIS workshops.

Bob Smyth

Bob Smyth is currently a Research Associate within the Information Technology Professional Services Research Program at Queensland University of Technology (QUT).

After a short career as a high school maths teacher, in January 1969, he joined IBM in its Brisbane Service Bureau, where he worked as a systems analyst. In August 1972, he started as a lecturer in data processing in the Department of Management at Queensland Institute of Technology (QIT). In 1978, after completing a graduate diploma in information processing at the University of Queensland and an MSc at Aston University, he was appointed head of the data-processing section in the School of Business Studies at QIT.

During these formative years of information systems (IS) in Australian tertiary education, QIT had a prominent place—a status maintained after 1989 when QIT became the QUT. It should be said that these early developments of IS at QIT took place in the context of passive resistance from Queensland's Board of Advanced Education, which sought to limit perceived challenges to the domain of existing universities. In 1980, he introduced QIT's first stand-alone postgraduate IS course, a Graduate Diploma in Commercial Computing. He also had some small influence on the development of IS in other colleges of advanced education (CAEs) in the region, serving on advisory committees at Darling Downs Institute of Advanced Education, Capricornia Institute of Advanced Education and Northern Rivers College of Advanced Education. He was also an advisor in business computing to Darwin Community College (the predecessor to Charles Darwin University), and a long-time member of IT advisory committees to the Queensland Board of Senior Secondary School Studies.

His career in IS at QIT/QUT has been a long one. In 1989, he was awarded QUT's inaugural Award for Distinguished Academic Service 'for outstanding teaching and his contribution to major curriculum development in information systems'. Only later did he become involved in formal IS research, although he had regularly contributed papers to the CAE Computing Conferences. He completed his PhD at QUT at the end of 2001. In 2002, he retired from his position as Assistant Dean (Postgraduate) in the Faculty of Information Technology at QUT, returning to QUT later to work part-time in research in the School of Information Systems. His main research interests include IT professional services, computer-aided software engineering and enterprise systems. He has a particular interest in the case-study method. In his recent role as research associate, he has been involved heavily in the guidance of PhD candidates in IS.

Craig Standing

Craig Standing is Professor of Strategic Information Management in the School of Management at Edith Cowan University. He is currently Director of the Web Research Centre and was previously head of the School of Management Information Systems at Edith Cowan University. Craig's work has focused on the adoption and use of electronic markets and he has obtained funding from several sources to support this work, much of which has involved partners from industry. He has also been involved in the adoption of mobile services through his collaboration with academics from Finland. His work has appeared in journals such as *Information and Management, Information and Organization, IEEE Transactions on Engineering Management, European Journal of Information Systems* and the *International Journal of Electronic Commerce*.

He is Chief Editor of the *Journal of Systems and Information Technology* (Emerald) and, along with his co-author, Steve Benson, is the author of a widely adopted foundation text for information systems (IS) courses (published by Wiley). This textbook is now in its third edition. Craig is particularly keen on doctoral supervision and has won several awards for the quality of his supervision.

Paula Swatman

Paula Swatman currently has a double role—first as the Inaugural State Records of South Australia/Fuji Xerox/State Library of South Australia Professor of Business Information Management (BIM) at the University of South Australia. In a world first, this chair was created to develop leading-edge teaching programs that would link the hitherto separate areas of: information management, library studies, records management, archival management, information and communications technology (ICT) and business management.

Her second role is as the continuing Professor of Information Systems (IS) within the School of Computer and Information Science at the University of South Australia. She has significant academic and industry experience—as well as research and teaching interests—in the areas of e-business and e-commerce and many of the newer extensions of this area (such as m-commerce, e-health and e-learning). She spent more than 10 years working in the banking and information technology (IT) industries and developing her interest in e-commerce before returning to academic life in the late 1980s.

Her background lies in the areas of IS and electronic business. Her specialised interests are in the strategic use of e-commerce and e-business; the creation and diffusion of e-business models; the use and application of standards; the evolution of the digital content sector; e-markets and supply chain management; rural telecommunications and the impact of m-commerce on rural Australia; the implications of the World Wide Web and the online economy; and e-learning and education in the 'New Economy'. She returned to Australia at the start of 2004 after three years in Germany as Professor of E-Business and Foundation Director of the Institute for Management at the University of Koblenz-Landau, where she was responsible for setting up and managing the new, Bologna-style BSc and MSc degrees in information management. She won and managed a fifth framework European Commission research grant in the development of new business models for digital content during her time in Germany and, as an adjunct professor, remains involved in research and teaching activities at the University of Koblenz-Landau.

She is active in the program committees of a wide variety of e-commerce and IS conferences, and is also a member of the editorial board of a number of e-commerce and IS journals. As one of the founding members of the CollECTeR e-commerce into universities research group, she organises annual conferences and has managed a number of major research consultation projects for the group.

Jim Underwood

Jim Underwood is a Senior Lecturer in the Department of Information Systems within the Faculty of Information Technology, University of Technology, Sydney (UTS).

Born in Sydney, he began his academic career with an Honours degree in (very) pure mathematics at the University of New South Wales. He continued with tutoring and pursuing a PhD, but a feeling that he was learning more and more about less and less, the realisation that advances in mathematics were starting to depend on how big a computer you had and a belated discovery of the social aspects of university life necessitated a change of direction.

After one term of attempting to teach abstract mathematics to 14-year-old girls who couldn't wait to leave school for the check-out, he moved to English-Electric-Leo-Marconi (later subsumed by ICL), where he was taught to be an analyst programmer and learned about corporate restructuring, communicating with users and the joys of being attached to non-market-dominant technology (he is now a Mac user). This was followed by a happy and successful year with a small start-up consulting company. Nevertheless, disillusion with the ordinariness of most computer applications led to a return to the tertiary sector and another start-up: the computing course at Canberra Collage of Advanced Education, presided over by the incomparable Digby Pridmore. The course catered mainly to the needs of the Commonwealth Public Service and was deliberately labelled Bachelor of Arts in Computing because 'computing wasn't a science'. This was a time of optimism that computing could help promote equality in society. After 18 years, Canberra began to pall and he moved to UTS. This was a much 'harder' computer science environment, so old issues needed to be revisited.

In both these institutions, he was quite involved in administration and course development, and for several periods led the information systems (IS) group.

His academic life has centred on an inevitably fruitless search for a theoretical basis for the practice and teaching of systems analysis, design and development. His political philosophy required that models should be participative and non-hierarchical. Initial investigations involved information theory, control theory and general systems theory, with reference to the work of Ashby, Beer, von Bertalanffy and Emery. The problem that became apparent in the literature was a tendency to apply simplified mathematical or technological models in situations in which no data were available. The need to get focus out of the machine and onto the users and their 'problem' led to more social theories, such as Argyris's organisational learning and Jung's archetypes. On his second attempt at a PhD (finished in 2001), He discovered 'Actor-Network Theory' (ANT), which had the advantage of giving practical guidance to investigations without worrying too much about truth claims. For an understanding of IS development, ANT did need a few additions: Foucault provided a model of intersecting meanings and Deleuze suggested a dynamic for the trajectory of such intersections.

As a result of his complex journey, Jim Underwood, among IS researchers, has one of the widest repertoires of models for applying to real situations of information technology (IT) use, and is one of the least embarrassed at switching models as necessary. This is valuable in communicating with practitioners, understanding a wide variety of IS research and supervising students with diverse interests. Nevertheless, as his career reaches maturity, he is disappointed to see the resurrection of hierarchy and bureaucracy, the business dominance of IT research and the continual pressure to push the meanings of information, knowledge, process, interaction and even satisfaction back into the machine.

David Wilson

Associate Professor David Wilson has teaching and research interests in software quality assurance, software process improvement, project management and information systems (IS) management.

His research collaboration with Tracy Hall of the Department of Computer Science at the University of Hertfordshire spans 10 years. This research focuses on identifying practitioners' attitudes towards software quality and process improvement, determining how these attitudes affect behaviour within the quality process and establishing how that behaviour affects software quality and process improvement. The overall aim is to develop generic strategies and guidelines that organisations can use to improve software quality and software processes by managing software practitioners more effectively within the quality improvement process. Further information is available at http://homepages.feis.herts.ac.uk/~pppgroup/

His research collaboration with David Avison of ESSEC in France spans more than 10 years. This research focuses on IS management issues, particularly the people and cultural aspects of information technology failure.

THE CONTEXT

1. The information systems discipline in Australian universities: a contextual framework

Guy G. Gable
Faculty of Information Technology
Queensland University of Technology

Abstract

This chapter presents the contextual framework for the second phase of a multi-method, multiple study of the information systems (IS) academic discipline in Australia. The chapter outlines the genesis of a two-phase Australian study, and positions the study as the precursor to a larger Pacific-Asia study. Analysis of existing literature on the state of IS and on relevant theory underpins a series of individual Australian state case studies summarised in this chapter and represented as separate chapters in the book. This chapter outlines the methodological approach employed, with emphasis on the case-study method of the multiple state studies. The process of multiple peer review of the studies is described. Importantly, this chapter summarises and analyses each of the subsequent chapters of this book, emphasising the role of a framework developed to guide much of the data gathering and analysis. This chapter also highlights the process involved in conducting the meta-analysis reported in the final chapter of this book, and summarises some of the main results of the meta-analysis.

Introduction

This book represents the second phase of a multi-method, multiple study of the IS academic discipline in Australian universities (the 'IS-in-Oz' study). In the first phase, drawing on Whitley's theory of scientific change—as encapsulated in a framework proposed by Ridley (2006a)—the study analyses the degree of 'professionalisation' of the IS discipline, the overarching research question being, 'To what extent is IS a distinct and mature discipline in Australia?' Completion of the first phase of the study was marked by publication, in December 2006, of a special edition (vol. 14, no. 1) of the *Australasian Journal of Information Systems* (*AJIS*).

Features of the second phase

The second phase of the IS-in-Oz study, reported in this book, has sought to address several constraints and limitations in the first phase. To begin with, it was felt that the potential long-term significance of this first examination of the IS discipline across Australia warranted a more permanent documentation of its findings to complement the medium of the *AJIS* publication. A main aim of the IS-in-Oz study is to initiate a continuing, longitudinal evaluation of the state of the IS academic discipline in Australia. A book offers an appropriate form to set down an initial long-term reference.

A book format also offered the opportunity to extend the work. A limitation of the first phase of the study was that—from necessity rather than choice—the theory framework continued to evolve in parallel with the progress of the individual research tasks. Hence, there was some variation among first-phase papers in relation to application of the theoretical framework. The second phase of the study allowed the researchers to further analyse the data in terms of the more complete theoretical Ridley framework described in Chapter 3.

Articles in the first phase of the study were subject to the standard length constraint of the *AJIS*. These constraints are eased by describing the research outcomes in a book. A feature of the case studies reported in this volume is the addition of vignettes from selected, significant people in the development of the IS discipline. In the second phase of the IS-in-Oz study, it was decided that the history of the progress of IS in the Australian states could be honoured through brief vignettes of a sample of the men and women who had made major contributions to the advancement of IS in those states.

The first phase of the IS-in-Oz study did not extend to a consolidated analysis across the individual completed sub-studies. In phase two, a group of researchers undertook to examine the individual revised studies, with a view to arriving at an Australia-wide perspective. This analysis sought to evaluate collectively the data from the individual states in relation to the revised Ridley framework. The consolidated analysis also sought to highlight more striking Australian characteristics that emerged from the data but that could not be applied readily to the a priori theoretical framework.

This chapter presents the contextual framework for the study described in this book. As such, it provides an overview to put the following chapters in perspective. The chapter examines the place of the IS-in-Oz study as a pilot and subset of a wider study. It reviews the overall design of the study and the role of the component studies described in individual chapters of this book. Finally, it provides the reader with some understanding of the main focus of each of the sub-studies described in the following chapters.

The 'parent' IS in Pacific-Asia study (IS-in-PA) design

This Australian study was derived from a broader study of the state of the IS academic discipline in Pacific-Asia ('IS-in-PA'), the results of which have been published in a special issue of *Communications of the AIS* (*CAIS*). Note that the Association for Information Systems (AIS)—the main international association of IS academics, and sponsor of the IS-in-PA study—organises its activities around three world regions: 1) the Americas; 2) Europe, Africa and the Middle East; and 3) Pacific-Asia. Figure 1.1 depicts the main components of the 'parent' IS-in-PA study. The Pacific-Asia study (and its component Australian study) is motivated by a recognition that IS as an academic discipline has evolved differentially around the world. For example, there is regional variation in the strength of its presence as an academic discipline; it could take on identifiably different local forms—for example, from a soft-systems emphasis to a more technical focus; there could be regional differences in topics taught and researched (as was observed across Europe by Avgerou et al. 1999).

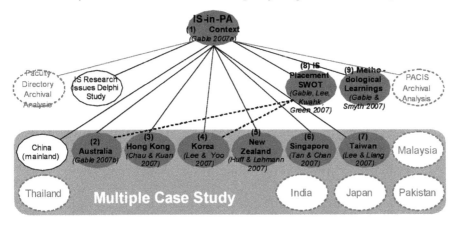

Figure 1.1 The IS in Pacific-Asia region study (IS-in-PA)

The IS-in-PA study includes nine main study components (see Figure 1.1), the principal of which is a multiple case study across six states of the Pacific-Asia (PA) region. It was decided early on to restrict the first iteration of the IS-in-PA study to those areas in the region where IS is relatively more visible internationally—Australia, Hong Kong (China), Korea, New Zealand, Singapore and Taiwan—the intent being in future to extend the study incrementally to other parts of the region (the study is currently being extended to Mainland China, with study initiation also in place in Japan, India, Malaysia, Pakistan and Thailand, for which tentative state study team leaders have been identified). Table 1.1 lists the main IS-in-PA study leaders.

Table 1.1 The IS in Pacific-Asia (IS-in-PA) study team

State	Study leader
Australia	Professor Guy G. Gable, Queensland University of Technology
Hong Kong (China)	Professor Patrick Chau, University of Hong Kong
Korea	Professor Jae-Nam Lee, Korea University
New Zealand	Professor Sid Huff, Victoria University of Wellington
Singapore	Professor Bernard Tan, National University of Singapore
Taiwan	Professor T. P. Liang, National Sun Yat-Sen University

The IS-in-PA and the IS-in-Oz studies have, from the outset, been designed and executed with the expectation that they will be extended and repeated over time. Shaded ovals in Figure 1.1 represent those components that were completed in the first execution, with the detailed Australian results reported in a special issue of *AJIS*. Unshaded ovals represent components that are in progress—for example, Mainland China Case Study, IS Research Issues Delphi Study—and dashed ovals represent planned components soon to begin (note that further study components are expected to evolve).

The phase one Australian study (IS-in-Oz) design

A meeting of a subgroup of the IS-in-PA study team in Auckland in January 2004 (Gable, Huff and Felix Tan, Auckland University of Technology, who was then the elected AIS Region 3 Council Representative) resulted in a proposal to conduct a multiple-case study of the Australian states—the IS-in-Oz study. Table 1.2 lists the main IS-in-Oz study team members. The components of the IS-in-Oz study are shown in Figure 1.2. Shaded ovals represent those components that were reported in the special issue of *AJIS*. Unshaded ovals represent components that were in progress at the time of the *AJIS* special issue. Initial findings of the IS Research Issues Delphi Study have since been reported elsewhere. Preliminary results of the Australasian Conference on Information Systems (ACIS) Archival Analysis are now available and are included later in this chapter rather than reported as a separate chapter.

The IS Research Issues Delphi Study—represented as an unshaded oval in Figure 1.1 and again in Figure 1.2—is an international study of the key issues facing IS researchers. The first round of this study resulted in 266 responses, articulating a total of 1241 issues. Analysis of these issues resulted in a comparatively succinct set of 56 issue statements being synthesised for presentation to IS researchers in the second round of the study. The second round of the study in March 2005 yielded more than 800 responses. Various results from this sub-study, although not reported in this book, have been presented at several workshops in Australia, Hong Kong and Shanghai, and as keynotes at the AIS SIG IS in Asia Pacific (ISAP) of ICIS 2005, and at the Information Systems and Management track (ISM '07) of the IEEE WiCOM 2007 conference in Shanghai (Gable, Stark and Smyth 2007).

Table 1.2 The IS in Australia (IS-in-Oz) study team

Home state	Team member
Queensland	Professor Guy G. Gable, Queensland University of Technology
	Dr Robert Smyth, Queensland University of Technology
Australian Capital Territory	Dr Roger Clarke, Principal, Xamax Consultancy Pty Ltd; Visiting Professor, The Australian National University
	Professor Shirley Gregor, The Australian National University
	Professor Ed Lewis, Australian Defence Force Academy, University of New South Wales
	Associate Professor Craig McDonald, University of Canberra
New South Wales	Professor Ernest Jordan, Macquarie University
	Dr Jim Underwood, University of Technology, Sydney
	Associate Professor David Wilson, University of Technology, Sydney
South Australia	Professor Andy Koronios, University of South Australia
	Associate Professor Mike Metcalfe, University of South Australia
	Professor Paula Swatman, University of South Australia
Tasmania	Dr Gail Ridley, University of Tasmania
Victoria	Dr Elsie Chan, Australian Catholic University
	Associate Professor Carol Pollard, Appalachian State University
	Professor Graeme Shanks, Monash University
Western Australia	Professor Janice Burn, Edith Cowan University
	Dr Chad Lin, Curtin University of Technology
	Professor Graham Pervan, Curtin University of Technology
	Professor Craig Standing, Edith Cowan University

There are 12 shaded ovals in Figure 1.2, corresponding with the 12 completed IS-in-Oz sub-studies reported in the December 2006 special edition of the *AJIS*. These include three conceptual papers ('The contextual framework', 'The history' and 'The theory base') and nine empirical papers (seven state case studies, a research survey and a 'contradictions' piece).

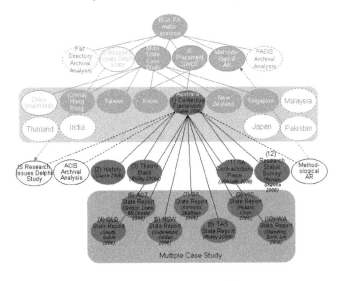

Figure 1.2 The IS in Australia (IS-in-Oz) study

Phase one of the IS-in-Oz study sought to draw on and complement other studies of the state of the IS discipline, notably those of Avgerou et al. (1999) in Europe, and Pervan and Shanks (2004) in Australia. The phase one IS-in-Oz study—being exploratory and descriptive, and to some extent a pilot—did not begin from a highly specific theory base. The Ridley (2006a) theory base evolved throughout the study, largely in parallel with and somewhat influenced by the study.

A key study aim was to evolve and apply (and 'test') a process of evidence collection and review, for future extension and possible replication within the region and across other world regions. This was to some extent addressing past concerns expressed—for example, by Phillip Ein-dor (Gable 2002)—about the lack of a methodology and indicators for tracking diffusion of the IS discipline. It was posited that the establishment of measures and indicators of the state of IS, and a baseline snapshot of its current state, would facilitate tracking of the state and monitoring the effect of initiatives to promote IS as a discipline. While emphasis here is on Australia, many of the ideas, mechanisms and aims are generalisable to all AIS regions. Thus, one overarching aim of the study is to contribute to a general methodology with which to describe and monitor the evolving state of the IS discipline in any region or country. Other more specific study aims included:

- to begin documenting characteristics of IS programs across universities in Australia
- to begin documenting characteristics of IS research across universities in Australia
- to begin assessing the strength of the IS presence in Australian universities
- to evaluate the maturity of IS as an academic discipline in Australia (as per the theory base)
- to identify emerging trends in IS in Australian universities
- to identify the main influences on IS in Australian universities.

Study questions in phase one of the IS-in-Oz study

Study questions and the units of analysis (sometimes the university; sometimes the state) evolved over time—along with the study design—with varying emphasis across the sub-studies.

Broad study questions implicit in the final case study protocol include:

- what is the relative size of the IS presence at the university
- what is the administrative placement of IS (including changes over time)
- to what extent has IS at the university been impacted on by local contingencies
- to what extent is IS identified as a separate field at the university
- what are the distinctive features of the IS curriculum at the university
- what are the distinctive features of IS research at the university

- who are the key people who have had an impact on IS in universities in the state?

The protocol includes a long list of more specific questions, based on each of these broad questions. The state teams varied in their reliance on the protocol.

Questions posed to intrastate reviewers of the state reports included:

- what do you believe to be the main challenges facing the IS academic discipline in your state today?
- what do you believe to be the main opportunities facing the IS academic discipline in your state today?

The next section briefly reviews literature on past studies of the IS discipline and relevant theory. The subsequent section summarises the overall study approach, with emphasis on repeatability—a key study aim. Overall study outcomes are then related. The final section describes study limitations and potential further research.

The literature

Past studies of the IS discipline

Articles discussing the state of IS tend to revolve around one of several themes: 1) the identity crisis within IS; 2) IS as an academic field; 3) the state of IS research; and 4) the evolution of the field of IS. (This section offers a very brief overview of past studies of the IS discipline. Individual chapters in this book make more specific reference to relevant literature.)

One dominant theme is the existence or otherwise of an identity crisis within IS, the concern being that the discipline's central identity is ambiguous (Benbasat and Zmud 2003). There are several articles debating the core and scope of IS. The debate in recent times culminated in a series of 11 articles published in the *Communications of the AIS (CAIS)*. This is an important debate, as the degree of convergence of a discipline can have political implications. 'Convergent communities are favourably placed to advance their collective interests since they know what their collective interests are, and enjoy a clear sense of unity in promoting them' (Becher 1989:160).

The academic field of IS is another recurring theme. Avgerou et al. (1999) comprehensively discuss the academic field of IS in Europe, while other authors tend to focus on one area: the status of IS as an academic discipline (Introna 2003; Khazanchi and Munkvold 2000); IS educational programs (Ang and Jiwahhasuchin 1998; Lo 1989); or the location of IS departments in universities (Sherer 2002).

Articles on the state of IS research include: paradigmatic and methodological examinations of IS research (Chen and Hirschheim 2004; Orlikowski and Baroudi

1991; Vessey et al. 2002); regional differences in IS research (Evaristo and Karahanna 1997); and themes of IS research (Bacon and Fitzgerald 2001; Palvia et al. 2004).

There are two types of articles on the evolution of IS: those that assess the current status of the field by tracing its historical evolution and the driving forces that shape it (Adam and Fitzgerald 2000), and those that gauge the status of IS development and evolution by examining changes over time in topics, themes and research strategies in the literature (Alavi and Carlson 1992; Claver et al. 2000; Farhoomand and Drury 1999).

Relevant theory

The study reported in this volume (as well as the phase-one study reported in *AJIS*) aims to investigate the IS academic discipline in Australia from historical and current perspectives, collecting evidence across a range of dimensions. To maximise the descriptive potential of the study, the results need to be capable of integration, so that the relationships within and across the dimensions and geographical units are understood. A meaningful theoretical framework helps relate the results of the different dimensions of the study to characterise the discipline in the region, and assist in empowering the Australian IS research community. The Ridley theory chapter (Chapter 3) reviewed literature on the development of disciplines, before deriving a theoretical framework for the broader study reported elsewhere in this book. The framework considered the current and past state of IS in Australian universities from the perspective of the development of a discipline. The components of the framework were derived and validated through a thematic analysis of the IS and non-IS literature. The framework developed in the Ridley paper—which has been guided partly by Whitley's theory of scientific change (1984a, 1984b)—was used to analyse data collated from the Australian regions.

Study approach

In this section, study logistics are described. The overall study design is reflected in Figure 1.2. Sub-study methods and methodology are addressed in the individual chapters of the volume. Some details of the case-study method are included below in order to avoid repetition across the seven state case reports.

Overview

The study process was a combination of deductive, top-down broad definitions of aims, questions and procedures, and inductive, bottom-up consideration of sources of evidence, project resources and feasibility. It could be said that early results were mainly inductive, these being followed by a more deductive, top-down review.

Project management

Individual state teams managed their respective case studies, with the overall project managed by Guy Gable (project leader) and Bob Smyth (project manager). The main mechanisms of project management were: 1) a project web site; 2) regular status meetings of the project leader and project manager and related project status reporting by e-mail; 3) face-to-face team meetings when feasible (on several occasions in conjunction with ACIS or the Australian Council of Professors and Heads of Information Systems [ACPHIS]); 4) several teleconference and Skype sessions, as a cost-effective alternative to face-to-face meetings; 5) the case-study protocol served as a valuable mechanism for coordinating the study teams.

Complexities and issues encountered

A range of complexities was encountered throughout the study, some of which were fully or partially overcome; others of which were not. Several pertained to the scope and object of the study: academia versus the profession versus both; teaching versus research; past versus present. There was discussion about the utility of 'state'-based case studies, it being mooted that other groupings of institutions might be more meaningful: for example, 'Sandstone' universities versus the others; large IS versus small IS—that is, based on numbers of undergraduate IS students).

Extending the phase-one study

At a meeting convened by Gable in Canberra shortly before publication of the December 2006 special edition of the *AJIS*, the possibility of extending the study was raised. The meeting agreed that a book would allow the results of the research to be available in a more permanent form—a desirable situation given the potential value of the studies to the IS discipline and given the plan to replicate the study over time. It was agreed that researchers who had authored papers in the *AJIS* special edition be invited to participate in this second phase.

Subsequently, 17 of the 18 researchers who had contributed to the *AJIS* special edition agreed to contribute to the second phase; only the second South Australian study, conducted by Metcalfe, was not taken to phase two. An additional contributor, however—Wilson—agreed to prepare an alternative view of IS in New South Wales, as a counterpoint to the earlier findings published in *AJIS*. As described earlier in this chapter, the extensions in phase two involved a new analysis of the state data in relation to the extended Ridley framework; they also provided for expanding on earlier material and focusing on a sample of important contributors to the development of the IS discipline, via selected vignettes.

The state case studies

The case studies were largely exploratory and descriptive, with relatively less emphasis on interpretation and the ability to be generalised. The case-study approach is well suited for investigation where there is little established theory on the topic (Yin 2003). The case-study method also has the advantage of allowing the researcher to develop a good feeling for the complexities of interacting forces and subtleties that are more difficult to detect with other methods. Walsham (1995) refers to the 'rich insight' possible from the case-study approach.

Team data gathering

The data collected in the case studies focused on questions implicit in the case-study protocol, as described earlier. It was planned that team members in Australian states and territories (referred to collectively as the study 'states') would gather qualitative data about each university (as well as relevant state-level data). The case-study method was agreed to as the research approach for the team study. The data gathered were intended to provide insights into the distinctive characteristics of IS in each university in relation to: the degree of administrative autonomy, size and influence, curriculum, research, local influences and significant people shaping IS at that university. Anchoring the data gathering and analysis in phase one was Gail Ridley's (2006a) evolving draft framework derived from theory on the emergence of disciplines. Team members in each state sought to analyse the data across the universities engaged in IS in that state, and to present general observations on the features of IS as an academic discipline in that state. Phase two provided further analysis of this state data, taking account of the updated version of Ridley's framework described in Chapter 3 of this volume. Phase two also entailed a consolidated analysis of the data from the study.

The protocol

Yin (2003) argues for the use of a case-study protocol to guide any study employing the case-study method. To this end, study team members developed a multi-state case-study protocol. An abridged version of the protocol is included in Appendix 1.1. A detailed version of the protocol was reported in the *AJIS* (Smyth and Gable 2006). It was intended that use of the protocol would contribute to:

- comparability across the states
- consistency across the individual case studies
- efficiency in the conduct of the case studies, with potential for data gathering and some analysis being delegated to research assistants or other junior researchers.

Yin (2003) strongly favours building a protocol around relevant theory. In this study, the protocol relies on a framework, the emergence of a discipline, developed by Ridley and articulated in preliminary form in the 2006 special edition of *AJIS*, and in expanded form in Chapter 3 of this volume.

Also, many of the tenets of general systems theory (Ackoff 1971) are implicit in the approach to data gathering and the themes and questions documented in the multi-state case-study protocol. The approach to data gathering advocated—based on semi-structured interviews utilising broad themes to tap the perceptions of interviewees—is consistent with general systems theory. This approach permits the researcher to take a more holistic approach to the topic, and allows the interviewee to touch on the multiplicity of interacting factors that might contribute to the distinctive characteristics of the IS presence in each university. The protocol directs the researcher to just some of the potential interacting factors that might determine the distinctive characteristics of IS at a given university: that the interaction of geography, the administrative structure and individuals from within and outside the university could, over time, influence curriculum and research at that university. This planned concern for pursuing a holistic view by calculated consideration of factors beyond those suggested by the guiding framework proved useful in the subsequent consolidated analysis of state data.

Mechanisms to increase representativeness

Given the descriptive and exploratory character of the overall study, the team harboured no illusions regarding the ultimate completeness of issues to be identified, related evidence to be gathered and analyses to be conducted. It was acknowledged that the study offered a mere starting point for continuing monitoring of the state of IS in Australia. Regardless, efforts were made to achieve some level of representativeness of the evidence and perspectives reported. Key mechanisms were: 1) selection of the study team; 2) review of draft state reports by interviewees; 3) review of state reports by intrastate experts; and 4) global review of the draft special issue by appropriate experts.

Selection of the study team

In establishing the study team, Australia-wide representation was sought; this suggested state-based case reports. Senior and long-standing IS academics were approached; in most cases, those contacted first welcomed involvement but with some changes to the composition of the team over the course of the study.

Review of draft state reports by interviewees

All interviewees received an early draft of the state report in which their views were recounted. Feedback was channelled through the project manager back to the state teams, and the state teams implemented changes.

Intrastate reviewers

In addition to careful review by state team members, interviewees, the project leader and the project manager, each state report was given further local exposure in draft form before wider circulation to cross-case reviewers. Selected 'local experts' were sent a copy of the draft report for review, the aims being to:

- minimise potential adverse reaction from perceived misrepresentation
- try to ensure the report was as representative of the state as possible
- enrich the report with further insights
- ensure that the process of peer review resulted in chapters of a strong academic standard.

Global reviewers

Two senior and internationally notable IS academics, Iris Vessey and Bernard Glasson, were sent a draft of the complete phase-one output—as prepared for the *AJIS* 2006 special issue—and were requested to review the material and respond to a brief set of questions pertaining to the historical evolution of IS-in-Oz, the current state and the possible future of IS-in-Oz. The aims of this survey included: 1) gathering further insights; 2) accounting for diverse perspectives; 3) keeping the study team accurate and seeking balance (soliciting third-party reactions to our areas of emphasis and our interpretations); and 4) maximising rigour.

Apologies for omissions or oversights

Though extensive measures have been pursued to ensure representative input and a balanced report, resource and time limitations have constrained what is possible. While such a report will unavoidably reflect certain emphases and biases and choices made at all stages of its production, the team nonetheless apologises for any omissions or oversights. Given the desire that this study be replicated in future, feedback on any such omissions or oversights is all the more welcome.

Methodological action research

The overall study effort was compounded substantially by the intention to document the approach for repeatability. Alvesson and Sköldberg (1999) use the term 'reflexive methodology' to refer to an evolutionary approach that aims to maximise the quality of study results. We prefer the term 'methodological action research' (MAR) whereby, in addition to results in relation to research questions posed, the study seeks generalisable contributions to knowledge as regards the research process. We define MAR as:

> an action research approach to studying the process of research; it is a reflexive process of progressive problem solving led by individual

researchers, possibly working with others in a team, to improve the way they address research issues and solve research problems. MAR is conducted above and behind the main research activity, with the researcher, on this second level, observing themselves (and their team) and their experience of the research process, the intent being to better understand and improve that process and to document related methodological learnings.

We therefore sought to establish a highly systematised and proceduralised approach, readily extended and repeatable across other countries and regions (and publication collections—for example, conferences or journals; see ACIS Archival Analysis in Figure 1.2). Note that there is a dotted arrow pointing up from the MAR oval in Figure 1.2 to a similar study at the IS-in-PA level of that figure. This reflects how MAR learning on the IS-in-Oz study informed the parent study by evolving, recording and piloting various methods, mechanisms, concepts and interpretations. It is noted that several of the IS-in-Oz research instruments and approaches needed only marginal adaptation for the purposes of the IS-in-PA study. It is noted also that much of the MAR learning from the IS-in-Oz study was reported in the 'Methodological learnings' article in the *CAIS* special issue (Gable and Smyth 2007).

Study overview

This section summarises the 12 chapters of this volume.

The IS discipline in Australian universities: a contextual framework

The contextual framework introduces the IS-in-Oz study, and the book, including background on study rationale and motivation, a summary of the study aims and conceptual design and main outcomes. Contributions include a cogent synthesis of the literature on previous studies of the IS academic discipline. The approach described offers valuable methodological guidance for the replication and extension of the overall study approach within Australia, the region and to other world regions, and represents one of few attempts to study methodically the evolution of a discipline. With 18 core team members in 12 sub-study teams, and in excess of 50 interviewees and a similar number of reviewers across Australia, the study serves also as a useful example of large-scale research project management. Most importantly, the contextual framework offers a meta-view of the underpinning sub-studies.

A retrospective of the IS discipline in Australia

In Chapter 2, Clarke, referring to three main eras, offers cogent discussion of the evolution of the IS discipline in Australia, suggesting that it did not follow on from development overseas, but rather emerged in parallel. During the 'emergence era' (up to 1965), a highly consequential federal government initiative was the Programmer-in-Training (PIT) scheme (from 1963), the syllabus of which emphasised systems analysis and design, and which produced hundreds of ultimately influential senior managers in the public and private sectors.

Early in the 'establishment era' (1965–73), departments were created in colleges of advanced education (CAEs) to assist practice with the application (particularly application development) of computers in business and government. In parallel, topics about how to apply the technology began to emerge in university accounting departments—these being relatively more concerned with the 'information' than with the system. The transfer of PIT to CAEs towards the end of this era heralded formalised IS education, which expanded to institutes of technology. Much of this early effort was service teaching, with IS in universities migrating forward from 'undergraduate service topics and units to sub-majors, majors and only later postgraduate teaching and research'.

At the outset of the 'consolidation era' (1974–90), the University of New South Wales (UNSW) appointed the first Professor of Information Systems, Cyril Brookes, and formed the first university IS department. In 1978, the first Australian was awarded a PhD in IS (Ron Weber at Minnesota under Gordon Davis's supervision). Weber was the second professor of IS (in 1981), with several further such appointments in the late 1980s and about 20 in the 1990s, resulting in more than 30 IS professors by 2005. Early published curricula from the United Kingdom and the United States was too comprehensive and either too computer-science or business-oriented for the mostly IS service subjects being taught; the 'local' IS curriculum thus sometimes became almost insular. Long-awaited recognition of IS within the Australian Computer Society (ACS) Accreditation Guidelines (Clarke and Lo 1989) proved to be a watershed—their core body of knowledge in 1990 evidencing 50 per cent IS content.

Clarke suggests that during the 1970s and the 1980s the vigour of the discipline in the United States resulted in that country establishing leadership in the IS discipline. Philosophies and methods of research were debated through this period, with some acceptance of pluralism. Clarke (in Maynard 1992) depicts IS as occupying 'space between the technical and business disciplines, encompassing a range of applied and instrumentalist topics, and interacting closely with many other disciplines and sub-disciplines'.

Clarke lists seven main clusters of topics or themes in Australian IS since 1965 (with much cross-fertilisation among the themes): 1) technology as enabler and driver; 2) applications of technology; 3) data management; 4) organisations; 5) systems thinking; 6) business-school thinking; and 7) information management. The apparent diversity of curricula and research domains appears perhaps more varied even than that of Europe or the United States.

Clarke's chapter reveals the slow emergence of a governance framework for the IS discipline in Australia, relative to the growth of the discipline itself. He points out that until 1990 the ACS guidelines for accreditation of tertiary-level courses made no specific provision for IS courses (as distinct from computer science courses). He observes also, however, that a person from an IS background has been president of the ACS for 34 of its 40 years' existence. Clarke observes that none of the business professional groups sought to assume a governance role over IS in Australia and that the business-oriented professional group, the Australian Institute of Systems Analysts (AISA), after prominence in the 1970s, ceased to have a role in IS governance in Australia. In 1990, the first Australian Conference in Information Systems (ACIS) was held, but it was not until 1994 that the *AJIS* was established. The ACPHIS was formally established in 1995; however, it was not until 2001 that an Australian chapter of the Association for Information Systems (AIS) was established.

Characterising academic IS in Australia: developing and evaluating a theoretical framework

Ridley's theoretical explorations are based on a review of the literature on the development of disciplines, ultimately deriving a theoretical framework for the broader study. The framework considers the current and past state of IS in Australian universities from the perspective of the development of a discipline. The components of the framework were derived and validated through a thematic analysis of the IS and non-IS literature. In the revised version of the framework employed for this second phase of the study, Ridley proposes that maturity of a discipline is characterised by the development of a core body of knowledge for the discipline and by the establishment by practitioners of that discipline of strong mechanisms of control leading to enhanced reputations and critical rewards. The framework also proposes that the degree of professionalism is inversely proportional to the extent to which a discipline responds to local contingencies. This *ad hoc* framework was applied as a guide to the collection and analysis of the state data.

The next seven studies are 'state' case studies, for Queensland, the Australian Capital Territory, New South Wales, South Australia, Tasmania, Victoria and Western Australia.

The IS discipline in Queensland, 2006

Data was gathered from all nine universities in Queensland (including the Australian Catholic University, which has common approaches in all its Australian campuses), as all teach IS on at least one campus (Table 1.3). The study found that the condition of IS in Queensland reflected the highly decentralised nature of the state. Relative to its population, Queensland has a large number of universities, each of which is engaged in IS teaching and research. The study reveals little evidence of a distinctive Queensland flavour of IS; rather, there is a diversity of curriculum approaches and an equally broad range of research topics and methods. Two of the state's regional universities are notable for the relative strength of their IS presence—in terms of the number of IS staff, the number of IS students and the range of campuses across which IS is taught. The breadth of topics and approaches to IS in Queensland is evidenced by the existence of separate, competing IS groups in each of two of the largest universities; in each case, one of the IS groups is highly technical in orientation while the other is business oriented. Across the eight Queensland universities, there is wide variability in terms of the administrative location of the IS academic staff in the university structure.

Table 1.3 Placement of the IS academic discipline in Queensland universities

Era	Type	University	First level down	Second level down	Third level down	Fourth level down	First level	Second level	Third level
			Location of IS within the university				Generic levels		
PU	C	Bond University	Faculty of Business, Tech and Sustainable Development	School of Information Tech	Information Systems Dept		Faculty	School	Dept
NU	C	Central Queensland University	Faculty of Business and Informatics	School of Information Systems			Faculty	School	
GT	2	Griffith University	Business (group)	Griffith Business School	Dept of Mgmt	(IS group)	Group	School (only in Business) or faculty	Dept (only in Business)
GT	2	Griffith University	Griffith Science and Tech (group)	Faculty of Engineering and Information Tech	School of Information and Comm Tech	(IS group)	Group	Faculty	School
GT	B	James Cook University	Faculty of Law, Business and Creative Arts	School of Business	Accounting and Finance Program	(IS group)	Faculty	School	Program
UT	T	Queensland University of Technology	Faculty of Information Tech	School of Information Systems			Faculty	School	

Type (Faculty type where IS resides): = B = Business, T = Technology, O = Other (e.g., Arts), 2 = Both (has IS groups in B and T), C = Combined (has B and T in a single faculty). Era: SS = Sandstone, RB = Redbrick, GT = Gumtrees, UT = Unitech, NU = New University, PU = Private University.

Table 1.3 Placement of the IS academic discipline in Queensland universities

Era	Type	University	Location of IS within the university				Generic levels		
			First level down	Second level down	Third level down	Fourth level down	First level	Second level	Third level
SS	2	University of Queensland	Faculty of Engineering, Physical Sciences and Architecture	School of Information Technology and Electrical Engineering	Data and Knowledge Engineering Research Division		Faculty	School	Research division
SS	B	University of Queensland	Faculty of Business, Economics and Law	UQ Business School	(IS group)		Faculty	School	Discipline
NU	B	University of Southern Queensland	Faculty of Business	Dept of Information Systems			Faculty	Dept	

Vignettes are presented of Ed Fitzgerald, Alan Underwood and Ron Weber, as three of the many individuals who have been important to the development of the IS discipline in Queensland. Fitzgerald can be seen to have been one of the powerful forces in the evolution of IS curriculum in Queensland, with an innovative practitioner-focused approach. Underwood for many years led the largest IS group at a Queensland university and promoted IS strongly through his involvement with the ACS. Weber has been perhaps the most prominent and admired Australian IS academic internationally. The study assesses the state of IS in Queensland universities in relation to criteria indicative of the maturity of a discipline. Measured against these criteria, IS in Queensland universities cannot be considered a mature, distinct academic discipline but emerges, nonetheless, as vigorous and innovative.

The IS discipline in the Australian Capital Territory, 2006

The ACT case study was prepared by three leaders in IS (Gregor, Lewis and McDonald) from the territory's three universities. The authors briefly discuss Roger Clarke, Igor Hawryszkiewycz, Errol Martin and Penny Collings as individuals who had—as well as the authors—contributed strongly to the development of the IS academic discipline in the Australian Capital Territory. The chapter depicts a vibrant IS group in each university but voices concerns about the disparate administrative locations of the IS academics (Table 1.4) and the relative lack of a strong identity for IS in the territory's universities.

Table 1.4 Placement of the IS academic discipline in ACT universities

Era	Type	University	Location of IS within the university				Generic levels		
			First level down	Second level down	Third level down	Fourth level down	First level	Second level	Third level
RB	B	Australian National University	College of Business and Economics	School of Accounting and Business Information Systems	Information Systems Discipline Group		College	School	Discipline
NU	C	University of Canberra	Division of Business, Law and Information Sciences	School of Information Sciences and Engineering	Information Systems Discipline		Division	School	Discipline
RB	T	University of NSW (ADFA)	Australian Defence Force Academy	School of IT and Electrical Engineering	(IS group)		Faculty	School	

Type (faculty type where IS resides): B = Business, T = Technology, O = Other (eg., Arts), 2 = Both (has IS groups in B and T), C = Combined (has B and T in a single faculty). Era: SS = Sandstone, RB = Redbrick, GT = Gumtrees, UT = Unitech, NU = New University, PU = Private University.

Information systems is prominent at all three universities, each having a distinctive background that reflects its position in Canberra, the seat of Australia's federal government. The Australian Defence Force Academy (ADFA, University of New South Wales) is essentially a private university for the Australian Defence Organisation; The Australian National University was set up to be a national research institution; and the University of Canberra group for many years focused on meeting the training needs for computing professionals for the federal government. Despite these distinguishing characteristics, the subject matter taught and researched in the three groups has much in common and 'each group regards itself as "vibrant" and happy with what it does'. Nonetheless, a low degree of professionalisation is reported relative to longer-standing disciplines, it being suggested that this is to some extent due to the fact that there exists 'a disjunction between what is taught as core knowledge and what is taught as research methods', a lack of social prestige and a lack of acceptance as a discipline with a unique symbol system.

The IS discipline in New South Wales, 2006, and response

The main NSW chapter, by Underwood and Jordan, identifies 12 separate IS academic groups across nine universities in the state. Unlike in the other state reports, the authors choose to address only a subset of the NSW universities—those they consider the most prominent in IS (some might disagree with their selection). They observe that students undertaking strongly identified IS undergraduate degrees can be found at few universities, with most offering a variety of majors within other programs. The size of the IS presence would therefore appear to depend on the university's enrolment in the core programs that offer the majors and the extent of compulsory IS subjects in their programs. Large accounting programs mean that many students will need to do IS, thereby requiring larger IS staff numbers. Growing enrolments in commerce during two decades has advantaged IS units and staff in that faculty. Nonetheless, IS would appear not to have a common home, but resides in a variety of locations—especially science and computer science—as shown in Table 1.5. Most IS groups remain as *ad hoc* or informal groups within larger departments.

Table 1.5 Placement of the IS academic discipline in NSW universities

Era	Type	University	Location of IS within the university				Generic levels		
			First level down	Second level down	Third level down	Fourth level down	First level	Second level	Third level
			Type (faculty type where IS resides): B = Business, T = Technology, O = Other (eg., Arts), 2 = Both (has IS groups in B and T), C = Combined (has B and T in a single faculty). Era: SS = Sandstone, RB = Redbrick, GT = Gumtrees, UT = Unitech, NU = New University, PU = Private University.						
NU	C	Charles Sturt University (Albury) from 2007	Faculty of Business and Computing	School of Business and Information Tech	(IS group)				
NU	C	Charles Sturt University (Wagga Wagga) from 2007	Faculty of Business and Computing (proposed name)	School of Computing and Mathematics (proposed name)	(IS group)		Faculty	School	
GT	2	Macquarie University	College of Science and Tech	Division of Information and Comm Sciences	Dept of Computing	(IS group)	College	Division	Dept
GT	2	Macquarie University	College of Commerce	Division of Economics and Financial Studies	Dept of Accounting and Finance	(IS group)	College	Division	Dept
GT	2	Macquarie University	College of Commerce	Macquarie Graduate School of Mgmt	(IS)		College	Division	Dept
NU	B	Southern Cross University	Faculty of Business	School of Commerce and Mgmt	(IS group)		Faculty	School	
GT	B	University of New England	Faculty of Economics, Business and Law	New England Business School	(IS)		Faculty	School	
GT	T	University of Newcastle	Faculty of Science and Information Tech	School of Design Comm Information Tech	Information Tech Discipline	(IS group)	Faculty	School	Discipline
RB	B	University of NSW	Faculty of Commerce and Economics	School of Information Systems, Tech and Mgmt	(IS group)		Faculty	School	

Table 1.5 Placement of the IS academic discipline in NSW universities

| Era | Type | University | Location of IS within the university | | | | Generic levels | | |
			First level down	Second level down	Third level down	Fourth level down	First level	Second level	Third level
SS	2	University of Sydney	Faculty of Science	School of Information Technologies	(IS group)				
SS	2	University of Sydney	Faculty of Economics and Business	School of Business	Discipline of Business Information Systems		Faculty	School	Discipline
UT	T	University of Technology, Sydney	Faculty of Information Tech	Dept of Information Systems			Faculty	School (only in the Business Faculty) or dept	
NU	2	University of Western Sydney (E-Business)	College of Business	School of Mgmt	Business Systems Group		College	School	
NU	2	University of Western Sydney (IS)	College of Health and Science	School of Computing and Mathematics	(IS group)		College	School	
GT	B	University of Wollongong	Faculty of Commerce	School of Economics and Information Systems	Discipline of Information Systems		Faculty	School	

The NSW chapter includes vignettes from Dubravka Cecez-Kecmanovic and Igor Hawryszkiewycz. Cecez-Kecmanovic has made a significant contribution to IS research through her effective promotion of critical theory-informed IS research. Hawryszkiewycz has had a long-term impact on IS curriculum and research and has authored IS textbooks important to the development of IS in Australia. While the universities reported by Underwood and Jordan display some structural recognition of IS as a separate field, it was widely believed by their interviewees that the distinctiveness of IS was not well known in the wider university communities. Indeed, the interviewees themselves appeared to hold diverse definitions of IS. Research activity tends to be fragmented and diverse. Small research groups, especially of doctoral students, have tended to exist without undergraduate programs to build the staff numbers to critical mass.

Wilson provides a response to the conclusions developed by Underwood and Jordan. While Underwood and Jordan conclude that the prospects for IS in most NSW universities are poor—they speak of 'an environment threatening the continuing existence of IS in some of the state's universities'—Wilson argues for a much more positive future. Wilson's arguments are that New South Wales has by far the largest information and communications technology (ICT) presence in Australia and that the greatest demand among ICT graduates is for those with 'a business-centric focus'—that is, IS graduates.

IS in South Australia: a critical investigation

The South Australian chapter emphasises the leading role of the University of South Australia. Data gathered suggest that South Australia's IS offerings were influenced heavily during the 1990s by the soft systems and critical systems approaches to the discipline—a situation that began to change at the turn of the century—and that the curriculum depended more heavily on industrial than on political factors. Though the authors report several substantive research centres or labs, it is also noted that there is little local funding for research, and while the three universities work together fairly well and have created some highly successful technical joint ventures, with IS playing such a minor role in the state, obtaining funding for any research activities is extremely difficult. The administrative placement of IS in South Australian universities is shown in Table 1.6.

Table 1.6 Placement of the IS academic discipline in SA universities

Era	Type	University	Location of IS within the university				Generic levels		
			First level down	Second level down	Third level down	Fourth level down	First level	Second level	Third level
Type (faculty type where IS resides): B = Business, T = Technology, O = Other (eg., Arts), 2 = Both (has IS groups in B and T), C = Combined (has B and T in a single faculty). Era: SS = Sandstone, RB = Redbrick, GT = Gumtrees, UT = Unitech, NU = New University, PU = Private University.									
GT	T	Flinders University	Faculty of Science and Engineering	School of Informatics and Engineering	(IS group)		Faculty	School or dept	
SS	B	University of Adelaide	Faculty of the Professions	School of Commerce	(IS group) 3 staff		Faculty	School	
UT	T	University of South Australia	Division of Information Tech, Engineering and the Environment	School of Computer and Information Science	(IS group)		Division	School	

A vignette is provided from Terry Robbins-Jones, head of the first School of Information Systems in South Australia and innovative leader in the promotion of IS.

The IS discipline in Tasmania, 2006

The Tasmanian case study is distinctive in several respects. First, it reports on just one university. Also, the data-gathering approach applied is somewhat different. Where reports in the other states used interviews from one or two senior academics in each university, in Tasmania it was possible to draw on data from a wide range of academics—current and former staff members from the University of Tasmania. The chapter includes vignettes from Chris Keen, a man who had a formative impact on the development of the IS discipline in Tasmania, and Arthur Sale, one of the father figures of ICT in Australia and a major proponent of IS at the University of Tasmania. The author of the Tasmanian report is also the author of the framework developed for the overall case-study protocol. The administrative placement of IS at the University of Tasmania is shown in Table 1.7.

Table 1.7 Placement of the IS academic discipline in the University of Tasmania

			Location of IS within the university				Generic levels		
Era	Type	University	First level down	Second level down	Third level down	Fourth level down	First level	Second level	Third level
Type (faculty type where IS resides): B = Business, T = Technology, O = Other (eg., Arts), 2 = Both (has IS groups in B and T), C = Combined (has B and T in a single faculty). Era: SS = Sandstone, RB = Redbrick, GT = Gumtrees, UT = Unitech, NU = New University, PU = Private University.									
SS	B	University of Tasmania	Faculty of Business	School of Information Systems			Faculty	School	

The Tasmanian case-study findings suggest that an inverse relationship exists between the impact of local factors and the degree of professionalism in this IS setting. A surprising finding was that the relationship found varied for research and teaching issues.

The IS discipline in Victoria, 2006

Victoria—more than any other state—was impacted heavily by the Dawkins reforms to Australian tertiary education. Amalgamations, mergers and take-overs were widespread in Victoria, sometimes bringing together strong IS groups with different cultures and different aspirations. Although most interviewees expressed the view that local industry had had negligible influence on curriculum, universities in Victoria appeared to be universally seeking increased collaboration with the local community and industry as part of their strategic direction. Distinctive themes taught within the many programs identified varied considerably. Despite diverse topics of research being pursued, IS research output in universities in Victoria was perceived as lesser than in other departments. Efforts are, however, under way to bolster research output. Interestingly, the Victorian report states, 'The mode of IS research in universities in Victoria is predominantly interpretive.' Only one university reported using 'multi-method, with an emphasis on quantitative techniques'. Although research is considered a high priority at almost all universities in Victoria, available funding appears to have a negative correlation with the avowed importance of research. Perceptions of 'very little funding', 'dwindling funding' and 'having trouble attracting ARC [Australian Research Council] and other external funding' were evident in the data. A diversity of administrative placements for IS groups in Victorian universities is shown in Table 1.8.

Table 1.8 Placement of the IS academic discipline in Victorian universities

Era	Type	University	Location of IS within the university				Generic levels		
			First level down	Second level down	Third level down	Fourth level down	First level	Second level	Third level
	Type (faculty type where IS resides): B = Business, T = Technology, O = Other (eg., Arts), 2 = Both (has IS groups in B and T), C = Combined (has B and T in a single faculty). Era: SS = Sandstone, RB = Redbrick, GT = Gumtrees, UT = Unitech, NU = New University, PU = Private University.
GT	B	Deakin University	Faculty of Business and Law	School of Information Systems			Faculty	School	
GT	B	Deakin University	Faculty of Business and Law	Deakin Business School	Information Systems Discipline Group (3 staff)		Faculty	School	
GT	T	La Trobe University	Faculty of Science, Tech and Engineering	School of Engineering and Mathematical Sciences	Dept of Computer Science and Computer Engineering	(IS group)	Faculty	School	Dept
RB	T	Monash University	Faculty of Information Tech	Caulfield School of Information Tech	(IS group)		Faculty	School	
RB	T	Monash University	Faculty of Information Tech	Clayton School of Information Tech	(IS group)		Faculty	School	
UT	B	RMIT University	Faculty of Business	School of Business IT			Faculty	School	
NU	T	Swinburne University of Technology	Faculty of Information and Comm Technologies	Information Systems Academic Group			Faculty	Academic group	
NU	T	University of Ballarat	School of Information Tech and Mathematical Sciences	(IS group)			School		
SS	T	University of Melbourne	Faculty of Science	Dept of Information Systems			Faculty	School or dept	
NU	B	Victoria University	Faculty of Business and Law	School of Information Systems			Faculty	School	

The Victorian chapter presents vignettes from two individuals as representatives of many important figures in the development of IS in Victoria. The two are Graeme Shanks, a significant contributor to IS research and early representative on the ARC College of Experts, and Gerald Murphy, 'one of the founding fathers of Australia's IT education sector'.

IS teaching and research in WA universities

The West Australian chapter identifies a degree of isolation, attributable to the size of the state and its relative remoteness from the universities elsewhere in Australia. The report suggests how these factors have impinged on the development of IS in the state's universities and how responses to local contingencies inhibit the perception of IS as a mature discipline. Research focus within the four universities is very different and this could be one of the reasons why all interviewees identified a low level of collaboration between WA universities. Interviewees stressed the real need for IS leadership and active involvement in IS research by the professoriate. Information systems groups without a professor tended to have a significantly lower profile in their home university than those with a professor. Administrative placement of the IS groups is shown in Table 1.9.

Table 1.9 Placement of the IS academic discipline in WA universities

Era	Type	University	Location of IS within the university				Generic levels		
			First level down	Second level down	Third level down	Fourth level down	First level	Second level	Third level
Type (faculty type where IS resides): B = Business, T = Technology, O = Other (eg., Arts), 2 = Both (has IS groups in B and T), C = Combined (has B and T in a single faculty). Era: SS = Sandstone, RB = Redbrick, GT = Gumtrees, UT = Unitech, NU = New University, PU = Private University.									
UT	B	Curtin University of Technology	Curtin Business School	School of Information Systems			Division	School	
NU	B	Edith Cowan University	Faculty of Business and Law	School of Information Systems			Faculty	School	
GT	O	Murdoch University	Division of Arts	School of Information Tech	(IS group)		Division	School	
PU	B	University of Notre Dame	College of Business	School of Business	(IS)		College	School	
SS	B	University of Western Australia	Faculty of Economics and Commerce	Business School	Information Mgmt Discipline	(IS group)	Faculty	School	Discipline

The chapter discusses briefly the roles of Richard Watson, Graham Pervan and Janice Burn as three major contributors to the development of IS in WA universities.

A longitudinal study of IS research in Australia

As part of a study to investigate the state of IS research in Australia, surveys of the heads of all IS discipline groups in Australian universities were conducted in 2004, 2005 and 2006. This chapter relates to the findings of the 2006 survey. The study revealed a wide range of topics researched (with rapid growth in electronic commerce and knowledge management), a range of foci, a balance between positivist and interpretive research; that surveys were the most frequently used research method, and that most research was directed towards informing IS professionals.

The IS academic discipline in Australian universities: a meta-analysis

This chapter provides a consolidation and broad interpretation of the data from the sub-studies described in the earlier chapters. The analysis identifies the recent and current positions of the IS discipline in Australian universities. It uses the revised Ridley framework to guide analysis of the consolidated data from each of the sub-studies, in particular from the case studies from each state.

At a basic level, it is worth noting from this chapter that not all universities across Australia have an IS presence. It is in Western Australia, South Australia and New South Wales that universities are found that do not have a definable IS academic group. Victoria was notable as the state with by far the strongest IS presence in its universities; Queensland has a strong IS presence relative to its population. Universities across Australia reported declines in student enrolments and in IS academic staff numbers.

A diversity of research methods and standards is seen in IS groups across Australian universities. Similarly, there is much variety in teaching curricula for IS courses in Australia. This is most evident in the variability of the relative emphasis on 'technical' content among universities; however, the variability does not appear to be based on state-to-state differences.

In relation to the criteria used to evaluate the relative maturity of IS as a discipline, the consolidated data suggest that IS is yet to achieve full maturity. Some of the qualities observed, however, relating to local variability and innovative curriculum, could be viewed as healthy, although they are at odds with the maturity criteria.

The consolidated data show a higher proportion of IS groups administratively separate from business faculties than would be the case in the United States, for instance. The data suggest, however, some slight trend for IS groups in Australian universities to move back to administrative placement within business.

Beyond the assessment of observed data against the proposed framework, this meta-analysis seeks to draw from the Australian data some observations on trends and unresolved tensions, with an emphasis on national and international factors impacting on the status of IS in Australian universities. Among factors discerned was a growing impact on IS groups as a consequence of the proposed introduction of the Research Quality Framework (RQF). The proposed RQF was seen to be affecting, in particular, preferences for research outlets and staffing patterns. Other influences are discussed in the meta-analysis chapter.

The Australasian Conference on Information Systems

The Australasian Conference on Information Systems (ACIS) ran for its eighteenth consecutive year in December 2007 in Toowoomba. The first conference was held at Monash University in 1990 with the name 'First Annual Conference on Information Systems'. In 1991, it was called the 'Second Annual Conference on Information Systems and Database Special Interest Group'. In 1992, it became the 'Australian Conference on Information Systems' and, in 1994, in recognition of the substantive involvement of New Zealand, the name was changed to the 'Australasian Conference on Information Systems'. Until the advent of the Pacific Asia Conference on Information Systems (PACIS) in 1993, ACIS was the only substantial IS conference in the region. Since 1993, ACIS and PACIS have coexisted happily, attracting a large overlap in delegates.

Attendance has stabilised at about 250 people during the past three years; paper submissions at about 250 and paper acceptances about 100 (50 per cent acceptance). Though a less international conference than PACIS, ACIS tends to attract papers and delegates from more than a dozen countries each year (the majority of the papers from Australia and New Zealand).

The first ACIS doctoral consortium on record was in 1995 at Curtin University of Technology. The consortiums began to run regularly from 2001. In 2005, the consortium was extended from one to one-and-a-half days. A doctoral thesis prize from the ACPHIS was introduced in 2004 and is now awarded each year at ACIS.

The conference organisation structure has evolved over time. Until the end of 1994, an interim committee ran the conference. The members of the interim committee were: Roger Clarke (The Australian National University), Igor Hawryszkiewycz (University of Technology, Sydney), Ross Jeffery (University of New South Wales), Ron Weber (University of Queensland) and Peter Weill (University of Melbourne). The decision to finally anoint a rolling ICIS-style ACIS committee and disband the interim committee was made at the end of 1994.

Table 1.10 summarises key characteristics of ACIS over time. Although these data have been vetted carefully by several knowledgeable individuals—including all who reviewed this chapter—it must be acknowledged that the data were compiled from multiple and diverse sources across which inconsistencies were observed. For example, conference dates were expressed differently in some materials depending on what was being included: in 1995, the doctoral consortium was held on 26 September, but papers were really presented on 27–29 September. The *Proceedings* show the dates for the conference as 26–29 September. In other years, the doctoral consortium dates might be included in some places and excluded in others. The terms 'organising chair', 'conference chair' and 'executive chair' seem to be used inconsistently, even for a single conference. There were differences in the counts of papers for some conferences on different pages of the proceedings, and the counts given did not always correspond to the real number of papers in the proceedings (though they were always very close).

Table 1.10a Australasian Conference on Information Systems, 1990–98

Year	1990	1991	1992	1993	1994	1995	1996	1997	1998
City	Melbourne	Sydney	Wollongong	Brisbane	Melbourne	Perth	Hobart	Adelaide	Sydney
Sponsoring university	Monash Uni	Uni of NSW	Uni of Wollongong	Uni of Queensland	Monash Uni	Curtin Uni of Technology	Uni of Tasmania	Uni of South Australia	Uni of New South Wales
Program chair(s)					Graham Shanks	Mike Newby	Cathy Urquhart	David Sutton	R. Edmundson D. Wilson
Conference chair(s)	I. Hawryszkiewycz		Rob MacGregor		David Arnott	Graham Pervan	Chris Keen	Terry Robbins-Jones	Ross Jeffery
Organising chair(s)	R. Jeffery K. Dampney			Paul Ledington	David Arnott	Graham Pervan			
Dates	6 Feb	4–5 Feb	5–8 Oct	28–30 Sept	27–29 Sept	27–29 Sept	11–13 Dec	29 Sept–2 Oct	29 Sept–2 Oct
Duration	1 day	2 days		3 days	3 days	3 days	3 days		
Number of submissions			79	80+	85	82	112		98
Number of countries (first author)	1	2	8	6	6	8	6	9	3
Acceptance rate			57%	<75%	66%	77%	50%		61%
Parallel streams	1			3	3	3			
Papers in proceedings	15	29	45	60	56	63	56	62	60
Panels	None in proceedings	None in proceedings	9		3	5	2		
Tutorials									
Keynote speakers	None indicated in proceedings	None indicated in proceedings	(1) T. W. Ollie (2) R. A. Stamper	(1) D. E. Avison (2) B. Glasson (3) G. Shanks	(1) R. Hirscheim, Klein, Lyytinen (2) G. Fitzgerald (3) S. Ingram	(1) R. D. Galliers (2) M. Shanahan (3) K. Kumar	(1) L. Willcocks (2) G. Burke	(1) M. C. Jackson (2) K. Myers	
Number of delegates					120	169			
Doctoral consortium						26 Sept			
Number of consortium students									
Consortium chair(s)						P. Marshall J McKay	M. Vitale	M. Broadbent	M. O'Connor

Table 1.10b Australasian Conference on Information Systems, 1999–2007

Year	1999	2000	2001	2002	2003	2004	2005	2006	2007
City	Wellington	Brisbane	Coffs Harbour	Melbourne	Perth	Hobart	Sydney	Adelaide	Toowoomba
Sponsoring u.	Victoria Uni of Wellington	Queensland U of Technology	Southern Cross Uni	Victoria Uni	Edith Cowan Uni	Uni of Tasmania	Uni Technology Sydney	Uni of South Australia	Uni Southern Queensland
Program chair(s)	B. Hope P. Yoong	G. Gable M. Vitale	D. Cecez-Kecmanovic G. Finnie	M. McGrath F. Burstein A. Wenn	C. Standing P. Love	S. Elliot M.-A. Williams S. Williams	B. Campbell D. Bunker	E. Fitzgerald	M. Toleman
Conference chair(s)	David Keane		Bruce Lo	Arthur Tatnall	Janice Burn	Carol Pollard	David Wilson	A. Koronios S. Spencer	D. Roberts
Organising chair(s)		Alan Underwood		Geoff Sandy	Nick Lethbridge	Leonie Ellis	Jim Underwood		A. Cater-Steel
Dates	1–3 Dec	6–8 Dec	5–7 Dec	4–6 Dec	26–28 Nov	1–3 Dec	30 Nov–2 Dec	6–8 Dec	5–7 Dec
Duration	3 days	3 days	3 days	3 days	3 days	3 days	3 days	3 days	3 days
No. submissions		180	165	151	246	227	262	218	176
No. countries (first author)	8	13	6	9	11	9	11	20	14
Acceptance rate	53%	50%	52%	67%	60%	53%	43%	53%	65%
Parallel streams	4		6	4	6	3	6	5	5
Papers in proceedings	103	94	86	104	147	120	113	114	115
Panels		6	8	6	7	5			6
Tutorials							3 workshops		0
Keynote and invited speakers	(1) R. B. Gallupe (2) M. L. Markus (3) R. Norris	(1) D. Avison (2) Gordon Davis	(1) P. Coroneos (2) E. M. Trauth (3) M. Vitale	(1) B. Jones (2) M. Broadbent (3) C. Bennett (4) W. Wojtkowski	(1) N. Bjorn-Andersen (2) D. Vogel (3) V. Adamson	(1) B. Galliers	(1) D. Gwillim (2) K. Kautz	(1) P. Grant (2) J. Peppard (3) G. Gable	(1) J. Minz (2) R. Winter (3) S. Gregor (4) C. Steele
No. of delegates		250	220	283	255	236		185	
Doctoral consortium		4 Dec	4 Dec		25 Nov	30 Nov	30 Nov–2 Dec	4–5 Dec	4 Dec
No. consortium students			32	23	29	28		18	21
Consortium chair(s)	Bob McQueen	Michael Myers	Kit Dampney	Mike Metcalfe	Graham Pervan	Sid Huff	I. Hawryszkiewycz	J. Fisher	G. Gable

ACIS archival analysis

A study of ACIS proceedings during its 18-year history has the potential to reveal a good deal about research in Australian (and New Zealand) universities. To this end, the author of this chapter has initiated an archival analysis of ACIS proceedings. To date, the papers from the first 16 ACIS events have been converted to electronic format and salient data from each of the papers have been captured in an EndNote database. A database that is more conducive to data analysis is being built.

Though analyses of the ACIS archival material are in progress, we are able to report some preliminary findings. Counts reported here were done using 'Search References' in EndNote and are for the years 1990–2005. More reliable counts will be available once the data are loaded into the intended database.

All papers have been classified using the classification options:

- technical
- behavioural/managerial
- educational (that is, IS curriculum related)
- other (predominantly research methodology papers).

The papers have also been coded according to topic. This coding is preliminary, and it is our intention that the codes be confirmed by the authors of papers. A 32-topic coding scheme was used based on Barki et al. (1993) and Palvia et al. (2004). The choice of the coding scheme was intended to facilitate the comparison of topics covered at ACIS with those covered in IS research topic studies elsewhere.

In the years 1990–95, about 30 per cent of the papers were classified as technical while in the years 2000–05 only 12 per cent were classified this way. In the years 2000–05, the percentage of papers that were coded as 'organisational environment' or 'external environment' was approximately double that of the years 1990–95. These changes support the premise that research in IS has been moving away from a more technical emphasis in the early years and is now placing more importance on context.

There has been no real pattern to the inclusion of curriculum-related topics. Most commonly, 7–8 per cent of papers are curriculum related. The first five years of the conference include the years with the highest and the lowest percentages of such papers. At the First Annual Conference on Information Systems, three of the 15 papers (20 per cent) were curriculum related; in 1994, there were no curriculum-related papers.

As new technologies have developed, new topics have emerged, interest in other topics has fallen away and previously discussed topics have taken on a new focus. For example, in recent years research into electronic commerce/inter-organisational systems has peaked, research interest in databases/DBMS has waned somewhat and there are new stirrings of interest in hardware due mainly to research into mobile devices such as PDAs.

The most popular topics have been:

- IS development/methods and tools: 14 per cent
- theory of IS: 9 per cent
- electronic commerce/inter-organisational systems: 6 per cent
- resource management/IS management issues: 6 per cent
- IS education: 5 per cent
- IS application areas: 5 per cent.

The universities that have contributed most papers (as of 2005) are:

- Monash University: 8.3 per cent
- University of Melbourne: 5.2 per cent
- Edith Cowan University: 5.1 per cent
- Curtin University of Technology: 4.7 per cent
- Deakin University: 4.5 per cent
- Queensland University of Technology: 4.3 per cent
- University of Wollongong: 4.1 per cent
- University of New South Wales: 4 per cent
- University of Tasmania: 3.9 per cent
- Victoria University: 3.8 per cent.

While the majority of ACIS papers were from Australian and New Zealand authors, there was a significant presence of authors from countries elsewhere in the world. The non-Australasian countries that have contributed the most papers between 1990 and 2005 (using first-author country affiliation) are (the number of papers from each country is in parentheses):

- United States (15)
- United Kingdom (13)
- Hong Kong (China) (10)
- Germany (9)
- Norway (9)
- Singapore (7)
- Finland (7)
- South Africa (7).

Conclusion

In conclusion, it is reiterated that this Australian study is the first component in a wider, continuing, longitudinal study of the IS academic discipline around the world. As reflected in the existing literature, owing to its youth, IS has understandably been soul-searching for the past two decades. Information systems as a separate academic discipline is relatively young and yet maturing. The extensive variation observed across the state case studies in curriculum and research foci—as well as the placement and levels of IS in universities in Australia—further attests to its formative stage of evolution. Following are described: 1) the communication of study results; and 2) study limitations.

Communicating study results

An initial vehicle for communicating the Australian study results was the December 2006 special issue of the *AJIS*. A consolidation of the Australian state case studies appears (Gable 2007b) in the September 2007 special issue of *CAIS*, as the Australian state case study in the Pacific-Asia region multiple case study. Many of the lessons learned in relation to research methods and tools are also reported in a 'Methodological learnings' paper (Gable and Smyth 2007) in the same special edition of *CAIS*.

Limitations

As acknowledged at various points in this chapter, the study was a learning experience, a major aim being to evolve an approach that could be repeated across time and across regions; as such, its limitations are many, several of which have been specified throughout this chapter.

References

Ackoff, R. 1971, 'Towards a system of systems concepts', *Management Science*, vol. 17, no. 11, pp. 661–71.

Adam, F. and Fitzgerald, B. 2000, 'The status of the information systems field: historical perspective and practical orientation', *Information Research*, vol. 5, no. 4, viewed 12 March 2006, <http://informationr.net/ir/5-4/paper81.html>

Alavi, M. and Carlson, P. 1992, 'A review of MIS research and disciplinary development', *Journal of Management Information Systems,* vol. 8, no. 4, pp. 45–62.

Alvesson, M. and Sköldberg, K. 1999, *Reflexive Methodology: New Vistas for Qualitative Research*, Sage, London.

Ang, A. Y. and Jiwahhasuchin, S. 1998, 'Information systems education in Thailand: a comparison between the views of professionals and academics', *Journal of Global Information Management*, vol. 6, no. 4, pp. 34–42.

Avgerou, C., Siemer, J. and Bjørn-Andersen, N. 1999, 'The academic field of information systems in Europe', *European Journal of Information Systems*, vol. 8, no. 2, pp. 136–53.

Bacon, C. J. and Fitzgerald, B. 2001, 'Research contributions: a systemic framework for the field of information systems', *ACM SIGMIS Database*, vol. 32, no. 2, pp. 46–67.

Barki, H., Rivard, S. and Talbot, J. 1993, 'A keyword classification scheme for IS research literature: an update', *MIS Quarterly*, vol. 17, no. 2, pp. 209–26.

Becher, T. 1989, *Academic Tribes and Territories*, Society for Research into Higher Education and Open University Press, Milton Keynes, England.

Benbasat, I. and Zmud, R. 2003, 'The identity crisis within the IS discipline: defining and communicating the discipline's core properties', *MIS Quarterly*, vol. 27, no. 2, pp. 183–94.

Chau, P. Y. K. and Kuan, K. K. Y. 2007, 'The information systems academic discipline in Hong Kong—2006', *Communications of the Association for Information Systems*, vol. 21, no. 3, pp. 49–60.

Chen, W. and Hirschheim, R. 2004, 'A paradigmatic and methodological examination of information systems research from 1991 to 2001', *Information Systems Journal*, vol. 14, no. 3, pp. 197–235.

Clarke, R. 2006, 'Key aspects of the history of the information systems discipline in Australia', *Australasian Journal of Information Systems*, vol. 14, no. 1, pp. 123–40.

Clarke, R. & Lo B. 1989, *Accreditation Requirements for Information Systems Courses for the Australian Computer Society*, ACS, November 1989.

Claver, E., Gonzalez, R. and Llopis, J. 2000, 'An analysis of research in information systems (1981–1997)', *Information & Management*, vol. 37, no. 4, pp. 181–95.

Evaristo, J. R. and Karahanna, E. 1997, 'Is North American IS research different from European IS research?', *The Data Base for Advances in Information Systems*, vol. 28, no. 3, pp. 32–43.

Farhoomand, A. F. and Drury, D. H. 1999, 'A historiographical examination of information systems', *Communications of the AIS*, vol. 1, no. 19, pp. 1–27.

Gable, G. G. 2002, *State of the Information Systems Academic Discipline in the Pacific Asia Region: A Survey and Multiple Case Study*, Proposal to Association for Information Systems (AIS) submitted to AIS Council at ICIS 2002 in Barcelona, [data file], available from http://sky.fit.qut.edu.au/~gable/

Gable, G. G. 2006, 'The information systems discipline in Australian universities: a contextual framework', *Australasian Journal of Information Systems*, vol. 14, no. 1, pp. 103–22.

Gable, G. G. 2007a, 'The information systems academic discipline in Pacific Asia 2006: a contextual analysis', *Communications of the Association for Information Systems*, vol. 21, article 1, pp. 1–22.

Gable, G. G. 2007b, 'The information systems academic discipline in Australia 2006', *Communications of the Association for Information Systems*, vol. 21, article 2, pp. 23–48.

Gable, G. G. and Smyth, R. W. 2007, 'The state of the IS academic discipline in Pacific Asia 2006: methodological learnings', *Communications of the Association for Information Systems*, vol. 21, article 9, pp. 166–94.

Gable, G. G., Lee, J.-N., Kwahk, K.-Y. and Green, P. 2007, 'Administrative placement of the information systems academic discipline: a comparative SWOT analysis', *Communications of the Association for Information Systems*, vol. 21, no. 8, pp. 137–65.

Gable, G., Stark, K. and Smyth, R. 2007, 'IS researcher issues', *Proceedings of the International Conference on Wireless Communications, Networking and Mobile Computing (WiCom 2007)*, Shanghai, China, 25–28 July.

Gregor, S., Lewis, E. and McDonald, C. 2006, 'Case study: the state of information systems in Australian Capital Territory universities', *Australasian Journal of Information Systems*, vol. 14, no. 1, pp. 177–92.

Huff, S. and Lehmann, H. 2007, 'The information systems academic discipline in New Zealand—2006', *Communications of the Association for Information Systems*, vol. 21, no. 5, pp. 87–103.

Introna, L. D. 2003, 'Disciplining information systems: truth and its regimes', *European Journal of Information Systems*, vol. 12, no. 3, pp. 235–40.

Khazanchi, D. and Munkvold, B. E. 2000, 'Is information systems a science? An inquiry into the nature of the information systems discipline', *Database for Advances in Information Systems*, vol. 31, no. 3, pp. 24–42.

Koronios, A. and Swatman, Paula 2006, 'The state of information systems in Australian universities: South Australia report', *Australasian Journal of Information Systems*, vol. 14, no. 1, pp. 201–10.

Lee, C.-C. and Liang, T.-P. 2007, 'The information systems academic discipline in Taiwan—2006: a focus on top-tier universities', *Communications of the Association for Information Systems*, vol. 21, no. 7, pp. 116–36.

Lee, J.-N. and Yoo, S.-W. 2007, 'The information systems academic discipline in Korea—2006: a focus on leading universities', *Communications of the Association for Information Systems*, vol. 21, no. 4, pp. 61–86.

Lo, B. W. N. 1989, *A Survey of Information Systems Educational Programmes in Australian Tertiary Institutions*, Working Paper Series No. 1, Department of Information Systems, University of Wollongong.

Metcalfe, M. 2006, 'Using contradictions to appreciate the history of IS education in South Australia', *Australasian Journal of Information Systems*, vol. 14, no. 1, pp. 261–72.

Orlikowski, W. and Baroudi, J. J. 1991, 'Studying information technology in organizations: research approaches and assumptions', *Information Systems Research*, vol. 2, no. 1, pp. 1–28.

Palvia, P., Leary, D., Mao, E., Pinjani, P. and Salam, A. F. 2004, 'Research methodologies in MIS: an update', *Communications of the Association for Information Systems*, vol. 14, pp. 526–42.

Pervan, G. and Shanks, G. 2004, *IS Research Activity in Australia: Results of the 2004 ACPHIS research survey*, Presentation to Australasian Conference on Information Systems, December 2004.

Pervan, G. and Shanks, G. 2006, 'The 2005 survey of information systems research in Australia', *Australasian Journal of Information Systems*, vol. 14, no. 1, pp. 273–80.

Pollard, C. and Chan, E. S. K. 2006, 'A review of information systems programs in universities in Victoria', *Australasian Journal of Information Systems*, vol. 14, no. 1, pp. 231–50.

Ridley, G. 2006a, 'Characterising information systems in Australia: a theoretical framework', *Australasian Journal of Information Systems*, vol. 14, no. 1, pp. 141–62.

Ridley, G. 2006b, 'The state of information systems in Australian universities—Tasmanian report', *Australasian Journal of Information Systems*, vol. 14, no. 1, pp. 211–30.

Sherer, S. A. 2002, 'Academic departments of information systems faculty in the US', *Journal of Information Systems Education*, vol. 13, no. 2, pp. 105–16.

Smyth, R. and Gable, G. 2006, 'Case study: the state of information systems in Queensland universities', *Australasian Journal of Information Systems*, vol. 14, no. 1, pp. 163–76.

Standing, C., Burn, J. and Lin, C. 2006, 'Information systems in Western Australian universities', *Australasian Journal of Information Systems*, vol. 14, no. 1, pp. 251–60.

Tan, B. C. Y. and Chan, T. 2007, 'The information systems academic discipline in Singapore 2006', *Communications of the Association for Information Systems*, vol. 21, no. 6, pp. 104–15.

Underwood, J. and Jordan, E. 2006, 'The state of IS in Australian universities—New South Wales report', *Australasian Journal of Information Systems*, vol. 14, no. 1, pp. 193–200.

Vessey, I., Ramesh, V. and Glass, R. L. 2002, 'Research in information systems: an empirical study of diversity in the discipline and its journals', *Journal of Management Information Systems*, vol. 19, no. 2, pp. 129–74.

Walsham, G. 1995, 'Interpretive case studies in IS research: nature and method', *European Journal of Information Systems*, vol. 4, pp. 74–81.

Whitley, R. 1984a, 'The development of management studies as a fragmented adhocracy', *Social Science Information*, vol. 23, no. 4–5, pp. 775–818.

Whitley, R. 1984b, *The Intellectual and Social Organization of the Sciences*, Clarendon Press, Oxford, UK.

Yin, R. K. 2003, *Case Study Research: Design and Methods*, 3rd edn, Sage Publications, Thousand Oaks.

Appendix 1.1: The information systems academic discipline in Australian universities—a multi-state case-study protocol

Overview of the multiple case study

The project involves a study of IS academia in Australia. From individual case studies in each of the Australian states, and the Australian Capital Territory, an Australian multiple case study report will be prepared to be published in the *AJIS* (phase one of the study). This research project is planned as a preliminary to a similar study across the Asia-Pacific region.

The study team

QLD	Guy Gable (editor)	Bob Smyth		
WA	Janice Burn	Craig Standing	Chad Lin	
NSW	Jim Underwood	Ernie Jordan		
ACT	Shirley Gregor	Ed Lewis	Craig McDonald	
SA	Paula Swatman	Andy Koronios	Mike Metcalfe	
VIC	Carol Pollard	Elsie Chan		
TAS	Gail Ridley			

Purpose of the case-study protocol

Since separate researchers will undertake the individual state case studies, this protocol seeks to be somewhat more detailed than might otherwise be necessary. It is hoped that this protocol will facilitate some:

1. comparability across the states
2. consistency across the individual case studies
3. efficiency in the conduct of the case studies, with potential for data gathering and some analysis being delegated to research assistants or other junior researchers.

The protocol draws heavily on the approach suggested by Yin (2003), incorporating some of the ideas of Walsham (1995). In particular, this protocol seeks an interpretive approach directed at what Walsham calls 'rich insight'.

Type of case study

Each case study should be viewed as an opportunity to collect and record perceptions of the interviewees (as well as other forms of evidence). In keeping with an interpretive slant, subjectivity on the part of the interviewees and the researchers is accepted. The case studies are to be descriptive and to focus on perceived points of differentiation across universities within a state (other, more readily comparable data might be available from existing surveys). The framework used to guide the study provides a theoretical context for the study, and was derived from the PhD thesis of team member Gail Ridley. It is expected that a historical perspective on the evolution of IS in each university will inform the current state of IS in the university and across the state.

Background to the current study

This Australian multi-state case study is a precursor to a wider Pacific-Asia study ('IS-in-PA'). This study seeks to draw on, and complement, other recent or planned studies of the state of the IS discipline, notably those of Avgerou et al. (1999), Huff and Lehmann (2007), and Pervan and Shanks (2006).

Theoretical framework

There is a body of knowledge that suggests that many of the characteristics of IS are consistent with those observed across emerging disciplines in the early stages of their development. For example, some of the characteristics that manifested themselves in the early evolution of management as a discipline have been seen more recently in the development of IS. Some of these characteristics include:

- a heavy reliance on reference disciplines
- a paucity of theory specific to the discipline
- a perceived lower status than for established disciplines, leading to the adoption of methods from the higher-status disciplines
- limited numbers of textbooks that review the discipline
- poor definition of the boundaries of study
- incorporation organisationally as a subset of an established discipline.

The framework proposed is based on two constructs: 1) the degree of professionalism as a discipline, and 2) maturity as a scientific field. Both are derived from Whitley's theory of scientific change (1984a, 1984b).

The first construct concerns the degree of 'professionalisation' of the discipline, which is expected to increase as the impact of local contingencies decreases. Where a discipline is not highly professionalised, local contingencies such as political pressures have a high impact. Consequently, the degree of professionalisation of IS can be evidenced by the extent of variation in the nature of its research among the 'states' of Australasia over time.

The second construct has been derived from Whitley's three conditions for the establishment of a distinct scientific field:

- scientific reputations become socially prestigious and 'control critical rewards'—that is, those in the discipline have the potential for prestige and power through prominence in that discipline
- standards of research competence and skills become established

- a unique symbol system is developed that allows the exclusion of outsiders and unambiguous communication between initiates within the discipline.

Approach to data gathering

Based on evidence deriving from interviews conducted, and supplemented by documentary and other archival evidence, it is expected that you will ultimately develop a rich description of the state of IS across your state. It is intended that interviews be used as the principal form of data gathering. Where available, existing documentary and archival material should be gathered to supplement the interview data and to provide some triangulation of observations. The interviews are to be semi-structured, with emphasis on factors relating to the emergence of IS, broad perceptions of the interviewee on IS in his/her university, points of differentiation and distinctive features of IS in that state. You should seek answers to the broad themes outlined below, using the supplementary questions only as deemed appropriate. Each interview should last about one hour. Where face-to-face interviews are impractical, telephone interviews will suffice. They will normally be of shorter duration (30 minutes plus) than the face-to-face interviews.

Ethical considerations

You should ensure that all interviews are conducted with due concern for the ethical standards that guide research procedures at the Queensland University of Technology and at your university. Before starting the interview, you should seek from interviewees their written approval to participate in a recorded interview. You should retain one copy of the signed consent, to be stored with the interview recording. The recorded interview need not be transcribed. The recording should be referenced by the interviewer to assist in the preparation of summary interview notes.

Preparation for the interview

Prospective interviewees should be selected from academics within each (if possible) university running IS courses in your designated state. A minimum of one interviewee per institution is recommended where this is practical. In states where there are several universities, a feasible approach to data gathering might involve just two or three 'full' interviews supported by shorter interviews in the other universities. Where resources permit, it will be useful to interview more than one person from each university as a means of gaining a more balanced perspective. In states with few universities, one-to-one interviews might be better replaced with focus groups.

Starting interviews

1. Start the interview by introducing yourself and explaining the purpose of the interview viz. to gather data on the condition of IS in universities in the state. Emphasise that we are seeking particularly broad perceptions on points of differentiation in the approach to IS in the interviewee's university.
2. Outline our agreed definition of IS, as distinct from other ICT disciplines such as computer science and computer engineering.

The original 1994 *Asia Pacific Directory of Information Systems Researchers* (*APDISR*) observed, 'The question, "Who is an Information Systems academic?" is not easily answered.' The *APDISR* goes on to 'loosely define an IS researcher as "one concerned with analysis, design, implementation, evaluation, and management of information systems, from a managerial or user perspective, rather than from a computer science perspective"'. In consultation with your interviewees, therefore, you will need to decide which organisational entities, which parts of the curriculum and which people you consider to relate to IS for the purposes of this study.

Recommended data to be gathered from each interview

Note that rich data are to be sought as indicated by the italicised headings below. The interviewer might use the specific questions to elicit the sort of data that might be useful if this is overlooked by the interviewee. It is not vital that each question below be asked. We accept that the individual state teams will likely have differing emphases in their data collection and interpretation. We feel this will give richness to the individual reports without unduly affecting comparability. Where interviewees can access relevant statistical data outside the interviews, these matters can be considered by the interviewer without being sought during the interview. You might, however, confirm any such statistical data with interviewees, either at the time of the interview or when interview notes are sent to the interviewee for checking.

Get identifying data and the scope of relevant knowledge.

1. Confirm the name of the interviewee; the institution the interviewee represents; and the position of the interviewee in that institution.
2. Explain that you are seeking information about IS courses and IS research. Check whether the interviewee is comfortable answering questions about each area in his/her institution. Where the interviewee has knowledge principally with regard to either research or teaching only, you should try to get the name of, and an introduction to, a suitable person to subsequently cover the other area.

Get a picture of the relative size of the IS presence at the university and the administrative placement of IS.

3. How many people teach IS subjects at the institution?
4. Which administrative groupings (for example, business faculty, school of IT) do the IS teaching staff belong to? Outline how this has evolved over the years.
5. What is the total number of students in your institution? (What is the full-time equivalent?)

    Look for approximate numbers. Do not let the discussion bog down in details. Use existing statistical sources if they are readily available to you.

6. What are the undergraduate and postgraduate IS courses offered at your institution (separate course-work courses from research-based courses)?
7. How many students are currently enrolled in each of the IS courses just referred to?

    Look for approximate numbers. Do not let the discussion bog down in details. Use existing statistical sources if they are readily available to you.

Get a feeling for the extent to which IS at the university is impacted on by local contingencies.

8. Discuss the extent to which IS curriculum and research at your university is affected by local factors (for example, local industry, political pressures).
9. Do you think that IS is any more or less affected by local factors than other disciplines at your university?

Get a feeling for the extent to which IS is identified as a separate field at the university.

10. Discuss the extent to which IS has a separate identity at your university.
11. What factors distinguish IS subjects and research from those that would be found in business and computer science at your university?
12. Do you feel that your position as an IS academic gives you greater or lesser status in your university relative to your colleagues in business and computer science?
13. Is there anything about the terminology of IS at your university that would be foreign/unfamiliar to your business and computer science colleagues?

Get a picture of the distinctive features of the IS curriculum at the university.

14. Discuss the extent to which IS curriculum and research at your university is affected by local factors (for example, local industry, political pressures).
15. Discuss the place of service teaching of IS at your institution, as opposed to teaching in IS courses.

16. What do you see as distinctive features (if any) of IS as taught at your institution? Themes?

17. How do you see your institution's IS courses in relation to those offered by other institutions in your state? Similar in emphasis? Complementary? Sharply different?

18. Are there particular tools, techniques or technologies used in the teaching of IS at your university that are distinctive?

19. Approximately what percentage of your IS course-work students are 'international students'? Which nations are represented most strongly? Has there been any significant change in this pattern in the past three years?

20. Approximately what percentage of your IS research students are 'international students'? Which nations are represented most strongly? Has there been any significant change in this pattern in the past three years?

21. What proportion of IS students at your institution are taught by 'distance education'? Discuss the form/s of distance education used and where most of these distance students are located (locally, interstate, overseas). Is your university distinctive in its approach to IS distance education?

22. To what extent have enrolments in IS at your institution been affected by the recent downturn in ICT employment?

23. What do you see as the main issues relating to the teaching of IS in your institution?

24. What changes are planned for teaching/curriculum in IS in your institution in the next three years?

Get a picture of the distinctive features of IS research at the university.

25. How would you rate the average level of research output across the IS staff in your institution? Discuss your assessment.

26. What is the balance between IS research and IS teaching in your institution, with respect to incentives for each?

27. How is IS research primarily funded in your institution?

28. What are the main areas of focus in IS research in your institution?

29. What are the main IS research methods used in your institution?

30. How many students are currently enrolled in IS PhDs in your institution? Has there been a decrease or increase in these numbers in the past three years?

31. To what extent do you think that the emphasis of research in your institution is consistent with IS research themes in other institutions in your state?

32. Discuss conference attendance by IS researchers in your institution: on average, how many conferences a year would your IS researchers attend? Which conferences are most popular with your IS researchers, and why?

33. What local factors have an impact on IS research in your state?
34. What do you see as the main issues related to IS research in your institution?
35. What changes are planned for IS research in your institution in the next three years? Changes of focus? Changes in funding? Changes in research group structure?

Get interviewee's perception of the characteristics of IS in universities in that state.

36. What general information can you provide about IS teaching and research across tertiary education institutions in your state?

Get interviewee's perception of the key people in their region who have had an impact on IS in universities in that state.

37. Can you name some significant individuals (politicians, bureaucrats, academics, members of professional societies, members of advisory committees) who have had a significant impact on IS in your university? Outline the nature of the impact in each case.
38. Can you give names of suitable people from other institutions in your state who might be usefully interviewed for this study?

Conclude the interview, with thanks to the interviewee. Give a commitment on when the interview notes will be made available to the interviewee for checking. Seek permission for access to the interviewee again for any incidental follow-up.

Acknowledgements

This study of the IS academic discipline in Australian universities has made significant demands on Queensland University of Technology (QUT), in terms of the time and efforts of Professor Gable, Dr Robert Smyth and Karen Stark; the provision of the study team web site; facilities for conferencing; and numerous other resources to support the project. I wish to acknowledge here my appreciation to QUT and the Faculty of Information Technology for this significant provision of resources to make the study achievable.

A project of this magnitude involves a large number of people. Many have contributed their valuable time to the study. In addition to the core study team members, we express our sincere thanks to: 1) state report reviewers, who reviewed a draft of one (or more) of the state case reports; 2) interviewees, who gave their time for evidence collection; and 3) special issue reviewers. We offer our special thanks to the special issue reviewers, who reviewed the complete special issue, offering ideas and advice that were particularly valuable and influential in finalising the papers. Thanks also to the AIS for endorsing the study and for seed funding. Thanks are due also to the ACS for supporting and seed funding the ACIS Archival Analysis.

Finally, my personal thanks to Bob Smyth for his untiring support as project manager throughout the study duration. We could not have made it without him; his input throughout has been substantial. My sincere thanks also to Karen Stark, who crafted sections of the overview, whose due diligence ensured maximum accuracy and completeness and whose meticulous eye introduced a level of presentation quality otherwise not possible within the project's scope.

2. A retrospective of the information systems discipline in Australia

Roger Clarke
Xamax Consultancy Pty Ltd
Canberra, Australia

Abstract

Information systems (IS) emerged as a discipline in the 1960s. It has struggled to define itself, its scope and its relationship with its neighbouring disciplines in the computing and management arenas. Despite that, it has grown into a diverse and busy community. The discipline in Australia numbers some 700 people, and it has had impacts on the international stage. This chapter charts key events in its first four decades, identifies what appear to the author to be the key themes, provides a body of references for future historians to consider in greater detail and from other perspectives and raises questions for the future.

Introduction

The IS discipline has mostly been too concerned about ensuring its future to spend much time celebrating its past, or even understanding it. As pioneers retire, however, the time has come to consolidate sources and memories and provide some historical background to this vibrant but often troubled field.

Research into the discipline's birth led to 1965 and 1967 as the most tenable start dates. The analysis reaches beyond 1995 only selectively. This is partly because of the scale of the undertaking, and partly because lack of perspective makes it much more difficult to write convincingly about 'recent history' than about 'ancient history'. For further comments on author bias, see the acknowledgements.

A history can be approached from a variety of directions. Because it is something of a 'trail-blazing' exercise, this chapter is intentionally eclectic. It blends (or perhaps muddles) the approaches of the chronicler (Who did what when?), the historian of ideas (Where were concepts, models and theories appropriated from? What scope has been evident? Which topics have been important? Which propositions were debated?) and the political historian (What power bases existed? What skirmishes were fought? Who won?). Little time is spent on historiography or critical thinking (Who wrote what, with what biases, and for what purpose?). First, we need some sources. Only then can the battle to own history begin.

The author's own perspectives and biases regarding the scope of the IS discipline will become apparent progressively through the chapter, but two aspects need to be addressed at the outset. Rather than beginning with a discussion about what IS is and what it should be, this chapter sets out with the pragmatic approach that 'IS is what IS does'. Reflection on the rich and at times tumultuous debates about those questions belongs elsewhere. The second limitation is that the traditions with which the author is most familiar are those of Australian IS, US management information systems (MIS), UK IS and information management (IM) and *Wirtschaftsinformatik* in German-speaking countries (which is translated most appropriately as 'business information systems'). These provide ample evidence, firstly, of different flavours but secondly of a measure of unanimity about the discipline's scope in action, and the matters that, at any given time, have been proper topics to be considered by the discipline's members.

The research method adopted was based heavily on secondary research, starting with the author's own substantial archives dating from 1970, followed by searches for relevant published resources. The modest literature that was uncovered is listed in the bibliography in Clarke (2007). Information from publications was supplemented with face-to-face interviews with a number of key players during the early years and e-mail exchanges and telephone conversations with a substantial number of people—in Australia and overseas. Many of these discussions resulted in further references that needed to be reviewed. The acknowledgements section lists the individuals on whom the author has placed greatest reliance. The now-compulsory 'web trawl' delivered some hits of consequence. Relevant resources are also listed in Clarke (2007). The intended review of IS departments' sites for historically relevant material was not undertaken, because the sampling that was performed suggested that there were more promising avenues in which to invest the available time. The only formalised departmental histories that were unearthed were Greig and Levin (1989) regarding computing at Caulfield/Chisholm (1965–88), Dreyfus (2004) regarding the University of Melbourne's IS department (1994–2004) and Burrows (2006) regarding the same university's accounting department (1925–2004).

The 'IS-in-Oz' team reviewed and provided substantial feedback on the proposal in March 2005, on a sketch in May 2005, on an interim report in November 2005 and on a draft in January 2006. The version of May 2006 was released with a request for comment sent to about 40 senior members of the discipline in Australia and overseas. This elicited important feedback, which has been reflected in this version. An article-length version was extracted and published (Clarke 2006).

The chapter begins by considering the intellectual origins of the IS discipline. Building on this foundation, key events are identified that are associated with the establishment of the discipline—overseas and in Australia. The development of the discipline is then traced, using a variety of metrics. The later parts of the chapter identify some key themes, of a political and an intellectual nature.

Origins and nature of the IS discipline

The foundations of IS can be traced back to the late nineteenth and early twentieth-century rational-management stream of thought, associated with Fayol and Taylor. Although usually interpreted as being about efficiency in the use of physical resources through understanding of the 'time and motion' of agents, the movement is reinterpreted easily as also being about the use of information. Drucker (1968) included a large section on what he called 'the knowledge economy' (which would currently be referred to as 'the information economy'). Drucker (1968:328) argued that 'the idea that knowledge, systematically acquired, could be applied systematically to work is no more than 200 to 250 years old', and first occurred in tool makers and tool designers in the eighteenth and early nineteenth centuries, who laid the foundation for the Industrial Revolution.

Automated equipment—in particular, punched-card handling devices—were in use in large-scale applications at the very beginning of the twentieth century, in particular for the US census (for example, Kistermann 1991). The invention, articulation, application and rapid improvement of electro-mechanical and then electronic computers in the period 1935–50 is well documented (for example, Campbell-Kelly 2003; Norberg 2005). These initiatives were motivated by the processing of ephemeral data into significant results, rather than what we would now call data management. Technologies to provide permanent storage quickly came to be seen as an important adjunct to computation, and the complex of technologies needed to support what became computer-based IS quickly emerged.

The use of electronic computers for the processing of administrative data brought a substantial impetus to the emergence of the IS discipline. Applications of this kind began simultaneously in the United Kingdom and the United States in 1951, with Leo at the Lyons Tea Company, and Eckert and Mauchly's Univac 1 at the US census (Caminer et al. 1998; Land 2000b; Johnson 2006). The first installation of a computer in a US company expressly for administrative purposes appears to have occurred only in 1954, for payroll at General Electric in Louisville, Kentucky (Mason 2005).

To extract a comprehensive history of the early years of business applications of computing, it is necessary to read beyond the substantial US literature on the subject. Many US publications subscribe to the myth that very little of consequence happened outside the United States, and they merely footnote German and particularly British work, even though it was vital from the 1930s into the 1960s. On the other hand, the tempo in the United States picked up very quickly, as banks and airlines recognised opportunities, and even more quickly after the emergence of computer architectures designed for business applications—particularly the IBM 360 series from 1964. From about 1960 onwards, US energy dominated innovation in information technology (IT) in Australia, as elsewhere.

The emergence of the IS discipline was in historical terms brisk, but to an observer at the time it would have appeared laboured and wayward. It appears to have followed somewhat different paths in various countries and regions, with distinct flavours discernible in the United States, the United Kingdom, Germany, Scandinavia and Australia. The myopia of the author—and of English-language cultures generally—makes it likely that critical ideas from other countries have been overlooked, or inaccurately attributed.

Differences also occurred within countries, particularly those of substantial geographical size. The term 'the tyranny of distance' (coined by Australian historian Geoffrey Blainey in his 1966 book of that name) might seem quaint to post-Internet generations, but it afflicted countries the size of Australia, Canada and the United States. During the early years of the IS discipline, with no coordinative mechanisms such as an information infrastructure any more sophisticated than the voice-only services over the Public Switched Telephone Network (PSTN) and textual data over the telegraph and telex networks, and with no accreditation panels, no curriculum committees, no textbooks, few conferences and relatively high airfares, there was ample scope for strong, energetic and visionary individuals to have significant local, regional and national impact.

It was natural that the new interest in information would draw on existing disciplines and professions for which data and their processing were already an interest, and on emergent disciplines that were adopting new approaches made feasible by the new technology. The dominant strands appear to have been accounting and the emergent computer science, together with threads arising from a range of other sources. The following were of particular importance.

- *Organisation and methods (O&M)*, a branch of industrial engineering that applied a form of 'rational management' to organisations' internal operations. This was influential particularly in the United Kingdom, and in some areas of Australia.
- *Operations management*—although this was far less influential in Australia than it was in the United States.
- *Operations research*, as it developed in the United Kingdom and the United States during World War II, and its applications in the business arena as management science and decision sciences. Particularly influential authors were Simon (1960) and Miller and Starr.

- *Management accounting*—particularly Anthony (1965) and Prince (1966, 1970). Similarly traceable to Taylorism and industrial engineering, this approach focuses on applications of micro-economics that are useful within the organisation, measurement schemes to enable the discovery and analysis of exceptions and ways to manage measurements and communicate them to the managers who need them.

- *Systems thinking*, which drew originally on von Bertalanffy and Boulding and the Society for General Systems Research in the United States from the mid-1950s onwards (Mason 2005), Emery, Churchman, Jay Forrester, and Katz and Kahn (1966); and in the United Kingdom von Bertalanffy in 1950, and later Peter Checkland. Closely related to this movement was cybernetics, as pioneered by Norbert Wiener, further developed by Ashby and applied by Stafford Beer. This focused on the feedback and control aspects of systems. There was much interest in these bodies of theory in Continental Europe as well, centred on the International Institute for Applied Systems Analysis (IIASA) conferences in Schloss Laxenburg, south of Vienna. The emphases and patterns of development on the two sides of the Atlantic, and within Continental Europe, were rather different, and no history has been located to date that integrates them.

- *Socio-technical systems*. This thread developed in the United Kingdom from the 1950s onwards—initially at the Tavistock Institute—and was adopted and extended particularly in Britain and Scandinavia. It represented a reaction against the reductionist thinking inherent in the previous strands, and resulted in (sophisticated) mechanistic designs: 'If a technical system is created at the expense of a social system, the results obtained will be sub-optimal' (Mumford 2006, attributed to the Tavistock Institute). The soft-systems school of thought followed. Publications that documented and consolidated this movement included Mumford and Banks (1967), Bjorn-Andersen (1980), Checkland (1981), Mumford (1983) and Wood-Harper et al. (1985).

- *Management theory* placed expectations on the new and expensive technology. Drucker was particularly influential, as were Ackoff and Likert, and Macfarlan, and Scott Morton (1971) at the Harvard Business School. A range of what could be called 'thinking manager's gurus' had substantial influence on DP/IS/IT managers, including EDP Analyzer (later I/S Analyzer), Dearden, Auerbach, Infotech 'State-of-the-Art' Reports and James Martin. Their impact on IS academics was less substantial, but Martin in particular provided syntheses of material that were much used as IS textbooks.

Beyond the intellectual sources were those dictated by pragmatism. The application of computers to administrative, commercial, industrial and government purposes required the development of software. The necessary rapid production of new software developers depended on the expression and structuring of know-how into what would now be called 'codified knowledge' about what came to be called analysis, design and programming. From 1967 until about the mid-1980s, this practical need had a substantial impact on the conception of the scope of the IS discipline. Since then, applications development has drifted away from the mainstream of IS—and IS from it. Programming has been reduced to an industrial skill, and design has become either the independent, cognate discipline of software engineering or a substantial component of the adjacent discipline of computer science—or both. It is unclear which discipline 'owns' analysis, if any. To many IS academics, the perspective typified by the Institute of Electrical and Electronic Engineering (IEEE) is far too narrow and mechanical, with its reductionist conception of systems analysis as 'requirements engineering'.

As the frame within which the remainder of this chapter is developed, some clustering of the themes and topics can be suggested, as follows.

- *Technology as enabler and driver*, including computers, electronic data processing (EDP), applications, applications development, the software development life cycle (SDLC), the systems life cycle (SLC), computer usage, usability, technology adoption and impediments to adoption.
- *Organisations*, as the primary context within which information systems are developed and operated, and for whose purposes they are applied, including organisational behaviour, requirements elicitation, business process analysis, usability, technology adoption and impediments to adoption.
- *Systems thinking*, including O&M, GST and cybernetics leading from SDLC to SLC, socio-technical theory, soft-systems methods, incorporation of human factors, usability, adoption and merging with human behaviour and communications into semiotics and perhaps ontological foundations.
- *Business school thinking*, including operations research (OR)/management systems (MS), management accounting, controls and auditing, management of DP/IS/IT/IC&T, information management, usability and adoption.
- *Data and information management*, including database management systems (DBMS), data modelling, data dictionaries, information resource dictionary systems (IRDS) and, later, the absorption from librarianship of key concepts about meta-data.

It is stressed that this clustering is a clumsy classification, not a clean taxonomy. As evidenced by the appearance of such terms as 'adoption' in multiple clusters, there was continual cross-feeding and co-evolution of thinking. Particularly during the formative years, the process and the product were highly eclectic, as each local leader sought to make sense of the domain and contribute to progress.

The foundation years overseas

This section reviews briefly the beginnings of IS in Europe and North America. It is not intended as a contribution to a broad IS history (because that would require much deeper treatment). Its purpose is to provide a backdrop to the early years in Australia.

The dominance of North American contributors in the published literature suggests that the United States was first in the field. The evidence as a whole, however, suggests that the emergence of IS could have been slightly earlier in Europe—and lagged only slightly in Australia. No material has been located at this stage in relation to the early years in Canada. Clarke (2007) provides time-lines of key events in Australia and overseas.

Europe

Borje Langefors was appointed Professor in Information Processing at the University of Stockholm in 1965. He proposed a theoretical basis for IS based on 'the infological equation $I = i (D, S, T)$, where I stands for information, D data, S the recipient prior knowledge as result of the individual's life experience, T the time, and i the interpretation process' (Shen 2003). His early texts (Langefors 1963, 1966) were translated into English, although it is not easy to judge the extent of their impact on thinking in English-speaking countries. The 'infological equation' is reflected in Mason (2005:14), which refers to information as 'data interpreted within a point-of-view', and in this author's own explanation of information as 'data that has value [that] depends upon context' (Clarke 1992). Both also appear to relate to Wiener's conception of information as 'data that an organisation could employ for the direction of its activities' (Mason 2005). It is in stark contrast with Shannon and Weaver's conception of information as 'a measure of one's freedom of choice when one selects a message'. That works brilliantly when applied to the transmission of data over a noisy channel, but very poorly in the contexts addressed by IS. Scandinavia has also had a long and strong association with the organisation and human behaviour aspects of IS, including from Niels Bjørn-Andersen, who, after completion of his PhD with Enid Mumford in Manchester, returned to Copenhagen in 1972.

In Germany, *Wirtschaftsinformatik* (roughly translated as 'business data processing' or 'business informatics') emerged within *Betriebswirtschaftslehre* (roughly, 'business administration') from the late 1950s and was influenced later much by *Informatik* ('computer science'). The earliest claim that has been found for the establishment of IS is the Institute for Business Organisation and Automation at the University of Koeln (E. Grochla) in 1963. The first German-language doctoral thesis on an IS topic was in 1966 (Peter Mertens); the next in 1968 (Lutz Heinrich). The first chairs in German-speaking countries were at Linz in Austria (Mertens, 1968–69; Heinrich, 1970–2004), then at Karlsruhe,

Erlangen-Nürnberg, Darmstadt, Muenchen and Speyer. The first full majors were at Wien and Linz in 1974–75, and in the 1980s large schools emerged in Berlin, Köln, Frankfurt-am-Main, Mannheim, Münster, Nürnberg and Saarbrücken. A national conference has existed since 1987. The leading German-language journal has been called *Wirtschaftsinformatik* since 1990, but was established as *Elektronische Rechtanlagen* ('electronic computing systems', 1959–72) and, between 1972 and 1990, was named *Angewandte Informatik* ('applied computing').

Wirtschaftsinformatik has had a sustained and strong orientation towards data processing and software development, with substantial practical work, but also a significant information management stream (Heinrich 1993; Avgerou et al. 1999; Mertens et al. 2002). Patterns in other German-speaking countries have been not dissimilar. Distinctions between the German and other styles are drawn out by this quotation: 'To what extent will Anglo-American researchers adopt the prototypical IS approach being cultivated in Germany and to what extent will German IS research better adapt to the survey-oriented Anglo-American research culture?' (Mertens et al. 2002).

In the United Kingdom, key appointments occurred in 1967: Frank Land at the London School of Economics (LSE) and Peter Keen at the London Business School (LBS). Together with Enid Mumford, already at Manchester, there were now three separate and rather different flavours. A key publication appeared in the same year: *The Computer and the Clerk* (Mumford and Banks 1967). This greatly influenced the conception and scope of IS in the United Kingdom, which has generally been attuned to a human-oriented interpretation of systems thinking that reflects the intrinsic ambiguity of the contexts in which information is used and IT applied, and the existence of a range of perspectives that need to be factored into analyses. This relatively 'soft' nature was noticeable in the contributions of Ronald Stamper at LSE from 1972, Peter Checkland at Lancaster and later Trevor Wood-Harper. The discipline in the United Kingdom has, however, come to reflect a wide diversity of approaches.

North America

The history of the IS discipline in North America (and, to a considerable extent, the world as a whole) is associated by many people with the appointment of Gordon Davis to a chair at Minnesota in 1967. The context was accounting within a graduate school of business, but impregnated with systems thinking. The field was described as 'management information systems' (MIS). Mason (2005:21) traces the origins of that term at least as far back as a 1962 book by James D. Gallagher.

Davis had already published an introductory textbook on computers for business students (Davis 1965), but his key intellectual contributions were encapsulated in his 'conceptual foundations' text (Davis 1974; Davis and Olson 1984). Davis spent close to four decades at Minnesota, from 1967 to 2004. Many of the people whose doctorates he supervised have also been active supervisors and, by the time of his retirement in 2005, the 'family' had reached the fourth generation and a total count of more than 100.

The year 1967 also saw the appointment of Bill King at Pittsburgh, who brought an OR perspective, but grafted on from other disciplines as appropriate. MIS was established at the University of California at Los Angeles (UCLA) by no later than 1968, also growing out of accounting, but with a strong 'systems thinking' emphasis (Mason 2005). Dan Couger published on systems analysis and development techniques—also in a manner imbued with systems thinking. Jim Emery published foundation textbooks (Emery 1969, 1971). Macfarlan and Scott Morton at Harvard Business School published on management aspects of IS from the late 1960s onwards.

Banker and Kauffman (2004) note that the journal *Management Science* started a column on 'information systems in management science' in 1967, edited by Harry Stern, and included IS in the first departmental structure of the journal in 1969. The Society for Information Management (SIM), which has always targeted the needs of the senior IS executive (in contemporary fashion, the chief information officer or CIO), was an important supporter from 1968. The Association for Computing Machinery (ACM), particularly through its Special Interest Group for Business Data Processing (SIGBDP) and The Institute for Management Science (TIMS) also provided support and considerable influence—from the computing and the operations research perspectives respectively. A perspective on the origins and evolution of MIS is in Dickson (1981).

In the United States, MIS has been imbued with a rationalist approach to systems thinking. Rationalism can be 'bounded', but 'satisficing' is still rational. There is limited scope for looseness and soft systems, little attention is paid to contexts that lack a single powerful entity that can dictate a requirements statement, and limited credence is granted to serendipity and what Ciborra called 'bricolage'. Strategically successful IS have to be attributed to intelligent management and cannot be seen to be the semi-accidental result of complex interactions. Tensions between perspectives are in principle capable of being balanced out, but in many cases they are simply overridden in deference to some 'greater good'. The greater good is by definition determined rationally, but from some particular perspective—generally that of the most powerful player or alliance of players.

Clearly, this stark juxtaposition of 'hard US' versus 'soft British and Scandinavian' philosophies in IS is an over-simplification that is subject to many qualifications, particularly in recent years as the level of trans-Atlantic communications, interactions and alliances has increased. In particular, a number of US writers have argued the case for interpretivism—for example, Boland (1978), Lee (1994) and Chen and Hirschheim (2004). Nonetheless, the tension between the 'hard' and the 'soft' exists; and it is not infrequent that the distinction is a regional one.

The first 40–50 years in Australia

A retrospective needs to adopt a largely chronological presentation, and to divide the period covered into digestible pieces. One possibility is to apply an interpretation of the phases of the IT, such as that in Table 2.1.

Table 2.1 Information technology history and its implications

	1940–80	1980–2000	2000–40
Processor technology	Grosch's Law: bigger is more efficient	VLSI/micros: more is more efficient	Commoditisation: chips with everything
Network technology	Star: centralised	Multi-connected: decentralised	Wireless: ubiquitous
Processor interrelationships	Master–slave: control	Client–server: request–response	P2P: collaboration
Organisational form	Hierarchies	Managed networks	Self-managing market/networks
Software and content	Closed, proprietary	Confusion and tension	Open
Politics	Authoritarianism: intolerance	Confusion and tension	Democracy and frustrated intolerance

Source: Clarke, R. 2004, 'Origins and nature of the Internet in Australia', Xamax Consultancy Pty Ltd, viewed 22 March 2007, <http://www.anu.edu.au/people/Roger.Clarke/II/OzI04.html> [at Exhibit 3.7]

Such an interpretation would, however, be unsatisfactory because although technology has been a driver—and even the major driver—it has not been determinative of the development of the IS discipline. This section presents what appear to the author to have been the key events in the emergence of the discipline in Australia, divided into three chunks of time that are proposed as being useful rather than decisive. Mason (2005) uses a related but somewhat different division:

- pre-formation: mid-eighteenth century to 1954 (addressed above)
- gestation: 1954–68 (addressed below)
- birth: 1968–2000 (subdivided below for reasons specific to the Australian context)
- rebirth: 2000 (addressed in the closing sections of this chapter).

Until 1960

Australia has something of a history in automated computation. In particular, the world's first totalisator—for 'totalling up' wagers, particularly on horse-races, and sharing the pool among the winning bets (and extracting fees and taxes)—was invented in Western Australia by George Julius about 1913 (Bennett et al. 1994). Although this was originally an entirely mechanical system, electrical components were later added. Julius's company enjoyed a world-wide monopoly for some time.

Later, the fourth electronic digital computer, CSIR Mk 1 (1948–56), was entirely 'home grown' in Australia—at the Council for Scientific and Industrial Research (CSIR) Division of Radiophysics in Sydney (Pearcey 1988:12–19, 160. See also Bennett et al. 1994:15–58, esp. 16–30). Mk 1's successor, CSIRAC, ran from 1956 until 1964 at the University of Melbourne. The University of Sydney's locally designed and built SILLIAC ran from 1954 until 1968, and the university also designed and built SNOCOM for the Snowy Mountains Authority (1960–67). Adapted versions of imported machines ran at the University of New South Wales (UNSW) (UTECOM, 1956–66) and at the Weapons Research Establishment (WRE) (WREDAC, 1956–66). There is a persistent mythology in Australia that the Commonwealth Scientific and Industrial Research Organisation (CSIRO, which succeeded the CSIR in 1949) abandoned investment in computing in favour of cloud seeding. This story is all the more poignant when it is appreciated that the last CSIRO-developed computer, from about 1963–68, was called the Cirrus (Pearcey 1988:66). A recent international perspective on the early years is in Chapter 7, 'Wizards of Oz', in Hally (2005:161–84). The predominant influences throughout this formative period were British rather than American, which derived in considerable measure from John Bennett's work on the earliest machines in the United Kingdom, including the first stored-program computer, EDSAC, at Cambridge.

Pearcey (1988:157) and Bennett et al. (1994:26) identify the first computer conference in Australia as having been held in March 1951 in Sydney, run by the University of Sydney and CSIRO. Bennett et al. (1994:28) cites papers in the *Proceedings* of an April 1952 conference on automatic computing machines, run by CSIRO, although this could have been a late publication of the papers from the 1951 event.

The second Conference on Automatic Computing and Data Processing was held in June 1957 at WRE (later renamed the Defence Science and Technology Organisation—DSTO) at Salisbury, north of Adelaide. It had three sections, one of which was 'Business applications'. The conference chair, John Ovenstone, contributed a paper on 'Business and accountancy data processing' (Pearcey 1988:47–8). This was only six years after the first commercial use of a computer in the United Kingdom and the first governmental use in the United States, and only three years after the first commercial use in the United States.

Until 1957, the circa-8 computers in Australia were all in universities and the WRE. By 1960, however, there were 34 within government alone and, by 1963, about 80 computers (Pearcey 1988:137, 159) or 'nearly 100' (Bennett et al. 1963:11). Bennett claimed that the count per million of population was on a par with Sweden, West Germany and the United Kingdom, and was exceeded only by the United States, Canada and Switzerland.

Few of the computers were intended exclusively for research. Commonwealth government agencies—beginning with the Department of Defence and the Australian Bureau of Statistics (ABS)—had installed computers for administrative tasks. In defence, for example, Ovenstone, an immigrant from the United Kingdom, was appointed to the new position of Controller of Automatic Data Processing at senior level (Band 2 SES), and drove the project from 1958 to 1964 (Pearcey 1988:72–4). The organisationally logical way for bureaucracies to integrate programmable computers into their ways of working was to conceive of them as super-tabulators, and manage them in a similar way.

The first Australian companies to install computers are understood to have been the two insurance companies AMP and MLC—both in 1960, nine years after the first in the United Kingdom, and six years after the first in the United States. In interview, Bill Caelli said that BHP had IBM 1401 and 1440 models installed in Newcastle and Wollongong by no later than 1962, and applied them to a variety of operations-management and commercial functions.

From 1960 to 1973

The Australian National Committee on Computation and Automatic Control (ANCCAC) was formed in 1959, with John Bennett as chair. It appears that 'the First [Australian computer] Conference was held at the University of Sydney and the University of NSW on 24–27 May 1960 under the chairmanship of Dr. J. M. Bennett of SILLIAC fame' (McDowell 2002). According to McDowell, 43 of the 158 papers at the event were focused on 'commercial applications'.

This was very early in the international history of computing outside the confines of closed military institutions. The first international congress was held only in 1959, in Paris. The International Federation for Information Processing (IFIP) was formed in 1960—and John Bennett was one of the key instigators of its formation.

Computing was a new field and suffered the classic 'bootstrapping' problem. Very few staff with the necessary background were available for hire—although migrants from the United Kingdom who could claim some relevant background, such as cryptanalysis, were in demand. Tertiary institutions could not yet offer courses, because they had no staff who could develop teaching materials and provide instruction. Agencies depended heavily initially on such training as was available from the suppliers of the technology they had purchased, and on the internal training schemes that they put together. A limited set of design techniques was available at this stage; however, Caelli recalls Fred O'Toole at BHP Newcastle being a strong fan of decision tables in 1963.

The second conference in 1963 included 20 such papers, primarily case-study reports, including one by Ovenstone on the Department of Defence, and others on the Snowy Mountains Authority Stores System, insurance and banking.

Training within the Commonwealth public sector was formalised as the Programmer-in-Training (PIT) scheme, beginning in 1963 (White and Palfreyman 1963; Bennett et al. 1994:108; ABS 2005; interview with Gerry Maynard in 2005). This 'was oriented toward training staff for establishing and running commercial and administrative applications of computing' (Pearcey 1988:122), and involved 'a full year at about twenty hours per week of class time, and effectively more than twenty hours per week of related private study' (p. 121). The scheme was run at least in Canberra and Melbourne. In Canberra, the Department of Defence ran it for its own staff and the then Commonwealth Bureau of Census and Statistics (CBCS, soon after renamed the ABS) ran it for itself and other agencies. The Postmaster General's Department (PMG) ran the Melbourne courses. Coordination was provided by the Public Service Board (PSB, disestablished in 1987).

The CBCS/ABS variant was what would later be called a 'sandwich course', including 'two ten-week stints of on-the-job training'. In an interview, Gerry Maynard said that the content was about 50 per cent programming and 50 per cent systems analysis and design. The 1965 CBCS syllabus included two languages, FORTRAN and COMPASS (CDC's Assembler), and the 1971 ABS syllabus somehow managed to cram in COBOL as well. 'Exams at the end of the year included a major systems analysis and design exam for which a time was allowed of "up to seven hours if required"' (ABS 2005).

Some hundreds of people entered the industry through these courses, primarily into the Commonwealth Public Service, but with substantial ripple effects into state government agencies and the private sector. This author's professional life in IS began in 1971, when he was hired into the Sydney industrial corporation Wormalds by Neville Clissold, a 1965 PIT scheme graduate.

By the mid-1960s, courses that were the precursors to what became 'computer science' were emerging in various tertiary institutions in various departments, including physics (Sydney), engineering (UNSW) and mathematics (Newcastle). The author and several reviewers were subjected to primitive versions and crippled subsets of FORTRAN about 1967.

In Australia, as elsewhere, the computer science discipline largely avoided applications, particularly those in business and government. This provided space for the emergence of data-processing specialisations and the IS discipline.

In 1965, the Caulfield Institute appears to have established the first specialist department, called Electronic Data Processing (EDP). The foundation staff were John McClelland, Doug Mills, Jack White and Pearl Levin, joined soon afterwards by Peter Juliff, Bob Grant and Gerry Maynard. Trevor Pearcey joined as head of department in 1972. The courses combined instruction about technology with teaching about how to apply it. Programming was a central feature, because all applications had to be custom built, few utilities were available and the era of code libraries was yet to arrive (Greig and Levin 1985).

Meanwhile, IS topics were emerging in university accounting departments. These were isolated, and the period was poorly documented. From interviews, it appears that the first mover was Ted Dunn, from 1965 to 1973, at the University of Tasmania, using Algol (interview with Stewart Leech). From the author's personal knowledge, Phil Grouse was offering full units at UNSW by no later than 1968, the purpose of which was to enable commerce students to understand computers, software and their applications, programming languages and software development. At the University of Melbourne, John McMahon and Stewart Leech offered an EDP unit in 1970, but this grew out of earlier fee-paying courses for industry (interview with Stewart Leech in March 2005; Burrows 2006). Interviews have also unearthed mentions of the then Wollongong College of UNSW, and of Douglas V. A. Campbell, of the Monash Accounting Department during the late 1960s.

Sydney and Melbourne were major world cities, and Wollongong was one of the major centres in the then very large steel industry. Hobart's early activity was presumably stimulated by the installation at the Tasmanian Hydro-Electric Commission.

Further Australian Computer Conferences (ACCs) were organised by ANCCAC—the second in Melbourne in 1963 and, in 1966, the third in Canberra (Pearcey 1988:130). Meanwhile, various state-based associations of practitioners emerged during the first half of the 1960s. The early movers were generally well educated and scientific in outlook. The Australian Computer Society (ACS) was formed in 1966 through the federation of those associations.

The PIT scheme was operated by at least the ABS until 1972. In interview, Cyril Brookes said that he arranged for a course to be run in Port Kembla in the late 1960s, to support the BHP steelworks and local industry on which it depended. Beginning in the late 1960s, a transition was begun to several colleges of advanced education (CAEs). For example, the ABS conducted training in conjunction with the Canberra College of Advanced Education (CCAE), with an internal bureau exam. By 1972, Caulfield Institute in Melbourne, Bendigo College and the CCAE were all operating award courses whose origins could be traced to the PIT scheme (Gerry Maynard in interview; Pearcey 1988:121–2; Greig and Levin 1989). Caulfield developed the course into a formal Graduate Diploma in Data Processing, and then expanded into a range of other specialised postgraduate courses.

Internal training courses continued to have their advantages (for example, Fiedler 1969, 1970), but gradually what would later come to be called 'outsourcing' was applied. For new entrants, courses were provided primarily by universities and CAEs, although training in specific programming languages and software products was offered by suppliers. Universities, CAEs, suppliers and the emergent private-sector training companies conducted continuing professional development courses.

The ACS established the *Australian Computer Journal* (*ACJ*) in 1967, and for many years also published a second-tier, non-refereed *Australian Computer Bulletin* (*ACB*). Until the establishment of the *Australasian Journal of Information Systems* (*AJIS*) in 1994, these were the only directly relevant domestic outlets for Australian IS academics.

The ACS also took over the Australian Computer Conferences, and ran well-attended events beginning with the fourth conference in August 1969 and the fifth in Brisbane in May 1972; it then ran the conferences biennially and then annually with the last of the 18 held in 1991 (Bennett et al. 1994:296). By the early 1990s, the computing community had become the IT community, and had splintered into a great many specialist conferences. With that, the attractiveness of a focal event waned. An annual Computing in CAEs Conference also ran from the late 1960s until the late 1980s. The papers presented at these conferences were lightly refereed in comparison with the *ACJ*, but the topics were of relevance to an analysis of the preoccupations of the profession and discipline at the time—for example, this author's first paper at the seventh ACC in Perth was entitled 'Top-down structured programming in COBOL' (Clarke 1976).

A measure of the explosion in business applications between the mid-1960s and mid-1970s can be gauged from the once-fraught area of payroll processing. Large government agencies and corporations wrote the earliest payroll applications in the early to mid-1960s. In interview, Caelli recalled using the patch-panel of an IBM 407 in late 1962 to program payroll for IBM Newcastle. In 1971–72, working as a systems analyst for an industrial company, this author had little option but to design and write a payroll application to run on the company's GE405. In 1975, however, working for a shipping company with 400 employees and a Honeywell 2000, there was a choice of several packages, one of which was adapted to satisfy some specific requirements, and converted to run on the company's machine, with little difficulty or delay. In short, the passage from custom-built assembler applications, via custom-built COBOL applications, to a mature market of packaged applications required, for this particular application, little more than a decade. This had substantial implications for the nature of market demand, and hence IS syllabi.

An important step in the maturation of the computer industry was the 'unbundling' of software from hardware. Until IBM's announcement in 1969, computers had been purchased for a single price, with such software included as the supplier could offer. As the sophistication and significance grew, software needed to be priced separately. That in turn led to greater visibility, and what would now be called application programming interfaces (APIs) and 'open source', such that specialist software developers could offer add-on and replacement software (for example, Campbell-Kelly 2003).

Although academics in foundation disciplines such as mathematics and physics had played a considerable part in the establishment of the ACS, its primary role quickly became that of a professional association. Its most direct relationship with tertiary institutions was as an accreditation body, assessing the suitability of courses as a basis for professional membership of the society. As Pearcey (1988:131) put it, '[T]he direction of development of the ACS moved away from its early, more academic style to represent the wider interests of [its] new membership more directly.' This encapsulates nicely the way in which the relationship between profession and discipline has seemed frequently to be as much about tension and distance as about mutual respect and cooperation.

The ACS has played an important role in the International Federation for Information Processing (IFIP), whose working groups run important international conferences in the computer science and IS disciplines. Several Australians have been major players in IFIP, including Ashley Goldsworthy as president, Bill Caelli as chair of TC11, Guy Gable as chair of WG 11.2 and similar contributions by others to TC8 and its working groups. Several major IFIP conferences were held in Australia, including the World Congress in 1980, and major TC8 conferences in 1984 and 1988.

By about 1970, IS was becoming a recognisable disciplinary activity within universities. At the University of Queensland, computer science offered a postgraduate diploma in IS, and accounting offered an Honours unit taught by British academic Peter Richards. Ross Jeffery and Ron Weber were in the same University of Queensland Honours class in 1970–72, and both submitted Honours theses on IS topics. Weber's, in 1972, was entitled 'An examination of file structures for information processing systems'. Other institutions active about this time included the New South Wales Institute of Technology (NSWIT, later the University of Technology, Sydney; Philip Stanley) and Queensland Institute of Technology (QIT, now Queensland University of Technology; Alan Underwood).

The author's Honours thesis at UNSW, also in 1972, was on an IS-related management accounting topic. It is noteworthy that, of the strands noted in the origins section of this chapter, almost all were represented in the readings set for the UNSW Management Accounting Honours unit in 1972, which was designed by liberal accounting professor Bill Stewart. The exceptions were O&M (which had already been covered in undergraduate IS), management theory (represented by Ackoff and Likert, but not yet by Macfarlan and Scott Morton) and socio-technical and soft-systems thinking (which were yet to make their impact in Australia, and in any case did not fit well with the then strongly numerate and rational patterns of management accounting and the emergent

IS/MIS discipline). The author has no record or memory of the Minnesota School having an influence at that stage, although it did soon afterwards; nor is this author aware of contact between the Queensland and UNSW schools until after 1972. Ross Jeffery did, however, move to the latter in 1975.

Although much of the intellectual basis of the IS discipline in Australia was provided by Americans, the materials used for teaching professional knowledge to undergraduates during the foundation years were much more eclectic. In this author's experience, some came from technology suppliers (mostly American, but some British), much was home grown and at least as many texts and articles had UK origins as US ones. In interview, Caelli referred to early systems analysis courses deriving from the Leo experience in the United Kingdom, and Cyril Brookes bemoaned the lack of appropriate textbooks as late as the end of the 1970s.

It is instructive to compare developments in IS with the emergence of computer science. Although computer science units emerged from the late 1950s in departments of physics, electrical engineering, mathematics and statistics, the growth was very slow until the mid to late 1960s. In 1963, there were 18 full-time staff in eight universities, with only John Bennett occupying a chair (Bennett 1963:14). According to Pearcey (1988:103–18), departments of computer science emerged in the following order: Basser at the University of Sydney (out of physics, John Bennett, about 1956 and independent from 1959); Adelaide (John Ovenstone, 1964); UNSW (out of electrical engineering, M. W. Allen, emergent from 1965); Monash (initially information science, C. S. Wallace, 1968); Queensland (G. A. Rose, 1969); Melbourne (Peter Poole, 1972); and Tasmania (Arthur Sale, 1974).

Offerings in computer science in most cases migrated from postgraduate diplomas back to final-year undergraduate, eventually expanding into full majors. It appears that the first full computer science majors became available only in 1975, at the Universities of Melbourne and Tasmania (Bennett et al. 1994:152). Information systems units were well established by then, because demand had ensured that many universities offered IS service units, at least the Universities of New South Wales and Tasmania already offered IS majors and others were emergent, and many CAEs and institutes offered postgraduate diploma courses in various areas of computing, including IS. As Pearcey (1988:116) put it, '[I]n some institutions special courses which concentrate upon administrative uses in computing are offered outside the formal computing departments and centres.'

It was to prove crucial that, by the end of 1973, there were at least six professors of computer science, but none of IS.

From 1974 to 1987

The development of computer science was explosive. Sufficient full professorships existed, and more were established. The Australian Computer Science Conference (ACSC) was established in 1978, the Australian Association of Professors of Computer Science (AAPCS) was formed in 1982 and the total academic staff-count more than trebled from 1981 to 1990—to 388 (Sale 1994). By 1988, there were about 1200 computer majors graduating from departments of computer science or similar, in 17 universities and 22 CAEs (Pearcey 1988:124). The political development of the IS discipline, on the other hand, lagged computer science by more than 15 years, hamstrung by the absence of the political power associated with a department and at least one full professor.

Only in 1974 was the first professor of IS appointed (Cyril Brookes) and the first university IS department formed (at UNSW). This was almost a decade after the CAE sector had started to form departments of computing and data processing. The move was a strategic measure by UNSW's Dean of the Faculty of Commerce and Economics, Athol Carrington. The *Australian Financial Review* reported at the time that 'the appointment was the first at an Australian university specifically directed towards the financial and managerial applications of computers and operations research technology' (McGregor 1974).

In interview in mid-2005, Brookes said that, in the mid-1970s, there was no body of knowledge and no clear foundation on which to build it. The SDLC and DBMS had emerged in the late 1960s, but it required years of experimentation and refinement before they matured and merged into structured analysis and design. Only then was a framework available for which project management could be overlaid, as a basis for teaching and research. In addition, no prior student knowledge of technology could be assumed, so a considerable amount of time had to be spent on introductory computing topics. Brookes suggested that UNSW was an innovator in placing data analysis in an entry unit in the mid to late 1970s, to establish disciplined thought at an early stage. Many institutions had great difficulty breaking the road-block presented by long-standing and powerful competitor departments that prevented IS from occupying more than one narrow thread in first year.

In interview, Gerry Maynard indicated that curriculum development at Caulfield was largely insular, with little input coming in from overseas. Course committees were more effective in communicating what needs industry had. Ron Weber also considered that the published curricula that progressively emerged—primarily in the United States but also in the United Kingdom—while informative, were not well fitted to the Australian context. They were comprehensive and oriented towards either computer science or the specifically US form of graduate schools of business. Because limited time was available within IS service units, topics had to be selected and integrated into local course environments, particularly 'accounting information systems'.

A major report on computer-education needs and resources was published in late 1975 (Smith and de Ferranti 1975, usually referred to as the *Barry-Barry Report*). The report, for the Australian Commission on Advanced Education, presaged the rapid growth in small business computer systems and packaged software.

Demand for IS graduates, and hence the growth of the IS discipline, were driven by corporate endeavours to exploit the use of computing by individuals. This was associated with the explosion in the accessibility of inexpensive devices beginning in 1975 (particularly the Apple II in 1977, Visicalc in 1979 and the IBM PC in 1981) and lasting to about 1995. This was reinforced by the rapid improvements in the interconnectivity of PCs from about 1985 (internally) and 1995 (externally).

About 1975, postgraduate contributions beyond Honours began to emerge. This author's Masters sub-thesis, completed at UNSW in 1976, appears to have been one of the first. Its title, 'The implementation of functional system design and development techniques in a COBOL environment', is indicative of maturity in the software development phase of IS, but not of any broadening out towards what IS was to become.

The late 1970s saw progress internationally, with the first IS-specific refereed journals in 1977 (*MIS Quarterly* and *Information & Management)*, the conversion of the long-standing IS journal *Database* to refereed form in 1979 and the first International Conference on Information Systems (ICIS) in 1980. (Because the author was in professional positions in London and Zürich from 1977 to 1982, his archives and memories of the IS discipline of that time are limited.)

From about 1980, as skills became more structured and teachable, and as large volumes of product-related training became necessary, the vocational-education sector and particularly colleges of Technical and Further Education (TAFE) became active in the IT area. A number of private colleges also emerged, a few of which have been active for an extended period.

The first local textbook appears to have been Brookes et al. (1982). It had few competitors, and had some success overseas as well. The orientation in universities was most commonly towards application software development, particularly analysis and design, in order to draw the focus of development away from programming and achieve relevant and effective information systems. There were parallel developments in IS management, and in decision support. Over time, information management became a distinguishable body of knowledge, and intellectual relationships developed with library science.

After UNSW's pioneering move, other early movers at departmental level were QIT and NSWIT. There was, however, a long delay before recognition of the discipline was sufficient for further full professorial positions to be created. The next professorship did not emerge until 1981, and even then Ron Weber's position at the University of Queensland (1981–2004) was throughout a joint accounting and IS role. The next appointments were not until 1988 (Bob Galliers at Curtin); in 1990, at UNSW (Ross Jeffery), the University of Queensland (Maria Orlowska), the University of Technology, Sydney (UTS) (Igor Hawryszkiewycz), and Monash (David Arnott, Peter Juliffe and Phillip Steele); in 1991, at UNSW (Michael Lawrence); and in 1992 at the University of Tasmania (Stewart Leech). Monash University, when it absorbed Chisholm in 1988, took over the mantle from QIT/QUT as the largest concentration of computing-related academics in Australia. Snapshots of IS professorships in Australia are provided in Appendix 2.1.

Arguably, the first doctorate completed by an Australian in IS was that by Ron Weber, supervised by Gordon Davis, and awarded by the University of Minnesota in 1978. The first IS doctorates completed in Australia appear to have been those by Errol Iselin in 1982 and Iris Vessey in 1984, both at the University of Queensland and both supervised by Weber. Ross Jeffery completed his at UNSW in 1986 under Cyril Brookes, and Rick Watson completed his at Minnesota in 1987 under Gerardine DeSanctis. Appendix 2.2 lists the IS PhDs known to have been completed by Australians, from the first in 1978 until 1995. For most Australian IS academics, however, the first opportunity to become acquainted with American and European professors was created by the ACS/IFIP TC8 conferences in Sydney in April 1984 and March 1988.

The prior computer-usage experience of first-year students changed significantly from year to year during this period. The author conducted surveys of first-year accounting students from 1984 until 1992. The first commoditised personal computing device (the Apple II in 1977) and the accompanying first spreadsheet modeller (Visicalc) had laid the foundations, but it took a further 15 years—until the early 1990s—for matriculating students entering Australian business faculties to have sufficient exposure that computing basics could be switched from core to remedial mode. Although entrants to IS courses tended to have had greater exposure to IT than had entrants to business courses, 'introduction to computing' groundwork consumed a considerable proportion of the limited available curriculum space in IS until at least the end of the 1980s.

Meanwhile, between the 1970s and the 1990s, there was considerable growth in the proportion of matriculants continuing to post-secondary studies, and then in the numbers of mature-age candidates returning to post-secondary education—at bachelor and postgraduate levels. During the next decade, a considerable proportion of these undertook at least some IT-related study, including IS.

By the mid to late 1980s, a moderate collection of textbooks was emerging to encapsulate the mainstream knowledge in the discipline and facilitate its transfer to the next cohorts of students. Clarke (1987) provides a snapshot of one person's assessment of the list of books that should have adorned 'the computing professional's bookshelf' at the time.

Since 1988

The orientation in universities was—and continues to be—towards theory and the intellectual aspects of disciplines. There was a tension between this orientation and the government's wish to produce rapidly increasing numbers of graduates. The government wanted people whose secondary-school performance had been lower than the highest rank to emerge as graduates who were familiar with the new and rapidly mutating hardware and software technologies, and who had an understanding about what to do with them.

The needs of these more practically oriented candidates were serviced mostly by the institutes of technology and CAEs, which had existed since the previous sectoral reorganisation in the mid-1960s. The CAE sector performed a role midway between the abstract, education-oriented work within universities and the concrete training provide by technical colleges. This resulted in a wide array of courses and units relevant to IS. On the other hand, staff in CAEs had longer contact hours (typically 13–16 rather than seven–eight hours a week), they were not funded to perform research and they had limited opportunity to attract external research funding. The CAEs accordingly provided a home to only a minority of the research-oriented academics in the IS discipline, and there was something of a cleft within the still-emergent discipline.

Rather than focusing its attention and resources on the CAEs, the government chose to demolish the highly valuable distinction between institutions with industry-oriented mission statements and those with primarily academic orientation. The restructuring of the tertiary education sector, initiated by the Labor government in 1987, has been highly disruptive and massively wasteful. The diktat saw the disestablishment of the 40 or so CAEs and 25 other smaller elements and the amalgamation of their operations variously into the existing 19 universities and six some-time institutes of technology, or into one of about 15 new combinations (AVCC 2004). Substantial and vital differences among the missions of the various types of institution were ignored, and remain confused even now. The previously more industry-oriented institutions came to perceive substantial roles for themselves in research and sought better access to research funding. The sector has been in more or less continuous flux since, driven by a culture of interventionism by the relevant agency, most recently the Department of Education, Science and Training (DEST). Flurries of additional administrative responsibilities have been imposed on universities, drawing resources away from teaching and research.

Among other things, the 1990s saw the death of the concept of a university as a collegial undertaking, and the imposition of managerial rationalism. To a considerable extent, profitability and return on investment are now the measures of worth of universities' senior executives. Academic ideals of all kinds—such as the pursuit of knowledge, freedom to research, open access to research outcomes and tenure—have become constraints rather than objectives. Pluralism has been deeply compromised by 'mission statements', 'key performance indicators' and the simplicity of 'the bottom line'. Oxford, Bologna and Tübingen wept; the Harvard Business School exulted.

Meanwhile, the per-student funding of all institutions was progressively slashed. Institutions were forced to seek funding from external sources, predominantly by attracting foreign fee-paying (FFP) students onto their campuses or into their existing distance education offerings, or by earning revenue from foreign campuses in excess of the costs involved in running or participating in them. Many strategic manoeuvres have been attempted—many in amateurish fashion—with the result that a number of universities are in dire financial straits. Multiple experiments with strategic alliances have been tried (including the Group of Eight, Innovative Research Universities Australia, Open Universities Australia, New Generation Universities and Regional Universities), most with limited impact. The dislocation arising from this massive change in business models is still being felt, many institutions have worrisome exposure to the vagaries of the education export market and the quantity of research is less than it might otherwise have been. Meanwhile, with staff-counts down and student–staff ratios much higher than they were two decades ago, it is unlikely that the quality of teaching has improved.

In 1990–92, a government review was undertaken of what were styled the 'computing studies and information sciences disciplines'. It was referred to popularly by the name of the committee chair, Hudson (1992). The submissions by the ACS and the ANU utilised a graphic, prepared by this author, which sought to convey the scope of IS and its relationship to the other relevant disciplines (Figure 2.1). Information systems was depicted as occupying vital space between the technical and business disciplines, encompassing a range of applied and instrumentalist topics, and interacting closely with many other disciplines and sub-disciplines. During the intervening 15 years, the topics might have changed somewhat, but the general framework arguably still provides a reasonable representation of the relationships.

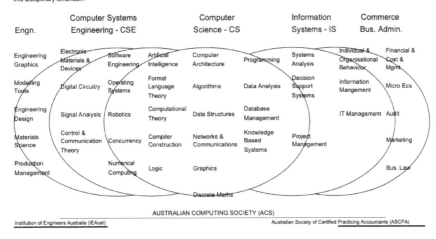

Figure 2.1 Location of the IS discipline, as perceived in 1991

Source: Australian Computer Society (ACS) 1992, *Report of the Task Force on the ACS Towards 2000*, Australian Computer Society, Sydney, Attachment 5.

Well into the 1980s, communications within the discipline in Australia were informal and somewhat haphazard. An early step to draw the scattered individuals and groups together was the development of a directory (Clarke 1988, 1991; Gable and Clarke 1994, 1996). This was merged, together with the North American directory (Davis and DeGross 1983) and the European directory (Bjørn-Andersen and Hansen 1993), into the world-wide online directory that was launched by Dave Naumann at Minnesota in 1995.

A critical initiative was the establishment of a regular national conference, the Australian Conference in Information Systems (ACIS). The first was held at Monash in 1990, chaired by Ross Jeffery, and it has run annually since then. During the first few years, the standing committee comprised Ross Jeffery, Ron Weber, Roger Clarke, Peter Weill and Igor Hawryszkiewycz. The committee then migrated to the ICIS pattern of rotating membership involving recent, current and upcoming organising and program committee chairs.

The mid-1990s saw maturation of the IS discipline at the international level. As the Internet was grasped as an opportunity for international communications and publication, the ISWorld mailing list and web site were established—both in 1994. The international Association for Information Systems (AIS) was also formed in that year. The regional forums (the Pacific Asia Conference on Information Systems, PACIS, from 1993; the European Conference on Information Systems, ECIS, from 1993; and the American Conference on Information Systems,

AMCIS, from 1995) provided a broader geographical frame for ACIS. Australians were active contributors to ISWorld, the AIS and the directory project, and to ECIS, PACIS, AMCIS and other international conferences.

Meanwhile, Rob McGregor established the national specialist journal, the *AJIS*, in 1994 at Wollongong University. Liaison among professors and departmental heads had been emergent, and was formalised through the ACPHIS in 1995. An ISWorld page for Australia was established by this author in 1996. A chapter of AIS was established in 2001.

The discipline continued to consolidate and expand through the second half of the 1990s, but it has suffered a substantial set-back since 2000. A later section of this chapter considers some aspects of this, but to a large extent the focus is the period 1965–95.

The early sections of this chapter have provided a largely chronological presentation of the development of the discipline. The remaining sections adopt a thematic structure, picking out aspects of the story that appear to have been of particular significance.

Drivers and scope

Critical among the questions addressed in this section are where the heartland of the discipline is to be found, and why. There can be little doubt that technology has been the biggest driver of change, qualified by organisational concerns. Whether technology is more than just a driver—and perhaps the core of the IS discipline—is considered progressively through the remainder of the chapter and is also reflected on in Chapter 12 of this book.

This section enumerates and briefly describes important aspects of what IS has done, and is doing, paying particular attention to changes in flavours over the years. Inevitably, the themes and the manner in which they are presented reflect this author's perspective on the discipline; it has, however, been cross-checked for completeness and structure against Culnan (1986, 1987), Land (1992), Barki et al. (1993), Avgerou et al. (1999), Pervan and Cecez-Kecmanovic (2001), Galliers and Whitley (2002) and Banker and Kauffman (2004).

Beginning slowly in the 1950s, accelerating through the 1960s and exploding in the 1970s, computers were being installed and organisations were beginning to spend considerable sums of money on them. They needed people to apply them and the resources committed had to be managed in order to contribute to the needs of the organisation. Initially, the opportunities were perceived in terms of business operations. Throughout its history, therefore, the IS discipline in Australia has had a strong focus on application software and technology in use, and seldom on hardware or even systems software.

Because the bare machine had to be oriented to business needs, software development was an essential focus from the emergence of IS, through the 1970s and until the late 1980s. A long-running strand of the discipline has focused on development tools and methods (often referred to using the inappropriate term 'methodologies', even in the key reference work, Olle et al. 1988). The software development life cycle (SDLC) was important in the IS departments of universities and was central to the many computing and (E)DP departments in more vocationally oriented institutions. Considerable attention has also been paid to the productivity and quality aspects of software development, giving rise to specialised strands within the discipline that overlap with—and are seen by some to have migrated across to—software engineering.

Through the 1980s, the 'structured era' matured. A comprehensive set of methods and associated tools was accumulated, which ensured completeness across the three dimensions of system designs: procedures, data models and control structures.

Concern had arisen, however, about the slowness and resource intensiveness of development using the structured techniques. Theories emerged about 'rapid-application development' (RAD). This sacrifices quality in order to gain speed and cost savings in the development process, and hence some prefer the more descriptive title 'quick and dirty' (QAD). During the 1990s, RAD and 'object-oriented' techniques overran the structured techniques, and they remain the technological mainstream.

During the same period, there was a substantial de-skilling of designers and programmers as their roles were converted into commodities (as encapsulated by the expression 'everyone thinks they can design an e-commerce web site'). These changes have resulted in a reduction in the quality of software, with large numbers of fragile and poorly and even undocumented applications, continued project failures and overruns and—particularly since the explosion of Internet-based applications—seriously low security.

During the 1980s—and in parallel with the rise of the structured techniques—the SDLC gradually matured into a systems life cycle (SLC). This distinction reflected the importance of non-software elements. It also acknowledged the need for maintenance and enhancement, and not just of software, but of business processes that integrated the manual, automated and intellectual elements. The area has been revisited and rebadged from time to time, most successfully during the 'business process re-engineering' phase.

Although programming and software engineering have eased away to the very edge of IS, and even systems design has become a boundary topic, systems analysis has remained within the IS discipline's scope. The approaches adopted within Australia have tended to moderate the hard-line, technology-driven approaches, which have emanated primarily from the United States, by adopting elements of the more tolerant and ambiguous notions of the UK school of thought. Therefore texts such as the Yourdon series during the 'structured' era, Booch and Rumbaugh during the later 'object-oriented phase' and Kendall and Kendall, have lined up with and against texts such as Avison and Fitzgerald. The extreme end of the mechanistic/reductionist approach, characterised by IEEE 'requirements engineering' and championed by software engineers and computer scientists, continues to have some hold in the IS discipline. At the other extremity, there has been some penetration by participative design notions.

In interview, Cyril Brookes perceived DBMS, data management and data modelling to have been among the key enablers of the separation of IS from computer science in the mid to late 1970s: '[T]here was only so far you could go with structured programming.' For some years, data schemata, data dictionaries and information resource dictionary systems (IRDS), coupled with more abstract entity-relationship modelling and enterprise data modelling, were central concerns. In recent years, however, these too have drifted toward the edge of IS, and information management has been more prominent, with its emphasis on semantics, meta-data, information retrieval and information architecture.

During the 1960s and 1970s, and well into the 1980s, the work of most IS practitioners was focused on support for business operations. This involved using data to represent relevant events that occurred in the organisation's world. A useful generic term for these kinds of applications was 'transaction data-processing systems' (TDPS). The first specialist newsletter, the *Data Base for Advances in Information Systems* (usually shortened to *Database*), was launched in 1969. It was, and continues to be, published under the auspices of the ACM Special Interest Group on Business Data Processing (SIGBDP), which changed its name to SIGMIS in 1991. It became a refereed journal in 1979 (Canning 1994). The term 'BDP' was little used in Australia, the more mainstream expressions being electronic data processing (EDP) in most of the private sector, and automatic data processing (ADP) in the public sector.

Progressively, the belief arose that the information needs of managers and executives could and should be served; this gave rise to the MIS movement. The term was associated with Gordon Davis and his colleagues at Minnesota, and much of the drive for it emerged from there. The concept reached Australia very quickly (Aiken 1971). This author has always considered that the key text that set the agenda was Davis (1974), entitled *Management Information Systems: Conceptual Foundations, Structure, and Development*. In its later form, Davis and

Olson (1984), it was still listed as a student reference for later-year undergraduates as late as the mid-1990s. *MIS Quarterly* began during this phase—in 1977—run out of Minnesota and supported by OR/MS and business organisations.

A key distinction between MIS and TDPS was the extraction of information from data, in particular through aggregation and exception reporting. The original concept is a natural extension of management accounting, but Davis and others quickly developed it much further. As noted earlier, MIS is the common term in the United States for the IS discipline as a whole.

Specialist conferences emerged about that time, with ICIS beginning in 1980. All of these activities were—and continue to be—heavily US-dominated, although many non-Americans travelled to the event, particularly from Europe and Australia, and the conference has been more meaningfully international since about 1990, with five of the last 15 conferences held outside North America. Since 1983, there has been a Minnesota-run North American Directory of Faculty ('faculty' in the American sense of 'academic staff' rather than the British and Australian sense of a collegial organisational unit).

The decision support systems (DSS) movement then augmented MIS. An ACM SIGBDP Conference in January 1977 addressed the topic (see also Keen and Scott Morton 1978 and Sprague 1980; although Banker and Kauffman 2004 claim that it was emergent in the management science community since the mid-1950s). DSS can be differentiated from MIS in two main ways. First, data extracted from TDPS and MIS is used in conjunction with models of current and possible future business, incorporating ideas from OR/MS. Second, data are used that derived from outside the organisation (such as demographics and costs of transport and of capital) and 'out of thin air' (as models were applied to 'what-if' analysis).

Subsequent developments included executive information systems (EIS), business intelligence (BI) and knowledge management (KM). Each was a fad driven by management consultants—'new bottles for old wine'—but each has brought focus to particular aspects of the whole, and has drawn insights into the IS discipline from other disciplines and research domains.

Figure 2.2 provides a diagrammatic representation of the relationships among these building blocks of the IS discipline.

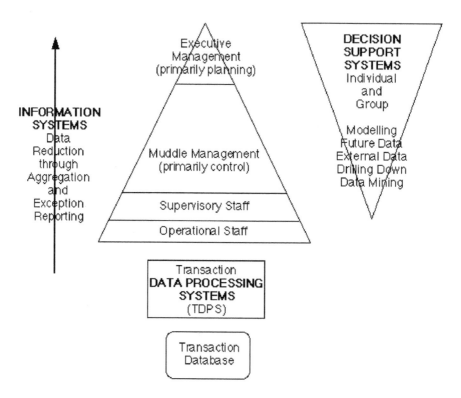

Figure 2.2 Building blocks of the IS discipline

Source: Clarke, R. 1990, 'Information systems: the scope of the domain', Xamax Consultancy Pty Ltd, viewed 22 March 2007, <http://www.anu.edu.au/people/Roger.Clarke/SOS/ISDefn.html>

A further strand reflected the inter-working of multiple individuals; this was group decision support systems (GDSS) and its correlation at the tactical level, computer-supported cooperative work (CSCW). This area is a good example of the way in which continuous technology-driven redefinition of scope has resulted in disciplinary splintering and scattered alliances. Other examples include human–computer interaction (HCI) and enterprise modelling. Such splintering has been a significant contributor to the inability of the IS discipline to build a substantial and stable power base.

Project management—although always a focus for the IS profession—has been performed poorly. This throws doubt on the quality of the teaching and research performed within the IS discipline. The need for formalised instruction in project management is higher now than ever before, because people in their twenties and younger have grown up with even less orientation towards planning than previous generations, because of their dependency on their mobile phone to perform just-in-time scheduling for everything that they do.

As a consequence of increasing application complexity and low-quality project management, project failure and application failure have long been major concerns among executives. Mandata and the Bank of New South Wales' CS90 were very public examples of failure in the 1970s and 1980s. They have been a less significant focus of research work than might have been expected of a discipline closely attuned to business needs, although Chris Sauer's doctorate and book were important contributions. Much stronger focus has been needed on the balance between quality, whole-of-life cost and risk management on the one hand, and speed and development cost on the other. That focus has not, however, been forthcoming, and high levels of project failure and application failure therefore continue.

The application of IT to particular categories of data (for example, text, numerical data and geographical data), and in particular industry sectors (for example, logistics/supply chain, health, justice and air traffic control), has tended to be at the fringe of the IS discipline. The intersection with the discipline of accountancy through accounting information systems has been crucial to a significant minority of the discipline's members, but has been seen as largely irrelevant by many others.

Applications in the 1960s and early 1970s were conceived within limited functional areas (in accounting contexts, the 'sub-ledgers' such as debtors, creditors, inventory, payroll and general ledger). The 1970s saw more effective interfacing between what began as stand-alone applications. Through the 1980s, applications were progressively integrated into larger products (such as, initially, financial management information systems, FMIS, and, later, the poorly named enterprise resource planning products, ERP).

During this period, a major change that had implications for the discipline's focus was the transformation from custom-built to packaged applications. As software became more complex, and more expensive, the focus switched from development to the acquisition of packages, and the customisation and integration of pre-written components. As indicated earlier, this transition occurred in areas such as payroll during the early 1970s, and for larger and more complex applications as late as the early to mid-1990s.

Theorists appreciated from the outset that, as the number of elements and the size of the source code grew, there would be an exponential growth in difficulties (such as bug content, the incidence of new bugs arising from fixes of old bugs, fragility, comprehensibility, the investment required in application-specific staff training, inflexibility and non-adaptability). Large-scale products have not reflected these insights sufficiently well, and the tendency to move from modularity towards monolithism has resulted in enormously expensive, highly integrated software products. The quality of the many large-scale applications has become a progressively larger problem, the lead time for adaptation (frequently of the organisation and its business processes, rather than the software) has become very long and project risk continues to be very high.

Progressively, a wide array of IT-related services has come to be regarded as commodities as unrelated to organisations' core competencies as are cleaning services. What was once referred to as data-centre management—and now as server hosting—was an early candidate for outsourcing. User support—and more recently customer support through 'help centres'—has followed them, in some cases offshore. Inadequacies in service delivery and loss of managerial control have resulted in instances of subsequent re-sourcing. The concept of 'right-sourcing' resurfaces from time to time.

The management of computers, data processing, data centres and, progressively, IS, was a focus in some schools from the outset (through such leaders as Dickson at Minnesota and Anthony, Macfarlan and Scott Morton at Harvard). It expanded progressively into a broader IT management thread. By the late 1980s, the opportunities that communications technologies had created caused a great deal of attention to be paid to IS that crossed the boundaries of organisations—originally inter-organisational systems (IOS—1-to-1), then multi-organisational (MOS—m-to-n) in various configurations, particularly in the form of 'industry value chains'. The combination of DSS and IOS/MOS resulted in increased capacity to contribute to the work of the most senior executives in large organisations. From the late 1980s, the strategic information systems (SIS) strand became important, and 'strategic alignment' became a preoccupation.

Appreciation grew that enormous harm arises from mechanistic application of technology without sufficient attention to its use by people and organisations, and to its first-order impacts on, and second-order implications for, people and organisations. This was investigated by the socio-technical movement, associated with Mumford, Checkland, Wood-Harper and Bjørn-Anderson. The tension between the 'managerial paradigm' and the 'humanistic paradigm' is examined in Land (2000a). These have had much more substantial influence in Australia than in North America. A few specialist journals exist, such as *Information Technology & People* and *The Information Society*, but they are somewhat marginalised.

The rationalist correlation of socio-technics and soft-systems techniques has been change management, which has loomed large in recent years for several reasons. One is the rapidity of technological advance. Another is the inevitable tendency of organisations to fall behind 'the technology curve', and then lurch into catch-up mode, with equally inevitable negative impacts on staff morale. A further factor is the entrenched distinction between management and operational staff, and the limited involvement of operational staff in the analysis of requirements and the design of new systems. Scandinavian 'participative design' and Japanese 'quality circles' and *kaizen* ('continuous improvement') have all made limited headway in breaking down simplistic top-down management notions.

By the late 1980s, the convergence of computing with communications was making rapid progress. Local-area networking (LAN) and later wide-area networking changed the scope of the industry that IS was bound up with from 'the computer industry' in the 1970s to 'the IT industry' in the 1990s. Subsequently, user satisfaction, technology use, technology adoption and impediments to adoption have been major focal points of IS research. The theory of reasoned action (TRA) and the technology-adoption model (TAM) are examples of theories drawn into IS from reference disciplines, and much applied—although with limited practical impact.

A range of economic perspectives and tools has been applied, resulting in sub-disciplines, or perhaps research domains, of the economics of IS and of IT. These focus on topics such as the productivity of developers, of user organisations and of industry sectors; the processes of technology diffusion; and the balance between hierarchies and markets.

Indications of the current structure of the body of knowledge are provided by the current ACS Accreditation Guidelines (Underwood 1997, under revision) and current curriculum guidelines, in particular, recent references such as Gorgone and Gray (2000), Gorgone et al. (2002, 2005).

From this necessarily brief outline, it is clear that the scope of the discipline has broadened over the years, and has been driven largely by technological change—and to a lesser extent by organisational needs. There has been only limited evidence of leadership by the IS discipline in technological innovation, although somewhat more evidence of contributions to the management of applications of technology.

Political dimensions

This section draws together some key aspects of the difficulties that the IS discipline in Australia has encountered, in relation to its international context, its organisational location within universities, its relationships with the IS profession and with industry more generally, its political weakness and the resultant resource constraints.

International orientation and impact

Australians have always been acutely aware of the need to be in contact with the discipline elsewhere in the world, and have been active travellers since the late 1970s, as conference contributors, participants and program committee members, as doctoral candidates, as seminar speakers and in short-term visiting positions.

A small number of Australians have held positions overseas for extended periods, particularly in the United States, including Ted Stohr at New York University from the late 1970s, Iris Vessey at Pittsburgh, Penn State and Indiana from the late 1980s, Rick Watson at Georgia from the late 1980s, and more recently Peter Weill at Massachusetts Institute of Technology (MIT). (All were to a considerable extent Australian educated, and all except Vessey were born in Australia). The flow has been far from one way. Migrants and visitors have included Britons Philip Yetton (at the Australian Graduate School of Management from 1976, although active in IS only from 1993), Bob Galliers (1982–89 at the West Australian Institute of Technology/Curtin, and subsequently Dean of the Warwick Business School) and Janice Burn (1997–2005 at Edith Cowan University); Canadian Guy Gable (since 1995 at QUT); and American Michael Vitale (1995–2001 at Melbourne University and subsequently Dean of the Australian Graduate School of Management).

Australia has also attracted many visits from leading overseas IS academics. The 1984 and 1988 ACS/IFIP Conferences were an important stimulus. Some who have made multiple and/or lengthy visits include Frank Land (LSE, LBS), Bill Olle (London), Neils Bjørn-Andersen (Copenhagen), Leslie Willcocks (Warwick), Trevor Wood-Harper (Salford), Rudy Hirschheim (Houston), Doug Vogel (Arizona, later City University of Hong Kong), Felix Hampe (Koblenz) and Michael Schrefl and Gerald Quirchmaier (both of Linz).

Given that Australia represents about 0.3 per cent of the world's population and about 1 per cent of global gross domestic product (GDP), Australia tends to punch above its weight in many fields. For example, three of the 13 AIS presidents have been Australian born (Ron Weber, Richard Watson and Philip Ein-Dor). Although the impact of Australia's approximately 700 IS academics has been noticeable, it has, however, been dwarfed by the energy of the United States. Appendix 2.3 provides an analysis in support of that conclusion.

One reason for this doubtless is the slow emergence of doctoral programs in Australia. Until the 1990s, most candidates had to either manage their own preparation with support from one or more supervisors but little formal preparatory study or leverage as best they could off relevant (and often not so relevant) units of study in adjacent disciplines. Even at the end of that decade, however, Metcalfe and Kiley (2000) found it necessary to argue for PhD course-work. Frank Land provided an important perspective—which confirms the author's experience—that at least during the period to 1995, Australian PhDs in IS were generally expected to submit to examination by top-quality international figures. This might be explained by the high standards demanded of pioneers in an emergent discipline, or by the exquisitely Australian concept of 'cultural cringe'—or more likely by a combination of both.

A range of institutions in Australia now offers more structured preparation for IS doctoral candidates. There might therefore be an expectation of some acceleration in Australians' contributions in the most heavily weighted journals and the ICIS. That development might be confounded, however, by the continuing high productivity of American scholars, the higher productivity of journal publication by European scholars in recent years, the explosion in doctoral programs in other countries and the prevalent attitude that there are only about five top-level journals (despite the explosion in IS and IS-relevant journals in the past 15 years—565 currently, according to Lamp 2004—and the high quality of far more than a mere five of them).

Discipline size and staff location

The organisational location of IS staff has been highly varied from the outset. A large proportion of IS academics has always been in departments dominated by other disciplines, for which IS was, and in many cases still is, perceived to fulfil a service role. The dominant disciplines have been variously welcoming and hostile to the IS discipline and the staff working in it.

Almost all institutions had specialist organisational units focused on IS by the end of the 1980s. The last two of the major institutions to create them were regarded widely as being among the most conservative: the University of Melbourne (1995) and the University of Sydney (2001).

The statistical data in Table 2.2 were extracted from the various editions of the printed *Directories of Australian Academics* (Clarke 1988), *Australasian Academics* (Clarke 1991) and *Asia Pacific Researchers* (Gable and Clarke 1994, 1996), and the online directory as of 2 May 2005 and 22 March 2007. The entries in the printed directories were managed, whereas those in the online directory have been, and remain, self-reported and unaudited. There is known to be a substantial 'staleness' factor, with many individuals not amending their entries when they move, and particularly when they leave the discipline altogether. There is also clear under-reporting—for example, only 30 of the 52 identifiable professors had entries in March 2007. The data have been analysed notwithstanding such issues, because to some extent the inaccuracies cancel one another out, but primarily because (in what might be regarded as a parable of the relevance-versus-rigour debate) that is all that is available to analyse.

Table 2.2 Institution and staff statistics

	IS depts	Departments	%	Institutions	Individuals	Professors
1988	9	55	16	41	175	2
1991	22	76	29	39	521	7
1994	32	84	38	38	640	13
1996	39	88	44	39	630	15
2005	28	103	28	42	670	30
2007	24	85	28	41	396	30

Note: The counts of individuals in 2005 and 2007 have been adjusted to remove PhD students and adjuncts, in order to sustain comparability with the earlier figures

Table 2.2 shows that, by 1988, when the first *Directory of Information Systems Academics* was produced, the 175 individuals who could be identified readily were in 55 separate departments in 41 educational institutions. Only nine of those 55 departments were recognisable as IS, with a further eight in computing or (electronic) data processing. In a pattern that has continued to the present day, 25 of the departments were dominated by business disciplines (six each of commerce, accounting and business; three each of management and economics; and one of administration); and computer science departments dominated the remainder, with some information science (in the technical rather than the librarianship sense) and mathematics. A significant difference from the patterns that are evident in the United States has been the relatively limited involvement of and interest in IS by Australian graduate schools of business, especially until about the mid-1990s.

The proportion of departments hosting IS staff that were named IS or similar grew steadily to nearly half, but plummeted after the end of the 1990s. This followed the 'dotcom implosion' about 2000 and the external financial pressures on universities, which have encouraged the imposition of departmental amalgamations in the hope that this will result in cost savings.

Analysis requires care. The count of individuals in 2005 included people who were no longer active in the IS discipline but whose entries had not been deleted. In early 2007, a purge of old records was undertaken, removing those that had not been updated since 2000 and where a message to the email address elicited no response, or a bounce message that indicated it no longer existed. This author (who was an editor of the directory from its establishment in 1988 until 1996) estimates that the 1996 figures over-counted by 10 per cent and under-counted by about the same amount, whereas, under the subsequent self-managed online scheme, over-reporting increased (until corrected in 2007) and the under-reporting increased as well (with no correction made as yet). Taking these factors into account, the contraction post-2000 would appear to have been 25–35 per cent. This is broadly consistent with anecdotal evidence and examination of a sample of institutions—although there was considerable variance among institutions in the timing and the scale of the contraction.

The approximately 400 people in the directory in 2007 under-reports the total count. If the under-reporting for all levels of staff is the same as that by professors, a factor of 52/30 or 1.73 needs to be applied, suggesting that in 2007 there were close to 700 people for whom IS was their dominant disciplinary affiliation, scattered across at least 85 departments (of which only 28 were distinctly IS or similar in name), in almost all institutions. This is broadly consistent with the finding in Pervan and Shanks (2006) of 460 staff in 24 respondent institutions of an estimated 36 (after allowing for probable over-sampling of the larger institutions). On the basis of directory entries in March 2007, the largest concentrations of IS academics appear to be at (in descending order) Melbourne, Monash, QUT, the University of South Australia, Edith Cowan, Deakin, Griffith and UNSW.

Pearcey wrote nearly two decades ago (1988:125) that '[t]he demand for people with computing expertise has always outstripped the capacity of the tertiary sector to supply it, and the situation seems unlikely to change'. Based on personal experience, that was the case for at least three decades, from the late 1960s until the end of the 1990s. About 2000, several factors conspired to dramatically reduce demand. The burst of the dotcom bubble about 2000 undermined the attractiveness of all IT-related courses. In addition, offshore outsourcing had been extending progressively from data capture to programming and even detailed design work. The commoditisation of many skills has also resulted in transfer from the university sector to the vocational education and training (VET) sector.

The publicity accompanying this large market correction was followed by substantial reductions in enrolments from domestic students—although it appears to have had a smaller impact on foreign fee-paying numbers. As is the way with 'the invisible hand' so beloved of economists, it appears likely that the slump will have been an over-correction, and that there will soon be shortages in graduates and in IS staff.

Relationships with the IS profession

Few members of the IS discipline would regard it as being intellectually remote and abstract. On the contrary, it is generally regarded as a professional discipline. One indicator of this is the fact that major contributions to the foundations of IS by Ron Weber and Canadian colleague Yair Wand (for example, Weber 1997) have been admired widely, but also ignored widely.

A professional discipline needs to be clear about who the professionals are whom the discipline needs to educate, interact with and conduct research for. The nature of the profession has, however, changed considerably over the years. It began with strong scientific credentials in the 1960s, but many of the people who surged into the field in the 1970s and even more so in the 1980s had no degree in a relevant discipline. The endeavours of the ACS to ensure appropriate preparation for careers in IS have been only partly successful, not least because of the rapid technology-driven changes in work patterns, business needs and IT management fashions.

Professional job titles and job definitions have changed a great deal in the four decades that the profession and discipline have existed. The original roles were computer operator (now largely defunct), systems analyst (now more commonly called business analyst), systems designer (often referred to as systems analyst/designer, and sometimes business process engineer, but diminished due to the contemporary dominance of packaged software) and programmer. The senior staff member was once called an electronic or automatic data-processing (EDP or ADP or just DP) manager. The executive to whom that manager reported was most commonly the finance director.

Chief technology officers (CTOs) and CIOs emerged at executive level only from the mid to late 1980s onwards, as the strategic significance of IT grew—and as the amount of money spent on it sky-rocketted. CIOs, who should be a natural connection point for senior IS academics into the world of business and government, commonly have no qualifications in IS, but rather are generalised executives thrust into a particularly challenging role.

Because graduates from IS courses are intended to move into the profession, the professional body, the ACS, has long run an accreditation program. Most institutions have felt the need to have their computing courses accredited by the ACS—as a form of review and as a means whereby graduates can be assured of qualifying for membership of the relevant professional body. For many years, the ACS's accreditation guidelines mentioned the term 'information systems', but were oriented heavily towards computing and were dominated by computer science thinking (ACS 1985, 1987). Through the 1980s, many IS courses achieved accreditation only through the exercise of the discretion that the guidelines permitted the assessors. A mature IS discipline and profession needed more than this.

In 1989, this author and Bruce Lo proposed that the accreditation requirements for IS be distinguished from those of computer science, and that they reflect technology and business needs (Clarke and Lo 1989). The proposal was adopted in ACS (1990), and retained in Maynard and Underwood (1996). Underwood (1997) provides a more detailed description of the 'core body of knowledge for IT professionals', and reflects the computer science and IS perspectives on the domain.

The tension between the technology driver and the organisational aspect was exemplified by the competition between the ACS and the Australian Institute of Systems Analysts (AISA) during the 1970s. In this case, the computing end of the spectrum won by a very wide margin. The AISA, despite its organisational orientation, never grew into an association with significant membership or influence. Nor did any of the larger business-oriented professional associations ever make a significant move to capture the business-analysis profession. Despite this, membership of the ACS has remained fairly steady in the past several decades (between 12 000 and 16 000), reflecting a reduction in the proportion of people active in the field who are members.

Influence by the IS discipline on the ACS has been muted. For example, the presidency has been held by people outside IS for only six of the society's 40 years. For 32 of the 40 years, the president has been a senior IS professional (Ashley Goldsworthy's five years preceding the period he spent in academia). For a total of only two years has a member of the IS discipline been president (Alan Underwood, in 1990–91).

Relationships with industry

The IS discipline needs linkages broader than the IS profession, reaching out to other business functions and to executive levels of business and government. One form of linkage has been course and departmental advisory committees, which facilitate input from industry to the discipline. Information systems departments have also tended to draw heavily on people within industry for sessional tutors, sessional lecturers, guest lecturers and sometimes for adjunct appointments. In interview, Gerry Maynard mentioned the use by Caulfield Institute of 'pleasant Friday afternoons', which were used as a means of drawing DP managers in industry and government into contact with staff and students. A primary motivation for employers was the attraction of good graduates, whereas educational institutions stood to gain funding support and intellectual interaction.

The Australian Computer Users Association (ACUA) operated from 1968 onwards. Although it was a potential linkage point for senior academics, it does not appear that it was much used in that manner. UNSW ran a very successful IS forum from 1977 onwards, which drew in senior executives from industry and government. This was much easier than for many other institutions because Cyril Brookes had moved into academia from what was arguably the top private-sector computing position in Australia: Manager, Corporate Data Processing, for what was then the country's largest company, BHP. Only a small number of IS departments appear to have been able to build and sustain linkages of this nature, primarily those in the more prestigious graduate schools of management.

The ACS/IFIP TC8 Conferences in Sydney in April 1984 and March 1988, organised by UNSW's Brookes and Ross Jeffery and the senior IS professional and ACS officer Ann Moffatt, had the express purpose of establishing a bridge between industry and academia. That team's success with industry linkage was reflected in the Institute of Information Technology, run at UNSW for IBM from 1987 to 1992.

During the 1980s, there was considerable emphasis among employers on 'sandwich courses', and flagship degrees were very successful at UNSW and UTS in Sydney, and at Monash and Swinburne in Melbourne. The perception in industry was that, particularly at the more applied end of computer science and the technical end of IS, quality graduates were being confronted by real-world problems too late. Sandwich courses provided students with early exposure to the work environment, enabled theory to be leavened with practice and created the possibility that practice could leverage off theory.

Course-work was originally entirely the responsibility of academics. There has been a drift in recent years towards outsourcing, as resource pressures in universities increase. A larger proportion of units of study appear to be being taught directly from textbooks, chapter by chapter, with less bespoke design to fit local needs. In addition, industry-provided product-specific units have come to be accepted for credit within some universities (for example, networking by Cisco and .NET development by Microsoft). The eternal relevance-versus-rigour tussle in research is mirrored by the training-versus-education battle in the learning context.

Political weakness and resource constraints

For an extended period, there was competition for dominance in the IS discipline between computer science on the one hand and business, commerce or accounting on the other. Dreyfus (2004) chronicles the establishment of the last IS department, at the University of Melbourne, which occurred during the period 1994–96. The Vice-Chancellor, David Penington, requested a report from a committee chaired by Peter Weill (who was an IT management professor in the Graduate School of Management). The Weill report stressed that there was no one standard structure for IS across the universities, with some courses management oriented, while others were highly technical. Penington opted to put the new IS department in the science faculty, at least for the short term, although housed close to computer science. The IS degree was to have five major themes: information systems, organisations, IT, analytical skills and personal competency. Later-year specialisation was to be in one of three streams: organisations, IT or custom (Dreyfus 2004:1–6). As it has transpired, the department quickly developed a sufficient scale and power base, and more than a decade later its faculty location remains unchanged.

A comparison between the experiences of the Australian IS and computer science disciplines is instructive. In 1990, the numbers of academic staff in IS and computer science were comparable; however, whereas computer science staff were concentrated in departments bearing that or a similar name, IS staff were distributed through many departments, in many cases without a senior academic post allocated to the IS discipline. The diffusion of IS staff has meant that for many years IS has lacked political clout, and even now has less political clout than other disciplines with similar total numbers. Computer science, for example, has demanded and attracted far greater funding and support staff, and it has always been far more influential and better recognised than IS.

One implication of the lack of political power has been a lack of resources for educational functions. In most institutions, there was a long-term struggle to gain sufficient funding and staff positions (and then to find people with appropriate education and experience to fill them). In some contexts, the computer science discipline was powerful and resisted the emergence of IS. In others, economics and management disciplines did the same. The joint majors and double degrees that the market needed emerged very slowly, and the silo effects of faculties, schools and even departments resulted in students often having to devise ways to construct programs that suited their interests, and their perceptions of current needs.

Another problem has been the serious difficulty of acquiring sufficient resources to support research programs, or even individual projects of significant scale. Members of the discipline in Australia were under-trained in research, they were highly diverse in their orientations, domains of study and research techniques, and they were scattered geographically. The development of consortia to develop quality bids was difficult, and remained so well into the era of widespread e-mail that began with the launch of AARNet in mid-1989 (Clarke 2004).

The primary source of funding, the Australian Research Grants Scheme (ARGS), later the Australian Research Council (ARC), created a sub-topic of IS only in the late 1990s. Until then, those few who were successful in their bids submitted under either computer science or management headings, and were generally assessed by academics with no affinity with the IS discipline.

Since 1998, IS has been recognised within the ARC RFCD Code as one of 139 disciplines and 898 subjects. The 17 most directly relevant subjects are listed in Table 2.3. The first 13 are in the discipline of IS, within the information, computing and communication sciences cluster, and the other four are applications within particular disciplinary areas, including business. It appears, however, that a revision of the RFCD Code could be placing these IS-specific classifications under threat.

In 2001, after lobbying by ACPHIS and the then new AAIS, the IS discipline gained a member of the ARC's College of Experts. Panel members from the IS community since then have been Janice Burn (Edith Cowan), 2001–03, Graeme Shanks (Monash), 2004–05, and Michael Rosemann (QUT), 2006–07.

Table 2.3 ARC codes for IS, from 1998

Code	Description
280101	Information Systems Organisation
280102	Information Systems Management
280103	Information Storage, Retrieval and Management
280104	Computer–Human Interaction
280105	Interfaces and Presentation (excl. Computer–Human Interaction)
280106	Inter-Organisational Information Systems
280107	Global Information Systems
280108	Database Management
280109	Decision Support and Group Support Systems
280110	Systems Theory
280111	Conceptual Modelling
280112	Information Systems Development Methodologies
280199	Information Systems not elsewhere classified
291004	Spatial Information Systems
321203	Health Information Systems
350202	Business Information Systems (incl. Data Processing)
390301	Justice Systems and Administration

Intellectual dimensions

The IS discipline in Australia faces serious challenges, and this chapter needs to offer a greater contribution than merely a historical recitation and analysis. This section addresses the important questions about the future: 'What do we regard as appropriate domains in which to conduct research?' and 'What research techniques are appropriate?'. It also lays the foundation for a further question discussed in Chapter 12: 'What unresolved tensions remain at the end of the discipline's fourth decade?'.

The research domain

An earlier section considered the drivers and scope of the IS discipline primarily from the teaching perspective. This sub-section considers the related, but somewhat different, question of what IS academics have considered appropriate areas of research.

Early endeavours to define the scope included Mason and Mitroff's (1973) program for research on MIS, Ives et al.'s (1980) framework for research in computer-based MIS, Galliers' manifesto for Australian-based research (1987) and Jeffery and Lawrence's special issue on current research directions in IS (1986). Reviews of the research undertaken in IS include Culnan (1986, 1987), Alavi et al. (1989), Alavi and Carlson (1992), Glass (1992), Avgerou et al. (1999), Galliers and Whitley (2002), Vessey et al. (2002) and Banker and Kauffman (2004). Each of these draws attention to the enormous breadth of the topics addressed. The diversity arises in at least two dimensions:

- cross-sectionally, reflecting:

  the diversity of origins

  the diversity of host disciplines and co-located disciplines
- longitudinally, as drift occurs over time, driven by changes in technology, in fashion, in management and in management disciplines, and increasingly in fashion within the IS discipline itself.

A few attempts have been made to adopt the encyclopaedists' approach of enumerating the topics that are within the scope of the IS discipline. More adventurously, a few have attempted taxonomies, in order to impose some order on the chaos. The most successful work of this kind is that by Barki et al. (1988, 1993). The second paper reported that articles published in just seven major journals in 1987–92 identified about 2000 different keywords. Barki et al.'s revised classification scheme of 1993 included 1300 keywords under nine major and 56 minor groupings—an increase of 175 on their original 1988 version. It appears that the Herculean task has not been repeated since. Moreover, the use of the Barki scheme appears to have subsided, as reliance on brute-force, free-text search engines has increased. Nonetheless, it is a highly valuable tool of historical analysis.

As Table 2.4 shows, about only half of the Barki et al. (1993) keywords were concerned directly with the core areas of the IS discipline; one-quarter were associated with reference disciplines, and one-quarter with external drivers and constraints. The discipline could be described, kindly, as being strongly professional in its orientation and sensitive to its environment and the needs of its clientele. Alternatively, it could be depicted more critically, as lacking confidence, being derivative, lacking in fundamentals and driven mercilessly by its rapidly changing context.

Table 2.4 Barki et al.'s 1993 keyword list for IS

Category		%
Reference disciplines		25
Drivers and constraints		25
Information technology	12	
Organisational environment	6	
External environment	7	
IS core research areas		47
IS management	16	
IS development and operations	14	
IS usage	5	
Kinds of information systems	11	
IS education, research, etc.		3

A later analysis examined articles published in *Information & Management* and *MIS Quarterly* from 1981 to 1997, using the Barki high-level structure. Claver et al. (2000) found that the largest concentrations of publications were IS development (13.2 per cent of 1121 papers), DSS (8.9 per cent) and IS evaluation (7.8 per cent). Avgerou et al. (1999) evaluate research foci and methods in Europe, and Galliers and Whitley (2002) analyse the papers accepted at ECIS conferences.

Studies of this nature conducted in Australia include Galliers (1987), Ridley et al. (1998), Pervan and Cecez-Kecmanovic (2001) and Pervan and Shanks (2004, 2006). Pervan and Cecez-Kecmanovic (2001) reported on the results of a survey of heads of IS groups regarding the research profiles of their groups. The heads of 21 of the 36 targeted IS groups responded. This represented more than 400 of the approximately 700 IS academics thought to be active in IS in Australia. The responses confirmed that Australian IS reflects the enormous breadth of scope elsewhere. Similar diversity was detected in relation to the unit of analysis of the research conducted. The primary beneficiaries of the research were identified as being predominantly IS professionals and managers—consistent with the notion of being a professionally oriented discipline—although the subsequent data in Pervan and Shanks (2004, 2006) suggest a strong focus on writing for other academics as well. The average publication count disclosed was about two for each staff member per annum, of which one-third was in journals and two-thirds in conferences. The research funding available was generally small, but Pervan and Shanks (2004) suggested that it was growing.

Research techniques

The diversity apparent in research topics is just as evident in IS academics' choice of research methods. Taxonomies of research techniques include Alavi and Carlson (1992) and Palvia et al. (2003, 2004). The 1980s saw an extended period of intolerance and mutual distrust and dislike between groups who adopted particular research techniques. The tensions were variously methodological, philosophical and transatlantic. While differences remain, there is sufficient mutual respect and 'agreement to disagree' that little energy has been wasted during the past decade. The discipline has become catholic, in one of the positive senses of the expression.

In the IS community internationally, Claver et al. (2000) found that 'theoretical studies' (as defined by Alavi and Carlson 1992) fell from 56 per cent to 20 per cent between 1981 and 1983 and 1996 and 1997, while empirical studies rose from 44 per cent to 80 per cent. 'Field studies' (although in many cases mere questionnaire-based surveys) rose from 18 per cent to 52 per cent, while case studies rose to a high of 23 per cent but fell back to their original 18 per cent.

In Europe, Avgerou et al. (1999) found that the techniques used varied widely between countries, and differed from those prevalent in the United States. A large proportion of German researchers focused on technology development and testing, whereas those in many other countries conducted a great deal more qualitative analysis.

In Australia, Pervan and Cecez-Kecmanovic (2001) reported that 'responses revealed dominance of a positivist paradigm, but the interpretivist paradigm was also often used'. Further, 'the full range of research methods are being used, from survey to action research, to technology development and testing'. Pervan and Shanks (2004, 2006) suggest that interpretivist approaches have been growing in popularity. Critical-theory approaches remain little used.

Conclusions

The purpose of this chapter has been to provide a chronicle of the early years of the IS discipline in Australia, in the process identifying important themes. It is arguably inappropriate in a review of this nature to draw conclusions; this section accordingly focuses on key questions that confront the discipline early in the twenty-first century.

The first cluster of questions relates to the discipline's intellectual survival. Is IS really a discipline? And does it matter if it isn't? Is there a core? Is it so heavily dependent on technology and management fashion that it can never have the stable core necessary for a recognised discipline? Put another way, are IS academics destined to wander forever, as Rosencrantz and Guildenstern to Hamlet, backstage bit actors to host discipline leads? Is IS not a discipline, but merely a research domain that needs to be viewed through the lenses of a variety of genuine disciplines? Has its value been ephemeral? Does it need to be absorbed by broader disciplines on either side of it? Does it need to continue to exist much as it does now, but with less energy wasted on existential angst?

In this author's view, we need to be far less nervous, and far more positive about the quality of our work; to be far less internally focused, and far more outward-looking and professionally oriented; to be far less interested in 'the IT artefact', and far more committed to 'information' and 'systems' as the once and future core of the IS discipline. We need to be far less mechanistic in our outlook, and far more humanistic; and we need to be far less servile to corporations and the State, and far more socially responsible.

If IS is a discipline with a long-term future, further questions arise. In interview, Frank Land said, 'We're fragmenting intellectually and methodologically, and our language is becoming confused, because words are increasingly being used in method-specific senses.' He sees this as leading to mistaken inferring and perhaps an outright inability to comprehend what someone from a different intellectual or methodological school of thought is trying to say. This author sees this as being a consequence of the dominance of rigour over relevance, and the resultant research technique-driven selection of research questions and even research domains.

If the discipline is intellectually worthy and sound, there remains the issue of economic survival. Can a still relatively young and politically weak discipline survive in the face of massively reduced government funding for institutions, new business models exposed to the vagaries of market conditions and a new mechanism for the distribution of research funds that is hostile to new and non-traditional disciplines? The market overreacted to the dot.com implosion—as markets do—and local demand for IT-qualified graduates could well exceed supply in the near future. The implosion in enrolments, however, confirmed the belief among university administrators that IS is ephemeral and/or unimportant. Will the recovery come soon enough and forcefully enough to ensure that IS survives as a distinct discipline? Political survival depends on many factors, but adjustment of the scope of the IS discipline, and maturation of its orientation, would deliver intellectual integrity, which would certainly help.

The first four decades of the IS discipline in Australia saw progress and growth achieved, but in a context of multi-dimensional change, uncertainty and adversity. The next decade promises more of the last three, but quite possibly more of the first two as well.

Select bibliography

Ackoff, R. L. 1967, 'Management misinformation systems', *Management Science*, vol. 14, no. 4, pp. 147–56.

Aiken, J. D. 1971, 'An introduction to management information systems', *Australian Computer Journal*, vol. 3, no. 3, pp. 98–105.

Alavi, M., Carlson, P. and Brooke, G. 1989, 'The ecology of MIS research: a twenty year status review', *Proceedings of the International Conference on Information Systems*, pp. 363–75.

Alavi, M. and Carlson, P. 1992, 'A review of MIS research and disciplinary development', *Journal of Management Information Systems,* vol. 8, no. 4, pp. 45–62.

Anthony, R. N. 1965, *Planning and Control Systems: A Framework for Analysis*, Harvard University Press.

Australian Bureau of Statistics (ABS) 2005, *Informing a Nation: The Evolution of the Australian Bureau of Statistics*, Australian Bureau of Statistics, cat. 1382.0, November 2005.

Australian Computer Society (ACS) 1985 *Guidelines for Course Accreditation*, Australian Computer Society.

Australian Computer Society (ACS) 1987 *Guidelines for Course Accreditation*, Australian Computer Society.

Australian Computer Society (ACS) 1990, *Guidelines for Course Accreditation*, Australian Computer Society.

Australian Computer Society (ACS) 1992, *Report of the Task Force on the ACS Towards 2000*, Australian Computer Society, Sydney.

Australian Vice-Chancellors' Association (AVCC) 2004, *Australian Higher Education Institutions*, Australian Vice-Chancellors' Association, viewed 22 March 2007, <http://www.avcc.edu.au/documents/universities/ AustralianHEMerges-Amalgamations.pdf>

Avgerou, C., Siemer, J. and Bjørn-Andersen, N. 1999, 'The academic field of information systems in Europe', *European Journal of Information Systems*, vol. 8, no. 2, pp. 136–53.

Banker, R. J. and Kauffman, R. J. 2004, 'The evolution of research on information systems: a fiftieth-year survey of the literature in management science', *Management Science*, vol. 50, no. 3, pp. 281–98.

Barki, H., Rivard, S. and Talbot, J. 1988, 'An information systems keyword classification scheme', *MIS Quarterly*, vol. 12, no. 2, pp. 299–322.

Barki, H., Rivard, S. and Talbot, J. 1993, 'A keyword classification scheme for IS research literature: an update', *MIS Quarterly*, vol. 17, no. 2, pp. 209–26.

Bennet, J. M. 1963, 'EDP—the universities' role', *Proceedings of the Australian Computer Conference, Group A—Commercial Data Processing*, A. 16, pp. 1–16.

Bennett, J. M., Broomham, R., Murton, P. M., Pearcey, T. and Rutledge, R. W. (eds) 1994, *Computing in Australia: The Development of a Profession*, Hale & Iremonger/Australian Computer Society.

Bjørn-Anderson, N. (ed.) 1980, *The Human Side of Information Processing*, North-Holland, Amsterdam.

Bjørn-Anderson, N. and Hansen, H. 1993, *European Information Systems Directory*, Copenhagen Business School.

Boland, R. 1978, 'The process and product of system design', *Management Science*, vol. 28, no. 9, pp. 887–98.

Brookes, C. H. P., Grouse, P. J., Jeffery, D. R. and Lawrence, M. J. 1982, *Information Systems Design*, Prentice Hall, Sydney.

Burrows, G. 2006, *Promise Fulfilled: The History of the Accounting Department at the University of Melbourne*, Melbourne University Press.

Caminer, D., Aris, J., Hermon, P. and Land, F. 1998, *LEO—The Incredible Story of the World's First Business Computer*, McGraw-Hill, New York.

Campbell-Kelly, M. 2003, *From Airline Reservations to Sonic the Hedgehog: A History of the Software Industry*, MIT Press.

Canning, R. C. 1994, 'History of the *DATA BASE Journal*', *Database*, viewed 22 March 2007, <http://www.baylor.edu/databaseJrnl/index.php?id=4298>

Checkland, P. 1981, *Systems Thinking, Systems Practice*, Wiley, Chichester.

Chen, W. S. and Hirschheim, R. 2004, 'A paradigmatic and methodological examination of information systems research from 1991 to 2001', *Information Systems Journal*, vol. 14, no. 3, pp. 197–235.

Clarke, R. (ed.) 1988, *Australian Information Systems Academics: 1988/89 Directory*, The Australian National University, November 1988.

Clarke, R. (ed.) 1991, *Australasian Information Systems Academics: 1991 Directory*, The Australian National University, April 1991.

Clarke, R. 1976, 'Top-down structured programming in COBOL', *Proceedings of the 7th Australian Computer Conference*, Perth, September 1976.

Clarke, R. 1987, 'The computing professional's bookshelf', *Australian Computer Journal*, vol. 19, no. 4, pp. 222–3.

Clarke, R. 1990, 'Information systems: the scope of the domain', Xamax Consultancy Pty Ltd, viewed 22 March 2007, <http://www.anu.edu.au/people/Roger.Clarke/SOS/ISDefn.html>

Clarke, R. 1992, *Fundamentals of 'Information Systems'*, Xamax Consultancy Pty Ltd, viewed 22 March 2007, <http://www.anu.edu.au/people/Roger.Clarke/SOS/ISFundas.html>

Clarke, R. 2004, 'Origins and nature of the Internet in Australia', Xamax Consultancy Pty Ltd, viewed 22 March 2007, <http://www.anu.edu.au/people/Roger.Clarke/II/OzI04.html>

Clarke, R. 2006, 'Key aspects of the history of the information systems discipline in Australia', *Australasian Journal of Information Systems*, vol. 14, no. 1, pp. 123–40.

Clarke R. 2007, *A Retrospective on the Information Systems Discipline in Australia—Appendices*, Xamax Consultancy Pty Ltd, viewed 22 March 2007, <http://www.anu.edu.au/people/Roger.Clarke/SOS/AISHistApps.html>

Clarke, R. and Lo, B. 1989, *Accreditation Requirements for Information Systems Courses for the Australian Computer Society*, Australian Computer Society, November 1989.

Claver, E., Gonzalez, R. and Llopis, J. 2000, 'An analysis of research in information systems (1981–1997)', *Information & Management*, vol. 37, no. 4, pp. 181–95.

Culnan, M. 1986, 'The intellectual development of management information systems, 1972–1982: a co-citation analysis', *Management Science*, vol. 32, no. 2, pp. 156–72.

Culnan, M. 1987, 'Mapping the intellectual structure of MIS, 1980–1985: a co-citation analysis', *MIS Quarterly*, vol. 11, no. 3, pp. 341–53.

Davis, G. B. 1965, *Introduction to Electronic Computers*, McGraw-Hill.

Davis, G. B. 1974, *Management Information Systems: Conceptual Foundations, Structure, and Development*, McGraw-Hill.

Davis, G. B. and DeGross, J. 1983, *Information Systems Faculty Directory for North America*, University of Minnesota.

Davis, G. B. and Olson, M. H. 1984, *Management Information Systems: Conceptual Foundations, Structure, and Development*, 2nd edn, McGraw-Hill.

Dearden, J. 1972, 'MIS is a mirage', *Harvard Business Review*, January–February, pp. 90–9.

Dickson, G. W. 1981, 'Management information systems: evolution and status', in M. Youts (ed.), *Advances in Computers*, Academic Press, New York.

Dreyfus, S. 2004, *The University of Melbourne Department of Information Systems—1996–2004*, University of Melbourne.

Drucker, P. F. 1968, *The Age of Discontinuity*, Pan Piper.

Emery, J. C. 1969, *Organizational Planning and Control Systems: Theory and Technology*, Crowell Collier and Macmillan, New York.

Emery, J. C. 1971, *Cost–Benefit Analysis of Information Systems*, The Society for Management Information Systems, Chicago.

Fiedler, M. R. G. 1969, 'Education for commercial ADP staff—I skills required and existing facilities', *Australian Computer Journal*, vol. 1, no. 5, pp. 277–84.

Fiedler, M. R. G. 1970, 'Education for commercial ADP staff in Australia II the solution in-house training', *Australian Computer Journal*, vol. 2, no. 1, pp. 32–8.

Gable, G. and Clarke, R. (eds) 1994, *Asia Pacific Directory of Information Systems Researchers: 1994*, National University of Singapore.

Gable, G. and Clarke, R. (eds) 1996, *Asia Pacific Directory of Information Systems Researchers: 1996*, National University of Singapore.

Galliers, R. D. 1987, 'Information systems planning: a manifesto for Australian-based research', *Australian Computer Journal*, vol. 19, no. 2, pp. 49–55.

Galliers, R. D. and Whitley, E. A. 2002, 'An anatomy of European information systems research ECIS 1993–ECIS 2002: some initial findings', *Proceedings of the 10th European Conference on Information Systems*, Gdansk, Poland, June 2002.

Glass, R. L. 1992, 'A comparative analysis of the topic areas of computer science, software engineering and information systems', *Journal of Systems and Software*, vol. 19, no. 4 (1992), pp. 277–89.

Gorgone, J. T. and Gray, P. 2000, 'MSIS 2000: model curriculum and guidelines for graduate degree programs in information systems', *Communications of the Association for Information Systems*, vol. 3, no. 1.

Gorgone, J. T., Davis, G. B., Valacich, J. S., Topi, H., Feinstein, D. L. and Longenecker, H. E. jr 2002, *IS 2002: Model Curriculum and Guidelines for Undergraduate Degree Programs in Information Systems*, Association for Information Systems.

Gorgone, J. T., Gray, P., Stohr, E. A., Valacich, J. S. and Wigand, R. T. 2005, 'MSIS2006 curriculum preview', *Communications of the Association for Information Systems*, vol. 15, pp. 544–54.

Greig, J. and Levin, P. 1989, *Computing at Chisholm: The First Twenty-Five Years, 1965–1989*, Chisholm Institute of Technology.

Hally, M. 2005, *Electronic Brains: Stories from the Dawn of the Computer Age*, Granta, London.

Heinrich, L. J. 1993, *Wirtschaftsinformatik—Einführung und Grundlegung*, Oldenbourg, Muenchen/Wien.

Hudson, H. R. 1992, *Report of the Discipline Review of Computing Studies and Information Sciences Education*, Australian Government Publishing Service.

Ives, B., Hamilton, S. and Davis, G. B. 1980, 'A framework for research in computer-based management information-systems', *Management Science*, vol. 26, no. 9, pp. 910–34.

Jeffery, D. R. and Lawrence, M. J. (eds) 1986, 'Current research directions in information systems', *Australian Computer Journal*, vol. 18, no. 4, pp. 157–8.

Johnson, L. R. 2006, 'Coming to grips with Univac', *IEEE Annals of the History of Computing*, vol. 28, no. 2, pp. 32–42.

Katz, D. and Kahn, R. L. 1966, *The Social Psychology of Organizations*, Wiley.

Keen, P. G. W. and Scott Morton M. S. 1978, *Decision Support Systems: An Organizational Perspective*, Addison-Wesley, Reading, Mass.

Kistermann, F. W. 1991, 'The invention and development of the Hollerith punched card: in commemoration of the 130th anniversary of the birth of Herman Hollerith and for the 100th anniversary of large scale data processing', *IEEE Annals of the History of Computing*, vol. 13, no. 3, pp. 245–59.

Lamp, J. W. 2004, *The Index of Information Systems Journals*, Deakin University, Geelong, viewed 22 March 2007, <http://lamp.infosys.deakin.edu.au/journals/index.php>

Land, F. 1992, 'The information systems domain', in R. Galliers (ed.), *Information Systems Research: Issues, Methods, and Practical Guidelines*, Blackwell, pp. 6–13.

Land, F. 2000a, 'Evaluation in a socio-technical context', in R. Baskerville, J. Stage and J. DeGross (eds), *Organizational and Social Perspectives on IT*, Kluwer, pp. 115–26.

Land, F. 2000b, 'The first business computer: a case study in user-driven innovation', *IEEE Annals of the History of Computing*, vol. 22, no. 3, pp. 16–26.

Langefors, B. 1963, 'Some approaches to the theory of information systems', *BIT Numerical Mathematics*, vol. 3, no. 4, pp. 229–54.

Langefors, B. 1966, *Theoretical Analysis of Information Systems*, Studentlitteratur, Lund, Sweden.

Lee, A. S. 1994, 'Electronic mail as a medium for rich communication: an empirical investigation using hermeneutic interpretation', *MIS Quarterly*, vol. 18, no. 2, pp. 143–57.

Lyttinen, K. and King, J. L. 2004, 'Nothing at the center?: academic legitimacy in the information systems field', *Journal of the Association for Information Systems*, vol. 5, no. 6, pp. 220–46.

McDowell, I. 2002, 'Computing history—the first ANCCAC Conference', *PC Update*, March 2002, Melbourne PC User Group, Australia, viewed 22 March 2007, <http://www.melbpc.org.au/pcupdate/2203/2203article10.htm>

McGregor, K. 1974, 'University claims a computer first', *Australian Financial Review*, 29 January.

Mason, R. O. 2005, *Putting 'Systems' Back into Information Systems: An Essay in Honor of Gordon Davis*, Working Paper, May 2005.

Mason, R. O. and Mitroff I. I. 1973, 'A program for research on management information systems', *Management Science*, vol. 19, no. 5, pp. 475–87.

Maynard, G. B. and Underwood, A. 1996, *Guidelines for Accreditation of Courses in Universities at the Professional Level*, Australian Computer Society.

Mertens, P., König, W. and Barbian, D. 2002, 'The German information systems perspective', *Systémes d Information et Management*, vol. 7, pp. 39–47.

Metcalfe, M. and Kiley, M. 2000, 'Arguing for PhD coursework', *Australasian Journal of Information Systems*, vol. 7, no. 2, pp. 52–9.

Mumford, E. 1983, *Designing Human Systems*, Manchester Business School.

Mumford, E. 2006, *Socio-Technical Design*, viewed 22 March 2007, <http://www.enid.u-net.com/Sociotech.htm>

Mumford, E. and Banks, O. 1967, *The Computer and the Clerk*, Routledge Kegan Paul.

Norberg, A. L. 2005, *Computers and Commerce: A Study of Technology and Management at Eckert-Mauchly Computer Company, Engineering Research Associates, and Remington Rand, 1946–1957*, MIT Press.

Olle, T. W., Hagelstein, J., Macdonald, I. G., Rolland, C., Sol, H. G., van Assche, F. J. M. and Verrijn-Stuart, A. A. 1988, *Information Systems Methodologies: A Framework for Understanding*, Addison-Wesley.

Palvia, P., Leary, D., Mao, E., Midha, V., Pinjani, P. and Salam, A. F. 2004, 'Research methodologies in MIS: an update', *Communications of the Association for Information Systems*, vol. 14, no. 24.

Palvia, P., Mao, E., Salam, A. F. and Soliman, K. S. 2003, 'Management information systems research: what's there in a methodology?', *Communications of the Association for Information Systems*, vol. 11, no. 16.

Pearcey, T. 1988, *A History of Australian Computing*, Chisholm Institute of Technology.

Pervan, G. and Cecez-Kecmanovic, D. 2001, 'The status of information systems research in Australia: preliminary results', *Proceedings of the 12th Australasian Conference on Information Systems*, December 2001.

Pervan, G. and Shanks, G. 2004, *IS Research Activity in Australia: Results of the 2004 ACPHIS Research Survey*, Presentation to Australasian Conference on Information Systems, December 2004.

Pervan, G. and Shanks, G. 2006, 'The 2005 survey of information systems research in Australia', *Australian Journal of Information Systems*, vol. 14, no. 1, pp. 273–9.

Prince, T. R. 1966, *Information Systems for Management Planning and Control*, Richard D. Irwin, Homewood.

Prince, T. R. 1970, *Information Systems for Management Planning and Control*, Richard D. Irwin, Homewood.

Ridley, G., Goulding, P., Lowry, G. and Pervan, G. P. 1998, 'The Australian information systems research community: an analysis of mainstream publication outlets', *Australasian Journal of Information Systems,* vol. 5, no. 2, pp. 69–80.

Sale, A. 1994, 'Computer science teaching in Australia', in J. M. Bennett et al. (eds), *Computing in Australia: The Development of a Profession*, Hale & Iremonger/Australian Computer Society, pp. 151–4.

Scott Morton, M. S. 1971, *Management Decision Systems*, Harvard University Press.

Shen, Z. 2003, *Langefors_Review*, Wiki for IS Scholarship, viewed 22 March 2007, <http://isworld.student.cwru.edu/tiki/tiki-index.php?page=Langefors_Review>

Simon, H. A. 1960, *The New Science of Management*, Harper, New York.

Smith, B. A. and de Ferranti, B. Z. 1975 *Computer education needs in Australia - the next ten years*, Commission on Advanced Education, Canberra, 6 vols.

Sprague, R. H. jr 1980, 'A framework for the development of decision support systems', *MIS Quarterly*, vol. 4, no. 4, pp. 1–26.

Underwood, A. 1997, *The Core Body of Knowledge for Information Technology Professionals*, Australian Computer Society.

Vessey, I., Ramesh, V. and Glass, R. L. 2002, 'Research in information systems: an empirical study of diversity in the discipline and its journals', *Journal of Management Information Systems*, vol. 19, no. 2, pp. 129–74.

Walstrom, K. A. and Leonard, L. 2000, 'Citation classics from the information systems literature', *Information & Management*, vol. 38, no. 2, pp. 59–72.

Weber, R. 1997, *Ontological Foundations of Information Systems: Coopers & Lybrand Research Methodology Monograph No. 4*, Coopers & Lybrand, Melbourne.

White, J. D. and Palfreyman, E. H. 1963, 'Electronic data processing in the Commonwealth Public Service staff training', *Proceedings of the Australian Computer Conference, Group A—Commercial Data Processing*, A. 10, pp. 1–12.

Wood-Harper, A. T., Antill, L. and Avison, D. E. 1985, *Information Systems Definition: The Multiview Approach*, Blackwell, Oxford.

Appendix 2.1: Professors

This appendix identifies individuals who are known to have occupied full professorial posts in Australia and whose background and role appeared to place considerable weight on IS. It was compiled during 2005–06 and revised in early 2007 with further edits in late 2007. It reflects the period up to early 2007. The confidence level is moderate—at an individual and an aggregate level.

In summary:

- in early 2007, the current count appeared to be 52 professors in 28 of the 42 widely recognised universities in Australia, although five of the 52 could be argued not to be professors in IS
- 70 individuals were identified as having held chairs, in 32 of the 42 institutions, although six could be argued not to be professors in IS
- the first 18 chairs appear to have been created between 1974 and 1995, as follows: 1974 (UNSW); 1981 (University of Queensland); 1987 (Curtin); five in 1990 (three at Monash, one each at UNSW, University of Queensland); 1991 (UNSW); 1992 (Tasmania); four in 1993 (Australian Graduate School of Management, Griffith, Macquarie Graduate School of Management, QUT); two in 1994 (Bond, Wollongong); two in 1995 (Macquarie, Charles Sturt University).

The three sections of this appendix are:

- an explanation of the basis on which the information was compiled
- a list of institutions, showing people known to have held full professorships there
- a list of people known to have held full professorships in IS, by surname, with such information as is known about their appointment(s).

The basis of the compilation

The starting points for this collection were the Australian and Asia-Pacific directories (Clarke 1988, 1991; Gable and Clarke 1994, 1996). It is of the nature of the early, printed directories and the self-maintained *ISWorld Online Directory* since 1995 that omissions and misclassifications occur. The proportion of IS professors who have established and maintained their own entries is very low (only 33 of 70). A '(D)' indicates that the person had an entry in the directory in March 2007 and '(NO)' means there was no entry.

The universities include all 38 that are members of Universities Australia (until 2007 known as the AVCC), together with four further institutions generally accepted as being universities.

Appointments in cognate disciplines such as accounting and computer science have been included, where the author judged the association with the IS community to be significant. One person listed has indicated that he no longer feels a close affinity with the IS discipline (Jeffery in empirical software engineering). At least five people would be regarded by some as being adjacent to rather than within IS (Gaffikin in accountancy, Henderson-Sellers in software engineering, Newton in computer science/OR, Orlowska in database and data management, Yetton in management and decision making).

The list does not include any of the following: associate professors, visiting professors, adjunct professors and professorial fellows (unless they were known to be full time for an extended period). The intention is to identify long-term, full-time positions and the people who occupy or have occupied them.

The years shown are only those during which the person is known to have held a chair—it is a list of professors, not an attempt to show each person's full career. This appendix includes the corrections and updates that were communicated to the author in response to a request for comment distributed to a large number of people in early 2007.

List by institution

Underlining indicates that the appointment was current in early 2007.

- Australian Catholic University (-)
- Adelaide (-)
- Australian Defence Force Academy (ADFA)—2001—Newton (1)
- Australian Graduate School of Management (AGSM)—1993, 2001—Yetton, Vitale (1)
- ANU—2001—Gregor (1)
- Ballarat (-)
- Bond—1994, 2003—Goldsworthy, Morrison, Finnie (2)
- Canberra (-)
- Charles Darwin University (CDU)—2004—Lueg, Haynes (1)
- Charles Sturt University (CSU)—1995—Cornish, Poon (-)
- Central Queensland University (CQU)—2000—Hovenga (1)
- Curtin—1987, 1996, 2002—Galliers, Pervan, Lloyd, Chang (3)
- Deakin—2000, 2002—P. A. Swatman, Corbitt, Castleman, Warren (2)
- Edith Cowan University (ECU)—1997—Burn, Standing (1)
- Flinders (-)
- Griffith—1993—Cecez-Kezmanovic, Davies, Gammack, Eklund (1)
- James Cook (-)
- La Trobe (-)
- Macquarie—1995, 1997, 1998—Jordan, Johnson, Offen (3)
- Melbourne—1996, 1997, 2000—Vitale, Morrison, Sonenberg, Ferguson, Shanks (3)
- Melbourne Graduate School of Management—1993, 1999—Vitale, Weill (-)

- Monash—1990, 1990, 1990—<u>Arnott</u>, Steele, Juliff, <u>Dooley</u>, Shanks, <u>Weber</u> (3)
- Murdoch (-)
- Newcastle—2000—<u>Aisbett</u> (1)
- University of New England (UNE) (-)
- UNSW—1974, 1990, 1991—Brookes, <u>Jeffery</u>, Lawrence, <u>Low</u>, <u>Cavaye</u>, <u>Cecez-Kezmanovic</u> (4)
- Notre Dame—2000—Glasson (-)
- Queensland—1981, 1990—Weber, <u>Orlowska</u>, <u>Green</u> (2)
- QUT—1993, 1999—Papazoglou, <u>Gable</u>, Underwood, <u>Rosemann</u> (2)
- Royal Melbourne Institute of Technology (RMIT)—2003, 2007—Swatman, <u>Corbitt</u>, <u>Smith</u> (2)
- University of South Australia (UniSA)—2002, 2003, 2003—<u>Koronios</u>, <u>Swatman</u>, <u>Swatman</u> (3)
- Southern Cross University (SCU)—2000—Cavaye, <u>Murugesan</u> (1)
- University of Southern Queensland (USQ)—2007—<u>Toleman</u> (1)
- Sunshine Coast—2003—<u>Fitzgerald</u> (1)
- Swinburne—2000—<u>Grant</u> (1)
- Sydney—1998, 2002, 2002—<u>Patrick</u>, <u>Elliot</u>, <u>O'Connor</u> (3)
- Tasmania 1992, 1999—Leech, Keen, <u>Marshall</u>, <u>Lueg</u> (2)
- UTS—1990, 1998—<u>Hawryszkiewycz</u>, <u>Henderson-Sellers</u> (2)
- Victoria University (VU)—2002, 2002—<u>McGrath</u>, <u>Zeleznikow</u> (2)
- University of Western Australia (UWA) (-)
- University of Western Sydney (UWS)—1998—Cecez-Kezmanovic (-)
- Wollongong—1988, 1994—<u>Gaffikin</u>, Winley, <u>Eklund</u> (2)

List by person

Underlining indicates that the appointment was current in early 2007.

- Janet <u>AISBETT</u> (NO)— <u>Newcastle</u>, 2000?–
- David <u>ARNOTT</u> [7] (NO)—<u>Monash</u>, 1990–
- Cyril BROOKES [1] (NO)—UNSW 1974–94
- Janice BURN (D)—ECU, 1997–2005?
- Tanya <u>CASTLEMAN</u> (D)—<u>Deakin</u>, 2002–
- Angele <u>CAVAYE</u> (D)—SCU 2000–02?, <u>UNSW</u>, 2002?–
- Dubravka <u>CECEZ-KEZMANOVIC</u> (D)—Griffith, 1993–97?, UWS 1998?–2002?, <u>UNSW</u> 2002?–
- Elizabeth <u>CHANG</u> (NO)—<u>Curtin</u>, 2002?–
- Brian <u>CORBITT</u> (NO)—Victoria University of Wellington 1998?–2000?, Deakin 2000?–2003?, <u>RMIT</u>, 2003?–
- Brian CORNISH (NO)—CSU, 1995?–2000?
- Lynda DAVIES (NO)—Griffith, 1995?–2000?
- Laurence <u>DOOLEY</u> (D)—<u>Monash</u>, 2000?–

- Peter EKLUND (D)—Griffith 1998–2002, Wollongong, 2004–
- Steve ELLIOT (NO)—Sydney, 2002?–
- Colin FERGUSON (D)—Melbourne, 2004–
- Gavin FINNIE (NO)—Bond, 2005–
- Ed FITZGERALD (D)—Sunshine Coast, 2003–
- Guy GABLE (D)—QUT, 1999–
- Michael GAFFIKIN (D)—Wollongong, 1988 (accountancy)–
- Bob GALLIERS [3] (NO)—WAIT/Curtin, 1987–88
- John GAMMACK (D)—Griffith, 2000–
- Bernie GLASSON (D)—Notre Dame, 2000–03?
- Ashley GOLDSWORTHY (NO)—Bond, 1994?–99?
- Doug GRANT (D)—Swinburne, 2000?–
- Peter GREEN (NO)—UQ, 2002?–
- Shirley GREGOR (D)—ANU, 2001–
- Igor HAWRYSZKIEWYCZ [6] (NO)—UTS, 1990–
- John HAYNES (NO)—CDU, 2005?–
- Brian HENDERSON-SELLERS (NO)—UTS, 1998?–
- Evelyn HOVENGA (D)—CQU, 2000?–
- Ross JEFFERY [4] (NO)—UNSW, 1990–
- Michael JOHNSON (D)—Macquarie, 1997?–
- Ernest JORDAN (D)—Macquarie, 1998?–
- Peter JULIFF [7] (NO)—Monash, 1990–97?
- Chris KEEN (NO)—Tasmania, 1999–2007
- Andy KORONIOS (D)—UniSA, 2002–
- Michael LAWRENCE [10] (NO)—UNSW, 1991–2004?
- Stewart LEECH [11] (NO)—Tasmania, 1992–2000, Melbourne, 2000–
- Ashley LLOYD (NO)—Curtin, 2002–
- Christopher LUEG (D)—CDU, 2004–05, Tasmania, 2005–
- Graham LOW (D) —UNSW, 1998?–
- Michael McGRATH (D)—VU, 2002–
- Peter MARSHALL (D)—Tasmania, 2001–
- Iain MORRISON (NO)—Melbourne, 1997?–2003?, Bond 2003?–
- San MURUGESAN (D)—SCU, 2002–
- Charles NEWTON (NO)—ADFA, 2001?–
- Marcus O'CONNOR (NO)—Sydney, 2002?–
- Raymond OFFEN (NO)—Macquarie, 1995?–
- Maria ORLOWSKA [5] (NO)—UQ, 1990–
- Mike PAPAZOGLOU (NO)—QUT, 1993?–99?
- Jon PATRICK (D)—Sydney, 1998–
- Graham PERVAN (NO)—Curtin, 1996–
- Simpson POON (D)—CSU, 2001?–04?
- Michael ROSEMANN (D)—QUT, 2004–

- Graeme <u>SHANKS</u> (NO)—Monash, 2003–06, <u>Melbourne</u> 2006–
- Ross <u>SMITH</u> (D)—<u>RMIT</u>, 2007–
- Liz <u>SONENBERG</u> (D)—<u>Melbourne</u>, 2001?–
- Craig <u>STANDING</u> (D)—<u>ECU</u>, 2003?–
- Phillip STEELE [7] (NO)—Monash, 1990–2001?
- Paul A. <u>SWATMAN</u> (NO)—Deakin 1997–2000, SIMT in Germany, 2000–03, <u>UniSA</u>, 2003–
- Paula M. C. <u>SWATMAN</u> (D)—RMIT 1998–2000, Koblenz 2000–03, <u>UniSA</u>, 2004–
- Mark <u>TOLEMAN</u> (NO)—<u>USQ</u> 2007–
- Alan UNDERWOOD (D)—QUT, 2004–06
- Michael <u>VITALE</u> (D)—Melbourne, 1996–99?, MGSM 1999?–2001?, AGSM, 2001?–
- Matthew <u>WARREN</u> (NO)—<u>Deakin</u>, 2004–
- Ron <u>WEBER</u> [2] (D)—UQ 1981–2004, <u>Monash</u> 2004–
- Peter WEILL (NO)—MGSM, 1993–2002?, MIT 2002?–
- Graham WINLEY (NO)—Wollongong, 1994–2002
- Philip YETTON (NO)—AGSM, 1993–2006
- John <u>ZELEZNIKOW</u> (D)—<u>VU</u>, 2002–

Appendix 2.2: Early Australian PhDs in IS

This appendix lists Australians known to have been awarded PhDs before the end of 1995, whose work was clearly in or directly relevant to IS. Sources used include the *ISWorld Dissertation Database*, the *Australian Digital Theses Program*, the author's memory, interviews with Ron Weber and Cyril Brookes and e-mail discussions with several other people.

This list excludes people who entered the IS discipline with doctorates in other areas, and those who migrated to Australia after completing a doctorate elsewhere.

1977 Ron Weber: Auditor decision making: a study of some aspects of accuracy and consensus and the usefulness of a simulation decision aid for assessing overall system reliability, University of Minnesota, supervisor Gordon Davis.

1982 Errol Iselin: [re information overload], University of Queensland, supervisor Ron Weber.

1984 Iris Vessey: [re psychological processes underlying program debugging], University of Queensland, supervisor Ron Weber.

1986 Ross Jeffery: A comparison of models describing third and fourth generation software development environments, with implications for effective management, University of New South Wales, supervisor Cyril Brookes.

1987 Rick Watson: A study of group decision support system use in three and four-person groups for a preference allocation decision', University of Minnesota, supervisor Gerry DeSanctis.

1987 Bob Galliers: Information systems planning in Britain and Australia in the mid 1980s: key success factors, London School of Economics, supervisor Frank Land.

1988 Peter Clayton: User involvement in academic library strategic planning: congruence amongst students, academic staff and library staff at the Canberra College of Advanced Education [very close to IS!], University of Canberra, supervisor unknown.

1989 Patricia Willard: The personal computer and the public library: a study of the absorption of new technology and an analysis of librarians' opinions about the present and future impact on Australian public libraries [very close to IS!], University of New South Wales, supervisor unknown.

1990 Marianne Broadbent: The alignment of business and information strategies', Graduate School of Management, University of Melbourne, supervisor Peter Weill.

1992 Chris Sauer: Information systems failure: the problem of managing support for a flawed innovation process, University of Western Australia, supervisor unknown.

1992 Paul Swatman: Increasing formality in the specification of high quality information systems in a commercial context, Curtin University of Technology, supervisor Roger Duke.

1993 Paula Swatman: Integrating electronic data interchange with existing organisational structure and internal application systems: the Australian experience, Curtin University of Technology.

1994 James Popple: SHYSTER: a pragmatic legal expert system, The Australian National University, supervisor Roger Clarke.

1994 Graham Pervan: A comprehensive model of group support systems application: development and initial testing, Curtin University of Technology.

The year 1995 was selected as the cut-off point on the pragmatic grounds that the numbers increased significantly from then onwards, with at least seven PhDs in 1996 (D'Ambra, Gould, Gregor, Green, Kirlidog, Mackay and Sayer) and at least five in 1997 (Clarke, Klobas, Parker, Shanks and Williams). It would appear that, by 2002, about 20–30 IS PhDs were graduating from Australian universities each year (Pervan and Shanks 2004).

Appendix 2.3: The early international impact of Australian IS

This appendix reports the results of a brief analysis undertaken of the international impact of Australian IS scholars.

The period considered is limited to 1965–95. The measures used have been limited to publications in the discipline's flagship journals and conferences.

The following people have been excluded, because their work during the relevant period was undertaken elsewhere or they were only visiting: Janice Burn, Angele Cavaye, Philip Ein-Dor, Bob Galliers and Michael Vitale.

The first specialist journal, *MIS Quarterly*, has been published since 1977. Authorship was strongly American during its first two decades. The first Australian author appears to have been Iris Vessey, in June 1980 (vol. 4, no. 2) and again in June 1981 (vol. 5, no. 2). (She could also have been the first non-American author and/or the first non-American PhD to publish there.) Ted Stohr followed in December 1983 (vol. 7, no. 4). Vessey published again in March 1988 (vol. 12, no. 1), this time in conjunction with Peter Tait of Touche Ross, Brisbane. Rick Watson appeared for the first time in September 1988 (vol. 12, no. 3), Eric J. Walton (then at UWA) in December 1988 (vol. 12, no. 4), Peter Weill in March 1989 (vol. 13, no. 1), Watson again in June 1990 (vol. 14, no. 2), Michael Lawrence and Graham Low from UNSW in June 1993 (vol. 17, no. 2), and Watson again in June 1995 (vol. 19, no. 2). Tellingly perhaps, Ron Weber appears only as an editor—and only from 2002.

In *Information & Management*, the first paper by an Australian was by Ross Jeffery and Iris Vessey in 1980, the next by Ross Jeffery and Michael Lawrence in 1981, then Bob Edmundson and Ross Jeffery in 1984, Vessey again in 1986, Michael Sager in 1988, Bill Cundiff in 1989 and then Guy Gable in 1991.

Information Systems Research (*ISR*) was a relative late comer on the journal scene—in 1989. Australians were slow to break into it as well, with the first published appearing to be Iris Vessey in 1995 (vol. 6), Ron Weber twice in 1996 and Peter Seddon in 1997.

Brisk analysis of the early years in *Management Science* identified no papers before 1996 (vol. 42), when Ron Weber and Guy Gable published. Rick Watson published there in 1998.

Communications of the ACM was an outlet for quality refereed articles in IS from the late 1970s until it adopted a lower-quality magazine format in the early 1990s. Early Australian IS authors were Iris Vessey and Ron Weber in February 1983 (vol. 26, no. 2) and again in January 1986 (vol. 29, no. 1), Ron Weber in January 1988 (vol. 31, no. 1) and Roger Clarke in May 1988 (vol. 31, no. 5).

The first *ICIS Proceedings* in 1980 included a paper by Ted Stohr (already of NYU); although the 'I' stands for 'international', the first *ICIS* was addressed exclusively by people resident in the United States. The 1981 proceedings included six papers with non-American authors (from the Netherlands, Belgium, Canada and Israel); 1982 included a similar number, with Finland, Sweden, Israel, Canada and Singapore represented; 1983 was similar, but Norway and Italy made their first appearance, and Ted Stohr again contributed.

The first contributions from Australia were in 1985: by Iris Vessey and Ron Weber and by Vessey as sole author (both at that stage were at the University of Queensland); and by Rick Watson, then of the West Australian CAE. Weber reappeared in 1988. In 1989, Australia was represented by Weber, Peter Creasy (also of the University of Queensland) and Peter Weill (at that stage of the University of Melbourne). Rick Watson appeared in 1989, although by then he was at Georgia. In 1990, Weber appeared again, as did Weill and Marianne Broadbent. In 1991, Weber (twice), Weill and Broadbent, and Watson again featured, and Paula and Paul Swatman made their first appearance. The steady increase in competition for space has meant that Australian representation on the *ICIS* program, although consistent, has seldom been as high since then. It did include the Best Paper Award in 1996—awarded to Broadbent and Weill (with two non-Australian co-authors).

The ECIS conference has also had high standards since it began in 1993, and the involvement of Australians has been considerable. Galliers and Whitley note that, in the first 10 years (1993–2002), '[T]he UK [had] by far the largest proportion of papers [398, 24 per cent], the second largest contributors [being] Australia (153, 9 per cent] and the USA [143, 9 per cent, ahead of Germany 134, 8 per cent and the Netherlands 103, 6 per cent].'

In summary, by 1995, it appears that only two resident Australians had published in *MIS Quarterly*, *Management Science* and *Information Systems Research* combined, and only a further three in *Information & Management* and two in *Communications of the ACM*. Moreover, Walstrom and Leonard's (2000) 'Citation classics' article did not appear to include any contributions by Australians (although of course the same can be said for most countries, as the research arena has been dominated so heavily by US academics). On a proportional basis, Australians did not figure strongly in the early years of the discipline, but a small number of individuals forged substantial international reputations.

In more recent years, Australians have been well represented in international conferences, particularly in Europe and to a lesser extent in North America. Their impact in major journals continues to be swamped, however, because of the large and in part very professional population of American, and to a lesser extent Canadian and European, IS researchers. The United Kingdom is probably the next most influential country, after which Australia can probably claim its place—at worst on a per capita par with Hong Kong and Singapore, and with the Netherlands and Germany. Many countries in Europe, Asia and South America are, of course, held back by the very strong English-language bias in the IS discipline.

Acknowledgements

Acknowledgement of bias

The author has been active in the IS discipline since 1970—that is to say, not from the very beginning, but from very shortly afterwards. Because the author was a contemporaneous observer of many of the phases that the chapter deals with—and often a participant and even a protagonist—his perspectives are inevitably embedded in the analysis. In addition, the author is not a trained historian. For these reasons, the chapter is entitled 'a retrospective' rather than 'a history'. It has, however, drawn on a wide variety of sources and will hopefully make a contribution to an emergent 'court history' of the discipline.

An attempt has been made to present information dispassionately; the degree to which that could be achieved is qualified, however, due partly to the author's inherent and unavoidable biases, but partly because of the conflicting aim of achieving at least some degree of readability and stimulation.

Acknowledgements of others

My thanks to Guy Gable and Bob Smyth for providing the stimulus for this chapter, and for the important inputs provided by them and other members of the IS-in-Oz project team.

The chapter has benefited greatly from interviews with the following key players in IS in Australia, listed in alphabetical order: Cyril Brookes, Bill Caelli, Frank Land, Stewart Leech, Gerry Maynard, Graham Pervan and Ron Weber. Many other senior members of the discipline made important contributions, including Dick Mason, Ann Moffatt, Phillip Ein-Dor, Iris Vessey and Bob Galliers. In relation to the PIT scheme, my thanks to Gerry Maynard, John Austin, John Growder, Rob Thomsett, Jonathan Palmer and Kerry Webb.

Responsibility for the errors, the omissions, the unfortunate phrasings and the judgementally impregnated expressions rests with the author. The electronic version of the chapter is intended to be a living document for a while at least, and suggestions for improvement of all kinds should be submitted to the author. It is intended that this chapter and the supporting documents will be mirrored on appropriate web sites. A living version of this document is available at http://www.anu.edu.au/people/Roger.Clarke/SOS/AISHist.html

Vale Cyril Brookes

As this chapter was going to press, word arrived of the death by accident of Cyril Brookes. Among many other things, Brookes was the first Professor of Information Systems in Australia—at UNSW from 1974 to 1994. It would appear that he is the first Australian professor of IS to pass on.

Brookes became the Founding Professor of Information Systems at UNSW in 1974 after a distinguished decade with BHP, culminating in his role there as Manager, Corporate Data Processing. The IT faculty grew to be one of the largest in Australia, with 30 academics and 1000 students during his 20-year tenure. His practical experience and professional determination to reinforce technological alignment with business and government supported the university's drive into cooperative education schemes with industry. He was involved as well in the design of advanced computer-based production systems, the work later leading to his establishing grapeVINE and BI Pathfinder as successful commercial enterprises. Brookes also worked to promote sound governance of ICT in Australia; he was NSW chair of the ACS, an executive committee member for several years and he served on IFIP's IS committee for a decade from 1975. He was made an ACS Fellow in 1972, and was founding director and later chair of the Australian Association of Chief Information Officers. His contribution to IS in Australian universities was massive. His untimely passing is lamented greatly.

3. Characterising academic information systems in Australia: developing and evaluating a theoretical framework

Gail Ridley
IT Control Research Group
School of Accounting and Corporate Governance
University of Tasmania

Abstract

The study reported in this monograph aims to investigate the state of the information systems (IS) academic discipline in Australia from a historical and current perspective, collecting evidence across a range of dimensions. To maximise the strategic potential of the study, the results need to be capable of integration, so that the relationships within and across the dimensions and geographical units are understood. A meaningful theoretical framework will help relate the results of the different dimensions of the study to characterise the discipline in the region, and assist in empowering the Australian IS research community. This chapter reviewed literature on the development of disciplines, before deriving a theoretical framework for the broader study reported in this volume. The framework considered the current and past state of IS in Australian universities from the perspective of the development of a discipline. The components of the framework were derived and validated through a thematic analysis of the IS and non-IS literature. This chapter also presents brief vignettes of the development of two other related disciplines. The framework developed in this chapter, which has been guided partly by Whitley's theory of scientific change, has been used elsewhere to analyse data collated from the Australian states and the Australian Capital Territory. The degree of variation in Australian IS as an indication of its 'professionalisation', the nature of its body of knowledge and its mechanisms of control will be used to frame the analysis. Information systems is acknowledged as a discipline that is subject to frequent change. Pragmatism is used as an example to test the framework's capability of accommodating future changes in IS. Information systems scholars from three other world regions—North America, the United Kingdom and Scandinavia—have commented on the application of the framework to their own region. Research reported in the chapters and the meta-analysis that follow in this monograph have drawn on the theoretical framework presented below.

Introduction

Information systems is a relatively new discipline in the Australian context, as is discussed in Clarke elsewhere in this monograph. Its contribution to Australia has increased with the growing understanding of the importance of computer systems in assisting organisations and individuals to achieve their goals. Given the growing contribution of the IS academic discipline to Australia, the study reported in this publication is timely, as it aims to investigate the state of IS in the universities of the region. The strategic benefits of gathering data in order to access increased power, status and resources for the IS discipline in Australia in the future are obvious. To maximise the future strategic benefits of doing so, however—particularly as this Australian study could act as a pilot for future Association for Information Systems (AIS) studies in other regions—the investigation needs to consider common questions in common ways. This chapter develops a theoretical framework to provide a common way of looking at data collected over a range of dimensions from different geographical areas in Australia. It also considers whether the framework is capable of accommodating future changes to the nature of IS.

It is tempting to view the development of IS in Australian universities as a unique case. There is, however, a body of knowledge that attempts to explain changes in fields of knowledge, including the emergence of new disciplines. An understanding of the past development of IS will help those in the discipline to better position the future of IS in Australia. Much of the literature on the development of disciplines comes from the sociology and philosophy of science and dates from the 1950s to the early 1980s. Since that period the philosophy of technology has emerged as another branch of philosophy, which includes study of the role of technology within the development of society (Gorokhov 1998). Some literature from both sources is relevant to a consideration of IS, as it is possible that many characteristics of its development arose because it was a new discipline, with involvement in technology. Therefore, the features and milestones of the development of IS might be typical of the early development of all or many disciplines and not unique. This reasoning was supported in the IS literature by Farhoomand (1992), who contended that the nature of progress in a discipline needed to be examined within a framework of the philosophy of science. The concept accords with Popper's (1959) argument that discovery needs to be directed by theory, instead of theory being derived from empirical observation. The development of IS as a discipline has been considered in several waves (Fitzgerald 2003) since its first emergence—most recently in 2006. This work has examined the origins and the future of IS. Bauman (1992:76), however, believed that 'only a [flawed] discipline...feels the need to justify its...exist[ence]'. Neither position, however, has been influential in Australia, where there has been little examination of the nature and development of IS.

At least two different views could be taken on the state of academic IS: an external view from outside the academic field, which includes the view of IS practitioners, and an internal one, as seen by IS academics (Hirschheim and Klein 2003). This chapter, like much of the literature, focuses largely on the internal view of IS, leaving the external view to another time, after an initial examination of the IS discipline in Australian universities has been undertaken. When taking an internal perspective, research and teaching perspectives could be considered in a discussion of the state of IS in Australian universities. Most of the literature on the state and development of IS concentrates on research issues, rather than teaching. Consequently, the review of the literature presented below regarding the state and development of IS places emphasis on research issues rather than on teaching issues.

Many people view IS as an applied science, as evidenced by the accreditation of IS programs in US business schools by ABET (formerly referred to as the Accreditation Board for Engineering and Technology) (Challa et al. 2005). Science has been described as a convention, in which the norms, expectations and values of the group while searching for understanding are relevant (Klein et al. 1991). As such, social characteristics are important to the development of science. Bunge (1979) differentiated between culture-free pure science and scientific technology, where the latter was applied in nature and involved ethics, while later writers saw science and technology as being interdependent or hybridised (Pitt 2000; Latour 2003). There has been much debate about how scientific progress comes about (Lee 1989) with many explanations put forward. The methods proposed for scientific progress include, for example, incremental verifications (the logical positivists), the increasing consensus of researchers (Polanyi 1958), the use of falsifications (Popper 1959), revolutions that overturn previous paradigms (Kuhn 1970), progressive or degenerative research programs conducted over extended periods (Lakatos 1970), political practices (Foucault 1977) or research trails versus tinkering (Chubin and Connolly 1982).

An overview of some of the literature related to scientific progress and the development of disciplines is presented in this chapter, particularly where it has been linked in the past to IS. It is believed that the literature provides a theoretical context for a study designed to characterise the state of the IS academic discipline in Australia. After an examination of the literature, a framework will be developed to guide the collection and analysis of data for the study reported elsewhere in this monograph. The framework is then examined to assess whether it is sufficiently dynamic to accommodate a more recent development in IS.

IS as a discipline or field

There are different ways of defining a group of researchers undertaking related research. At least five definitions have been applied to IS. Keen (1991) saw nothing unique in IS research in its topics, theory or methodology, and referred to IS as a 'self-defined community' as researchers 'declare[d] themselves as members'. King (1993) viewed IS as 'not even a field', but as 'an intellectual convocation that arose from the confluence of interests among individuals from many fields'. A 'field' has been defined as

> an area of knowledge and learning which is not yet accepted as a discipline. Fields of study tend to be more recent areas of scholarship with somewhat fuzzy boundaries; significant numbers of concepts within them are open to debate; and researchers and scholars in the area tend to draw heavily on old-established disciplines for their methodologies and conceptualisations. (Tardif 1989)

A discipline has sharper boundaries. Tardif (1989) saw a discipline as

> a body of knowledge, definitions, and concepts built up over a long period and receiving consensus recognition by scholars; theories which interrelate the concepts and provide explanations of observed phenomena and permit predictions from them; and well established research methodologies.

Keen (1991) and King (1993) saw IS as a sub-field; Hirschheim et al. (1996) referred to IS as a field. Even more recently, little consensus has been reached on whether IS is a discipline or some other grouping. In 2002, Paul viewed IS as a 'subject seeking a body of knowledge' (p. 175). The next year, Fitzgerald (2003:225) saw IS as not 'even close to being a discipline', but as a perspective placed between technology and some other subject areas such as management. More recently, Bryant (2006) argued for reorienting the discipline of IS—as informatics.

A review of the literature suggests that researchers are still unsure about how to label IS. Many IS researchers have used the terms 'field' or 'discipline' interchangeably, avoiding the issue. Whether to label IS as a discipline, a field or as something else is likely to become clearer with greater awareness and understanding of its nature and development. Consequently, no attempt will be made in this chapter to label IS in the Australian context as a discipline or otherwise. It is more appropriate to leave this analysis until after review has been undertaken of the study findings.

Approaches to the development of disciplines

A number of different approaches have been taken to account for the nature of different disciplines and their development. A review of the literature identified that three of the approaches were largely considered independently of other approaches; these were theory, social processes and research methods and standards. More holistic approaches have, however, also been used to explain disciplinary nature and progress, by considering two or more of theory, social processes, research methods and standards, topics of knowledge, symbol sets for communication, the impact of local factors and the degree of professionalism. Literature that deals with theory, social processes and research methods and standards to explain the nature and development of disciplines will each be examined in turn below, followed by literature that takes a more combined approach.

Largely independent approaches to explain disciplinary development

Interestingly, some of the approaches to explain disciplinary development have waxed and waned in popularity at particular times in the past 50 years. In 1959, Popper argued that it was only through the generation of theories that scientific progress could occur. The importance of theory to a discipline has been recognised up to the present.

Theory

Kuhn (1970:182) used the word 'paradigm' in different ways, including 'universally recognised scientific achievements that for a time provide model problems and solutions to a community of practitioners'. He argued that scientific progress arose as a result of new observation or experience that necessitated a 'reconstruction of prior theory' and resulted in a paradigm shift. 'Normal science' represented the body of theory, practice and methods of inquiry that were accepted by a group of researchers, typically expounded in textbooks of the discipline. Wernick and Hall (2004) analysed the textbooks of a discipline allied to IS, software engineering, to examine the underlying belief system of authors from that discipline, to find that it was pre-paradigmatic with a common core of knowledge supplemented by competing sets of beliefs. It has been claimed by many researchers that there is limited theory in IS (for example, Grant 1991; Keen 1991; Paul 2002), while few textbooks have been published that provide an overview of the discipline. Hirschheim and Klein (2003), however, saw a 'generalisation deficit' (p. 257) in IS, rather than a lack of 'theoretical knowledge' (p. 268). Kuhn saw the presence of paradigms as a sign of maturity in a discipline, as they gave researchers a basis for choosing problems as well as guiding them in their investigation. Despite frequent discussion of Kuhn's work in articles about its development, IS has also been classified as pre-paradigmatic (Culnan 1987; Seddon 1991). Consequently, from this perspective it appears that IS might not have achieved the state of normal science—at least not by 1991.

Kuhn's (1970) analysis of physical optics before the time of Newton is illuminative. As that discipline had 'no common body of belief...each writer...[built] his field anew from its foundations...[and] there was no standard set of methods or of phenomena'. Kuhn saw early fact gathering that was not guided by some 'theoretical and methodological belief that permits selection, evaluation and criticism' as a 'nearly random activity'. He saw the result of undirected research as a morass of 'mere facts' that was too complex to be integrated with theory. Senior IS researchers have recognised the problem in IS for decades. For example, 'We seem to randomly generate research projects with the outcome that we have a scattering of results which presents a severe problem of pattern recognition' (Dickson et al. 1982). More recently, it has been claimed that IS is characterised by the problems it studies more than by a body of knowledge, or theories (Paul 2002). It could be that some IS research is guided more by the ease with which data can be gathered rather than by other criteria. It appears that, from Kuhn's perspective, IS could be at a very early stage in the development of a discipline.

Elias (1982) referred to the nature of theory in traditional physics as 'law-like theories' rather than 'process theories', which could be more appropriate in other sciences. The ideas regarding theory types might be interesting ones to apply to IS, even though not all researchers in the area—including Fitzgerald (2003)—would refer to the discipline as a science. The development of theory in IS has been acknowledged as difficult (Fitzgerald 1993; King 1994; Paul 2002; Fitzgerald 2003), despite a well-known proponent of the philosophy of technology, Bunge, seeing technology as 'philosophically productive' (Ihde 2004:120), with technological systems putting 'forth...philosophically significant theories' (Bunge 1979:172). Just one part of the difficulty could be that the origin of IS in technology and its past link with computer science has given those within and outside the discipline an expectation that law-like theories are appropriate for it. While the nature of IS stresses organisational issues rather than technical ones (Avison and Fitzgerald 1991; Galliers 1992; Hirschheim 1992; Fitzgerald 2003), the more recent emphasis on 'interpretivism' has not produced more general theory than the positivist approach (Hirschheim and Klein 2003). Another researcher (Zahedi 2004) has proposed a list of theories for IS, but argued for their greater consolidation. Fitzgerald (2003:226), when discussing theory in IS, distinguished between rules (or laws), evidenced guidelines and normative guidelines, where the last is 'an interpreted view of something a practitioner developer might consider doing, under appropriate circumstances, but...[that] would not necessarily lead to success'. Fitzgerald held that only the last kind of theory was possible in IS. Furthermore, the location of management information systems (MIS) in business schools in the United States and, to a degree, in Australia, also suggests that law-like theories and scientific method might not be the only, or even the most appropriate, approach for IS. So a mismatch between expectation and achievement as well as the complexity of process theories could account in part for the limited production of theory in IS.

Regardless of what kind of theory is produced in IS, or what it is called, there is support for its development (Paul 2002; Fitzgerald 2003).

A decade after Popper referred to the role of theory in scientific progress, a very different view of the development of disciplines emerged. At that time, the role of social conditions in the production and assessment of scientific knowledge was recognised (Whitley 1984a).

Social processes

Even though Kuhn's views have been referred to in previous discussion on the contribution of theory to the development of a discipline, he is associated more with a different approach. In 1970, at a time of burgeoning science and higher education sectors in many Western nations, Kuhn published a seminal analysis of the social process of science, which is still referred to in the IS literature and elsewhere decades later (for example, Wernick and Hall 2004). Kuhn's treatise, *The Structure of Scientific Revolutions*, influenced the change in attitude to science and the nature of the development of disciplines. Kuhn emphasised the social mechanisms that created a scientific discipline (Ariav et al. 1987), such as conferences, journals and academic departments, which have also been referred to as 'mechanisms of control'.

Hirschheim and Klein (2003) saw the control of rewards and punishments by academics from other disciplines as driving IS research to become more theoretical and less applied. Although such pressure could increase the acceptance of IS as a discipline, Hirschheim and Klein considered that a less applied orientation reduced the relevance of IS to practitioners, and therefore its viability.

A link between knowledge and power was proposed by Foucault (1977), who also recognised the significance of social issues on the nature and development of a discipline. Foucault would see the status of IS as a political issue, rather than the achievement of ontological or epistemological positions. The supporters of this view see IS as becoming a discipline only once sufficient 'status has been conferred by institutional practices…[including] the ability to form departments, appoint chairs, organise conferences [and] edit journals' (Introna 2003), or the achievement of mechanisms of control. The nature of academic leadership is another way that social issues can impact on the direction of a discipline and its perceived status (F. Land, personal communication, 23 January 2006). It can be seen that one way to evaluate the status of IS as a discipline would be to examine whether it had the mechanisms of control normally associated with a discipline.

Research methods and standards

Other researchers have considered research methods and standards in the development of a discipline. This work has led some researchers to examine the relationship between disciplines, particularly reference disciplines. Elias (1982) argued that 'high-status sciences' retained their position by imposing their methods on other sciences. He considered it inappropriate for scientific method to be imposed on newly emerging sciences, particularly as it was developed for, and by, other disciplines. As the emphasis of one discipline could be on physical objects while in another discipline it could be on organisational issues, the scientific methods of some disciplines could be irrelevant to other disciplines.

Different disciplines rank more highly than others in the public and academic mind. As each has its own ideology and values that colour the knowledge it produces, Elias (1982) saw interdisciplinary collaboration as 'exceedingly difficult and almost impossible in many cases'. He argued that only low-status disciplines would take heed of interdisciplinary criticism. Moreover, Elias contended that modelling a low-status discipline on a high-status discipline or its characteristics, in an attempt to gain kudos for the field or researcher, usually failed. If this last proposition is true it could have ramifications for IS because of its close relationship with its reference disciplines. The use of theory and research approaches from reference disciplines could reduce the viability of IS as a discipline while it attempts to improve the rigour of its research. Furthermore, although it has been lamented that the IS literature is not read by those in its reference disciplines (Keen 1991), this characteristic could be a typical of any discipline.

The concept of 'restricted and unrestricted science' (Rip 1982) is relevant to an analysis of the nature of IS. In restricted sciences there is considerable control of the 'knowledge object', which allows a researcher to tightly restrict the behaviour of the object being studied, whereas in unrestricted science the reverse is true (Rip 1982). Rip argued that the high status of restricted sciences encouraged researchers from unrestricted sciences to become more like a restricted science by importing restrictedness. Signs of a restricted science include use of sophisticated instruments, standardised procedures and empirical generalisations that give increased credibility and allow research assistants or research students to undertake routine work.

There is evidence that points to IS as being unrestricted, despite technical IS research appearing more restricted. Criticism of IS research approaches indicated that many of the instruments that had been used were not sophisticated, research procedures were far from standardised (Straub and Carlson 1989; Boudreau et al. 2001) and a wide range of approaches from reference disciplines were considered appropriate (Ahituv and Neumann 1986; Culnan and Swanson 1986).

Although greater standardisation of some research procedures has been seen more recently—at a time when it has been suggested that IS is now itself a reference discipline (Baskerville and Myers 2002)—other researchers have pointed to the difficulty in reaching consensus on the most appropriate methods for IS (for example, Hirschheim and Klein 2003), and challenges associated with the diversity of methods in use (Frank 2006). Even though the view of the development of IS by practitioners is an external perspective, and this chapter has restricted itself to the internal view from IS academics, there will also be an internal perspective on the relevance and quality of IS teaching to future and current practitioners and other students.

Research education itself could be seen as a standardised procedure where it is specialised to a particular discipline. Relatively recent figures indicated that IS researchers in the United States had gained their highest degree across a broad range of disciplines (Walstrom et al. 1995), revealing that the research training process for IS academics trained before 1995 in that country was far from standardised. It appears that a similar diversity was found in the education of Australian IS researchers until 1996, but that this diversity has narrowed since then. An anonymous reviewer of this chapter contended that the diverse educational backgrounds of the 'fathers of the field' of IS are significant when examining the current nature of IS.

In addition to theory, social issues and research methods and standards, other approaches were identified in a review of the literature as having been proposed as contributing to an understanding of the nature and development of a discipline. These were more joint approaches, which combined two or more other approaches.

Combined approaches to explain disciplinary development

There is majority support for examining the body of knowledge along with the social processes, when considering the development of a discipline (Becher 1994), as 'we cannot...artificially separate the...substantive content from...social behaviour' (de Solla Price 1970). Becher (1987) examined the nature of three different disciplines by examining their tacit knowledge (which derived from the body of knowledge) along with their linguistic behaviour (a social process). Like Tardif (1989), Paul (2002) and Hirschheim and Klein (2003), Fitzgerald (2003) considered that a discipline required a core body of knowledge. Fitzgerald and Paul, however, saw a body of knowledge as being more than an agreed set of topics; it included the set of laws, rules or evidenced guidelines—that is, theory. Fitzgerald (2003:226) postulated that IS had 'the trappings of a discipline...[such as] mechanisms of control [which are social processes], but without the core body of knowledge or agreed theory'. Consequently, Fitzgerald viewed IS as a 'perspective' rather than a discipline.

Hirschheim and Klein (2003) saw the IS body of knowledge as incorporating some social processes and theory, when they proposed that its four components were technical, theoretical, ethical and applicative knowledge. Hirschheim and Klein saw the development of applicative knowledge, which 'required...[the application of] theoretical knowledge to specific circumstances' (p. 266), as being necessary to reach understanding and consensus in IS. They considered that the limited extent of applicative knowledge in IS threatened the viability of the discipline. The discourse needed to develop the body of knowledge for IS, particularly applicative knowledge, would increase communication and the relevance of IS—internally to the academic discipline and externally. In later work, Klein and Hirschheim (2006) saw IS at risk because it was made up internally of several 'communities of practice and knowing' (CoP&K), each with different values and legitimacy criteria, and because there was limited connection from academic IS' internal CoP&K to the outside. Discourse would, however, benefit the development of the discipline by helping to derive a common language across groups impacted on by IS, reducing the state of fragmentation in IS and overcoming its significant communication gaps (Hirschheim and Klein 2003).

Shinn (1982) considered concepts that related social processes, research procedures and theory development when he examined the intellectual and social structure of a range of disciplines, in particular looking at the intellectual division of labour. He found some disciplines to be highly formalised, with a dichotomy between the gathering and collation of findings on the one hand, and experimentation, theory and hypothesis on the other. One would expect that the more restricted a science (Rip 1982), the more formalised were its intellectual and social structures. As expected from its degree of restrictedness, IS is not as formalised in this way as are some other disciplines. Where interpretivist research is undertaken in IS, the data gathering and the theory building could be interleaved. Even in IS positivist investigations it is likely that the chief investigator/s will be involved in all stages of the process. The latter characteristic is dependent partly on the limited success of IS in attracting research funds (Ridley et al. 1998), which relates in turn to the perceived status of the discipline. Consequently, relatively few academic IS researchers have funding to employ assistants to carry out some of the research tasks.

The work of Chubin and Connolly (1982) allows further understanding of the combined pressures that have acted on the IS discipline. The authors argued that 'research trails' became institutionalised by offering potential rewards such as legitimacy and access to resources. On the other hand, 'tinkering' with new ideas or novel developments is normally opposed. Research trails are likely to use the epistemologies, research strategies, theory and perhaps even the topics of existing established research of reference disciplines. In IS, those who follow the existing research trails that were established by the reference disciplines might be more likely to be rewarded with tenure, promotion and access to research grants, as rigour is easier to demonstrate. Efforts to establish appropriate independent research approaches and traditions for IS could be seen as tinkering, as it is more difficult to claim that work is rigorous if it does not follow established traditions. Elias (1982) has, however, argued that greater independence of a discipline leads to its development and, it is assumed, eventual research rewards. It is possible that the path to the development of IS could involve breaking with some traditions established by the reference disciplines.

Whitley's theory of scientific change

Whitley's theory of scientific change (1984b), which viewed disciplinary development as a social process in combination with other approaches, has been applied to many disciplines, including IS (Banville and Landry 1992; Checkland and Holwell 1998). Whitley categorised some sciences as highly professionalised, with high task certainty, routinisation of activities and division of labour—a categorisation that echoed the work of Biglan (1973), Kolb (1981), Rip (1982) and Shinn (1982). Kuhn's (1970) 'normal science' fell into this category; however, other sciences were not highly professionalised, with high task uncertainty, decentralised control of work process and limited routinisation of tasks. Where a discipline was not highly professionalised, local contingencies had a high impact, such as the influence of local political pressure. Ruscio (1987) also found that local factors resulted in substantial variations among universities for the same discipline. Non-professionalised disciplines could account for Ruscio's finding.

In disciplines that are not highly professionalised, researchers investigate disparate problems that are likely to vary in nature and approach to those of concern to practitioners. Researchers work in flat non-hierarchical groups, or independently, rather than in highly structured teams with a clear division of tasks. Information systems appears to fit the mould of a discipline that is not highly professionalised. Furthermore, if local contingencies are likely to have a high impact on IS, it would be expected that considerable variation would exist in the nature of IS research between different universities and regions. There is evidence of considerable variation in the nature of IS research between nations, IS curricula and IS research education.

Whitley (1984b) suggested that three conditions needed to exist for the establishment of distinct scientific fields. These were the need for

1. scientific reputations to become socially prestigious and to 'control critical rewards'
2. the establishment of standards of research competence and skills
3. a unique symbol system to allow exclusion of outsiders and unambiguous communication between initiates within the field.

Whitley's first condition is a social process and relates to mechanisms of control. Scientific reputations are established, and critical rewards are obtained, through publication records and success at attracting research funding (Mingers and Stowell 1997. There were more IS publication outlets available in 1995 than in 1980 (Cule and Senn 1995), and many more in recent years (Hirschheim and Klein 2003). In general, these publication outlets are now administered by fellow

IS researchers. Access to funding, however, remains tenuous while external funding decisions are made by individuals outside the discipline—as has happened with the allocation of Australian Research Council (ARC) grants (Ridley 1997) during much of the development of the IS discipline in Australia.

Whitley's second condition—the establishment of research skills (and standards)—appears to be one component of a core body of knowledge, just as in the preceding discussion it has been seen that theory is also a component of the body of knowledge. Continuing debates regarding the quality of IS research and appropriate epistemologies and methodologies (Benbasat and Weber 1996; Boudreau et al. 2001) are signs that activity is taking place regarding Whitley's second criterion for the establishment of a field, but that it has not been resolved. More recently, however, there have been some signs of increasing consensus.

Whitley's third condition—the existence of a unique symbol set—appears to be another component of a core body of knowledge. Whitley's third criterion for the establishment of a field is hard to meet as long as reference disciplines remain important to IS. Because so many reference disciplines inform IS research (Walstrom et al. 1995; Baskerville and Myers 2002) and the symbolic systems of each vary and compete, a dedicated and accepted IS symbol system has yet to emerge. The *Framework of Information System Concepts* (*FRISCO*) report that was produced in 1996 to clarify important IS definitions (Verrijn-Stuart 2001) is one demonstration of attempts to satisfy the third criterion.

Interestingly, however, two other components that were identified in earlier discussion of the literature as contributing to a discipline's body of knowledge fall outside Whitley's three conditions for the establishment of a distinct scientific field. Theory (or laws, rules and evidenced guidelines) is not included within Whitley's conditions for the development of a distinct field; nor is an agreed set of topics.

In earlier work, Whitley (1984a) conceptualised seven stable categories to classify variations in the degree of mutual dependence between researchers of a field as against variations in the degree of task uncertainty. These seven categories can be used to differentiate the nature of one discipline from another. The categories have been applied to IS by researchers for two decades.

Researcher mutual dependency was defined as 'dependence upon particular groups of colleagues to make competent contributions to collective intellectual goals', while task uncertainty referred to 'the extent to which work techniques are well understood and produce reliable results' (Whitley 1984a:781). Where task uncertainty is low, there is an 'established set of research techniques' that 'can be acquired through formal training programmes' where 'success is easy to determine' (Whitley 1984a:781). Of the seven categories, IS has been classified as a fragmented adhocracy (Culnan and Swanson 1986; Banville and Landry 1992; Culnan et al. 1993; Swanson and Ramiller 1993; Checkland and Holwell

1998; Hirschheim et al. 1996; Hirschheim and Klein 2003; Kanungo 2004). Fragmented adhocracies display high task uncertainty with low researcher mutual dependence, so researchers from these disciplines make diffuse contributions to fluid goals that are contingent on local pressures (Whitley 1984a). Another characteristic of fragmented adhocracies is their openness to the general public (Whitley 1984a), as they tend not to have unique symbol sets that exclude the uninitiated. It is suggested that the characteristics of IS as a fragmented adhocracy work against it becoming a distinct scientific field.

It has been seen in a review of the literature that the establishment of theory, social processes, research methods and standards, a unique symbol set and a set of key topics have been used to explain the nature and development of disciplines in the past. A core body of knowledge appears to subsume theories, research methods and standards, the existence of a unique symbol set and a set of key topics. An examination of the relationship between the impact of local pressures and the degree of professionalism has also been used to help account for the nature of disciplines.

Although little literature was found that related teaching issues to the state of IS in universities, as an internal academic perspective must include teaching issues, any framework developed will need to be capable of encompassing this area. It is argued that for completeness, the relevance and quality of teaching need to be considered. The set of key IS topics must denote then, not only research topics but relevant teaching topics, and will be one means of achieving interaction between the internal and external perspectives of IS. Like research, teaching quality is also concerned with methods and standards.

Motivation to understand the nature and development of a discipline

The author de Solla Price (1961, 1963) believed it was possible to trace the history of a discipline through its artefacts, which included the number of researchers as well as the number of papers, journals and scientific societies it engendered. He referred to the difficulty of a new field in making progress, and the characteristic that large disciplines grew faster than small ones (1963). This could be because large disciplines are more able to control critical rewards and exert political power and so meet the first criterion for Whitley's establishment of scientific fields—controlling critical rewards through a range of mechanisms of control.

Taking a disciplinary perspective results in cross-fertilisation and an increased sense of unity (Becher 1994), which brings other benefits in turn. Disciplinary cultures frequently span institutional and national boundaries (Becher 1994). A social mechanism, the 'invisible college', was described by de Solla Price (1961; 1963). Culnan (1987) defined invisible colleges as the clustering of researchers into informal networks, 'which tend to concentrate on examining common questions in common ways'. De Solla Price (1963) saw membership of an invisible college as conferring power and status on an individual and the network. As these networks of researchers are better placed to lobby for better access to resources and funds (Ridley 1997) than individuals, individuals and researcher networks are likely to be advantaged by an increased awareness and understanding of their discipline.

The following brief examinations of two other disciplines are presented to demonstrate that it is possible to analyse disciplines from the perspective of their development and it is advantageous to do so. The reader is asked to note reference to approaches to clarify the nature and development of disciplines in the following vignettes, as identified from the review of the literature presented earlier.

Vignettes of disciplinary development

An examination of the early development of two other related disciplines could help clarify the development of IS.

Management

Whitley (1984a) tracked the development of management as a discipline. Like IS, management has been categorised as a fragmented adhocracy, but it has had a longer history. Management originated as a distinct discipline about 1960. Until the late 1950s, US business schools taught material from economics, mathematics and psychology. The distinct labour market that emerged after a critical mass of management doctorates graduated allowed the specification of a management doctorate and scholarly repute as criteria for appointment to academic positions and senior posts in management. These developments allowed management researchers to distance themselves from lay criteria and standards and increased their degree of mutual dependence. Consequentially, these changes limited their need to seek approval from non-management audiences for reputations and rewards (Whitley 1984a). It can be seen in this brief vignette that a specific doctoral qualification in management, and the achievement of a critical mass of doctoral graduates, were keys that led to the development of the management discipline.

Many management sub-disciplines experienced a need to debate the most appropriate traditions to direct their research and choice of research methods. This has been true of organisational behaviour, accounting, marketing, strategic management and policy, operations management and operations research (Klein et al. 1991). It is little surprise then that IS has not escaped similar debate.

Computer science

Computer science is another discipline that can be used to demonstrate that the concerns of the IS community for the future of its discipline are not unique. Computer science experienced problems associated with the youth of its academics (Gries and Marsh 1988), the diverse backgrounds of its researchers (Hopcroft 1987) and a need to 'cease its largely inward-looking activities and branch outward' (Gries et al. 1989). Doubts were later expressed about the future of the discipline and fears that computer science could become irrelevant (Freeman 1995). There were calls for computer science to develop its own disciplinary characteristics and to avoid emulating high-status disciplines such as physics (Hartmanis 1995b). Other researchers in the same discipline debated the nature of computer science and tried to determine if it was a subset of engineering, science, mathematics or something more (Denning et al. 1989; Hartmanis 1995a). King (1994a) observed that the majority of computer science departments were found within engineering schools, and that very few were completely independent with the same status as other schools.

An analysis of the literature to develop a framework

After having examined IS and non-IS literature that reviewed approaches to the development of disciplines, and considered two examples from related disciplines, a method was sought to develop a framework that could be used to guide the examination—to be conducted elsewhere—of the nature and development of IS in Australian universities. Not only did the components of the framework need to be identified, along with their relationship, an evaluation was sought of whether a framework of the development of a discipline from the general literature was consistent with that developed from the IS literature. In other words, would IS and non-IS researchers share a common view of the components that contributed to the nature and development of a discipline? It was reasoned that if the perspectives of each group of researchers on the nature and development of a discipline were consistent, this would act to validate the framework derived from the literature.

Methodology

A thematic analysis process for a structured review was followed (Dixon-Woods et al. 2005), in which relevant literature identified previously was classified as having discussed one or more approaches that contributed to an understanding of disciplinary development. A data-driven approach was adopted, in which the themes emerged from the data. The analysis did not reflect the frequency of the themes, but instead accepted themes that offered a 'high level of explanatory value' (Dixon-Woods et al. 2005:47). The relationship between the identified components was also examined. As it was considered necessary to examine the views of researchers from IS and other disciplines, it was acknowledged that any classification of approaches to disciplinary development derived from the literature was unlikely to be complete, due to the quantity of publications available on the topic. It is argued, however, that only sufficient analysis is needed to identify the main issues when reviewing disciplinary development, until theoretical saturation is achieved, as is done when working towards concept development in primary qualitative research (Dixon-Woods et al. 2005). Therefore any omission of literature in the area is unlikely to weaken the analysis and classification process. The purpose of distinguishing the themes identified from the IS literature from those of the wider literature was to allow an evaluation of the degree of consistency between IS researchers and those from other disciplines. If the framework developed matched the components identified from both groups of literature, and the relationship among the components, the robustness of the framework would be strengthened.

As classification is a largely subjective process, two trained IS researchers categorised the literature independently. Discussion took place where the classification differed, until agreement was reached. The major themes derived from the literature, social processes and a core body of knowledge, were used for analysis. As foreshadowed, the latter category was broken down into four subgroups: research and teaching methods and standards (or IS knowledge gain and transfer), a unique symbol set, key research and teaching topics (or IS knowledge domain) and theoretical issues. To acknowledge the importance to IS of providing professional training, any literature that considered teaching methods and quality in the development of the discipline was grouped with the research and teaching methods and standards category, while literature on teaching relevance was grouped with key research and teaching topics. The impact of local influences was also sought.

A record was made for each reference to these themes, by author. The results were delineated further by whether the author came from the IS discipline or elsewhere, as determined by the publication outlet. The relationship between the themes was captured by recording the combination of issues discussed with reference to disciplinary development, for each author.

Results

Table 3.1 sets out the results of the analysis of the literature, where the components explicitly examined in discussion of the nature and development of disciplines were identified and then classified. Themes taken from a review of the IS literature have been distinguished from those that were derived from the more general literature. The order of listing in the table matches that followed in the earlier discussion.

Table 3.1 Identification from the literature of framework components for disciplinary development

Published research	Social processes	Core body of knowledge		Research & teaching key topics	Theoretical issues	Local influences
		Research & teaching methods & standards	Unique symbol set for communication			
Popper (1959)					o	
Klein et al. (1991)	•					
Bunge (1971)	o					
Foucault (1977)	o					
Keen (1991)	•					
Paul (2002)				•	•	
Wernick and Hall (2004)	o			o		
Kuhn (1970)	o	o			o	
Elias (1982)		o		o	o	
Becher (1994)	o			o		
Hirschheim and Klein (2003)	•		•		•	
de Sola Price (1961, 1963, 1970)	o			o		
Tardif (1989)				o		
Fitzgerald (2003)	•			•	•	
Rip (1982)		o		o		
Shinn (1982)	o	o			o	
Ridley et al. (1998)	•	•				
Chubin and Connolly (1982)	o	o		o	o	
Banville and Landry (1992)	•					•
Checkland and Holwell (1998)	•					•
Biglan (1973)				o		
Kolb (1981)		o				
Whitley (1984b)	o	o	o			o
Ruscio (1987)						o
Cule and Senn (1995)	•					
Mingers and Stowell (1997)	•					
Verrijn-Stuart (2001)			•			
Culnan and Swanson (1986)	•					•
Culnan et al. (1993)	•					•
Swanson and Ramiller (1993)	•					•
Kanungo (2004)	•					•
Culnan (1987)	•	•				

• derived from IS literature
o derived from non-IS literature

Discussion and findings

As all the categories were found in the IS and the general literature, this finding was interpreted to mean that both groups shared a common view of the components used for explaining the nature and development of a discipline. Consequently, it was assumed that the components identified were robust and appropriate for inclusion in a framework of the development of a discipline. From the number of studies examined, and the results, it was assumed that saturation of topics had been reached. As many authors identified more than one component, a combination of components was considered most appropriate to account for the nature and development of the IS discipline.

Framework development

A framework to account for the nature and development of a discipline was prepared, using the components and their relationships identified in the review and analysis of the literature. Whitley's theory of scientific change and related concepts influenced the development of the theoretical framework. The framework has been used to consider the historical and present position of IS in Australian universities, in combination with a 'body of knowledge', using Fitzgerald's understanding of the term. The two constructs from Whitley discussed below were utilised in the framework.

The first construct that sets out Whitley's three conditions for the establishment of a distinct scientific field has been used in part for the theoretical framework. As set out earlier, these are: a) scientific reputations to become socially prestigious and to 'control critical rewards'; b) establishing standards of research competence and skills; and c) a unique symbol system to allow exclusion of outsiders and unambiguous communication between initiates within the field.

As outlined earlier, the first condition from Whitley is a collection of mechanisms of control, or social processes, while the second and third conditions relate in part to a core body of knowledge. Whitley's second and third conditions, however, were found insufficient to cover all aspects of a discipline's body of knowledge. For example, the second condition excluded teaching issues, even though IS academic teaching is largely the means by which an understanding of the discipline is imparted to future academics and practitioners. As demonstrated in the analysis of the literature, the 'laws, rules or evidenced guidelines' component of 'body of knowledge' (Fitzgerald 2003; Paul 2002), which has not been incorporated into the first construct above, also needs to be considered when examining progress towards the development of IS in Australia. Furthermore, key topics were also shown by analysis to be an essential component of the body of knowledge, and included relevant research and teaching topics. The second construct concerns the degree of professionalisation of the discipline, which is expected to decrease as the impact of local contingencies increases.

Consequently, a two-part framework was developed as a result of the literature analysis that includes mechanisms of control for the discipline and the core body of knowledge, or knowledge base—both considered against time. The framework has been used to guide some of the regional data collection and analysis for the Australian study. The second condition from Whitley was adapted and incorporated into the core body of knowledge, as research and teaching methods and standards (or knowledge gain plus knowledge transfer), while the third condition was included as the unique symbol set. Two additional components, laws, rules and evidenced guidelines (or knowledge types), and research and teaching key topics (or IS knowledge domain), have also been included in the framework. Figure 3.1 illustrates the first part of the framework used for the study and sets out the components that characterise the nature and development of a discipline. The second part of the framework is set out in Figure 3.2, which shows the inverse relationship between the impact of local contingencies on the IS discipline and the degree of professionalism.

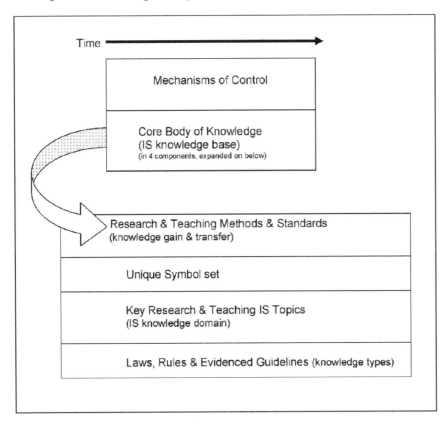

Figure 3.1 Framework for study: components of academic discipline

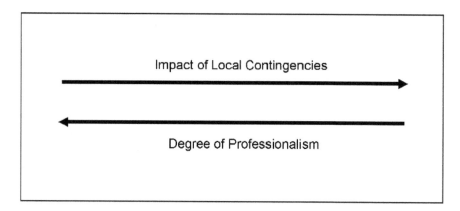

Figure 3.2 Framework for study: inverse relationship between impact of local contingencies on IS discipline and degree of professionalism

Adaptability of framework to future change in IS

Frequent and continuing change in the IS discipline has been well recognised and described frequently. For example, the major role of institutions that teach IS has been described as preparing graduates for an environment that changes continuously (Al-Imamy and Farhat 2005). Moreover, Kanellis and Paul (2005) remind the reader of a number of well-known IS researchers who have stressed that flexibility is a success variable for IS.

It follows then that the theoretical framework proposed to characterise IS in Australia will need to adjust to such change, or be modified on a continuing basis. An example of possible changes associated with each component of the framework is provided in Table 3.2, to illustrate the continuing pressures on the framework.

It is argued that the framework needs to be able to accommodate future developments in IS within one or more of the components listed in Table 3.2 without adaptation, if it is to be of value. A static framework will quickly become superseded, given the rate of change in the discipline. Therefore, a further way of validating the utility of the framework is to test whether it is dynamic enough to accommodate a new development in IS.

A number of topics have become influential in IS research or teaching in recent years, including design science and pragmatism. The design science paradigm places focus on the design, building and application of new artefacts for computing and communication (Hevner et al. 2004; Ramesh and Rao 2005), and has been linked to pragmatism. As an example of a new development in IS, the relatively recent interest in pragmatism in IS is examined below, after a review of the literature on this topic. The framework was then assessed to see whether it was possible to accommodate pragmatism in it without adaptation of the framework. If accommodation is possible, the process undertaken will be regarded as further demonstration of the robustness of the framework. If the framework needs adaptation in order to accommodate the example of change to the nature of IS, this finding will be regarded as a demonstration that the framework needs additional refinement.

Table 3.2 Example of possible change for each component of the framework

Level 1 component	Level 2 component	Example of change
Mechanisms of control		Introduction of new publication outlets for IS; change to the administrative placement of IS schools in Australian universities with changing enrolments
Core body of knowledge		
	Research and teaching methods and standards	Introduction of new methods of IS research or teaching, or standards, such as standardised use of Vista for teaching or the introduction of e-print repositories in universities
	Unique symbol set	Reaching agreement on a unique symbol set for the IS community
	Key research and teaching IS topics	Introduction of new IS topics for research or teaching, such as pragmatism and design science for research, or information technology (IT) control frameworks for teaching
	Laws, rules and evidenced guidelines	Development of new theory and its publication
Impact of local contingencies		Local contingencies impacting on the degree of professionalism, such as recent IS staffing retrenchments in universities reducing the degree of specialisation in collaborative research teams
Degree of professionalism		Linked through an inverse relationship; see above

Review of the recent literature on pragmatism

Classical pragmatism is a philosophy developed and popularised by the American philosophers Peirce, James and Dewey about the beginning of the twentieth century (Sundin and Johannisson 2005). Although the word 'pragmatic' is used by laypeople to indicate a concern with the practical outcomes of actions, the philosophy of pragmatism holds that theory needs to contribute to practice or experience, while utility can be used to test truth. The earlier classical pragmatism is distinguished from the more recent neo-pragmatism because the former places emphasis on the experience, while the latter focuses more on the role of language than the experience (Rorty 1999; Sundin and Johannisson 2005).

The term pragmatism has been used numerous times in the IS and related literature, where it is used most often in the lay sense (as a notable example by three Australian authors; see Darke et al. 1998). Particularly since 2003, however, in this same literature, pragmatism has also been used to mean 'a deep seated chosen philosophical stance rather than an approach to one-off events' (Martin 2004:28). Pragmatism is used often in conjunction with reference to action research and/or critical realism (as an example see Hjorland 2005). Mingers (2002:296) saw pragmatism as a 'view about the purpose of science...[as] it is essentially a practical activity aimed at producing useful knowledge rather than understanding the true nature of the world'. Put another way, in pragmatism, practical and political consequences were sought from research, not a contribution to 'foundational knowledge' (Brannick and Coghlan 2006:15).

That there is a connection between action research, critical realism and pragmatism is obvious, given that all three aim to bring about some change to a situation. Baskerville and Myers (2004) saw a more fundamental link between action research and pragmatism. They suggest that pragmatism is the philosophy that underpins most action research, as the following four pragmatist premises also underlie action research.

1. Establish the purpose of any action.
2. Practical action needs to be taken in response to the problem.
3. Practical action must inform theory.
4. The reasoning and the action need to be situated socially.

As there has been strong interest in action research (Baskerville and Myers 2004) and critical realism (Wikgren 2005) in recent years, it is not surprising that reference to pragmatism as a philosophy relevant to IS and its reference disciplines has also been noted recently. Is it possible, however, to incorporate this latter recent development into the framework for IS without modifying it?

Testing the placement of pragmatism in the framework

From the review above, it can be seen that pragmatism falls within the core body of knowledge component of the framework. Depending on how it is used, pragmatism can be classified within two of the sub-components of this core. Pragmatism can be regarded as a research and teaching method and standard, in a similar way that action research and critical realism are regarded as methods for undertaking research. When viewed as a topic on which research can be undertaken, however, pragmatism can also be considered a key research and teaching IS topic, just as action research is the topic of many research papers, including those invited by Baskerville and Myers (2004).

It can be seen that no changes need to be made to the framework to accommodate the recent interest in pragmatism. Although this finding suggests that the framework is robust, further testing will be needed by examining whether other new IS developments can be placed in the framework without its modification.

Applicability of the framework to IS in other world regions

As the framework components were derived and validated from literature that originated largely outside Australia, it seems reasonable to consider whether the framework can be applied to IS in world regions beyond Australia. It is premature to test the framework using data collected from IS in other world regions until it has been tested with data gathered in Australia, as modifications to the framework might be necessary. Examining the framework using data collected within Australia will be reported on elsewhere in this volume; however, the next section reports on a preliminary examination of the applicability of the framework to IS in world regions outside Australia, using the broad experiences of internationally known IS scholars from those regions.

Expert IS scholars from North America, the United Kingdom and Scandinavia were approached and were asked to comment briefly on the relevance of the framework to IS in their own region. The three international regions were chosen as they were viewed as being distinctive in their contribution, while also having had a major input to the development of IS. The framework chapter was sent to the international researchers, who read it before writing a commentary on the applicability of the framework to IS in their own region. The commentaries were broad ranging, and used the framework components to guide their discussion to a varying degree. Each of the commentaries is presented below, while a later subsection collates the views of the international commentators on the applicability of the framework to the three regions outside Australia. The contributions of professors Bob Zmud (giving a North American perspective), Frank Land and Antony Bryant (giving a perspective from the United Kingdom) and Karlheinz Kautz (giving a Scandinavian perspective) are acknowledged with gratitude.

Applying the framework to IS in North America: a comment from Professor Bob Zmud, from the Price College of Business at the University of Oklahoma, USA

It certainly is a fruitful exercise to apply (and, in doing so, assess) the proposed framework. The disciplinary status of the North American IS discipline has been a topic of great interest, as reflected in my article on the discipline's 'identity crisis' (Benbasat and Zmud 2003) and the ensuing reaction to this article (King and Lyytinen 2006).

It is perhaps most important to begin by recognising the progress that has occurred in developing the North American IS discipline in the past four decades. When I completed my doctoral studies in business administration (combining organisation theory with computer science) at the University of Arizona in 1974, there were few IS faculty members in North America and, at most, two or three freshly started IS doctoral programs. In North America today, IS faculty members are well represented at the majority of comprehensive universities and colleges, in schools of business, information science and technology. As my own experiences have been solely with schools of business, I will limit the ensuing discussion to this context. This is important to note as an essay written from the perspective of schools of information science and technology would be somewhat different, though the overall message would likely be quite similar. This is a nice example of the framework's 'impact of local contingencies' component.

The framework has four level-one components: mechanisms of control; core body of knowledge; impact of local contingencies; and degree of professionalism. This essay will unfold with my perspective of the North American experience with each of these. Concluding comments will then be provided on the usefulness of the framework in carrying out this exercise.

Mechanisms of control

The IS discipline in North America has developed quite well—in fact, surprisingly so given the relatively short time since the discipline's emergence—with regard to mechanisms of control and especially with regard to research. Mechanisms of control reflect the mechanisms put in place to facilitate the development, communication and regulation of research programs and the development, delivery and regulation of education programs and curricula.

The North American IS research community has achieved considerable success. The major conference, the International Conference on Information Systems (ICIS), is very successful and is recognised as a premier research conference. The major journals (*MIS Quarterly* and *Information Systems Research*) have achieved high Social Sciences Citation Index (SSCI) impact ratings, are respected by business school promotion and tenure committees and by institutions (*Business Week*, *Financial Times*) rating MBA programs, and are being cited increasingly by articles published in non-IS scholarly journals. In addition, a number of successful IS scholars are members of non-IS editorial boards.

The North American teaching community has also achieved success, though neither as consistent nor as substantial as observed with research. Information systems undergraduate and graduate degree programs are found in the majority of comprehensive universities and colleges, with a majority of business degree programs maintaining IS core requirements. While enrolments have gone up and down and up again in the past decade, this largely reflects the variability that characterises high-technology markets. Many universities and colleges have institutionalised IS faculties into their departmental structures; however, the control mechanism of accreditation processes has not shown much development. The widely adopted Association to Advance Collegiate Schools of Business (AACSB) accreditation process pays, at best, modest attention to IS.

Core body of knowledge

The IS discipline in North America remains surprisingly underdeveloped regarding its core body of knowledge. Essentially, a discipline's core body of knowledge reflects the consensually agreed-on research topics, research methods and teaching topics that distinguish it from other disciplines. While consensual agreement is likely to exist around a very limited core of topics regarding research and teaching, much debate continues to arise as one pushes beyond this very limited core. The focus of research programs therefore varies widely as does the content of IS courses and IS curricula. Still, three trends can be observed. First, over time, these 'limited cores' have been expanding, though slowly. Second, in terms of teaching, greater consistency does exist at the undergraduate level than at the graduate level. Third, regarding research methods, the North American IS discipline is increasingly receptive to the view that any research method is appropriate given that it fits with the research question(s) asked and is executed and interpreted well.

Local contingencies

Local contingencies are useful in understanding the developmental differences discussed above regarding mechanisms of control and the core body of knowledge. Again, the local context described is that situated within North American schools of business.

During the 1970s and 1980s, IS faculties in North American business schools tended to be associated with one or more of a limited number of scholarly societies: Operations Research Society of America/The Institute of Management Sciences (ORSA/TIMS; now the Institute for Operations Research and Management Sciences, INFORMS), the American Institute for Decision Sciences (AIDS; now the Decision Sciences Institute, DSI) and the Academy of Management. Each of these societies had strong research cultures and scholarly journals reflected the prevailing values and norms of faculty members across business disciplines. These values and norms were thus ingrained within IS faculties and institutionalised in the discipline's conferences, journals and doctoral programs.

No such institutional structures, however, existed regarding teaching IS in schools of business. This lack of institutional structures was exacerbated by the varied training (economics, management science, computer science, organisation theory and so on) of the faculties, the lack of pedagogical role models within local institutions and a strong bias towards research (rather than teaching) within the North American IS discipline's conferences and journals.

Degree of professionalism

Recognising the applied nature of the IS discipline and the need to align itself with prevailing school of business values and norms, the North American IS discipline has strived (with varied success) to balance the objectives of being rigorous—that is, developing and communicating new knowledge within academic communities—and being relevant—that is, developing and communicating knowledge that is actionable immediately by practice communities (Benbasat and Zmud 1999). While local contingencies (for example, local institutional values and norms, association with practice communities) are again key to explaining situational differences, the North American IS discipline has generally exhibited a bias that has and continues to favour rigour ahead of relevance—a bias held, generally, by North American schools of business.

Summary statement

While it is always dangerous to over-generalise, the framework does appear (at least at this very high level of analysis) useful in understanding the evolution and current state of the North American IS discipline.

Applying the framework to IS in the United Kingdom: a comment from Professors Frank Land, from the London School of Economics, and Antony Bryant, from the School of Information Management at Leeds Metropolitan University, UK

Gail Ridley has written a paper offering a framework for 'developing and evaluating the IS discipline in Australia'. This is a laudable undertaking, but it immediately raises the question: 'Why does the IS discipline need to be evaluated and developed?' And what is specific to the Australian context?

At first reading, one of the specific features of the Australian context is that IS appears to be thriving. At least there is no indication of any crisis—unlike the situation in the United States and most of Europe, where there is a steep and continuing decline in student numbers, a continuing threat to IS departments and university posts, and also to funding for teaching and research.[1] We suspect that it is unlikely that Australian IS is bucking the trend, and if the decline has not yet started, it will soon do so. This might appear to undermine the effort of developing a framework, yet we would argue that it might make it even more pertinent and important. First, however, a few provisos are in order with regard to the paper itself.

Much of the first part of the paper is concerned with the extent to which IS can be regarded as a discipline, yet the title and the bulk of the paper beyond the opening section assume that it is. This evades some key issues that have been raised elsewhere (see for instance Bryant 2006) and even some of those addressed in the opening section of the paper; but since the main focus is on the framework this is, perhaps, understandable.

As it is presented, the framework falls between offering a descriptive account of the current situation in Australian IS and a prescriptive one advocating what IS should be or should become. It might then serve as a useful basis for these considerations elsewhere in the world. On the other hand, many of the issues raised are already fairly well known outside Australia.

---

[1] Other chapters in this volume, in particular the state case studies, consider this issue.

Whether or not IS constitutes a discipline, it is evident that its status and role within the twenty-first century university is changing. Rather than seeking to fight some rearguard action to preserve whatever might make up the 'home turf' or territory of IS, it is far more important to raise awareness of the key issues around which IS-type activities—teaching, research and so on—gather. Some indication of these is given in the framework—for example, teaching, methods, theories and links to other disciplines. The next step might then be to offer some indication of the ways in which these foundations might be built on, within a recognised IS discipline and in cases and contexts where IS becomes (re)absorbed into one or other of its reference or kin disciplines—for example, business, management, computing and so on.

The paper in which the framework is presented discusses the issue of pragmatism—correctly distinguishing between the more common meaning of the term, in which something is pragmatic if it is of more-or-less immediate practical use and application, and the term used to evoke the work of American philosophers such as Peirce, Dewey and James, whereby concerns for truth and validity are seen against a background of practice and experience as well as against theories and concepts. Pragmatism is located within the framework in two respects; however, it is perhaps worth considering the framework as a whole from a pragmatic point of view. Does the core of the framework find any validity and authority among IS practitioners? Those involved in academic IS might spend a considerable amount of time agonising about disciplinary status, core concerns, reference disciplines and the like, but these are probably not even of passing interest to those working outside such narrow confines. Recent work in Germany on *Wirtschaftsinformatik* (WI) indicates that a practice-oriented discipline, gaining much of its findings and credibility from the commercial sector, continues to thrive. So a useful test of any framework might be its ability not only to capture this state of affairs, but to indicate how it might be applied elsewhere as well as be used in future developments. Ironically, reports on the current state of WI also suggest that in an effort to gain some international academic credibility WI academics are trying to mimic academic IS using the American-oriented approach, whereas precisely the inverse relationship appears to be the sounder strategy.

We offer the following example as an instance of the context that any framework or similar explanatory and exploratory project must seek to address. If we seek to understand the issues around Customer Relationship Management (CRM), our study will be concerned with the design of such a system, drawing on marketing theory and practice as well as systems theory and perhaps computer science and database theory. These 'outside' theories are not reference theories but part of our apparatus for the study. Moreover, if our study is intended to establish how effective a given CRM system has been, we will have to use different methods of analysis and draw on different theories to help in the explanation. These could include theories relating to the management of change and explanations of resistance to change. Further, they might have to link with theories of ethical behaviour.

There is another issue that arises from a consideration of the framework: the extent to which it focuses attention on the boundary between what is included within IS and what is excluded. In recent years, there have been various attempts to produce statements to this effect, and all have fallen foul of the complex interdisciplinary nature of IS itself. For instance, there would need to be some way in which attention was directed to topics such as computer games, including activities such as online casinos; also the impact of the market for online pornography on the development of information and communications technology (ICT). There is no evading the issue that many of the key technical developments in the 1980s and 1990s were clearly pushed through by the demand for sites with quickly loading graphics and secure online payment facilities—that is, porn sites. Similar advances have been achieved with gaming and gambling in mind. A host of antisocial applications ranging from pornography to spam and viruses to computer crime need to be seen as innovative and hugely successful application areas for IS, as well as features to be researched and overcome.

A framework must therefore include the capability of characterising the wide and complex nature of the phenomena that are being studied. Because the IS domain is undergoing constant change, as the paper notes—for example, the introduction of the phenomenon of mobile computing—what is in the framework under the heading 'nature of the phenomenon' is constantly changing. It could be that in such a friable context attempts to develop a framework are doomed from the start; on the other hand, a case might be made that in such circumstances it is imperative that some form of guidance and prescription is articulated. Perhaps the framework on offer here might serve as a useful starting point in such an endeavour.

Currently in the United Kingdom, IS departments are having to respond to considerable upheaval and change: the higher education sector is undergoing major transformation as a whole, and the number of students seeking IS-type courses, particularly at undergraduate level, is falling. On the other hand, demand for IS skills is likely to increase, but in combination with a range of other skills—technical, social and business oriented. In such an uncertain context, attempts to clarify key IS aims and characteristics are all the more critical.

Applying the framework to IS in Scandinavia: a comment from Professor Karlheinz Kautz, from the Copenhagen Business School, Denmark

Based on an intensive literature study, Ridley (2006) has developed a framework to characterise IS in Australia. Ridley considers whether related research undertaken by a group of researchers can be regarded as a discipline or a field. She has done so to support efforts that aim to determine whether IS is a scientific discipline. Such efforts are of course driven by the perceived need of some IS researchers to legitimise what they are doing, particularly in environments where such researchers are a minority grouping in university departments or schools and are permanently challenged by colleagues from other fields. Ridley's framework consists largely of four components, which she puts forward to characterise Australian IS: mechanisms of control, a core body of knowledge, the impact of local contingencies and the degree of professionalism. The question arises whether the framework can also be used in, and for, other geographical regions.

My comments are provided from a Scandinavian perspective. In Scandinavia, discussion about IS as a discipline has never really been dominant. Instead, there has been discussion about whether there is a unique Scandinavian approach to IS research. Scandinavian researchers settle comfortably with Lee's (2001) assessment that 'research in the information systems field examines more than just the technological system, or just the social system, or even the two side by side; in addition, it investigates the phenomena that emerge when the two interact'.

Ridley sees social processes as operating through conferences, journals and academic departments; these have also been referred to as mechanisms of control. The social process is important for the Scandinavian IS community, where numerous academic institutions have independent IS departments. These are rarely called 'department of information systems'. Although they operate under the name of informatics, information-processing science or information science, the majority of members of such departments feel like IS researchers and the different names might just be a matter of language, as all departments of course have names in the respective language of the country. The sense of community developed since as early as the late 1970s, while in 1978 the Information Systems Research Seminar in Scandinavia (IRIS) was founded. This working conference has been a meeting place for senior and junior researchers for nearly 30 years. The *Scandinavian Journal of Information Systems* (*SJIS*) has operated since 1989 and was started originally to give Scandinavian IS researchers their own voice.

Ridley's second IS component, core body of knowledge, in which she distinguishes between research and teaching methods and standards, a unique symbol set, key research and teaching of IS topics, theory/laws, and rules and evidenced guidelines, can be discussed from a Scandinavian perspective and its strong commitment to the social process.

Historically, IS research in Scandinavia took its starting point in IS development as opposed to computer science and software engineering research. Being embedded in formerly social democratic countries, Scandinavian IS research traditions emphasise engagement with practice. Like the editorial policy of the *SJIS*, however, Scandinavian IS values and welcomes theoretical and methodological pluralism. Although Scandinavian research seems to favour qualitative, interpretive or even action-based research, quantitative research of high quality can also be found. Early on, Bansler (1989) had already identified three Scandinavian IS research schools: a systems theoretical tradition, a socio-technical tradition and a critical tradition. The question arises whether such pluralism should be considered as a coherent whole or as a set of scattered methods and standards (or symbol sets). If the former is the case, IS in Scandinavia might be considered a discipline or research field, while if the latter is the case, it might not. The answers to these questions will help decide whether these elements of Ridley's framework make sense.

The key research topics in Scandinavian IS can also be examined. The *SJIS*—I am again citing its 2007 editorial policy statement—invites contributions on electronic commerce, IT diffusion, mobile and ubiquitous computing, organisational and societal issues, research approaches and methods and systems development methods, but explicitly states that the journal's topics are not restricted to these. Consequently, the journal has published work on other topics as well. Interesting research themes, fads and fashions come and go, but as long as IS development and use (as broad as they are) are accepted as the underlying key topics, Scandinavian IS fulfils this criterion for being a discipline. This is, of course, as long as the criterion itself can be used in such an expansive way.

Research in a discipline should certainly contribute to the body of knowledge about a phenomenon. Theories, laws, rules or evidenced guidelines also clearly contribute to a discipline. In Scandinavia, practical relevance has always had an important role in legitimate research. There is no one such 'theory of IS' or 'theory of IS development' or 'theory of IS use', and it is debatable whether there is a commonly accepted set of laws, rules and guidelines in IS. Information systems research has provided insights, guidelines and rules, often through the use of theories from reference disciplines. Even if these activities do not define theories in their own right, they at least contribute to theory building.

Finally, Ridley proposes that local contingencies and professionalism help characterise the IS discipline in Australia, and even influence each other. It is true that local contingencies and professionalism have an influence on the local manifestation of the IS discipline, but it is debatable whether they can be used to characterise the IS discipline itself. Whether the concept of locality should be considered in an examination of the nature of the IS discipline is questionable. Even if there is 'one' IS discipline in Scandinavia, with local differences from country to country, and even from university to university, this is also the case in other disciplines where there is no debate about their existence.

Overall, IS in Scandinavia—as is explained above—is influenced heavily by its social democratic heritage and its preference for relevance. Both factors have had an influence on the degree of professionalism in Scandinavian IS research, in the sense that the term 'professionalism' is used in the framework. The outcome has been that more qualitative, interpretive and action-oriented approaches have been favoured in Scandinavian IS until recently, with less emphasis on the rigour and generalisability of the results.

Do the differences discussed above regarding IS in Scandinavia mean that IS in that region can be characterised differently to the IS discipline in, for instance, Australia or North America? Although local contingencies might influence local incarnations of a discipline, they do not necessarily challenge the general definition of the IS discipline. Thus, if in general Scandinavian IS is the same as Australian IS, the elements of a framework to characterise the nature of the IS discipline in Australia have to be used with some caution.

Collating international views on the framework

This section reviews the experiences of the four international IS scholars in applying the framework to IS in their own region, drawing on their own expertise. Bob Zmud stepped through the four top-level components of the framework before concluding that, at least at a high level of analysis, it appeared useful 'in understanding the evolution and current state of the North American IS discipline'.

Tony Bryant and Frank Land from the United Kingdom questioned why the endeavour to characterise the IS discipline needed to be done for an Australian context. Consequently, their commentary focused on global issues, pointing to the need for IS to respond to pressures to change. These included the decline in student numbers and its impact on IS teaching and research, the status, role and structural location of IS, the connection with IS practitioners, the need for IS work to integrate with theory and practice from elsewhere and difficulties associated with the increasingly fluid nature of the boundaries of IS. Bryant and Land therefore considered that a framework of the nature of the IS discipline must be capable of 'characterising the wide and complex nature of the phenomena being studied' and, in particular, accommodating change, and they referred to aspects of the framework that noted some of these issues. While supporting the need for a framework to clarify key aims and characteristics for IS, the authors' commentary also laid down some of the challenges of doing so.

Karlheinz Kautz considered how to apply the framework to a Scandinavian perspective, after pointing out that there had been more interest in evaluating whether there was a unique approach to Scandinavian IS research than considering the state of IS as a discipline in that region. Like Zmud, Kautz was able to use the four top-level framework components to review the nature of IS in Scandinavia; however, while being able to identify what appeared to be distinctive characteristics of IS in Scandinavia, Kautz questioned whether it was relevant to consider 'local incarnations' when attempting to characterise the nature of the IS discipline.

It can be seen then that three of the four international scholars query the purpose of characterising the nature of IS in Australia, implying that global influences on the discipline will be more important than regional ones. In two of the international regions, the framework components appeared useful to review the nature of the IS discipline in those areas. These two perspectives suggest that the framework has some value in characterising the IS discipline outside Australia and/or it should be capable of doing so. Neither position is surprising, given the development of the framework from the international literature. After the framework has been tested on a range of case studies set in Australian 'states' and reported on elsewhere in this volume—then modified where necessary—it will be interesting to test the refined framework against international settings, using broader data gathered in those settings. Future iterations of the framework might need to accommodate the requirements suggested by the international scholars who commented above.

Conclusions

A body of literature exists that examines the theory of the development of disciplines. This literature suggests that the development of IS in Australian universities should not be viewed as a unique case, but instead a range of pressures need to be considered, which act on the discipline. A brief overview of the early development of the management and computer science disciplines was presented to illustrate the development of two disciplines related to IS. Although some reference has been made in IS to theory on the nature and development of disciplines, very little use of the material has been made to provide a context within which to view the past and present nature and position of IS in Australian universities.

The project reported on elsewhere in this monograph gathered data across a range of dimensions for universities in each large region in Australia. It has been argued that if such data collection is to be utilised in a strategic way to increase access to resources for the IS discipline, it will be necessary to integrate the data and findings from regions across the dimensions, so that the relationships within, between and among the regions and dimensions can be analysed, and the contributing factors better understood. A theoretical framework to guide data collection and analysis was developed from an analysis of the IS and non-IS literature on the development of disciplines and presented in this chapter. As the framework's components could be derived independently from the IS and non-IS literature, this characteristic strengthened the validity of the framework. The framework will integrate different aspects of the broader study and provide a common way of looking at data collected over a range of dimensions from a range of regions and Australian universities.

Data gathered from universities in the regions around Australia can be used to assess the extent to which mechanisms of control have been established in Australian IS, along with the four components of the body of knowledge (research and teaching methods and standards, the existence of a unique symbol set, key research and teaching topics and laws, rules and evidenced guidelines). In addition, the relationship between the impact of local contingencies and the degree of professionalism can be evaluated through an analysis of the extent of variation in the nature of IS in universities among the states of Australia over time and at present. Together, these two constructs will provide a means of tracking progress in the state and development of the IS discipline in Australian universities in the past and future, and will identify those issues that hinder progress.

The discipline of IS is subject to frequent change, including new research and teaching topics and methods. Pragmatism is one example of a recent development in the IS and related literature. The framework was examined to see whether it was capable of accommodating new developments in IS, such as pragmatism, without modification. As the framework remained robust as a result of this test, the results were interpreted as a further validation of the framework.

Future work will analyse the utility of the framework, based on its effectiveness to characterise the development of IS in Australian universities. This utility needs to consider more broadly whether change to IS can be fitted within the framework. The external view of the development of IS from those who are not IS academics will also need to be evaluated in future. Before applying the framework to examine the development of IS in other regions of the world, it might be necessary for further refinement, based on the outcomes from the framework's application to the Australian study.

Acknowledgements

I would like to thank a range of people for their valuable input on one or more aspects of this discussion and framework, including Rudi Hirschheim, Frank Land, Bob Smyth, Guy Gable, Shirley Gregor, Craig McDonald, Mike Metcalfe, Bob Zmud, Antony Bryant, Karlheinz Kautz and the anonymous reviewers.

Select bibliography

Ahituv, N. and Neumann, S. 1986, *Principles of Information Systems for Management*, 2nd edn, W. C. Brown, Dubuque, USA.

Al-Imamy, S. and Farhat, N. 2005, 'The MIS expectation gap in the UAE: industry expectations versus academic preparation', *Journal of American Academy of Business*, vol. 7, no. 2, pp. 78–85.

Ariav, G., DeSanctis, G. and Moore, J. 1987, 'Competing reference disciplines for MIS research', *Proceedings of the Eighth International Conference on Information Systems*, Pittsburgh, Pennsylvania, pp. 455–8.

Avison, D. and Fitzgerald, G. 1991, 'Editorial', *Journal of Information Systems*, vol. 1, no. 1, pp. 1–3.

Bansler, J. 1989, 'Systems development research in Scandinavia: three theoretical schools', *Scandinavian Journal of Information Systems*, vol. 1, pp. 3–20.

Banville, C. and Landry, M. 1992, 'Can the field of MIS be disciplined?', in R. D. Galliers (ed.), *Information Systems Research: Issues, Methods and Practical Guidelines*, Blackwell Scientific Publications, Oxford, UK.

Baskerville, R. and Myers, M. 2002, 'Information systems as a reference discipline', *MIS Quarterly*, vol. 26, no. 1, pp. 1–14.

Baskerville, R. and Myers, M. 2004, 'Special issue on action research in information systems: making IS research relevant to practice-foreword', *MIS Quarterly*, vol. 28, no. 3, pp. 329–36.

Bauman, Z. 1992, *Intimations of Postmodernity*, Routledge, New York.

Becher, T. 1987, 'Disciplinary discourse', *Studies in Higher Education*, vol. 12, no. 3, pp. 261–74.

Becher, T. 1994, 'The significance of disciplinary differences', *Studies in Higher Education*, vol. 19, no. 2, pp. 151–61.

Benbasat, I. and Weber, R. 1996, 'Research commentary: rethinking "diversity" in information systems research', *Information Systems Research*, vol. 7, no. 4, pp. 389–99.

Benbasat, I. and Zmud, R. W. 1999, 'Empirical research in information systems: the practice of relevance', *MIS Quarterly*, vol. 23, no. 1, pp. 3–16.

Benbasat, I. and Zmud, R. W. 2003, 'The identity crisis within the IS discipline: defining and communicating the discipline's core properties', *MIS Quarterly*, vol. 27, no. 2, pp. 183–94.

Biglan, A. 1973, 'The characteristics of subject matter in different scientific areas', *Journal of Applied Psychology*, vol. 57, no. 3, pp. 195–203.

Brannick, T. and Coghlan, D. 2006, 'To know and do: academic and practitioners' approaches to management research', *Irish Journal of Management*, vol. 26, no. 2, pp. 1–23.

Boudreau, M., Gefen, D. and Straub, D. 2001, 'Validation in information systems research', *MIS Quarterly*, vol. 25, no. 1, pp. 1–16.

Bunge, M. 1979, 'Philosophical inputs and outputs of technology', *The History of Philosophy and Technology*, University of Illinois Press, Urbana.

Bryant, A. 2006, *Thinking Informatically*, Edwin Mellen, Lampeter, UK.

Challa, C., Kasper, G. and Redmont, R. 2005, 'The accreditation process for IS programs in business schools', *Journal of Information Systems Education*, vol. 16, no. 2, pp. 207–16.

Checkland, P. and Holwell, S. 1998, *Information, Systems and Information Systems—Making Sense of the Field*, John Wiley & Sons, Chichester.

Chubin, D. and Connolly, T. 1982, 'Research trails and science policies: local and extra-local negotiation of scientific work', in N. Elias, H. Martins and R. Whitley (eds), *Scientific Establishments and Hierarchies*, D. Reidel Publishing Company, Dordrecht, Holland, pp. 293–312.

Cule, P. E. and Senn, J. A. 1995, 'The evolution from ICIS 1980 to AIS 1995: have the issues been addressed', *Proceedings of the Inaugural Americas Conference on Information Systems*, Pittsburgh, 25–27 August, Session MP-14.

Culnan, M. J. 1987, 'Mapping the intellectual structure of MIS, 1980–1985: a co-citation analysis', *MIS Quarterly*, vol. 11, no. 3, pp. 341–53.

Culnan, M. J. and Swanson, E. B. 1986, 'Research in management information systems, 1980–1984: points of work and reference', *MIS Quarterly*, vol. 10, no 3, pp. 289–301.

Culnan, M. J., Swanson, E. B. and Keller, M. T. 1993, 'MIS research in the 1980s: shifting points of work and reference', *Proceedings of the Twenty-Sixth Hawaii International Conference on Systems Sciences. Volume 3*, IEEE Computer Society Press, Los Alamitos, California, pp. 597–606.

Darke, P., Shanks, G. and Broadbent, M. 1998, 'Successfully completing case study research: combining rigour, relevance and pragmatism', *Information Systems Research*, vol. 8, no. 4, pp. 273–89.

Denning, P., Comer, D., Gries, D., Mulder, M., Tucker, A., Turner, J. and Young, P. 1989, 'Computing as a discipline', *Communications of the ACM*, vol. 32, no. 1, pp. 9–23.

de Solla Price, D. 1961, *Science Since Babylon*, Yale University Press, New Haven.

de Solla Price, D. 1963, *Little Science, Big Science*, Columbia University Press, New York.

de Solla Price, D. 1970, 'Citation measures of hard science, soft science, technology and non-science', in C. Nelson and D. Pollock (eds), *Communication Among Scientists and Engineers*, Health & Co., Lexington, Mass., pp. 3–22.

Dickson, G. W., Benbasat, I. and King, W. R. 1982, 'The MIS area: problems, challenges, and opportunities', *Data Base*, vol. 14, no. 1, pp. 7–12.

Dixon-Woods, M., Agarwal, S., Jones, D., Young, B. and Sutton, A. 2005, 'Synthesising qualitative and quantitative evidence: a review of possible methods', *Journal of Health Services Research & Policy*, vol. 10, no. 1, pp. 45–53.

Elias, N. 1982, 'Scientific establishments', in N. Elias, H. Martins and R. Whitley (eds), *Scientific Establishments and Hierarchies*, D. Reidel Publishing Company, Dordrecht, Holland, pp. 3–70.

Falkenberg, E. D., Hesse, W., Lindgreen, P., Nilsson, B. E., Oei, J. L. H., Rolland, C., Stamper, R. K., Van Assche, F. J., Verrijn-Stuart, A. A. and Voss, K. 1998, 'A framework of information system concepts', *The FRISCO Report* (web edition), viewed 28 October 1998, <ftp://leidenuniv.nl/pub/rul/fri-full.zip>

Farhoomand, A. F. 1992, 'Scientific progress of management information systems', in R. D. Galliers (ed.), *Information Systems Research: Issues, Methods and Practical Guidelines*, Blackwell Scientific Publications, Oxford, UK.

Fitzgerald, E. P. 1993, 'Success measures for information systems strategic planning', *Journal of Strategic Information Systems*, vol. 2, no. 3, pp. 335–50.

Fitzgerald, G. 2003, 'Information systems: a subject with a particular perspective, no more, no less', *European Journal of Information Systems*, vol. 12, no. 3, pp. 225–8.

Foucault, M. 1977, 'Truth and power', in C. Gordon (ed.), *Power/Knowledge: Selected Interviews & Other Writings 1972–1977*, Pantheon Books, pp. 109–33.

Frank, U. 2006, 'Towards a pluralistic conception of research methods in information systems research', *Institut fur Informatik und Wirtschaftsinformatik Research Report No. 7,* December, University of Duisburg-Essen, Germany.

Freeman, P. A. 1995, 'Effective computer science', *ACM Computing Surveys*, vol. 27, no. 1, pp. 27–9.

Galliers, R. D. 1992, 'Choosing information systems research approaches', in R. D. Galliers (ed.), *Information Systems Research: Issues, Methods and Practical Guidelines*, Blackwell Scientific Publications, Oxford, UK.

Gorokhov, V. 1998, 'A new interpretation of technological progress', *Society of Technology and Philosophy*, vol. 4, no. 1.

Grant, R. A. 1991, 'Issues in conducting a field study of computerized work monitoring', *Proceedings of the 1991 ACM SIGCPR Conference*, Athens, Georgia, USA, 8–9 April, pp. 68–79.

Gries, D. and Marsh, D. 1988, 'The 1986–1987 Taulbee Survey', *Communications of the ACM*, vol. 31, no. 8, pp. 984–91.

Gries, D., Walker, T. and Young, P. 1989, 'The 1988 Snowbird Report: a discipline matures', *Communications of the ACM*, vol. 32, no. 3, pp. 294–7.

Hartmanis, J. 1995a, 'The Turing Lecture, Computing Surveys Symposium on Computational Complexity and the Nature of Computer Science', *ACM Computing Surveys*, vol. 27, no. 1, pp. 5–15.

Hartmanis, J. 1995b, 'Response to the essays "On Computational Complexity and the Nature of Computer Science"', *ACM Computing Surveys*, vol. 27, no. 1, pp. 59–61.

Hevner, A., March, S., Park, J. and Ram, S. 2004, 'Design science in information systems research 1', *MIS Quarterly*, vol. 28, no. 1, pp. 75–105.

Hirschheim, R. 1992, 'Information systems epistemology: an historical perspective', in R. D. Galliers (ed.), *Information Systems Research: Issues, Methods and Practical Guidelines*, Blackwell Scientific Publications, Oxford, UK.

Hirschheim, R. and Klein, H. 2003, 'Crisis in the IS field? A critical reflection on the state of the discipline', *Journal of the Association for Information Systems*, vol. 4, no. 5, pp. 237–93.

Hirschheim, R., Klein, H. and Lyytinen, K. 1996, 'Exploring the intellectual structures of information systems development: a social action theoretic analysis', *Accounting, Management and Information Technologies*, vol. 6, no. 1–2, pp. 1–64.

Hjorland, B. 2005, 'Library and information science and the philosophy of science', *Journal of Documentation*, vol. 61, no. 1, pp. 5–11.

Hopcroft, J. E. 1987, 'Computer science: the emergence of a discipline', *Communications of the ACM*, vol. 30, no. 3, pp. 198–202.

Ihde, D. 2004, 'Has the philosophy of technology arrived? A state of-the-art review', *Philosophy of Science*, vol. 71, pp. 117–31.

Introna, L. 2003, 'Disciplining information systems: truth and regimes', *European Journal of Information Systems*, vol. 12, no. 3, pp. 235–40.

Kanellis, P. and Paul, R. J. 2005, 'User behaving badly: phenomena and paradoxes from an investigation into information systems misfit', *Journal of Organizational and End User Computing*, vol. 17, no. 2, pp. 64–92.

Kanungo, S. 1993, 'Information systems: theoretical development and research approaches', *Information Systems*, vol. 18, no. 8, pp. 609–19.

Kanungo, S. 2004, 'On the emancipatory role of rural information systems', *Information & People*, vol. 17, no. 4, pp. 407–22.

Keen, P. G. 1991, 'Relevance and rigor in information systems research: improving quality, confidence cohesion and impact', in H. E. Nissen, H. K. Klein and R. Hirschheim (eds), *Information Systems Research: Contemporary Approaches and Emergent Traditions*, Elsevier Science Publishers BV, North-Holland, Amsterdam, pp. 27–49.

King, J. L. 1993, 'Editorial notes', *Information Systems Research*, vol. 4, no. 4, pp. 291–8.

King, J. L. 1994, 'Rock and roll will never die', *SIGOIS Bulletin*, vol. 15, no. 1, pp. 25–8.

King, J. L. and Lyytinen, K. (eds) 2006, *Information Systems: The State of the Field*, Wiley, Chichester, England.

Klein, H. K. and Hirscheim, R. 2006, 'Further reflections on the IS discipline: climbing the tower of Babel', in J. King and K. Lyytinen (eds), *Information Systems: The State of the Field*, Wiley, Chichester, England.

Klein, H. K., Hirschheim, R. and Nissen, H. 1991, 'A pluralist perspective of the information systems research arena', in H. E. Nissen, H. K. Klein and R. Hirschheim (eds), *Information Systems Research: Contemporary Approaches and Emergent Traditions*, Elsevier Science Publishers, North-Holland, Amsterdam.

Kolb, D. 1981, 'Learning styles and disciplinary differences', in A. Chickering (ed.), *The Modern American College*, Jossey Bass, San Francisco, Calif., pp. 232–55.

Kuhn, T. S. 1970, *The Structure of Scientific Revolutions*, 2nd edn, University of Chicago Press, Chicago.

Lakatos, I. 1970, 'Falsification and the methodology of scientific research programs', in I. Lakatos and A. Musgrove (eds), *Criticism and the Growth of Knowledge*, Cambridge University Press, Cambridge, UK, pp. 91–196.

Latour, B. 2003, 'Do you believe in reality: news from the trenches of the science wars', in R. Scharff and V. Dusek (eds), *Philosophy of Technology: The Technological Condition*, Blackwell Publishing Ltd, pp. 126–37.

Lee, A. S. 1989, 'A scientific methodology for MIS case studies', *MIS Quarterly*, vol. 13, no. 1, pp. 33–50.

Lee, A. S. 2001, 'Editor's comments', *MIS Quarterly*, vol. 25, no. 1, pp. iii–vii.

Martin, A. 2004, 'Addressing the gap between theory and practice: IT project design', *Journal of Information Technology Theory and Application*, vol. 6, no. 2, pp. 23–43.

Mingers, J. 2002, 'Real-izing information systems: critical realism as an underpinning philosophy for information systems', in L. Applegate, R.

Galliers and J. I. DeGross (eds), *Proceedings of the Twenty-Third International Conference on Information Systems*, Barcelona, 15–18 December 2002, pp. 295–303.

Mingers, J. and Stowell, F. (eds) 1997, *Information Systems: An Emerging Discipline?*, McGraw-Hill, Maidenhead, Berkshire, UK.

Paul, R. 2002, 'Is information systems an intellectual subject?', *European Journal of Information Systems*, vol. 11, no. 2, pp. 174–7.

Pitt, J. 2000, *Thinking About Technology: Foundations of the Philosophy of Technology*, Seven Bridges Press, New York.

Polanyi, M. 1958, *Personal Knowledge: Towards a Post-Critical Philosophy*, University of Chicago Press, Chicago.

Popper, K. R. 1959, *The Logic of Scientific Discovery*, Harper Torchbook, London, England.

Ramesh, R. and Rao, H. 2005, 'Foreword design science and information systems', *Information Systems Frontiers*, vol. 7, no. 3, p. 215.

Ridley, G. 1997, 'The role of conferences and refereed journals in Australian information systems research', *Australian Journal of Information Systems*, vol. 5, no. 1, pp. 69–82.

Ridley, G. 2006, 'Characterising information systems in Australia: developing and evaluating a theoretical framework', *Australasian Journal of Information Systems*, vol. 14, no.1, pp. 141–62.

Ridley, G., Goulding, P., Lowry, G. and Pervan, G. 1998, 'The Australian information systems research community: an analysis of mainstream publication outlets', *The Australian Journal of Information Systems*, vol. 5, no. 2, pp. 69–80.

Rip, A. 1982, 'The development of restrictedness in the sciences', in N. Elias, H. Martins and R. Whitley (eds), *Scientific Establishments and Hierarchies*, D. Reidel Publishing Company, Dordrecht, Holland, pp. 219–38.

Rorty, R. 1999, *Philosophy and Social Hope*, Penguin Books, London, UK.

Ruscio, K. 1987, 'Many sectors, many professionals', in B. Clarke (ed.), *The Academic Profession*, University of California Press, Berkeley.

Seddon, P. 1991, 'Information systems: towards a definition for the 1990s', *Proceedings of the Second Annual Conference on Information Systems and Database Special Interest Group*, Sydney, pp. 372–82.

Shinn, T. 1982, 'Scientific disciplines and organizational specificity: the social and cognitive configuration of laboratory activities', in N. Elias, H. Martins and R. Whitley (eds), *Scientific Establishments and Hierarchies*, D. Reidel Publishing Company, Dordrecht, Holland, pp. 239–66.

Straub, D. W. and Carlson, C. L. 1989, 'Validating instruments in MIS research', *MIS Quarterly*, vol. 13, no. 2, pp. 147–64.

Sundin, O. and Johannisson, J. 2005, 'Pragmatism, neo-pragmatism and sociocultural theory: communicative participation as a perspective in LIS', *Journal of Documentation*, vol. 61, no. 1, pp. 23–44.

Swanson, E. B. and Ramiller, N. C. 1993, 'Information systems research thematics: submission to a new journal, 1987–1992', *Information Systems Research*, vol. 4, no. 4, pp. 299–330.

Tardif, R. (ed.) 1989, *The Penguin Macquarie Dictionary of Australian Education*, Penguin, Ringwood, Victoria, Australia.

Verrijn-Stuart, A. (ed.) 2001, *A Framework of Information System Concepts—The Revised FRISCO Report*, web document (draft).

Walstrom, K. A., Hardgrave, B. C. and Wilson, R. L. 1995, 'Forums for management information systems scholars', *Communications of the ACM*, vol. 38, no. 3, pp. 93–107.

Wernick, P. and Hall, T. 2004, 'Can Thomas Kuhn's paradigms help us understand software engineering?', *European Journal of Information Systems*, vol. 13, no. 3, pp. 235–43.

Whitley, R. 1984a, 'The development of management studies as a fragmented adhocracy', *Social Science Information*, vol. 23, no. 4–5, pp. 775–818.

Whitley, R. 1984b, *The Intellectual and Social Organization of the Sciences*, Clarendon Press, Oxford, UK.

Wikgren, M. 2005, 'Critical realism as a philosophy and social theory in information science?', *Journal of Documentation*, vol. 61, no. 1, pp. 11–23.

Zahedi, F. 2004, 'Consolidation and learning in IS: managing the research knowledge base', *Information Resources Management Journal*, vol. 17, no. 2, pp. 1–4.

THE STATE
CASE STUDIES

4. The information systems discipline in Australia's capital

Shirley Gregor
School of Accounting and Business Information Systems
The Australian National University

Edward Lewis
School of Information Technology and Electrical Engineering
University of New South Wales at the Australian Defence Force
Academy

Craig McDonald
School of Information Sciences and Engineering
University of Canberra

Abstract

The Australian Capital Territory (ACT) is the seat of Australia's federal government. The three universities studied—the University of New South Wales at the Australian Defence Force Academy (UNSW@ADFA), The Australian National University (ANU) and the University of Canberra (UC)—are all located in the nation's capital city, Canberra. Each group has a distinctive background that reflects this setting. The UNSW@ADFA is essentially a private university for the Australian Defence Organisation; the ANU was set up to be a national research institution; and the UC group for many years focused on meeting the training needs for computing professionals for the federal government. Despite these distinguishing characteristics, the information systems (IS) groups studied have some commonalities. Pedagogical approaches, epistemological approaches and research topics are all recognisably within the bounds of what is regarded as legitimate for the IS discipline. There is also a degree of commonality in the core knowledge topics offered to students. There are, however, also aspects that detract from the degree to which IS has developed as a discipline. Our field is not regarded as socially prestigious and there are few signs of mechanisms of control. A unique symbol set does not exist to exclude outsiders. The placement of the organisational units within the universities is a result of local contingencies, as is, to some extent, the nature of research undertaken.

Figure 4.1 Location of the Australian Capital Territory within Australia

Introduction

A study of the state of the IS discipline in the Australian Capital Territory could be expected to show some distinctive characteristics, as all universities are relatively small and are situated in Australia's national capital, Canberra, which is the home of the federal government. With this proximity to government and national institutions it would perhaps not be surprising to find the impact of local contingencies stronger than in other states.

In this chapter, we present our analysis of IS in three universities in the Australian Capital Territory, allowing for a comparison with other states in an accompanying chapter in this volume. The aim of the ACT study is to document commonalities and differences across the three universities in terms of teaching and research, to identify significant influences on the discipline and to consider emerging trends. The chapter concludes with an assessment of the degree of professionalism exhibited in the IS discipline across the ACT universities, based on a modified form of Ridley's (2006) framework.

It should be noted that the Australian Capital Territory differs from the Australian states in that it is a 'territory' rather than a state—a distinction shared also by the Northern Territory. The Australian Capital Territory was chosen as the seat of the Australian government and the home for Canberra in 1908. A neutral location for the capital and the new territory was selected between Sydney and Melbourne, because of the rivalries among the states that federated to form the nation of Australia in 1901. The territory covers just 2538 square kilometres and is tiny compared with the large state of New South Wales that surrounds it. The population of the Australian Capital Territory is approximately 300,000 and almost all its inhabitants live in Canberra, which is home to the three university institutions described in this report. The descriptions of the institutions should be read against this common background of being situated in a relatively new, planned, government city with a smaller population than all but one of the capital cities in the other states in Australia.

The three institutions represented are The Australian National University (ANU), the University of Canberra (UC) and the University College of the University of New South Wales (UNSW) at the Australian Defence Force Academy (UNSW@ADFA). The Australian Capital Territory also has campuses of the Australian Catholic University and Charles Sturt University but, as they do not have IS programs, they are not included.

The research method

The ACT study uses the case-study method, following Yin (2003). A detailed case-study protocol was employed, provided by the Queensland team. A research assistant, Ahmed Imran, interviewed each of the authors separately as an initial source of information, with each interview taking approximately one hour. The interview data were supplemented by archival research. The report was then extended and refined by additions from each of the authors and colleagues at the three institutions.

Each of the three authors of the report represented one of the institutions included and we were able to collaborate face to face in preparing the report as we were all located within such a small geographical area. The authors are used to working together and interacting around common interests on other occasions. It is acknowledged that what we have chosen to highlight in the concluding analysis of our case studies reflects our own experiences and personal insights. We have, however, passed draft versions of the chapter to our colleagues in our own departments and asked them to check our interpretation of our situation. This process resulted in some minor amendments.

The theoretical framework guiding the study

In common with the other chapters in this volume, our chapter utilised the framework proposed by Ridley (2006) for assessing the development of a discipline. This framework draws on Whitley's theory of scientific change (1984a, 1984b) and Fitzgerald's views (2003) on the different knowledge types in a discipline. Ridley's framework is relatively new and its use in the series of case studies in this monograph provides a means of assessing its applicability and for suggestions for potential refinement. We discovered in using the framework to analyse our own cases that some minor modification to the framework allowed our data to be better represented and we have used this revised framework.

The original work by Whitley (1984b) saw some sciences as highly professional, with high task certainty, routinisation of activities and division of labour. Where a discipline was not highly professional, local contingencies had more influence—for example, with the impact of local political pressure. Further,

Whitley (1984b) suggested that three conditions underlay the establishment of distinct scientific fields, namely:

1. scientific reputations become socially prestigious and are used to control 'critical rewards'
2. standards of research competence and skills are established
3. a unique symbol system allows exclusion of outsiders and clear communication between initiates within the field.

Further input to the original Ridley framework (2006) came from the work of Fitzgerald (2003), who characterised the 'body of knowledge' in the disciplinary units as being of different knowledge types:

1. rules or laws (as in the natural sciences)
2. evidenced guidelines
3. normative guidelines.

Table 4.1 shows the adapted Ridley framework as we have used it in this study. Note that although this revised framework is presented at the outset of our chapter, it arose during the course of our data analysis, where we adapted the labels and definition for the categories as a result of insights gained in studying our data—a process in keeping with the grounded-theory approach (Glaser and Strauss 1967).

The term 'knowledge base' was used as an overarching term for the category that included a number of elements relating to a knowledge base, including teaching methods. The term 'core body of knowledge' was not felt to be appropriate for the overarching construct as this term was reserved commonly for the core 'topics' or 'domain' of a discipline, as in the 'core body of knowledge' defined by the Australian Computer Society (ACS) (Underwood 1997)—that is, for element (d) within the overarching knowledge base construct (Table 4.1). Within the knowledge base construct, pedagogical approaches were separated from epistemological approaches, as our data analysis indicated that these were distinct sub-categories.

We have used this framework in our analysis, although we do not necessarily endorse the use of the words 'science' or 'scientific' to describe the IS discipline. This is not to say that IS research should not be rigorous, but the word science has many connotations and at least some of the work done in IS does not conform to common understandings of what makes a science, in terms of the natural and behavioural sciences (for example, see Nagel 1979).

Table 4.1 Framework for analysis of the IS discipline in ACT universities

Framework component	Definition
Mechanisms of control	Scientific reputations become socially prestigious and are used to control 'critical rewards' (Whitley 1984b).
Knowledge base	
a) Recognised pedagogical approaches	There is a common understanding of the methods needed to impart knowledge, whether experiential, laboratory, didactic and so on.
b) Recognised epistemological approaches	Established standards for research competence and skills exist (Whitley 1984b). There is some agreement on epistemological questions as they relate to the discipline. How is theory constructed? How can scientific knowledge be acquired? How is theory tested? What research methods can be used? What criteria are applied to judge the soundness and rigour of research methods (Gregor 2006)?
c) Unique symbol set	A unique symbol system allows exclusion of outsiders and clear communication between initiates within the field (Whitley 1984b).
d) Agreement on core knowledge domain topics	There is some agreement on the phenomena of interest in the discipline, the core problems or topics of interest and the boundaries of the discipline. As an example, Benbasat and Zmud (2003) proposed a core set of phenomena to define the IS field. See also Underwood (1997).
e) Range of knowledge types	A range of knowledge types are present: laws, rules and evidenced guidelines (theory) (Fitzgerald 2003).
Impact of local contingencies	The degree to which local conditions in regions, communities or nations influence the manner in which the discipline operates and is understood (Whitley 1984b).
Degree of professionalism	The extent of variation in the nature of IS research. The degree to which there is task certainty, routinisation of activities and division of labour (Whitley 1984b).

The universities in this study

Table 4.2 presents some summary statistics for the universities in this study.

Table 4.2 Demographics for the home universities for the IS groups, as of 2006

University	Number of full-time equivalent students	Approximate number of full-time equivalent staff (academic and general)
UNSW@ADFA	2 109 (988 u/g)[a] in 2006	300
ANU	>13 920 (8731 u/g)	>3 600
UC	6 000 (4 200 u/g)	>1 000

[a] u/g = undergraduate

The academic component of ADFA is the University College of UNSW, which has the status of a faculty. The UNSW has an agreement with the Department of Defence to provide tertiary education to officer cadets and midshipmen of the armed forces of Australia, New Zealand, Singapore and Thailand. In effect, it is a private university for the Australian Defence Organisation; however, it also offers postgraduate education to any qualified applicant, not necessarily with any defence affiliation.

The ANU differs from other contemporary Australian universities in that it was established by an act of federal parliament. On its establishment in 1946, it was given no undergraduate teaching responsibilities. Its mandate was to undertake 'postgraduate research and study both generally and in relation to subjects of national importance' (ANU 2005a, 2005b). Undergraduate teaching was gained only when the ANU joined with the Canberra University College in 1960. The Canberra University College had been in existence for some time as a college of the University of Melbourne. The ANU continues to be one of Australia's most research-intensive universities, with a high ratio of academic staff to students. The ANU was also given an unusual structure, with an Institute of Advanced Studies, which is engaged primarily in research, and 'the faculties', which undertake undergraduate teaching as well as engaging in postgraduate training and research. Information systems is situated in the faculties. The university structure has changed recently, with colleges formed in January 2006 that integrate more closely the component parts of the institute and the faculties.

The UC was formed by an act of the ACT government in 1990 from the Canberra College of Advanced Education (CCAE), which was established in 1969. As a college of advanced education (CAE), its educational programs focused on professional and para-professional disciplines. As a university, it has increased its focus on research.

Overview of the IS presence in the ACT universities

Table 4.3 gives an overview of the IS groups in the three universities.

Table 4.3 Demographics for the IS groups, as of 2006

University	Administrative entity	Home faculty	Number of full-time IS academics	Number of IS students[a]
UNSW@ADFA	IS Group in School of Information Technology and Electrical Engineering	University College	7.5 (2 vacant)	100
ANU	IS Group in School of Accounting and Business Information Systems	Economics and Commerce	6.5	100
UC	IS Group in School of Information Sciences and Engineering	Business, Law and Information Sciences	11	250

[a] Approximate numbers of full-time equivalent students in IS courses, including service courses, not IS programs alone.

ADFA

Computer science was taught at the Royal Military College (RMC) Duntroon for some time. Initially, it was presented by the Department of Mathematics but a separate Department of Computer Science, under Vance Gledhill, was in place in the mid-1980s. While still at RMC, the department introduced a first-year IS subject in 1985. In 1986, ADFA opened and the university moved to it from RMC. The UNSW@ADFA has provided education in IS since its inception in 1986, within the School of Computer Science. For each year since 1986, another year has been added to the IS curriculum, with an Honours year established in 1991. The first postgraduate research student also started in 1991.

In 1990, there were 120 students in IS first year, with 50 in second year. At that time, the defence force was encouraging students to undertake IS or computer science studies to at least second year. This 'encouragement' has dropped off since then and the numbers fell to about 30 in IS first year in 2003. The numbers have since risen in all years, despite the dip in enrolment in other institutions—to about 65 in first year and 30 in second year.

In 2003, the schools at the UNSW@ADFA were amalgamated and IS is now taught within the School of Information Technology and Electrical Engineering. The IS staff members also provide a service course to the second-year students in the School of Business (about 25 students).

Postgraduate enrolments have been the main increase in student numbers. These numbers have been increasing in the past four years. Currently, there are 14 PhD or DIT students and more than 100 course-work Masters students in the Master of Science in Information Technology (IT) or the Master of Management Studies. There are about 20 students undertaking the postgraduate course in the enterprise architecture stream, from certificate to DIT level. These postgraduate courses were the first in Australia. This year, the IS staff members have started to provide vocational education and training (VET) level training in enterprise architecture under contract to the Department of Defence.

Despite being part of the UNSW, the IS group at ADFA has little contact with the School of Information Systems, Technology and Management in the Faculty of Commerce at the main campus in Kensington, New South Wales.

The ANU

At the ANU, IS has been part of the Faculty of Economics and Commerce since courses in IS were first taught. An early influence was Ron Weber, who had an appointment in the then Department of Accounting and Public Finance in 1977–78. Professor Weber had just completed his PhD at the University of Minnesota and was identified as the first Australian to obtain a PhD in IS. He recalls that at that point there were few openings for an IS academic and he had to rely on his background in accounting and auditing to get a job. Information systems appears to have been taught first as a separate unit in 1982–83, by Michael McCrae and Roger Debreceny. In 1984, the faculty made the strategic appointment of a Reader in Information Systems. Roger Clarke led the discipline until 1995. Joan Cooper was also a reader in the department from 1990 until 1992.

The decade 1984–95 was marked by growth. A major was developed jointly with the separate computer science department, and successful joint Bachelor of Information Technology programs were introduced. These programs ranged from highly technical to highly business-oriented programs, and were linked to the Bachelor of Science and Bachelor of Engineering at one end, and the Bachelor of Commerce and Bachelor of Economics at the other. The foundations for a comprehensive postgraduate program were laid, four PhD supervisions were completed and bodies including the Australian Research Council (ARC) awarded external research grants.

From 1995, a number of pressures meant that the discipline contracted. Although the number of IS staff at one point briefly reached five, a number left in the mid-1990s. The faculty made no senior appointment and, for the next five years, the discipline languished. By 2000, the group had shrunk to just two staff. At that time the Dean of the Faculty, Professor Tim Brailsford, showed confidence in the future of IS and electronic commerce and appointed the first professor of IS, with an endowment from the central administration.

The group has now increased so that there are eight staff and a good number of PhD, Masters and Honours students. Research activity has increased considerably, with much output in the past few years. As at other institutions, research is driven by staff interest and grant funding. This has led to significant diversity in research output, with key papers in areas such as the philosophy of technology, technology adoption and use, decision making, business ethics, open-source software and market modelling.

The ANU also has a College of Engineering and Computer Science, which offers programs in IT, computer science and software engineering. The IS group works with the IT staff in offering joint degrees and in program specification and design.

The UC

Information systems is a discipline in the School of Information Sciences and Engineering alongside network engineering, software engineering and mathematics and statistics. The school is in a division with the business and law schools. The UC has two other divisions: Communication and Education and Health, Design and Science.

Computing was a founding discipline at the UC when the institution was created as a CAE in 1971. The major in-house course for IT in the Commonwealth Public Service, the Programmer-in-Training (PIT) program, became the core of the computing degree, initially as part of the School of Administrative Studies. The foundation head was Digby Pridmore and, within three years, computing became a separate school. Information systems has always been organisationally co-located with the technologists, who can reify designs, rather than with the user areas. This has allowed a concrete, effective approach to IS teaching and research rather than IS being an abstract discipline that 'someone else can actually do'. Staff initially did not belong to streams such as software engineering, IS or computer hardware; rather, they taught in one or more of many computing areas.

Separation has never been complete and IS is core to the Bachelor of Software Engineering and BIT as well as its own program, the Bachelor of Business Informatics. Information systems continues to teach a significant major into the business program and the major is available to the rest of the university—attracting, particularly, education students who want to become IT teachers. It also continues to teach its introductory unit into all disciplines. The postgraduate picture is similar, with IS teaching into the MIT as well as establishing the MBI and teaching into the MBA, M. Knowledge Management and so on.

In its 30-year history, IS has remained with its sister IT disciplines through a range of reorganisations. This history has allowed IS at the UC to integrate information, workflow and knowledge management to complement the traditional data management in organisations. There are some areas in the UC that teach IS-like units (the communications school teaches knowledge management and multimedia; the resources school teaches GIS; marketing teaches some Internet; education teaches some e-learning and so on). This teaching is coordinated mostly with the IS program.

Since becoming a university in 1990, the UC has emphasised its research program and has reached supervisory saturation point.

Distinctive features of the IS curriculum

Table 4.4 gives an overview of the programs offered at the three universities.

Table 4.4 Courses from which IS students are drawn, as of 2005

University	Undergraduate courses/programs	Postgraduate courses/programs
UNSW@ADFA	BSc, BA, service to BBus	MSc (IT), including streams in enterprise architecture and governance
ANU	BComm (IS major)	MInfSysSt
	BIT/BComm	MInfSys
UC	BSE, BIT, BBI[a], IS Major, double degrees, eg., B.Comm/BBI; BSE/BBI, BBI/Law	MIT, MBI

[a] BI = business informatics

ADFA

The UNSW@ADFA follows the Association for Computing Machinery (ACM)/Association for Information Systems (AIS) curricula for its undergraduate and postgraduate courses. It reviews its curriculum every three years, with the last review in 2004. As the third year designed by that review has just finished, so another review is just starting.

The IS group within the school uses problem-based learning as much as possible within its undergraduate courses. There is an emphasis on systems thinking, including Alter's 'work systems' concepts (as represented by the third-year subject 'Managing work systems'). The components of IT are not discussed until the 'Operating information systems' in second year. All first-year students are, however, expected to pass the International Computer Driver's Licence made available through the ACS.

There are no electives in the IS minor course and only one elective in the IS major. All students are required to undertake a project in the third year that acts as a capstone for the course. This project requires the students to work on tasks gathered through requests primarily to the Department of Defence. The sponsors of the projects are often senior defence officers.

The postgraduate courses are taught using 'flexible education'—that is, classes are available on campus but most of the students are distance students. WebCT is used at the moment to manage the courses, with student notes delivered as Word documents linked to WebCT or to a student portal or Wiki for some subjects. The college as a whole moved to OLIVE in 2007.

The ANU

The undergraduate IS curriculum is based on the ACS accreditation guidelines. Major curriculum reviews occur approximately every five years, with minor revisions occurring on a yearly basis. Staff levels have historically dictated the number of course offerings available, though recent increases in staff levels have meant more specialised classes can be offered at graduate and undergraduate levels.

Because of the group's proximity to the business disciplines, course delivery is frequently undertaken from a business and commercial perspective. Key undergraduate courses are offered in IS foundations (encompassing knowledge management, decision support systems, design and ethics), electronic business, analysis and design, IS management and project management. Graduate-level courses are offered in IS research issues, e-commerce for managers, strategic IS, communications technologies and issues in organisational IS. Staff members are encouraged to take their own approach to delivering course content, guiding students and providing pastoral care. This approach includes sharing course tutelage between staff members in order to support different perspectives and teaching styles.

The combined four-year BIT/BIS degree program that gives a business-focused IS major as well as the more technical knowledge in the IT major offered by the Department of Computer Science has been very popular with students until recently.

All undergraduate courses maintain at least one course web site. Content portals vary between staff members, classes and year levels. Some courses in the school use WebCT to manage and provide course content, while others maintain their own content web sites under a faculty web server model. Some courses are also using weblogs to furnish class content.

The UC

Information systems at the UC takes the position that there is a core of IS knowledge and that this facilitates responsible and effective technology-based systems creation and adoption by a wide range of professional disciplines. Business is one application area, and the UC runs courses at undergraduate and postgraduate levels in 'business informatics' that combine IS and business. The IS group also teaches into areas including health informatics and educational informatics, but to date with much lower numbers than for business. On the technology side, IS has majors and electives in the Bachelor of Information Technology and Bachelor of Software Engineering and a combined BBI/BIT course.

The IS core comprises typical IS units (IS in organisations, database design, human–computer interaction, systems analysis and modelling, document and workflow management, systems projects and quality management) plus electives (in human–computer interaction, usability evaluation, knowledge management systems, business intelligence systems, database systems, advanced information modelling, general systems theory, IS management, business informatics case studies, information security, information law and IT and business alignment).

The development of students who have an understanding of the interpersonal and group processes required of IS and IT professionals is a feature of IS teaching at the UC. Students engage in group projects, role-playing case studies, online virtual organisations and presentations and they develop visual and written communication skills, critical thinking and teamwork skills.

All units are required to show how they embody: a) current research literature, b) appropriate IT, c) industry participation, and d) pedagogical technique. All units have a web site for teaching material and to facilitate communications. Units are developed by teams and each academic is on several teams in order to keep the unit content coherent. Academics are encouraged to develop new units in the areas of their research.

Industry interaction is important so the UC has tutors and guest lecturers drawn from industry and panels to advise on curriculum content while the IS group teaches into specific industry courses (for example, with the Australian Bureau of Statistics and Kaz Computing). The BIT has an industry project and the Bachelor of Business Informatics has an industry-supported internship that is becoming a significant vehicle for industry interaction.

Distinctive features of IS research

The UNSW@ADFA

The UNSW@ADFA IS group prefers the 'design theory' approach to research, which focuses on knowledge and theory concerning effective methods and structures for the development of IS. All of its members have consultancy and information and communications technology (ICT) industry backgrounds, so they favour the development of tools and techniques that are useful and usable. These group members undertake several consultancies each year, which often act as feedstock for their research papers.

Generally, the IS group members avoid applying for external grants. They prefer to obtain industry funding for their research, usually in the form of consultancy activity, which can form the basis for papers about how the work was undertaken.

The research interests of the members of the IS group include systems planning (business cases, tender evaluation), enterprise architecture, ICT governance (strategic planning, performance measurement), aids to human decision making, social networks, value systems, viable systems theory, household IS and e-government. The members of the group work with other staff of the school in gaming, complex systems and optimisation.

Table 4.5 shows the main areas of research interest in the IS groups in each of the universities.

Table 4.5 IS research in ACT universities

University	Areas of IS research focus	IS research groupings
UNSW@ADFA	Governance, DSS for crisis/anti-terrorist management, risk management, tools for human thinking	Virtual Environment and Simulation Laboratory (part), Decision Support, ICT Governance and Enterprise Architecture group (see ADFA 2005c)
ANU	Strategic use of IT, e-government, technology adoption, intelligent systems/decision support, human–computer interaction, project management, theoretical foundations	National Centre for Information Systems Research
UC	HCI, ethics, ontology and systems modelling, virtual behaviour, informatics (e-research, e-learning, health informatics, e-law, e-government)	Human–Computer Communication Laboratory, Informatics Program (see UC 2005b)

The ANU

The ANU group is very active in research. The primary research concerns currently are the strategic use of IT across industry and government, IT adoption, e-government, intelligent systems and knowledge management, project management and network-centric warfare. The group is interested in the 'philosophy of technology' and argues for recognition of plurality in theory types and research methods in IS (see Gregor 2002, 2006; Gregor and Jones 2007; Fernandez et al. 2006).

Staff members have recently been increasingly successful in obtaining grants, receiving a number of ARC grants and applied research projects with government and industry. As an example, members of the group completed a large applied research project in 2005 commissioned by the Department of Communications, Technology and the Arts (DCITA) concerning the realisation of value from information and communication technologies. The report from this project was launched by the minister then responsible for DCITA, Helen Coonan, in Sydney in April 2005 and copies of the report were distributed nationally in conjunction with the ACS.

The group aims to focus on research issues that are of fundamental importance to the IS discipline and, to this end, hosts a biennial workshop on 'Information Systems Foundations'. The National Centre for Information Systems Research (NCISR), formerly known as the Electronic Commerce Research Group, is a vehicle for collaborative research within the IS group. Members include other faculty staff as well as external researchers and business figures. The centre has a regular seminar program that is designed to be of interest to a wide range of people.

The UC

In the 15 years since the UC became a university, IS research has been largely individual and therefore eclectic. Most of the IS staff come originally from industry, but have been in the education field for some time. Of the 11 staff, five have PhDs and two are enrolled. The group comprises roughly half active researchers, one-quarter occasional researchers and one-quarter who are not active in research.

In ARC terms, the research is not strong, but there is a history of work in human–computer interaction, modelling, ethics, IT education and e-government. Much of the research work is done in collaboration with Commonwealth government agencies and semi-government organisations such as Greening Australia and Kaz Computing.

The informatics theme is an attempt to bring the group's research work into a coherent framework, in particular to research informatics (or e-research—being the application of ICT to the research process and the use of its products), e-learning, e-law and health informatics.

The development of two research course-work units—research proposal and research methodology—and the weekly research seminar series have assisted in giving research students a better grounding and provided a forum for staff and visitor interaction with research students.

Key figures who have influenced IS in ACT universities

It is not possible to include all the people who have contributed to IS within the Australian Capital Territory, so just a few key people are included. The background for each of the three authors is given in accompanying vignettes. Each is currently a leader of IS at one of the three universities and so has some degree of influence on what is happening and what has happened, for varying lengths of time.

Several other names recur when contributions to the IS discipline in the Australian Capital Territory are discussed. Dr Roger Clarke led the establishment of IS at the ANU, where he was a reader in the Department of Commerce from 1984 to 1995. A vignette for Clarke is given separately.

At UC, Dr Igor Hawryszkiewycz was head of IS during the late 1970s and early 1980s and is now a professor at the University of Technology, Sydney, specialising in collaborative technologies. Dr Errol Martin was an associate professor and head of the school in which IS was located in the late 1990s. He maintained strong links with industry and chaired the ACS Information Systems Board for many years.

Penny Collings has been a long-time teacher and researcher at the UC after specialising in computer-supported collaborative learning and behavioural simulations. She became the head of the IS discipline (1992–2001) and was responsible for the development of several industry-based panels that provided input into the course redesigns that occurred every three years.

The status of IS as a distinct discipline in ACT universities

Mechanisms of control

Analysis of the vignettes accompanying this chapter show some signs of individuals in the IS groups studied taking up positions that have some prestige or degree of control. For example, Ed Lewis is currently the chair of the IT-030 Committee for Standards Australia that recently published *AS8015: 2005 Corporate Governance of Information and Communication Technology* and *AS8018: 2004 ICT Service Management* (now *AS/ISO 20000: 2007 Service Management*). McDonald is currently editor of the *Australasian Journal of Information Systems*. Professor Gregor was honoured with an award under the Australian honours system in 2005—possibly the first time that work in an IT field was recognised in this way (Gerry Maynard from Victoria received an honour at the same time).

The consensus of opinion among the authors, however, is that our field is not 'socially prestigious'. All of us have had experience with appointment and promotion committees where it is clear that the nature of work in IS is not well understood or regarded highly. Many of our staff have had experience in industry before joining academia so they have had relatively limited time to establish a scientific reputation in terms understood by committees of social and physical scientists who have worked almost their whole careers in universities.

To summarise, the best we could say about this aspect of our discipline is that it is possibly emerging, but it is 'early days'.

Knowledge base

a) Recognised pedagogical approaches

A wide range of pedagogical approaches is evident in the teaching at the three universities: lectures, seminars, tutorials, group projects, case studies, presentations, use of online learning management systems (WebCT) and laboratory sessions. There are some discernible differences. The UNSW@ADFA has a philosophy of 'problem-based learning', while the UC focuses more explicitly on industry involvement in course development and on team teaching.

b) Recognised epistemological approaches

A wide range of epistemological approaches is evident in the research undertaken, with the groups tolerant of approaches ranging through quantitative survey work, qualitative case studies, the grounded-theory method, design approaches and interpretive work.

c) Unique symbol set

Our view is that we are not accepted as a distinct field in terms of a unique symbol system by outsiders. We do have commonalities in our symbol system with parts of computer science and software engineering, which is understandable, as we are allied fields, with some degree of overlap. We have overlap, however, which is of more concern in that people in application areas, who use IS and IT as tools, also use much of our symbol system. We find it hard to 'exclude these people as outsiders' and many cannot see why they should not teach IS topics within their own areas, as in health informatics. People outside IS, even within universities, have very poor understanding of what the term 'information system' means, either in relation to the artefacts constructed or as the name of the discipline. The continuing debate within IS about how our discipline should be defined only adds to the confusion.

d) Knowledge domain

The domain of knowledge is examined by analysing the commonalities in syllabi across all three institutions. Table 4.6 shows the areas of knowledge that are common across all three of the universities in the core knowledge in their IS majors. Two of the three universities follow ACS guidelines in planning their curriculum but these guidelines, as described in Underwood (1997), leave a great deal of discretion to the institution applying them.

Table 4.6 Knowledge areas common to the core of IS at all three universities

ACS core knowledge area nomenclature[a]	UNSW@ADFA course (IS major in BA, BSc)	ANU course (IS major in BComm)	UC course (IS major)
Introductory unit[b]	Introduction to IS (problem-solving approach)	Foundation of IS and e-commerce	IS in organisations
Program design and implementation (or systems building/software construction)	Exercises in Perl within IS in organisation; web design within design of IS	Introduction to programming	Use of SQL in database design and system building in IT projects; some use of design tools in designing human–computer interaction and systems analysis and modelling
Systems analysis and design	Design of IS	IS analysis	Systems analysis and modelling, advanced information modelling, document and workflow management, knowledge management systems
Database management	IS in organisations; design of IS	Relational databases, database systems	Database design, database systems
Project management and quality assurance	Selection of systems; management of work systems	Project management and IS	Systems project and quality management
Managerial and organisational issues[b]	Management of work systems; selection of systems; project	IS management	IS management; IT business alignment
Specialist areas[b]	Application of IS (elective choice of topics, including e-commerce, data management)	Electronic business; accounting IS; electronic commerce strategic issues; IT in electronic commerce	Document and workflow management; knowledge management systems; business intelligence systems; general systems theory; informatics case studies
Ethics/social implications/professional practice	IS in organisations; management of work systems	In many courses	In many courses, especially IT project
Interpersonal communications	Introduction to IS; management of work systems; IS project—all courses	In many courses	Throughout; specialist unit (professional practice in IT) for international students
Industry project	Third-year team project, 50% load second semester, canvassed from defence	Project management and IS	IT project; business informatics internship

[a] ACS Core Body of Knowledge terminology unless noted
[b] not named as such in the ACS Core Body of Knowledge

It can be seen from Table 4.6 that there is some commonality across the institutions in the core of their courses, which is evidence of common understanding of the domain knowledge that is central to the discipline. The areas in common include systems analysis and design, database design and management, project management, managerial and organisational issues, ethics/social implications/professional practice and interpersonal communications. Each university also provides coverage of specialist knowledge and application areas that reflect the interests and capabilities of staff.

There is variation in the degree to which programming and software construction are required. At the ANU, an introductory programming course is mandatory.

The UNSW@ADFA provides little education in programming in its IS courses, with its computer science programs covering programming in more depth. The main reason for this is that the careers of the undergraduates are prescribed and they involve no programming on the job, rather the supervision of civilian or service trade-trained personnel. The UC requires no mandatory programming study, which, again, is covered in IT programs, but students do receive experience of systems building in their project courses.

e) Range of knowledge types

There is a range in the types of knowledge presented in the courses taught in common. In the terms of Fitzgerald (2003):

1. *Rules or laws (as in the natural sciences)*. Examining the common syllabi shows that there is relatively little core knowledge of the natural-science type—there are few, if any, law-like generalisations; rather the knowledge falls more into the second and third categories in Fitzgerald's taxonomy. The knowledge, however, does rely on underlying theories of the natural-science type for justification and explanation of system-building knowledge. For example, guidelines for the construction of decision-support systems rely on behavioural science knowledge of human decision making.

2. *Evidenced guidelines*. The common syllabi include knowledge that is in the form of guidelines arising from practice. For example, the project management courses include knowledge of project management tools and practices such as software cost estimation that are based on empirical observation.

3. *Normative guidelines*. The courses in the common syllabi include what can be termed normative guidelines or 'design theory' (see Gregor 2002, 2006; Gregor and Jones 2007). For example, Codd's relational database theory is taught in all the database courses across the institutions.

Our conclusion is that we have a recognised common domain that might be expressed in this way: the IS discipline analyses human activity, determines the kinds of data, information and knowledge needed to enable people to act effectively and responsibly, designs technology-based systems to support them and evaluates the impact of those systems. Our knowledge is based on theories of information, human activity and organisations, IS studies analysis techniques and methodologies, human–computer interaction, data and knowledge representation and design, systems construction and validation and the impacts of systems on people, organisations and society. In this unique role, IS bridges the essentially content-free information technologies with the content-rich but often unstructured domain knowledge. To perform this function, IS embraces types of knowledge and epistemologies that differ from those that are traditional in the natural sciences and exhibits a more well-grounded, participative style—congruent with a discipline that is at the intersection of science, technology and human and organisational behaviour.

Impact of local contingencies

Local contingencies have a fair degree of impact on how the discipline operates in the three universities. There are differences among the universities in terms of the faculties in which they are based and this positioning influences the types of subjects taught and the nature and practice of research. For example, the IS group that is in the College of Business and Economics at the ANU has a strong business orientation in its research and teaching. The case studies also show how the nature of ADFA and its role in educating personnel for the defence forces influences the choice of subjects offered to undergraduates.

Degree of professionalisation

Our reflection leads us to conclude that we have a relatively low degree of professionalisation in the discipline, using the criterion of the 'extent of variation in the nature of IS research'.

In terms of the content of our research endeavours, there is not a great deal of variation, as all our researchers focus on areas that are recognisably within the disciplinary bounds, and we have common understanding of one another's interests. A number of the people in our schools (and all the authors) do applied research, in that we build or help people to build artefacts.

In terms of the methods used in our research, however, there is very wide variation and the research methods taught to students do not necessarily suit the particular nature of IS as—at least in part—a discipline concerned with the construction of artefacts (as evidenced in our common syllabi). The IS students at the ANU are taught research methods in the same class as accounting, auditing, management and marketing students and do not currently have any exposure in these courses to 'design theory' (a shortcoming to be addressed in the near future). The situation at ADFA is similar, with only the UC explicitly addressing design-type research. This disjunction between what is taught as core knowledge and what is taught as research methods leads us to conclude that there is a low degree of professionalisation at the undergraduate level.

The UNSW@ADFA does teach research methods and professional practices as discrete units in its postgraduate courses. The emphasis on a professional approach is made evident in the tenor of the Doctorate of IT—an offering that is unique in the Australian Capital Territory.

At least in the UNSW@ADFA undergraduate courses, the focus is on providing 'well-informed users' rather than professional service deliverers. Few of its early graduates will serve as IS specialists while still in the military, except in some logistics or intelligence areas. More will end up as IS professionals after on-the-job training in more senior positions.

Table 4.7 Analysis of ACT cases against an adapted professionalisation framework

Framework component	Assessment
Mechanisms of control	Emerging, but 'early days'.
Knowledge base	
a) Recognised pedagogical approaches	Yes, but a wide range.
b) Recognised epistemological approaches	Yes, many recognised and used.
c) Unique symbol set	No.
d) Agreement on knowledge domain topics	A discernible common core, but also variation across complete range of offerings.
e) Range of knowledge types	Yes, although rules of laws as in the natural sciences are used primarily as support knowledge.
Impact of local contingencies	Yes, placement of groups in faculties within universities and proximity to federal government influences research and teaching.
Degree of professionalism	Low degree. Research methods taught to students do not necessarily suit the particular nature of IS. There is more professional emphasis in the postgraduate courses.

Conclusions

Table 4.7 summarises the analysis of the IS discipline in the three ACT universities against the modified Ridley (2006) framework.

To conclude, each of the universities has a vibrant IS group, which appears happy with the work they do themselves. There are areas of concern, however, reflected in the different organisational placements of each group and the disciplines with which they interact most within their university. It would be hard to argue that the groups have an unambiguous identity visible to those outside the groups.

Select bibliography

Australian Defence Force Academy (ADFA) 2005a, *UNSW@ADFA*, Australian Defence Force Academy, viewed September 2005, <http://www.unsw.adfa.edu.au/>

Australian Defence Force Academy (ADFA) 2005b, *School of Information Technology and Electrical Engineering*, Australian Defence Force Academy, viewed September 2005, <http://www.itee.adfa.edu.au/>

Australian Defence Force Academy (ADFA) 2005c, *ITEE Research*, Australian Defence Force Academy, viewed September 2005, <www.itee.adfa.edu.au/research/>

Australian Defence Force Academy (ADFA) 2005d, *Portal*, Australian Defence Force Academy, viewed September 2005, <www.itee.adfa.edu.au/~ejl/Portal>

Australian National University (ANU) 2005a, *Discover ANU: ANU profile*, The Australian National University, viewed September 2005, <http://info.anu.edu.au/discover_anu/About_ANU/Profile/index.asp>

Australian National University (ANU) 2005b, *Discover ANU: Vice-Chancellor's Welcome*, The Australian National University, viewed September 2005, <http://info.anu.edu.au/Discover_ANU/About_ANU/Vice-chancellor_XXs_Welcome/index.asp>

Benbasat, I. and Zmud, R. W. 2003, 'The identity crisis within the IS discipline: defining and communicating the discipline's core properties', *MIS Quarterly*, vol. 27, no. 2, pp. 183–94.

Fernandez, W., Martin, M., Gregor, S., Stern, S. and Vitale, M. 2006, *A Multi-Paradigm Approach to Grounded Theory*, Paper presented to the third Biennial ANU Workshop on Information Systems Foundations, Canberra, 27–28 September.

Fitzgerald, G. 2003, 'Information systems: a subject with a particular perspective, no more, no less', *European Journal of Information Systems*, vol. 12, no. 3, pp. 225–8.

Glaser, B. and Strauss, A. 1967, *The Discovery of Grounded Theory: Strategies for Qualitative Research*, Aldine Publishing Company, Chicago.

Gregor, S. 2002, 'Design theory in information systems', *Australian Journal of Information Systems*, Special Issue, pp. 14–22.

Gregor, S. 2006, 'The nature of theory in information systems', *MIS Quarterly*, vol. 30, no. 3, pp. 611–42.

Gregor, S. and Jones, D. 2007, 'The anatomy of a design theory', *Journal of the Association of Information Systems*, vol. 8, no. 5, pp. 312–35.

Nagel, E. 1979, *The Structure of Science*, Hackett Publishing Co., Indianapolis, Ind.

Ridley, G. 2006, 'Characterising information systems in Australia: a theoretical framework', *Australasian Journal of Information Systems*, vol. 14, no. 1, pp. 141–62.

Underwood, A. 1997, *The Core Body of Knowledge for Information Technology Professionals*, Australian Computer Society.

University of Canberra (UC) 2005a, *University of Canberra*, viewed September 2005, <http://www.canberra.edu.au/>

University of Canberra (UC) 2005b, *Information Sciences and Engineering: Research*, University of Canberra, viewed September 2005, <http://www.canberra.edu.au/schools/ise/research/programs_and_projects>

Whitley, R. 1984a, 'The development of management studies as a fragmented adhocracy', *Social Science Information*, vol. 23, no. 4–5, pp. 775–818.

Whitley, R. 1984b, *The Intellectual and Social Organization of the Sciences*, Clarendon Press, Oxford, UK.

Yin, R. K. 2003, *Case Study Research: Design and Methods*, 3rd Edn, Sage Publications, Thousand Oaks.

5. The information systems discipline in New South Wales universities

Jim Underwood
Department of Information Systems
University of Technology, Sydney

Ernie Jordan
Graduate School of Management
Macquarie University, Sydney

Abstract

This chapter, examining information systems (IS) in New South Wales (NSW) universities, highlights the significance of New South Wales as the most populous state in Australia. Rather than offering a comprehensive coverage of all IS courses in the state, the chapter gives a broad overview of IS in the state's universities while seeking to highlight the distinctive characteristics of some of the universities deemed to have particular significance in the state. The view portrayed is of an environment threatening the continuing existence of IS in some of the state's universities. Again, the condition of IS research in the state's universities is characterised by diversity and limited collaboration.

Introduction

The information and communications technology (ICT) industry is a significant part of the NSW economy, ranked seventeenth in the world according to a NSW government report (NSW Government 2001). This report also suggests that this significance is reflected in some 70 per cent of the top 250 Australian IT head offices being located in New South Wales. There are long-established university programs that support this economy. As New South Wales is the most populous state, it is natural that there are more universities and more programs to report on than in other states. This report will concentrate on those universities that have been most significant in the development of the IS discipline in New South Wales and give outline information for the others. The basis for this selection will be explained in the next section of the report. The universities that are reported on in detail are the University of New South Wales (UNSW), the

University of Sydney, Wollongong University, the University of Technology, Sydney (UTS), and Charles Sturt University.

Figure 5.1 Location of New South Wales within Australia

Overview of the IS presence in NSW universities

As some universities have more than one administrative entity that is concerned with IS, these are shown separately in Table 5.1.

The UNSW has had a historical place in the development of IS in Australia going back to the leadership of Cyril Brookes. This place has wavered over time but the school remains a significant player in IS research and education. The UTS also has a long history of IS that has complemented and competed with the UNSW. Both of these have organisational units with names including IS and the only other such unit is the formal 'discipline' of IS at Wollongong. This alone merits their in-depth treatment. The only other university that is considered in detail is the University of Sydney—for two reasons: first, the relatively recent establishment of a 'discipline group' of IS in the Faculty of Commerce is seen as a strategic move warranting consideration; and second, because of the significant status and historic role of the Department of Computer Science and its IS members. Charles Sturt University has long had IS-related courses and has been a major provider of distance learning. Here we discuss mainly the Riverina operation, which has been associated closely with library studies.

Dealing with the other units in turn, the University of Western Sydney (UWS) had a long-term role going back to data-processing days, but this has been much reduced today. Macquarie University has several IS degrees, including majors in the Bachelor of Business Administration (BBA), but the few IS faculties remain fragmented. Southern Cross University (SCU) has significant distance education enrolments and is a relatively new entrant in the market-place, with some significant innovation. Its influence on the discipline in New South Wales is as yet not large, but the research activity at SCU in particular could establish a future place for it. The University of New England (UNE) and Newcastle University are underdeveloped in terms of IS. We now present an outline of the five identified universities.

Table 5.1 IS presence in NSW universities

University	Administrative entity	Home faculty	No. of IS academics
UNSW	School of Information Systems, Technology and Management	Commerce and Economics	20
UNSW	Group	Australian Graduate School of Management (AGSM)	1
University of Sydney	Group in School of Information Technology (IT)	Science	ca. 5
University of Sydney	Business IS 'Discipline' in School of Business	Faculty of Business and Economics	12
UTS	Department of IS	Information Technology	20
University of Wollongong	'Discipline' of IS in School of Economics and Information Systems	Commerce	15
UWS	Group in School of Computing and Mathematics	Health and Science	ca. 10
Macquarie University	Group in Department of Computing	Information and Communication Sciences	ca. 5
Macquarie University	Group in Department of Accounting and Finance	Economic and Financial Studies	ca. 3
Macquarie University	Group	MGSM	1
Charles Sturt University	Group in School of Information Studies	Science and Agriculture	10 +
SCU	Group in School of Multimedia and IT	Commerce and Management	12
UNE	Nil [?]		
University of Newcastle	Group in School of Design, Communication and IT	Science and IT	ca. 3

The UNSW

The School of Information Systems, Technology and Management (SISTM) has a long and varied history (there was a Department of Information Systems in the early 1980s). Today, it is placed within the Commerce Faculty but does not have a core unit in that faculty's flagship BComm program. It has its own BSc in IS as well as a major in IS available in many degrees. High entrance scores are required in all programs. The distinctive BIT degree has industry training (which entails students spending time working in industry during the degree studies), industry-funded student scholarships and includes an Honours year. A Master's degree in IS is being established but there is support teaching for other Masters degrees.

The school has long been active in research, with strong performances in quantitative aspects of IS, especially in the 1980s and early 1990s. There have also been strong performances in major research grants and doctoral student completions. With the appointment of a new head of school (Dubravka Cecez-Kecmanovic), qualitative research methods in IS are likely to become more prominent. Highly rated IS research in management areas is conducted at the

Australian Graduate School of Management (AGSM), but there is no collaboration with SISTM. SISTM is seen to be distinct from computer science within the UNSW.

The University of Sydney

As a traditional university, the University of Sydney has until recently located IS primarily in computer science, with a Sybase Chair in Information Systems appointed there in 1998—although the position is now called 'language technology', reflecting the interests of the incumbent. Other areas, such as librarianship and informatics (in the Faculty of Arts), have developed independently. The major in IS offers the same units to various degrees. There are now some 30 students (out of 100) doing an IS project in their BSc Honours degree—the largest honours group in New South Wales. The computer science department is developing a masters in IT that will have an IS major.

In contrast, the newly established business IS 'discipline' (one of 10) in the Faculty of Commerce teaches the IS core to some 1000 students in the BComm program, aiming to recruit them to the IS major. Students in the accounting stream take additional IS units, also in MBus and MComm. A new MBusIS degree started in 2006. The establishment of this discipline was seen as a strategic move by the dean, to provide visibility and to promote interdisciplinary research. Five research areas have been selected to build strength in the group.

There is not much visibility of IS (in either incarnation) in the wider university community.

The UTS

From the days of the NSW Institute of Technology—the UTS predecessor institution—vocationally oriented programs have been developed. At the undergraduate level, all courses were in either part-time or 'sandwich' mode, requiring students to spend usually one year in suitable paid employment before graduation. In response to an increasing number of international students and the decline of employment opportunities, industrial experience became optional in 2002, and the number of students graduating with work experience has gradually decreased. To some extent this experience is now 'simulated' in a large group-systems development project.

Since 1968, computing has been taught in a variety of science-oriented faculties; a second Business Information Systems group developed within the Faculty of Business. These two groups were brought together in about 1980 in a Faculty of Mathematical and Computer Sciences; this faculty became the Faculty of Information Technology in 2000. A number of conflicts between the 'science' and 'business' groups in the 1980s are still having an impact on the faculty. In the Faculty of Information Technology, IS was established as one of three departments but with limited autonomy. As a matter of policy, all faculty courses are interdepartmental, as the 'integration' of computer science and IS is seen as a key strength of the UTS. In the late 1990s, the faculty grew rapidly and was a strong contributor to UTS income, but the faculty is now suffering from the reduced enrolments in IT common across the sector. This has impacted particularly on the IS department as it had a large number of students from the Faculty of Business enrolled in IS majors. In terms of research profile and general visibility within the university, the IS department remains relatively weak alongside the other departments. Research in the IS department has taken a lower profile historically and, even today, the proportion of staff without doctorates is comparatively high.

The University of Wollongong

The IS discipline has some 400 equivalent full-time students units (EFTSU) at the moment, making it probably the largest outside Sydney; there are undergraduate and graduate programs. Its history goes back to 1984 when an IS group from the then Wollongong Institute joined the commerce faculty. In 1991, a Faculty of Informatics was created but IS stayed with commerce. Programs were supported by the local presence of BHP, one of Australia's largest companies, and some research success was achieved in the 1990s. Currently, the discipline is perceived as suffering somewhat from the increasing proportion of overseas students, difficulties in attracting research students and lack of distinctive recognition within the university.

Charles Sturt University, Riverina

Charles Sturt is a multi-campus regional university, so the administrative position and visibility of IS depends to a large extent on cross-campus structure and politics. At present, IS lies within the Faculty of Science and Agriculture, which controls staffing, major funding and course and subject design. At Wagga Wagga, on the other hand, arrangements have remained fairly stable, with IS as a 'discipline area' in the School of Information Studies. In the past, this placement has encouraged an emphasis on the 'information science' aspects of IS (an aspect largely ignored elsewhere) but this specialisation is diminishing.

As a regional university, Charles Sturt has a majority of students studying in distance mode, and has good relationships with the community, TAFE and local business (which is not strong). Research projects are mainly individual, and a number of full-time academics are currently enrolled in PhDs. Collaboration tends to be with universities in the nearby Australian Capital Territory rather than with the rest of New South Wales. Researchers do not identify (or feel the need to identify) particularly with IS as such. There is a feeling that regional universities are (for political reasons) less threatened than others by fluctuations in student demand and research fashion.

Results

The next sections summarise and discuss the responses under the headings adopted by the survey instrument that is presented in Ridley (2006).

Relative size of IS presence

Students undertaking strongly identified IS undergraduate degrees can be found only at the UNSW. The UTS has an IT degree with IS as an 'equal' component, and a cross-faculty business/computing degree. These universities also offer a variety of majors in non-IS programs. This format—majors in other programs—is the bread and butter of IS in all the other universities. The size of the IS presence therefore depends on the university's enrolment in the core programs that offer the majors and the extent of compulsory subjects in those programs. Large accounting programs mean that many students will need to do IS and larger staff numbers are entailed. With more than 1000 students in commerce at the University of Sydney, a larger IS unit is created.

Another characteristic is the fragmentation of IS academics across departments or faculties.

Administrative placement of IS

With the growth of enrolments in commerce in the past 20 years, there has been some advantage to those IS units that are placed in that faculty; however, a variety of locations, especially science and computer science, persist. Most IS groups remain as *ad hoc* or informal groups within larger departments.

Local contingencies

It is noteworthy that when asking participants about 'local contingencies', responses reflect 'very local' issues, such as organisational politics, nearby employers and competitors. There were no 'NSW' issues that came up—for example, Wollongong's support from BHP, alternative perspectives at the UTS and the UNSW, or faculty rules at Sydney.

IS as a separate field

While the four universities highlighted had some structural recognition of IS as a separate field, it was held widely that this did not extend to the wider university communities. Indeed, the interviewees would be challenged to agree on a definition of IS that was mutually satisfactory. For example, the International Conference on Information Systems (ICIS) and the Australasian Conference on Information Systems (ACIS) were not universally agreed on as central conferences. The fragmented state of IS at Macquarie University (an *ad hoc* IS group in computing, an accounting IS group in accounting, information management taught in statistics and IS management in the management school) is symptomatic.

Distinctive IS curricula

The language technology emphasis in one group at the University of Sydney is the most distinctive. Support classes within commerce programs are possibly the least distinctive across universities. The UTS has systematically innovated with specialist programs over the years, especially at the Masters level. 'Cooperative' programs—that is, with an industrial training component—are offered only at the UTS and the UNSW.

Distinctive features of IS research

The IS group at the UNSW has been productive for a long period, particularly in quantitative aspects (some would describe this as software engineering). This emphasis has declined and qualitative research is growing there. Each group at the University of Sydney is pursuing independent research strategies, with the scam-detection project of Jon Patrick very large, although not labelled as IS. At the UTS, Igor Hawryszkiewycz leads a large continuing project on collaborative systems software, but few full-time IS staff are involved in this project. Ernest Edmonds' new 'creativity and cognition' studio is under the IS umbrella, but works with computer scientists as much as with other IS academics. Large research projects in IS are otherwise few in number. Research activity tends to be fragmented and diverse.

Small research groups, especially of doctoral students, at the AGSM and Macquarie Graduate School of Management (MGSM) have existed without undergraduate programs to build the staff numbers to critical mass.

Perceptions of other universities

The founding roles of the UNSW, UTS and Sydney were recognised widely although there was also some recognition of interstate universities and researchers.

Key people in the region

In the 'round up of the usual suspects', members of the Australian Council of Professors and Heads of Information Systems (ACPHIS) and ACIS regulars were the most widely cited. Ron Weber has been influential outside Australia—perhaps more than inside. Dubravka Cecez-Kecmanovic and Steve Elliott are in significant strategic positions in New South Wales at the moment.

Vignette—Igor Hawryszkiewycz

Professor Igor Hawryszkiewycz is head of the Department of Information Systems at the UTS, where he is responsible for teaching and research in the department. He completed a BE and ME degrees in electrical engineering at the University of Adelaide, and a PhD at the Massachusetts Institute of Technology. His expertise is in the area of design of information systems. He has developed methods for the design of systems that have been reported in more than 150 publications.

His widely adopted text in the mid-1980s on database analysis and design represents a significant early contribution to IS in Australian universities, as does his text on systems analysis and design, first published in 1987. This latter book was well accepted internationally, and was translated into several languages and offered in five editions. Later books, on relational database design (1990) and the design of networked enterprises (1997), have added to Hawryszkiewycz's standing as an IS researcher and educator.

Hawryszkiewycz was an important figure in the establishment, in 1989, of a national conference in IS. Through the early years of the ACIS he was a member of the conference standing committee.

Before joining the UTS, Hawryszkiewycz was a principal lecturer in IS at the University of Canberra and, before that, a research engineer at Telecom Australia and a senior systems officer at the Telecom Information Systems Branch.

He has also been:

- a visiting professor at the University of Sydney
- a visiting professor at the UNSW
- a visiting professor at the University of Maryland, College Park
- a visiting professor at the University of Vienna
- a visiting scientist at the FAW in the University of Ulm, Germany
- a visiting scientist at GMD, Bonn, Germany
- a visiting scholar at Tilburg University in the Netherlands
- a research fellow at the British Telecom Laboratories in Martlesham, UK.

His current emphasis is on the design of knowledge-based collaborative systems that are required to support process agility in the increasingly competitive environment. This focuses on developing requirements for collaborative systems and supporting them with technology that integrates collaboration into the business process. His work on collaboration has included research as well as industrial applications as, for example, setting up business networks or health research planning, as well as developing a workspace system.

Hawryszkiewycz is a member of the Australian Research Council (ARC) Research Network in Enterprise Information Infrastructure. Within this network, he is participating in a program on technology adoption and impact and is a senior member of a task force investigating major issues related to service computing and business process management.

Vignette—Dubravka Cecez-Kecmanovic

Dubravka Cecez-Kecmanovic is Professor of Information Systems and Head of Information Systems, Technology and Management in the Australian School of Business at the UNSW.

Cecez-Kecmanovic Dubravka earned her BSc in electrical engineering at the University of Sarajevo (1970), MSc in system sciences and IS at the University of Belgrade (1974) and a PhD in IS at the University of Ljubljana (1979). Until 1992, she was with the Informatics Department, Faculty of Electrical Engineering, University of Sarajevo, where she held positions as the head of the IS department, associate dean and dean of the faculty, among others. Since arriving in Australia in 1993, she has held the positions of Professor and Head of School of Information Systems and Management Science, and Deputy Dean of the Faculty of Commerce and Administration, Griffith University, Brisbane; Pro-Vice-Chancellor, Research and Consultancy, and Professor and Founding Chair in Information Systems at the UWS, Hawkesbury. She has been with the UNSW since January 2002.

Cecez-Kecmanovic has published in the field of social systems of information and government IS, decision support systems, web-enhanced cooperative learning and teaching and electronically mediated work and communication. Her recent research interests include the sense-making theory of knowledge as a foundation to study information and knowledge systems in organisations; evolutionary approaches to organisations and IS; autopoietic views of IS organisation relationships; IS and organisational learning; electronic democracy and the social aspects of electronic commerce. Cecez-Kecmanovic's major contribution has been to critical theory-informed IS research, including theoretical, methodological and empirical studies, for which she has been recognised internationally. Due largely to her contribution to the development and promotion of the critical approach to IS research, Australian and British researchers have together been leading the critical research project in the IS discipline.

Her major awards include Excellence in Research and Development from the University of Sarajevo (1988), Woman (Academic) of the Year 1989 (in the former Yugoslavia) and Research Excellence Award from the UWS (2000). In 2006, Cecez-Kecmanovic and her co-author, Marius Janson from the University of Missouri, St Louis, were awarded the Emerald Literati Network 2006 Award for Excellence for their paper 'Making sense of e-commerce as a social action' as the best paper published in the *Information Technology & People* journal.

Conclusion

The already fragmented condition of IS in most universities means that with further reductions in undergraduate recruitment their positions will not improve and could deteriorate further. In the view of the authors, the strong candidates for survival and prosperity are SISTM at the UNSW and Business IS at the

University of Sydney. The chasing pack is led by the Department of Information Systems at the UTS and the IS discipline at Wollongong, which face difficulties at the moment but do have the critical mass to move forward, if the way is clear. Postgraduate specialist programs remain strong at the UTS.

Research is characterised by almost no cross-institutional cooperation and little within institutions. The 'changing of the guard' at the UNSW and the University of Sydney could bring about revivals. The problem will be, however, to avoid the lost opportunities of the 1970s. New South Wales (and Sydney in particular) had at least two institutions with plenty of highly employable undergraduate students, the respect of the IT industry and other institutions, and proximity to a large part of the Australian IT industry for support and research opportunities, yet IS in the institutions failed to develop an identity or a presence. It can be argued that this was due partly to a premature desire to define a discipline. Elias (quoted in Ridley 2006) suggests that modelling low-status on high-status disciplines is bound to fail. The moves suggested by Ridley (2006) for establishing a discipline will, if pursued by individuals or specialised research groups, work against the establishment of a broadly supported discipline. Individual prestigious reputations are established at the expense of wide collaboration, and standard research methods and unique symbol systems are used to exclude rather than enrol. Information systems—and perhaps all new disciplines—defines itself by what it is not, particularly 'not computer science'. It is easy for those outside a developing prestigious group to think 'but that's not really IS'. The drive for academic recognition, particularly in the current university research climate, can also damage relations with industry—relations that are vital to the identity of IS. The question is how can we build a 'discipline that isn't a discipline'?

References

NSW Government 2001, *Skilling People for an Information Society*, Office for ICT, NSW Government, viewed March 2006, <http://www.oict.nsw.gov.au/pdf/3.4.1-ICT-Skills.pdf>

Ridley, G. 2006, 'Characterising information systems in Australia: a theoretical framework', *Australasian Journal of Information Systems*, vol. 14, no. 1, pp. 141–62.

Addendum: another perspective on the IS discipline in NSW universities

David Wilson, Faculty of Information Technology, University of Technology, Sydney

The ICT market in Australia is one of the largest in the world, rated in the top three in the Asia-Pacific and eleventh in the world (CeBit 2006). Australia's expenditure on ICT is between 4.6 per cent (Australian Information Industry Association and federal government reports) and 6.4 per cent of GDP (CeBit 2006), placing Australia ahead of countries such as the United Kingdom, Canada, China and Japan. New South Wales represents a significant proportion of this market, as it is home to 76 per cent of Australia's ICT regional headquarters and provides employment to more than 120 000 people—about 41 per cent of the Australian ICT total (NSW DSRD 2007). New South Wales accounts for 42 per cent of ICT businesses and 47 per cent of telecommunications services (NSW DSRD 2007). New South Wales leads all other Australian states and territories in ICT research capabilities, being the headquarters of five national centres of excellence in ICT-related research fields, two major national research facilities and three cooperative research centres, as well as accounting for 43 per cent of the business expenditure on ICT services research and development in Australia (NSW DSRD 2007).

The ICT industry is changing and exhibits a shift from a techno-centric focus with technology priorities to a business-centric focus with business priorities where client-facing capabilities allied with business and project management skills are critical (Abraham et al. 2006; Zwieg et al. 2006). This represents a shift from a technical computer science and software engineering focus to a business IS focus. Information systems professionals are now required to possess business domain knowledge and project management skills and to have the ability to work well with clients and colleagues to solve business problems; the emphasis is on the client-facing skills of analysis and design enhanced with good communication skills, functional area process knowledge and industry knowledge (Abraham et al. 2006). Information systems professionals will be versatile as they assume numerous new roles, assignments and experiences (Morello and Libman 2005). This view is supported by chief information officers (CIOs), who identify ineffective communication with IS as the top inhibitor of alignment between business and IS (Luftman et al. 2005). Zweig et al. (2006) identified that, in the past, technically skilled early career IS professionals transformed themselves into mid-career professionals with strong business and project management skills through experience gained over many years. In the twenty-first century, this change needs to be effected more rapidly and this will require changes in university curricula, career paths and the continued development and training of IS professionals. Zweig et al. (2006) conclude that, although the balance of technical, business and project management skills is unlikely to be found in a fresh undergraduate, CIOs want to hire graduates with foundation technical skills complemented by business knowledge and project skills and the ability to work closely with non-technical departments and users.

In summary, New South Wales occupies a prominent position in a significant industry sector that is experiencing a skills shortage, yet the prognosis in the NSW chapter of this book is generally one of doom and gloom. NSW IS university departments are well positioned to produce graduates with the business-centric focus where client-facing capabilities allied with business and project management skills are in demand, yet the numbers of applications and enrolments are, in general, falling. There appears to be no one simple answer for this, but possible reasons that have been advanced include:

- fears that the improvement is a 'spike' and will not be sustained
- a natural lag in students responding to the changed jobs situation; things could improve in 2008
- despite the improvement, IS/ICT has lost its 'golden glow'; it is no longer a discipline of choice
- the stereotype of IS/ICT being dominated by male 'nerds' is strong and puts off potential applicants
- current school students are computer literate and therefore do not appreciate the career opportunities in the industry
- IS/ICT does not appeal to the aspirations of 'Generation Y'.

Whatever the reason—and in reality all these factors might contribute to the issue—it is clear that IS (and ICT) has lost credibility. The Y2K 'fizzer', the dotcom bust, the trend towards offshoring and a poor understanding of the IS industry among the general public have all contributed to decreased interest in IS-related careers among young people. The immediate issue is to promote IS as an interesting and rewarding career option for young people and to return the discipline to being one of choice. NSW IS university departments can be in the vanguard of this recovery.

References

Abraham, T., Beath, C., Bullen, C., Gallagher, K., Goles, T. K. K. and Simon, J. 2006, 'IT workforce trends: implications for IS programs', *Communications of the Association for Information Systems*, vol. 17, pp. 1147–70.

CeBit Australia 2006, *Australian ICT Industry*, viewed June 2007, <http://www.cebit.com.au/main/CeBIT/australian_ict_industry.asp>

Luftman, J., Kempaiah, R. and Nash, E. 2005, 'Key issues for IT executives 2005', *MIS Quarterly Executive*, vol. 5, no. 2, pp. 81–99.

Morello, D. and Libman, P. 2005, *The IT Professional Outlook: Where Will We Go From Here?*, Paper presented to Gartner Symposium ITxpo, Cannes, November 2005.

NSW Department of State and Regional Development (NSW DSRD) 2007, *Industry Profiles: Information and Communications Technology*, viewed June 2007, <http://www.business.nsw.gov.au/industry/ict/>

Zwieg, P., Kaiser, K. M., Beath, C. M., Bullen, C., Gallagher, K. P., Goles, T., Howland, J., Simon, J. C., Abbott, P., Abraham, T., Carmel, E., Evaristo, R., Hawk, S., Lacity, M., Gallivan, M., Kelly, S., Mooney, J. G., Ranganathan, C., Rottman, J. W., Ryan, T. and Wion, R. 2006, 'The information technology workforce: trends and implications 2005–2008', *MIS Quarterly Executive*, vol. 5, no. 2, pp. 101–8.

6. The information systems academic discipline in Queensland

Bob Smyth
School of Information Systems
Queensland University of Technology

Guy G. Gable
School of Information Systems
Queensland University of Technology

Abstract

Relative to its population, Queensland has a large number of universities, each of which is engaged in information systems (IS) teaching and research. As elsewhere, powerful external forces have wrought substantive change to the IS discipline in Queensland in recent years. The highly decentralised nature of Queensland has also had an enduring impact on the IS discipline in the state. Nonetheless, beyond several instances of adaptation to distance and decentralisation, the study reveals little evidence of a distinctive Queensland flavour of IS. Rather, there exists a diversity of curriculum approaches and an equally broad range of research foci and approaches to research. Two of the state's regional universities are notable for the relative strength of their IS presence, in terms of the number of IS staff, the number of IS students and the range of campuses across which IS is taught. The breadth of topics and approaches to IS in Queensland is evidenced by the existence of separate, competing IS groups in two of the largest universities; in each case, one of the IS groups is highly technical in orientation while the other is business oriented. Across the nine Queensland universities there is wide variability in terms of the administrative location of IS academic staff in the university structure. The study assesses the state of IS in Queensland universities in relation to criteria indicative of the maturity of a discipline. Measured against these criteria, IS in Queensland universities cannot yet be considered a mature, distinct academic discipline. Profiles are presented of three people prominent in the development of the IS discipline in Queensland.

Figure 6.1 Location of Queensland within Australia

Introduction

For the IS community world-wide, this is a period of great turbulence. In 2002, there was an unprecedented downturn in demand for information technology (IT) skills, resulting in a sharp decline in student entry to university IT courses. Information systems courses have been among those affected by the downturn. The impact of the decline in demand for IS skills has been heightened by the fact that, unlike engineering for example, IT had never previously experienced anything but continuing growth. Indeed, in the years leading up to the IT downturn the demand for skills had been overwhelming, fuelled by the dotcom boom and the perceived Y2K crisis.

After the drop in demand for IS courses, there has been a major re-examination of IS. Old insecurities about the status of IS as a separate academic discipline have emerged. In universities in Queensland, as elsewhere in the world, IS curricula have been re-analysed with a view to repositioning IS in response to the fall-off in student demand. The changes to IS curricula have been accompanied in some instances by administrative restructuring of IS academic staff, driven by the goals of rationalising and economising.

In Australia, proposed Commonwealth government policy on research in universities has also had a profound effect on the IS discipline. The Howard government's proposed Research Quality Framework (RQF) caused IS groups in Australian universities to reassess academic staffing profiles and to reconsider research priorities.

In this setting of introspection and change, there is value in analysing IS in Queensland universities. From a position of soundly based understanding of the current status, and some feeling for how this status was arrived at, IS academics are better placed to plan to take advantage of emerging opportunities and to minimise the impact of identified threats to the IS discipline, to IS academics and to the programs of teaching and research guided by these academics. This chapter reports on such a study into the IS discipline in universities—in this instance, universities in the state of Queensland.

Purpose of the Queensland study

Queensland, one of the six Australian states, has a population of about three million people across an area roughly six times that of Britain. Brisbane, the capital of Queensland, has a population of about 1.2 million.

The Queensland study aims to document current characteristics of IS programs and research across universities in the state. As with the broader study, this one also seeks to assess the strength of the IS presence in the state's universities, to evaluate the maturity of IS as an academic discipline, to identify emerging trends in IS and to identify the main influences on IS in the state's universities. These aims are to be seen in the context of debate about what IS is and, significantly, whether IS can claim legitimately to be a distinct academic discipline.

The research method

The Queensland study utilises the case-study method. The specific case-study method applied draws heavily on the approach suggested by Yin (2003), incorporating some of the ideas of Walsham (1995). In particular, this version of the case-study method seeks an interpretive approach, directed at what Walsham calls 'rich insight'. Consistent with Yin's recommendation, the Queensland case study utilises a detailed case-study protocol. This protocol was developed by the Queensland study team members with input and consensus from all the Australian study team members. Major objectives of the detailed case-study protocol were to facilitate:

1. comparability across the states
2. consistency across the individual state case studies
3. efficiency in the data-gathering process.

The principal data-gathering method used in the case study was interviewing. Existing documentary and archival material was also gathered to supplement the interview data and to provide some triangulation of observations. The interviews were semi-structured, of about one hour's duration, with emphasis on broad perceptions by the interviewee on IS in his/her university, points of differentiation and distinctive features of IS in that university and in other Queensland universities.

Theoretical framework guiding the study

There is a body of knowledge that suggests that many of the characteristics of IS are consistent with those observed across emerging disciplines in the early stages of their development. For example, some of the characteristics that manifested themselves in the early evolution of management as a discipline have been seen more recently in the development of IS.

The framework proposed by Ridley (see Chapter 3) is based on two constructs: 1) the degree of professionalisation as a discipline, and 2) maturity as an academic discipline. Both are derived from Whitley's theory of scientific change (1984a, 1984b).

The first construct concerns the degree of professionalisation of the discipline, which is expected to increase as the impact of local contingencies decreases. Where a discipline is not highly professionalised, local contingencies such as political pressures have a high impact. Consequently, the degree of professionalisation of IS can be indicated by the extent of variation in the nature of IS curriculum and research.

The second construct—maturity as an academic discipline—has two components: mechanisms of control, and a core body of knowledge. The framework proposes increasing maturity as a discipline being characterised by increased control and prestige, as well as increases in the core body of knowledge associated with the discipline. The core body of knowledge, in turn, is viewed as having four dimensions:

- a common set of research and teaching methods and standards
- a unique symbol system that allows the exclusion of outsiders and unambiguous communication between initiates within the discipline
- a coherent set of key research and teaching topics
- a set of laws, rules and evidenced guidelines—some form of theory base.

The universities in this study

Data were gathered from all nine universities in Queensland, all of which teach IS on at least one campus. The universities and the campus locations where IS is taught are shown in Table 6.1.

Table 6.1 Campuses of Queensland universities where IS is taught

University	Campus locations for IS
Australian Catholic University	McAuley College, Brisbane
Bond University	Gold Coast
Central Queensland University	Rockhampton; Bundaberg; Gladstone; Mackay; Emerald; (International Colleges: Melbourne; Sydney; Gold Coast; Brisbane)
Griffith University	Brisbane; Logan; Gold Coast
James Cook University	Townsville; Cairns; Mackay
Queensland University of Technology	Brisbane (2 campuses); Caboolture
University of Queensland	Brisbane; Ipswich
University of the Sunshine Coast	Sunshine Coast
University of Southern Queensland	Toowoomba; Wide Bay

Relative size of the IS presence in Queensland universities

In total size, three of the Queensland metropolitan universities—the University of Queensland, Queensland University of Technology (QUT) and Griffith

University—rank with the largest universities in Australia. The University of Queensland and QUT have total student numbers of about 40 000, while Griffith students number about 32 000. At the other end of the range, Bond University has about 2600 students, the University of the Sunshine Coast (USC) has about 3200 students, while the Queensland branch of the Australian Catholic University (ACU), McAuley College, has fewer than 5000 students.

In terms of the number of IS students and academic staff, and the extent of degree programs and research activities, the IS presence in Queensland universities is, not surprisingly, aligned roughly with university size: larger universities tend to have a stronger IS presence. Table 6.2 approximates the size of the IS presence in each Queensland university.

Table 6.2 The size of the IS presence in Queensland universities

University	No. of IS academics	No. of IS students
Australian Catholic University	<5	<100
Bond University	5–10	<100
Central Queensland University	15–20	>1 000
Griffith University	>30	>1 000
James Cook University	<5	<100
Queensland University of Technology	>30	>1 000
University of Queensland	20–25	>1 000
University of the Sunshine Coast	5–10	100–200
University of Southern Queensland	25–30	>1 000

The use of broad ranges in Table 6.2 serves to overcome inconsistencies in terms of who respondents deem to be 'IS academics' and 'IS students'. In some instances, an IS academic might also teach subjects in related disciplines, or sessional staff might or might not be reported in full-time equivalents. Similarly, IS students might be seen by some to include only those students who are studying an IS major, or equivalent, while others will include all students studying even the equivalent of a minor in IS. The number of IS academics at a university is perhaps the better guide to the size of the IS presence.

In the two to three years leading up to 2006, the IS presence in Queensland universities was characterised by downsizing. After the global downturn in IT in 2002, all Queensland universities experienced a decline in demand for IS (and other IT) courses. With reductions in the number of full fee-paying students and in the number of international students, there was a decline in the revenue from these IS groups, thereby requiring a corresponding reduction in IS staff. Several Queensland universities offered voluntary early retirement packages to IT academics and associated professional staff as part of a strategy to reduce staff numbers. Although in 2006 there were some signs of a turn around and increasing demand from industry for IS and other IT graduates, by the end of that year this had not translated into a comparable increase in demand for IS places in Queensland universities. Several Queensland IS academics expressed the view that demand for IS places in universities was likely to continue to lag behind the returning demand from practice for IS skills.

Regardless, it can be said that IS has a relatively strong presence in Queensland universities. One effect of the IT downturn appears to be that, at least in some Queensland universities, the impact on IS has been relatively less than that on computer science.

While the larger universities tend to have the larger IS presence, two regional universities that are far smaller than the three large Brisbane-based universities are distinctive for the relatively large size of their IS groups. At the University of Southern Queensland (USQ), the Department of IS is by far the largest of seven departments within the Faculty of Business, with almost 25 per cent of the faculty's enrolment. One interviewee stated that 'the Department of Information Systems [has] more students than the whole Faculty of Engineering'. While the relative size of IS at Central Queensland University (CQU) is not quite as great as at the USQ, it is still disproportionately large in terms of student numbers, staff numbers and the range of programs/courses offered, compared with the overall size of the university.

The USQ and CQU have long pursued a strategy of heavy emphasis on external studies (70 per cent of USQ IS students are external), a feature largely absent from the other Queensland universities. The consequence of heavy external enrolments, allied with a policy of setting up study centres in the Australian east-coast capital cities, means that only very small proportions of their IS students attend the home campuses of Toowoomba (USQ) and Rockhampton (CQU). The strength of external studies in IS at these two regional universities can be seen as a distinctive feature of the state of IS in universities in Queensland. The presence of IS classes away from the home campus, often in other states and commonly making up the bulk of IS enrolments at the university, is also notable.

The administrative placement of IS in Queensland universities

Across the nine Queensland universities there is remarkable variability in the administrative location of IS academic staff in the university structure. Table 6.3 shows, first, the administrative entity with which the IS academics at that university are affiliated. It should be noted at this point that it is common to find academics involved with aspects of IS across a range of departments, schools and faculties in a given university—for example, health informatics in a health faculty, IS auditing in a school of accounting, and so on. In this study, data were collected only on groups who self-identified as teaching and/or researching IS in each university.

A feature of IS in Queensland universities (perhaps not distinctive to Queensland) is that from late 2004 to mid-2006, many of the IS groups had either just participated in restructuring or were about to begin a restructuring process. The CQU, Griffith, James Cook and USQ IS academics were about to begin a review process; Bond University IS staff members were involved in restructuring in June 2005 and QUT IS academics were in the midst of a restructuring. The downturn in demand for IT courses was cited as a major stimulus for restructuring.

It can be seen from Table 6.3 that five of the nine Queensland universities have IS academics in a separate school or department. A separate identity for IS might be associated with a higher level of academic control by the IS academics and with a higher level of prestige for the IS group. Interestingly, no two of these five universities use exactly the same terminology to describe their IS administrative entity. The remaining four universities—Bond, James Cook, the University of Queensland and the USC—have IS academic staff placed in administrative entities within other departments, schools or faculties. In these four instances, the administrative entities are identified as discipline groups.

Table 6.3 Administrative placement of the IS group in Queensland universities

University	Administrative entity	Home faculty
Australian Catholic University	School of Business and Informatics	Arts and Sciences
Bond University	Informal IS group within School of Information Technology	Business
Central Queensland University	School of Information Systems	Informatics and Communications
Griffith University	School of Information Communications and Technology/informal IS group in School of Management	Engineering and Information Technology/Business and Law
James Cook University	Informal IS group in School of Business	Law, Business and Creative Arts
Queensland University of Technology	School of Information Systems	Information Technology
University of Queensland	Information Systems Cluster in Business School; Data and Knowledge Engineering Division in School of Information Technology and Electrical Engineering	Business, Economics and Law/Engineering, Physical Sciences and Architecture
University of the Sunshine Coast	Information Systems Discipline Group in Faculty of Business	Business
University of Southern Queensland	Department of Information Systems	Business

In turn, the 'home' faculty for each IS group also shows some variability across the nine Queensland universities. At James Cook, Bond, USC and USQ, the home or parent faculty for the IS academics is business (or some variant of that title). At QUT, the home faculty for IS academics is a Faculty of Information Technology. Griffith University and the University of Queensland are distinctive in two respects in relation to the administrative placement of their IS academics: first, both universities are characterised by two separate IS groups. At Griffith, the smaller of the two groups is within the School of Management in the Faculty of Business and Law. The second, and larger, IS group at Griffith University is distinctive in being administratively alongside engineering, in a Faculty of Engineering and Information Technology. At the University of Queensland, the larger of the two IS groups is in the Business School, while the second IS group, somewhat akin to Griffith, is within a School of Information Technology and Electrical Engineering. The placement of the IS group at the ACU within a Faculty of Arts and Science appears anomalous until it is observed that ACU has only three faculties, the other two being health and education.

In terms of independent status for IS groups in Queensland universities, there is evidence of two contradictory trends. On the one hand, at such universities as the CQU, Griffith and QUT, IS academics have moved into separate, identifiable schools of IS. On the other hand, at the USQ, a separate School of Information Technology, formed in 1990 to include IS and computer science, was broken up in 1993, with IS returning to the business faculty. Similarly, the Faculty of Information Technology at Bond University, which incorporated the IS group (and computer science), was disbanded in June 2005, with all IT being absorbed into the Faculty of Business as a new School of Information Technology. Thus, while some IS groups have been moving out of business faculties in Queensland, others have been moving back into business. The moves cannot be linked easily to broad outside forces; while the movement to business at Bond seems clearly linked to the decline in demand for IT, at the USQ the move back to business occurred at a time when IT demand was booming.

Sherer (2002) asserts that the theoretical basis of the discipline and the curricular needs of the professional community influence the organisational placement of the IS group. The assertion seems most plausible. If we assume that the theoretical basis of the discipline and the perceived curricular needs of the local community are two significant determinants of the administrative placement of IS groups, it is possible to make inferences about these factors from the differing placements in universities across the state. These inferences can provide useful insights regarding the maturity of IS as a distinct academic discipline. The administrative placement of the IS group is significant in relation to the acquisition, by the IS group, of mechanisms of power—a prerequisite for maturity of a discipline within the Ridley framework. This matter of the maturity of the discipline is analysed in a later section of the report.

Distinctive features of the IS curriculum

The Queensland universities offer a wide range of undergraduate and postgraduate IS courses/programs. Table 6.4 summarises the main IS courses currently presented in the Queensland universities. It is clear from the table that there is much variety in IS courses across the state. At the coarsest level of analysis, it can be seen that the IS courses bear a wide range of nomenclatures. Within these obvious differences in degree names, in the Queensland universities there is considerable further variability in IS curriculum content. One obvious area of variability in curriculum content relates to the amount of 'technical' emphasis in different courses. At QUT and Bond University, for instance, at least 20 of the 24 units in the undergraduate IS degree course are from the Faculty of Information Technology. The IS units offered within the School of Information Technology and Electrical Engineering at the University of Queensland are characterised by the fact that every one of them has a technical focus. In contrast, the IS undergraduate degrees in the universities where the IS group is located within a business faculty tend to include a number (typically four to six) of compulsory business units. The same variability in IS curriculum content is to be observed in the course-work postgraduate IS courses across the Queensland universities.

Another aspect of the variability of IS curricula across Queensland universities is in the demarcation between IS and related discipline areas in relation to which discipline has curriculum responsibility for specific topic areas. For instance, at the CQU no programming subjects are controlled by IS staff; they are instead the domain of computer science staff. The CQU has, however, strong representation in its course curricula from such topic areas as management support systems and health informatics—topic areas covered by other faculties in some other Queensland universities. Topic areas such as database and data communications, as well as a range of web-related topics, are other examples of curriculum areas that lie within the ambit of the IS academic departments at some Queensland universities and, yet, with other departments at other universities.

The Ridley framework depicts the ready identification of a core body of knowledge—characterised in part by broad commonalities in the curricula of courses—as an important characteristic of a maturing discipline. It is clear from the data that in Queensland universities it is difficult to find evidence of consistency in the content of IS curricula across the state.

A phenomenon apparent in curriculum in Queensland, apparently in response to the overall decline in IT, has been an increased effort to develop courses closely aligned to the needs of business. For instance, at QUT during 2006 a Bachelor of Corporate Management degree was being developed for introduction in 2007. Similarly, at the USC a flexible new undergraduate IS structure, consciously aligned to the expressed needs of business, was being developed.

Table 6.4 IS courses in Queensland universities

University	Undergraduate courses/programs	Postgraduate courses/programs
Australian Catholic University	BIS	MIS
Bond University	BIS (discontinued after school's move to Faculty of Business) BIT (IS)	GradDipIT MIT (Prof) MIT (Exec) MIT (Hons) MITM MEC
Central Queensland University	BBus (IS) BEC BIT (Bio-informatics)	GradCertIS GradDipIS Management MIS GradCert Health Informatics GradDip Health Informatics Master of Health Informatics PhD
Griffith University	BIT BBus (Commercial Comp)	MIT MIT (Advanced) MeCom MIS MIS (Advanced) MSoftEng MStrategicInfSysMgt PhD
James Cook University	BCom	MCom MBA-MInfTech PhD
Queensland University of Technology	BInfTech (IS)	BInfTech (Hons) GradDipInfTech MInfTech MInfTech (Advanced) PhD
University of Queensland	BCom (IS) BBusMan (eBusiness) BInfTech	MCom (IS) MCom (eCom) MSc (Comp Sc) MEng MInfTech PhD
University of the Sunshine Coast	BBus (IS) BICT	GradDipIS MInfTech (Research) PhD
University of Southern Queensland	BBus BIT	GradDipInfTech GradDipInfSys MInfSys MIT (Research) MIT (Prof) PhD

Distinctive features of IS research

As with IS curriculum, diversity is a feature of IS research in Queensland universities. Table 6.5 summarises major foci for IS research in Queensland universities and the organisational approaches to promoting research. Again, the diversity of topics highlights the breadth that appears to characterise IS. Once again, the research foci of the individual universities also do not appear to be related closely to geographical factors local to each university. Instead, the research areas appear to reflect the specific interests and skills of the academic research leaders. Again, there is evidence from some of the Queensland universities of a policy to focus deliberately on global IS issues in preference to purely local ones.

There is also no consistent pattern in the organisational approaches of the universities in seeking to promote and support IS research in Queensland universities. While some universities have established formal groups and programs and research centres, others—such as the two IS groups at the University of Queensland, which has a long tradition of research—rely largely on voluntary collaborations. Some of the groupings have a tight IS focus, while others—such as James Cook University—foster broad cross-discipline collaborations.

The diversity of research topics, research methods and administration of the IS research function in Queensland universities is at odds with the requirement, as expressed in the Ridley framework, for

- a common set of research methods and standards
- a coherent set of key research topics.

Again, this observation sees the IS academic field in Queensland failing to meet another prerequisite for the acceptance of IS as a mature discipline.

Table 6.5 IS research foci and groupings for IS research in Queensland universities

University	Areas of IS research focus	IS research groupings
Australian Catholic University	Business requirements definition; software quality assurance; management of IS; systems modelling and simulation	Individual
Bond University	Smart supply chain; business intelligence	Smart Enterprise Centre
Central Queensland University	Health informatics; group solutions (GDSS); teaching and learning; multimedia	No research centres; research clusters from across schools in the faculty
Griffith University	Software quality; packaged software; decision support systems; programming methodology; gender and IT; IS analysis, design, development and implementation; IS security; IS strategy; end-user issues; knowledge management; rural IS	Software Quality Institute; Institute for Integrated and Intelligent Systems; IS Group in Department of Management
James Cook University	People, identity and place: intellectual, social, economic and cultural dynamics; gender and IT	Collaborative; cross-faculty
Queensland University of Technology	IT professional services: knowledge management; enterprise systems success factors; IT sourcing; the management consulting process; information management in business processes; ERP life cycle knowledge management; business process management; workflow patterns; workflow tools; web service design and implementation	Centre for Information Technology Innovation: IT Professional Services (ITPS) Research Program; Business Process Management (BPM) Research Program

Table 6.5 IS research foci and groupings for IS research in Queensland universities

University	Areas of IS research focus	IS research groupings
University of Queensland	Ontological analysis; data quality; e-commerce; knowledge management; computer forensics; IT governance; mobile communications (security aspects); enterprise computing (workflows, etc.); spatial databases	Voluntary collaborative groupings
University of the Sunshine Coast	Knowledge management; data mining	Faculty Research Centre, SCRIBE
University of Southern Queensland	Eclectic: e-business; IS education; knowledge management; IS development methodologies	eBARC—Electronic Business Advisory and Research Centre, faculty-wide

A feature of IS research in Queensland universities has been the response by the IS groups to the Commonwealth government's proposed RQF. Interviewees frequently referred indirectly to RQF with statements about 'the new research environment'. While details of RQF had not been fully determined, the general thrust was a new approach to assessing and rewarding university research output. Beyond this, there was widespread conjecture among Queensland IS academics that failure to reach certain government benchmarks in research might be followed by a removal of government financial support for research at that university. The new Labor government announced in December 2007 its abandonment of the RQF, while foreshadowing a replacement mechanism for assessing university research. Information systems academic groups can be expected to adapt to whatever new mechanisms are put in place. Some changes observed among Queensland IS groups in response to the RQF proposals included the following.

1. Major efforts were begun to win competitive research grants, particularly Australian Research Council (ARC) grants. Universities where there had been little history of ARC grant applications were vigorously gearing up to make themselves competitive in seeking such grants.

2. New staff members with established research records were being sought. The understanding regarding RQF was that prior research publications would count in assessing current research output; so, 'buying in' established researchers was seen as a mechanism for immediately boosting the measured research output of the IS group.

3. Publication in conference proceedings, even of the most prestigious international IS conferences, was being eschewed in favour of journal publication. The understanding was that publications in conference proceedings would carry far less weight in the measurement of research output.

Key figures who have influenced IS in Queensland universities

Senior academics in IS in Queensland universities cite a wide range of individuals as having been significant to the development of IS teaching and research in their universities. In most instances, prominent IS academics in the early days of IS at the university in question were viewed as having had the greatest impact—for example, Ed Fitzgerald at the USQ.

Vignettes are presented in this chapter of just three of the many figures who have made major contributions to the IS discipline in Queensland universities. A vignette of Ed Fitzgerald provides an overview of his achievements and his contribution to the IS discipline in Queensland, most particularly through his contribution to IS curriculum at the USQ and more recently at the USC. Less commonly, outside figures were cited. At Bond University, British academic Frank Land, an early advisor to Bond, was proposed as a most influential individual. At QUT, it was John Puttick, a prominent IT proprietor and practitioner and chair of the QUT Faculty of Information Technology Advisory Committee. At the USC and the University of Queensland, Ron Weber was nominated as a significant influence because of his prominence internationally, along with Alan Underwood, another Queensland IS academic who made a significant contribution to the Australian Computer Society (ACS). Vignettes of Ron Weber and Alan Underwood are also presented here, as examples of leading figures in the development of IS in Queensland. Weber's contribution to research and scholarship in Queensland has been outstanding; Underwood has been the major contributor in the development of the largest IS group in Queensland universities.

Vignette—Ron Weber

Ron Weber had a major impact on IS in Queensland during his 25 years as an academic at the University of Queensland. In his final role at the University of Queensland, he was Professor of Information Systems in the School of Business and Research Director for the Faculty of Business, Economics and Law. In 2004, he was appointed Dean of the Faculty of Information Technology at Monash University.

Weber's first degree was a Bachelor of Commerce, in which he obtained first-class honours from the University of Queensland in 1972. After working as a programmer, systems analyst and project manager, he undertook his MBA (1975) and PhD (1977) in Management Information Systems at the University of Minnesota. He had the privilege of having Gordon Davis as his advisor and of studying with a number of doctoral students who would go on to make major contributions to the IS discipline.

In 1977, Weber returned to Australia as Senior Lecturer in the Department of Accounting and Public Finance at The Australian National University. In 1979, he took up the post of Reader in Commerce at the University of Queensland. In 1981, he was appointed Professor of Commerce and, in 1988, he was the inaugural appointment to the GWA Chair in Commerce, which he held until 1993.

Weber has held visiting academic appointments at the University of Alberta, the University of British Columbia, the City University of Hong Kong, the University of Minnesota, Nanyang Technological University Singapore, New York University and the University of Otago.

His main research interests are in ontology (a branch of metaphysics), conceptual modelling, modelling of IS and IS management, auditing and control. He has published extensively in Australian and international journals, and many students and practitioners have used his book, *Information Systems Control and Audit*, internationally.

Weber is a Fellow of the ACS, the Institute of Chartered Accountants in Australia, CPA Australia, the Association for Information Systems and the Academy of the Social Sciences in Australia. In 2002, he was elected a life member of the Accounting and Finance Association of Australia and New Zealand. He was the first president from Region 3 of the Association for Information Systems. In December 2000, he was co-chair of the International Conference on Information Systems (ICIS). During 2001, he was chair of the ICIS Executive Committee.

His many awards include the University Medal (the University of Queensland), University of Minnesota Corporate Fellowship and the Prime Minister's Award for University Teacher of the Year (2000). In 1994, he won one of four Silver Jubilee Awards given world-wide by the Information Systems Audit and Control Association for contributions to the profession and the discipline of IS auditing. In 2000, he received the Accounting and Finance Association of Australia and New Zealand's inaugural Outstanding Educator Award and the Notable Contributions to the Accounting Literature Award.

Weber has worked on many editorial boards. He is a past senior editor for the *MIS Quarterly* and on, 31 December 2004, he ended a three-year term as Editor-in-Chief of *MIS Quarterly*—the first non-American resident to ever hold the position.

Vignette—Ed Fitzgerald

Ed Fitzgerald has 37 years' experience in the ICT industry, including 10 years working as a project manager/systems analyst/programmer, and 27 years in universities. His strong research background is supported by a PhD in IS strategic planning. He also maintains an active involvement in consulting in the public and private sectors.

In 1978—at a time when IS was still called data processing—Fitzgerald, along with two colleagues, began building what in the space of 10 years became the largest academic department in the USQ, the second-largest IS department in Australia at that time, and the first to offer IS courses by distance education. Starting with three data-processing staff providing 'service' subjects to a dominant (and domineering) accounting program, he led the establishment of a major in IS within the Bachelor of Business degree, then a Bachelor of IT, a Masters by course-work and a Masters by research. Always available to assist students and to explore ways of making possible what others said was impossible, he was nevertheless rigorous in his approach to academic standards in teaching and research.

Many of his students who now hold senior management positions in IT will tell you that Fitzgerald was demanding, but fair, and they still draw on key lessons learnt from him in his role as teacher and mentor. Some of those students benefited from the links Fitzgerald had established earlier when he was head of computer training in the Department of Defence in Canberra. At a time when IS jobs were few and far between in Queensland, Fitzgerald created Department of Defence opportunities, resulting in Canberra becoming home to hundreds of USQ IS graduates in the following years. Several IS professors will tell you how Fitzgerald also fostered their careers—encouraging them to enrol in Masters and PhD degrees, and supporting them personally and professionally through difficulties and successes.

After 25 years of managerial roles at the USQ ranging from foundation Head of the Department of Information Systems and Associate Dean (Academic) and Acting Dean to director of an e-business research centre, in 2003, Fitzgerald moved to the USC to take up the newly created role of Professor in Information Systems. Challenged to create in a new regional university an IS program that developed graduates with career opportunities equal to those of larger urban universities, he designed a degree with an 'industry studies' component that gave students the opportunity to target any one of the range of specific careers now available in the ICT industry. In the final four courses of the 12-course major, students select the combinations of internships, industry certifications and courses from other universities that deliver the career-specific knowledge and experience required for their chosen speciality. This innovative response is already being considered in some other Australian universities.

Fitzgerald is currently Dean of the Faculty of Business at the USC.

Vignette — Alan Underwood

Alan Underwood has been involved in most facets of the IT profession since starting out as a technical programmer in January 1967. After his recent retirement, QUT conferred on him the title of Emeritus Professor.

Underwood completed his first degree, a Bachelor of Business (Management), at Queensland Institute of Technology (QIT, the precursor to QUT) in 1974, while working in the industry as a programmer, systems analyst, project manager and operations manager. In 1975, he began at QIT as a lecturer in data processing. He completed a Master of Science (Management Information Systems) at Texas Technical University (1979) and an MBA at the University of Queensland (1982). After QIT's change to QUT in 1989 and an increased emphasis on research within the university, Underwood completed his PhD at QUT in 1995.

Until his retirement in 2006, Underwood was the academic and administrative head of the IS group at QUT, a position held almost continuously since his initial appointment as the Head of the Business Computing Section in October 1981. In 1983, Underwood helped create a new Faculty of Information Technology at QUT, which presented an opportunity to introduce an undergraduate degree in IS. Underwood's insistence on offering practically oriented IS courses with a business outlook, reflecting the needs of industry, was a catalyst for the excellent reputation that QUT enjoys today.

Underwood has always maintained strong links with the profession through the ACS; he was the national vice-president and president from 1988 to 1991. He served on the Queensland branch executive for 11 years in many capacities, including as vice-chairman and branch chairman from 1982 to 1985. Underwood was a member of the ACS National Council from 1984 to 1996, the National Technical Board Governor in 1989 and National Director of the Professional Development Board from 1995–96. He also served as the chairman of a number of national and international conferences including IFIP, ACC, SEARCC, ACIS and PACIS and he was a member of many national and international conference program committees.

Underwood is a fellow and an honorary life member of the ACS. During his term on the National Management Committee and as president, Underwood was instrumental in the society concentrating on professional issues. Consequently, the Practising Computer Professional (PCP) scheme was introduced in 1992 and a certification program was announced in 1993; both of these schemes still exist today.

Together with ACS colleagues, Underwood developed the core body of knowledge used by the ACS for the accreditation of IT courses in Australian institutions.

From 1988 until 2000, Underwood represented the ACS as a member of the Executive Council and as Assistant Secretary-General of the South East Asia Regional Computing Confederation (SEARCC).

In late 1988, Underwood, with a colleague from surveying, was successful in winning one of the first ARC grants awarded to QUT. His research interests now are in certification, professional ethics and IT project management.

The status of IS as a distinct discipline in Queensland

To analyse the status of IS as a distinct discipline, we turn initially to the two constructs from Whitley (1984a, 1984b) outlined earlier in this report viz. professionalisation and conditions for acceptance as an academic discipline. Where a discipline is not highly professionalised, Whitley argues that local contingencies have high impact. From the data collected in Queensland, there is little evidence of IS curriculum or research effort being focused on accommodating local community characteristics. Nonetheless, as has been pointed out in an earlier section of this report, within the Queensland universities there is high variability in curriculum content. It can be argued that this variability in IS content is attributable primarily to a specific local contingency factor. That factor is the IS leadership in each university. Even within a single university, sharp changes in curriculum content can be seen when leadership of the IS group changes. An example of this is the USC, where the curriculum moved abruptly from a focus on soft-systems approaches to a much more 'technical' curriculum after a change in the IS leader at that university. A similar phenomenon is evident in IS research in Queensland universities; research topics and methods at each university at any time can be seen to be dependent largely on the influence of a small number of key figures at that university. On these grounds, it can be argued, using the Ridley framework, that the IS discipline in Queensland is not professionalised. Clearly, local contingencies have a high impact.

Ridley's first component associated with discipline maturity is: increased influence over mechanisms of control. The evidence in Queensland is ambivalent on this. There are data pointing to IS groups in Queensland gaining a high degree of autonomy in teaching and research. Very often these highly autonomous groups are ones that have moved out of business faculties. In other instances, IS groups within business appear to have significant control over curriculum and research. On the other hand, there are data showing instances where, under the pressure of reduced demand for IT, IS groups have had a reduction in their autonomy. Further evidence of increasing control, power and prestige is reflected in more IS academics in Queensland achieving high status within their universities; there are a number of IS professors in Queensland now, where 20 years ago there would have been just one.

As observed in the earlier discussion on the IS curriculum in each of the Queensland universities, there is a lack of consistency across the universities with regard to subject areas that properly 'belong' to IS staff as opposed to staff from computer science, multimedia, business or some other academic group. This observation of the absence in Queensland universities of a core body of knowledge defining IS is consistent with the wider observations of Fitzgerald (2003). Fitzgerald concludes that the absence of such a core body of knowledge relegates IS to 'a subject with a particular perspective' rather than a discipline. Again, using the second indicator of discipline maturity in the Ridley framework, this diversity of curriculum, along with a comparable diversity in research topics and methods, further suggests IS is lacking maturity as an academic discipline. Nor was there evidence in the Queensland universities that IS possessed 'a unique symbol system'—in other words, a distinct language of its own, which differentiated it from related discipline areas.

Review of findings

While the study pointed to a considerable diversity in IS across the nine universities in Queensland, there was little evidence of sharply different 'philosophies' of IS, as was reported from a survey of IS in 18 European countries (Avgerou et al. 1999). The European study had, for instance, highlighted the strong socio-technical stance of the Scandinavian countries, in contrast with a pragmatic technical emphasis in German universities. In the curricula and research emphases of the Queensland universities there was evidence of an eclectic melding of the various European and American approaches. Only at the University of Queensland and at Griffith University—both of which maintain two strong IS groups, one 'technical' and the other 'business-focused'—is this blending of approaches to IS not in place in a single administrative unit.

In relating the Queensland data to Ridley's (2006) framework for assessing the maturity of IS as a discipline, it has to be said that the evidence from Queensland universities does *not* fully support IS being recognised as a mature discipline. Certainly, the data suggest that the IT field in Queensland is characterised as being subject to the high impact of local contingencies. According to Ridley's framework, this characteristic is typical of a field lacking a high degree of professionalisation.

Ridley's first criterion for maturity as a discipline—that those in the discipline have a high level of control, associated with the potential for prestige and power—would appear to be met at least partially. At several of the Queensland universities, where senior IS academics are recognised by their universities as Professor of Information Systems, these individuals are recognised, by virtue of their achievements in IS, as warranting the same prestige and decision-making power in the university as their colleagues in long-established disciplines. Similarly, the control that comes with increased autonomy is evident in many

Queensland universities, where IS academics have significant control over resources, IS curriculum content and IS research.

In relation to the second maturity criterion—that there should be evidence of a core body of knowledge for that discipline—the Queensland data indicate that no such clear core body of knowledge is identifiable. Information systems curricula are very diverse across Queensland universities, as are IS research topics and methods. Further, as reflected in debate within the wider IS community, there is little evidence in Queensland (or elsewhere) that IS yet possesses the 'theory base' that is also among Ridley's indicators of discipline maturity. Again, in relation to Ridley's criterion of a unique symbol system that allows the exclusion of outsiders and unambiguous communication between initiates within the discipline, there is limited evidence from the data to suggest that IS academics in Queensland share such a common unique symbol system. The wide variability in curriculum content and research foci would alone argue against this unique basis for communication among the IS academics.

In summary, the features of the IS activities observed in Queensland universities have much in common with features reported by Whitley (1984a) in relation to the early stages of the development of management as a discipline area viz.

- a heavy reliance on reference disciplines
- a paucity of theory specific to the discipline
- a perceived lower status than for established disciplines, leading to the adoption of methods from the higher-status disciplines
- limited numbers of textbooks that review the discipline
- poor definition of the boundaries of study
- incorporation organisationally as a subset of an established discipline.

Whitley uses the term 'fragmented adhocracy' to describe this immature stage of the development towards a distinct discipline.

The existence in each of two Queensland universities of separate IS groups, under the administration of different faculties and with quite different curricula and research foci, highlights the relative immaturity of the IS discipline in Queensland. Nonetheless, evidence of recent collaboration and cooperation between these previously rival IS groups suggests progress in this pursuit of discipline maturity.

Limitations and future research

The Queensland study draws only patchily on historical data related to the development over time of IS in the nine Queensland universities. In some universities there were historical data readily available, while in others there were not. Where historical data were available to the researchers, there was a richer context for analysis to understand the current situation. The value to the researchers of such limited historical data as were available points to improved insights from an extension of this study, incorporating a fuller historical analysis.

A feature highlighted in the execution of this study was the dynamic state of IS in Queensland universities at the time of the study. The study therefore represents a snapshot of a rapidly changing scene. To capitalise on the findings of this study, there is an imperative to replicate it over time. A longitudinal view of IS in Queensland will tell much about the progressive maturing of IS as a discipline. In particular, it will be of great interest to see how the IS discipline in Queensland is influenced by the apparent resurgence in demand for IT skills. The Excellence in Research for Australia (ERA) which replaces the RQF, has the potential to very much change the nature of IS research and the methods of communicating research findings.

General findings from the Queensland study

In conducting this Queensland study, there was recognition by the researchers of the intention to reflect on the procedures followed and the outcomes achieved; this and the other Australian studies were to inform subsequent, broader studies into the IS discipline. A similar study into the IS discipline in universities in the countries of the IS Pacific-Asia region is in progress, drawing to some extent on the Australian experiences. It is envisaged that similar studies of the IS discipline be carried out in other regions of the world. This might ultimately allow a useful global analysis of the discipline, highlighting regional similarities and differences.

A useful finding from the Queensland study relates to the approach to data gathering that was proposed in the study protocol. The intention was to have interviews with at least one key person from each university in the state as the prime source of data. These interviews were planned to take about one hour each. In the event, arranging face-to-face interviews at two of the Queensland universities proved impractical. For James Cook University and the ACU, telephone interviews were used, followed up with interview notes and other exchanges by e-mail between the researcher and the interviewees.

For future studies elsewhere, a revised study protocol has been prepared to accommodate telephone interviews. In addition, in recognition of the large time requirements for interviewing where there are many universities involved in the study, a survey instrument has been prepared as a substitute for each interview. The instrument attempts to provide some of the richness of an interview by minimising questions seeking specific numerical responses, in favour of questions teasing out the distinctive characteristics of the university. In recognition of a study environment in which, on the other hand, there are very few universities in the study, a guideline for conducting focus groups, based on the standard data-gathering framework, has been added to the study protocol.

The use of a theory framework to guide the data gathering and analysis, based on 'the emergence of a discipline', proved most helpful to conducting the Queensland study. It is envisaged that the Ridley framework will prove valuable to similar future studies.

References

Avgerou, C., Siemer, J. and Bjørn-Andersen, N. 1999, 'The academic field of information systems in Europe', *European Journal of Information Systems*, vol. 8, pp. 136–53.

Fitzgerald, G. 2003, 'Information systems: a subject with a particular perspective, no more, no less', *European Journal of Information Systems*, vol. 12, pp. 225–8.

Sherer, S. A. 2002, 'Academic departments of information systems faculty in the US', *Journal of Information Systems Education*, vol. 13, pp. 105–16.

Walsham, G. 1995, 'Interpretive case studies in IS research: nature and method', *European Journal of Information Systems*, vol. 4, pp. 74–81.

Whitley, R. 1984a, 'The development of management studies as a fragmented adhocracy', *Social Science Information*, vol. 23, pp. 775–818.

Whitley, R. 1984b, *The Intellectual and Social Organization of the Sciences*, Clarendon Press, Oxford, UK.

Yin, R. K. 2003, *Case Study Research: Design and Methods*, 3rd Edn, Sage Publications, Thousand Oaks.

7. Information systems in South Australia: a critical investigation

Paula M. C. Swatman
School of Computer and Information Science
University of South Australia

Andy Koronios
School of Computer and Information Science
University of South Australia

Abstract

This study aims to establish the state of information systems (IS) degree programs and research at Adelaide University, Flinders University and the University of South Australia—the three South Australian universities. It examines the location of IS as an academic discipline, its size and presence and the impact of local contingencies. The study reveals only a small IS presence at Flinders University and a modest IS presence, within commerce, at Adelaide University. The largest IS presence in the state's universities is at the University of South Australia, where the IS group is sited in a School of Computer and Information Science (CIS), located within a Division of Information Technology, Engineering and the Environment. The study concludes that although IS in South Australian universities meets some of the criteria for recognition as a mature discipline, the state's unique qualities have played a large part in the unusually low level of academic interest in IS.

Figure 7.1 Location of South Australia within Australia

Purpose of the South Australian study

South Australia is the fourth-largest of the Australian states, with a population of 1.7 million; and it is central to Australia, being the only state to share a border with all other mainland Australian states. It is often referred to as the driest state in the driest inhabited continent of the world. Instead of the convict past common to most of the Australian states, South Australia was settled freely as a British province and proclaimed officially in 1836. It also has a strong German heritage resulting from several decades of German migration in the early to mid-1800s, which has left a unique architectural and phonetic legacy. The capital is Adelaide, with a population of 1.2 million people.

The South Australian study aims to establish the state of IS degree programs and research in its three universities. It examines the location of IS as an academic discipline, its size and presence, the impact of local contingencies, and contributes to the debate about IS as a separate field.

The chapter begins with a discussion of the theoretical framework used to analyse IS research and teaching activities in South Australia, then provides an overview of the three South Australian universities and their teaching activities in the IS field. The chapter then discusses the aspects of IS relevant to this group of case studies—with a particular focus on the University of South Australia, as data were not obtainable from the other two universities on many of these topics.

Research approach

Theoretical framework guiding the study

Ridley's (2006) theoretical framework has been developed through a thematic study of IS and non-IS literature. Common components were identified and included in the framework, which was influenced by Whitley's (1984) theory of the establishment of scientific fields. Essentially, Whitley proposed three conditions necessary for the formation of a new field:

1. mechanisms of control such as publication records and an ability to gain research funding
2. research skills and standards
3. a unique symbol set.

Ridley (2006) suggests that Whitley's second and third conditions together comprise 'a core body of knowledge', and adds theory and an agreed set of topics as additional essential components. On this basis, she then constructs a two-tiered framework comprising mechanisms of control, a core body of knowledge, the impact of local contingencies and the degree of professionalism as the first level. The second level builds on the core body of knowledge drawn from Whitley and consists of research and teaching methods and standards, a unique symbol set, key research and teaching IS topics and laws, rules and evidenced guidelines.

Table 7.1 provides an abridged version of Ridley's own summary of this framework.

Table 7.1 Discipline nature and development framework (adapted from Ridley 2006)

Level 1 component	Level 2 component
Mechanisms of control	
Core body of knowledge	
	Research and teaching methods and standards
	Unique symbol set
	Key research and teaching IS topics
	Laws, rules and evidenced guidelines
Impact of local contingencies	
Degree of professionalism	

Ridley (2006) believes this framework is sufficiently robust to accommodate future developments in IS and has tested it (successfully) against the inclusion of pragmatism into the IS literature. This characterisation framework forms the basis for the present chapter.

Data analysis

This study of IS in South Australia takes the form of a positivist case study (Yin 2003), based predominantly on interviews conducted with IS teaching staff at the University of South Australia and the University of Adelaide,[1] and enhanced by data drawn from internal and external sources. Case studies of this type frequently make use of a detailed case-study protocol; Australasian study team members developed such a protocol at the time of the original *Australasian Journal of Information Systems* (*AJIS*) special issue paper preparation to ensure consistency of data collection across the universities studied. Major objectives of this protocol were to facilitate:

1. comparability across the states
2. consistency across the individual state case studies
3. efficiency in the data-gathering process.

Data were collected by a combination of personal interviews and e-mail questionnaires, filled in by staff and returned to the authors for analysis and review. Existing documentary and archival material was also gathered to supplement the interview data and to provide some triangulation of observations.

Data gathered from interviews and questionnaires were then analysed using the Ridley framework, so that qualitative data collected from participants and

---

[1] A description of Flinders University is included in this chapter for the sake of completeness but, since IS does not exist as a school, department or even a discipline within a school at Flinders University, detailed data were not gathered from Flinders for this study.

quantitative data collated from other sources could be integrated more effectively (Dixon-Woods et al. 2005; Ridley 2006).

The discussion that follows was 'weighted towards themes that appear to have a high level of explanatory value', rather than reflecting how frequently the themes were reported (Dixon-Woods et al. 2005:47).

The universities in this study

The University of South Australia

The University of South Australia (UniSA), the largest university in South Australia, was founded on 1 January 1991 through the amalgamation of the South Australian Institute of Technology and the Magill, Salisbury and Underdale campuses of the South Australian College of Advanced Education. It is one of the five Australian Technology Network (ATN) universities (http://www.atn.edu.au/), which have a focus on applied research and whose aim is to develop strategic partnerships between the academic and business sectors. Since its inception, UniSA has quickly earned a reputation as a national leader in collaborative research, it has been recognised nationally for innovation in teaching and it has South Australia's largest intake of international students (and one of the largest in the country). The UniSA has an overall student population of about 33 000 and employs more than 3000 staff. It offers almost 400 degree programs from diploma to postgraduate level across four divisions: Health Sciences; Education, Arts and Social Sciences; Information Technology, Engineering and the Environment; and Business.

The University of Adelaide

Adelaide's first and oldest university was established in 1874 and has approximately 20 000 students and 2500 staff. The University of Adelaide has something of a history of firsts, being the first Australian university to admit women to academic courses, in 1881, and the first Australian university to award degrees in science. Today the University of Adelaide, which is a member of the Group of Eight (Go8) universities (see http://www.go8.edu.au/)—eight of Australia's oldest and most research-intensive universities—extends across four campuses and accommodates more than 4500 international students. It has produced 100 Rhodes Scholars and has five faculties: Engineering, Computer and Mathematical Sciences; Health Sciences; Humanities and Social Sciences; Professions; and Sciences.

Flinders University of South Australia

Established in 1966 in the southern Adelaide suburb of Bedford Park, Flinders University has approximately 15 000 students and 1500 staff. The university takes its name from British explorer Matthew Flinders, who surveyed the South

Australian coastline in 1802. An early initiative was the decision to build the Flinders Medical Centre on land adjoining the campus and to house the university's medical school, which opened in 1976, within this new public hospital—the first such integration in Australia. When higher education was restructured in South Australia in 1991, Flinders merged with the neighbouring Sturt campus of the former South Australian College of Advanced Education. Flinders University comprises four faculties: Education, Law, Humanities and Theology; Health Sciences; Social Sciences; and Science and Engineering.

Flinders University does offer a Bachelor of Information Technology degree, which has definite similarities with UniSA's Bachelor of Information Technology program, but since both these degrees focus primarily on information technology (IT) rather than IS (offering a 'half-way house' between computer science and IS), this material has not been included in the present, IS-focused study. Flinders also offers a Bachelor of Arts (Geographical Information Systems, GIS) program, offering students enrolled in an arts degree the opportunity to include a major sequence in the area of GIS. This might well be seen as an attraction for students considering an IS degree, but is a rather more specialised offering and, again, is not included in the present chapter.

Size and presence of IS in South Australian universities

It proved surprisingly difficult to obtain accurate figures for IS student numbers at the three universities—largely because statistics were not available for IS in isolation and therefore had to be extrapolated from combined computing or commerce student numbers. Table 7.2 summarises the 'best guess' numbers provided by each of the universities. For this reason, numbers in this study are reported as 'students', rather than effective full-time student load (EFTSL).

Table 7.2 Numbers of IS staff and students in South Australian universities

University	No. of IS academics	No. of IS students
University of South Australia	12	>1 500
Flinders University	Not available	Not available
University of Adelaide	3	>500

IS at the University of South Australia

At the time the UniSA was founded, some members of antecedent organisations decided to form a School of Information Systems within the new Business Division. Some of these staff members came from the Institute of Technology, while others had previously been a part of the South Australian College of Advanced Education. One study participant commented:

> We had all been in Business Schools teaching IS topics. We believed it worthwhile to have an IS concentration and develop the area academically as it was useful for the uni and the citizens of SA. At the time IS had quite a high profile. I was a founding member along with approx 21–23

others. We were the first and only School of Information Systems in SA. Flinders University had nothing in the way of IS and Adelaide University had one subject in Computing Science. We developed a range of undergraduate programs which [was] very well received.'

In 1996, the university reduced funding to the school, which resulted in staff cuts and redundancies. In 1996, there were cuts across the Business Division, and IS staff were advised that the annual budget had been reduced from $2.8 million to $1.8 million. The group had significant financial problems at the time, although it had developed a successful industry placement program with about 40 industry partners and earned a very positive reputation for its engagement with industry. At least one respondent (now retired) believes the group had a mixed relationship with the Division of Business from its inception, claiming there were several attempts to move the discipline out of the Business Division. In that year, the IS discipline group was moved into an accounting and IS school, which also included a group of staff from the administrative management area, which had originally taught secretarial studies and was slowly evolving towards a new focus on the management of corporate administrative functions.

In 2004, a review of the Division of Business resulted in the restructuring of all the schools within that division. This review, combined with a strategic university-wide decision to combine all computing-related disciplines into one school, led to the IS discipline as a whole being transferred to the School of CIS, located within the Division of Information Technology, Engineering and the Environment, which had existed for the life of the university and was already a very much larger school. This merger has resulted in a large and vibrant computing school, based on two campuses (and with teaching offerings on four campuses), with a wide variety of programs covering the full range from computer science through software engineering and IT to IS.

Although some respondents believe that the IS group is smaller and less visible as a result of this merger, it now has three full-time IS professors and one associate professor—in addition to two European adjunct professors who are also IS focused. The combined School of CIS launched a Bachelor of Information Systems for the first time in the history of the university after the merger, and all degree programs offered by the school were reviewed and completely revamped, with significant changes taking place in all degree offerings.

The merger also allowed the UniSA to rationalise the location of the IS staff. Before the move to CIS, the majority of the IS discipline staff (12 academics) were based in the School of Accounting and Information Systems at the City West campus, which comprised three discipline areas: accounting, IS and administrative management. Some of the IS courses (those with an 'INFS' prefix) were taught by administrative management staff, while some of the administrative management courses were taught by IS staff. These blurred lines of control had simply evolved over time, but were rationalised at the time of the merger.

During the merger discussions, 11 of the 12 IS academic staff agreed to move to the new school and one of the former administrative management staff joined the group moving to CIS. Before the merger, some five IS academics were located in the 'old' CIS at the Mawson Lakes campus in the north of Adelaide, and their courses became part of the revised degrees offered by the enlarged, combined school.

The majority of the IS teaching takes place at the City West campus of the UniSA, where most of the IS staff are still located, with some (predominantly graduate) IS courses also being offered at Mawson Lakes. A number of the largest IS courses are also offered face to face at the Whyalla and Mt Gambier campuses, as well as being taught offshore as part of the transnational degrees being offered in Hong Kong and Malaysia.

The school has an industry advisory group, which has been very supportive of IS programs and has an excellent reputation with local business and with the public sector.

IS student and subject numbers at the University of South Australia

There is one major similarity between IS at the Universities of South Australia and Adelaide: both universities (as is common around Australia) offer a major, first-year subject to students enrolled in a business or commerce degree. In the case of the UniSA, this subject has an average annual enrolment of approximately 2000–2500 students and is taught over nine separate delivery channels (on-campus/off-campus in Adelaide; through Open University Australia; on-campus in Whyalla and Mt Gambier; as a service teaching offering through the business colleges of the South Australia Institute of Business and Technology [SAIBT] and EBIT; and on-campus in Hong Kong and Malaysia). Running a subject of this size through so many varying delivery methods is a major logistical exercise and involves two academic staff members. A senior member of teaching staff oversees the subject and provides the face-to-face and video-taped lectures, while a more junior member of staff is occupied full time as course manager, coordinating the tutors and off-site lecturers, tutorial material and coordinating/overseeing student contact activities.

Since many of the students enrolled in this subject are taking an accounting degree, the syllabus is influenced strongly by the requirements of the CPA, which accredits the Bachelor of Commerce degree. Nonetheless, this subject is designed and taught by full-time IS academics, who ensure that it provides a thorough grounding in IS for all business students.

Table 7.3 Course-work offerings within the School of CIS

Undergraduate courses offered	Postgraduate courses offered	No. of students enrolled in IS subjects
DBBI, DBEB, DBIN, DBIT, DBMS	DCMI, DGEC, DGMI, DMEC, DMIS, DMMI, LMCT	1 500 approx.

The bachelor degrees identified in Table 7.3 are all IS focused—DBIN is a complete Bachelor of Information Systems degree, while the other three are business degrees with an IS focus. The postgraduate offerings vary from being entirely IS focused (for example, DMMI) to having a major IS focus.

IS at the University of Adelaide

Information systems is located within the School of Commerce at the University of Adelaide and is considered a separate discipline with its own head. With a staff of only three (including the discipline head), IS is focused largely on the core foundation course for the accounting and business IT degrees. We were unable to interview the head of the discipline, and one of the staff members had arrived in South Australia only for the start of the first 2007 semester. The other staff member has been teaching IS for the past three and a half years and was a PhD student at the University of Adelaide before that appointment.

The IS subject is accredited by the CPA as a core component of the commerce degree and therefore has a large undergraduate enrolment (more than 500 students). At postgraduate level, IS is offered in the form of a number of elective subjects, with a current overall enrolment of about 250, including five Masters students and one PhD student. The university does not offer any degree majoring in IS and IS is regarded as a supporting area to other disciplines.

Interestingly, there was a 30 per cent growth in IS numbers in the first semester of 2007, which staff attributed to a combination of the recent lowering of the Tertiary Entrance Requirement (TER) and the university's status as a member of the Group of Eight. In addition, this growth reflects the increase in international students, particularly from China, studying IS.

Information systems at the University of Adelaide is of marginal status, reflected in the comparatively small number of staff and the lack of any IS degrees at either undergraduate or graduate levels. Although there is a compulsory IS subject for some degrees within the School of Commerce (generally for accounting students), its visibility as a discipline or field appears to be in decline at the University of Adelaide. Those teaching IS are strongly business oriented and are convinced of its supportive role within the school—and are not connected to the wider IS community, with the result that they are unaware of the discipline's struggle for survival in other universities. Unfortunately, no information could be gathered relating to the history of IS at this university so it is unclear whether IS has played a more important role in the past.

The final section of this chapter focuses on influences and issues specific to IS within South Australia. Much of this material relates to activities at the UniSA, because IS at the University of Adelaide is predominantly service teaching for the accounting students and is therefore driven by the needs of the accounting profession and its accreditation practices.

Issues for IS within South Australia

Characteristics of IS in the state

South Australia has very few corporate head offices; instead, it has a number of very innovative and successful smaller businesses working in the ICT sector. Even EDS, which had a sizeable representation in Adelaide under the former government (having won a contract to handle all government ICT outsourcing), has now 'right-shored' its South Australian operations to a significant extent, after the current state government's change of its outsourcing policy to one in which government ICT activities are outsourced predominantly to interstate and offshore companies. The lack of a single minister responsible for ICT activities in the state (South Australia has six ministers who share the various aspects of the ICT field) has also helped to create an unusual profile for IS in the state—with many IS activities focused on the activities of imaginative and innovative small companies in such areas as computer gaming, defence or consultancy.

The major ICT group within South Australia is, of course, the defence industry. The decision to build 'smart ships' (air warfare destroyers) in Adelaide has bolstered the existing activities of many high-tech defence companies, which had been working with ASC (formerly the Australian Submarine Corporation) on the development of the Collins-class submarines.

The impact of local contingencies on IS education

Although the curriculum is naturally affected by industry requirements, IS academics also endeavour to provide industry leadership, rather than simply responding to industry demand.

Local demand does affect IT and IS teaching structure within the state, particularly in terms of content, because students must have certain skills to be employed by local and interstate businesses. It is, however, probably no more affected by industry than other applied disciplines, such as tourism or oenology.

The UniSA has made significant structural changes that affect the teaching of IS—specifically, the move of the IS group from the School of Accounting and Information Systems within the Division of Business, to the School of Computer and Information Science within the Division of Information Technology, Engineering and the Environment. This has enabled the development of a Bachelor of Information Systems degree (IS was formerly offered only as one alternative within the Bachelor of Business degree). As it is the only university in South Australia offering IS degrees, there is little (if any) political pressure on the school to provide any particular offerings, although the BBIS/MBIS program (a funded joint program with industry, which takes high performers and fast-tracks them via a combined academic/industry placement scheme) has had an influence on academic outcomes, as most of the brightest students choose this alternative in place of doing an Honours degree.

Like all other Australian states, South Australia has suffered from the ICT downturn in terms of local student numbers. Employment in South Australia in the ICT industry is particularly difficult because of the lack of large corporate head offices (the majority of which are still located in Sydney or Melbourne), and the current state government's decision to outsource major ICT developments to interstate and/or international companies has made this situation still more difficult. Many South Australian graduates are forced to seek work in other states, so that we are probably suffering more from the downturn than any other state in the sample. Recent moves to source staff for major Commonwealth government projects from South Australia are, however, likely to have a positive impact on student placements and have been welcomed warmly.

Recent events, such as the large defence contractor presence in South Australia and the South Australian government's memorandum of understanding with the defence studies arm of Cranfield University and the public policy and ICT programs of Carnegie Mellon University have the potential to be advantageous to all South Australian IS programs.

The extent to which IS is identified as a separate field of study

The University of Adelaide

The status of IS within the School of Commerce is complex and contradictory. Staff were unaware of funding issues affecting IS and did not feel its status was inferior to that of any other discipline within the school, with one member commenting, 'Status is what you make it. You have to earn it.' Information systems is not, however, listed as a separate discipline on the university web site under the School of Commerce and appears only as a separate area when conducting a search of staff and contacts within the school. Although one staff member definitely considered IS a discipline rather than a field, he was also keen to emphasise that IS was only a supporting course of management, accounting and marketing.

The location of IS within the School of Commerce appears to be unproblematic. The CPA broadly controls its curriculum and there is therefore little opportunity for substantial debate or change in its structure and content. It would appear that IS at the University of Adelaide confirms the view of IS as fragmented and lacking a 'set of shared assumptions and language' (Hirschheim and Klein 2006:94), which has led to its virtual dissipation within the School of Commerce.

The University of South Australia

In contrast, IS at the UniSA has a long and rich history originating from its development as part of the Graduate School of Management, through to its current incarnation in the School of Computer and Information Science. This reflects IS as a dynamic field, with a flexible identity referencing a plethora of academic disciplines (Markus 1999; Galliers 2006; Robey 2006). The shift in IS from the School of Business to the School of CIS signifies what Lyytinen and King (2006) refer to as a 'market of ideas' where free-flowing views regarding the management of information and affiliated technologies are exchanged. Instead of IS being fixed rigidly in its curriculum and research practices, it is positioned ideally as a more fluid concept capable of adapting to change and keeping abreast of industry.

In its former existence as part of the School of Accounting and Information Systems and in its current existence as part of the School of CIS, IS at the UniSA has been a component of a larger school; it has been many years since there was a School of Information Systems at the UniSA. To a large degree this can be traced to the comparative lack of local student interest in IS; the fact that neither the University of Adelaide nor Flinders University even bothers to offer IS at all provides further evidence for this atypical lack of interest, which pre-dates the current IS student crisis. This is in stark contrast with the West Australian situation, where all four of the universities offer an IS degree and see IS as an area of strategic importance. Since these two states have a number of common features (distance from the east coast 'power base' and a strong focus on the resource and agriculture sectors, for example), it is curious that such a markedly diverse attitude to the importance of IS has arisen over such a long period.

The move from the Business Division to the Division of Information Technology, Engineering and the Environment forced the UniSA IS group to think very carefully indeed about the composition of its degrees. The School of CIS went through a complete degree restructuring in 2004–05 and now has an entirely new suite of offerings right across the field of computing: CS/SE/IT/IS. This exercise also required the school to distinguish its offerings very carefully from those of administrative management, which teaches some of the material offered by the IS discipline in other universities; so awareness of the specific role of IS in the computing spectrum is probably focused more finely at the UniSA than it is at other universities.

Research in the IS domain is led by the three IS professors and their research groups (laboratories), as the majority of the other IS staff have still to complete their doctorates. The foci currently include requirements engineering/computer-supported cooperative work (CSCW) and electronic business/business information management, which are wide enough to include any members of staff interested in becoming involved in the Information Systems Laboratory (InSyL).

In terms of winning Australian-based competitive grants, it is obviously much more difficult for IS academics than for computer science academics in Australia—especially since the creation of National ICT Australia (NICTA), which absorbs the lion's share of Australian IT research funding.

Distinctive features of IS within the curriculum

The University of South Australia

The School of CIS endeavours to provide a suite of offerings that covers the entire computing spectrum, from computer science right through to IS. Degree programs therefore—at undergraduate and postgraduate level—offer a wide range of options. The school provides significant incentives for teaching and research; indeed, the School of CIS at the UniSA is well above average in terms of providing incentives for research.

The newly developed Bachelor of Information Systems is a broadly based degree, with specialisations possible in a variety of more finely targeted areas. At the graduate level, the school offers conversion Masters degrees, which are extremely popular with international students, as well as an advanced Masters degree in IS. It is also developing a range of double degrees, with the Business Division in areas such as accounting and marketing, and with the Health Studies and the Education, Arts and Social Sciences Divisions. Identifying niche markets is a major focus of IS strategic planning and is likely to become increasingly important over time.

A major new venture has been the industry-funded Chair of Business Information Management, which was established within the school at the start of 2006. Funded by State Records of South Australia, Fuji Xerox and the State Library of South Australia—and with significant support from the UniSA itself—the chair has been funded to provide an entirely new approach to education and research opportunities for the management of corporate information in the twenty-first century. The four partners are aware that the previously separate disciplines of library management, preservation, records and archival management and ICT are becoming increasingly intertwined. The sponsors have funded the development of a suite of new degree programs (a graduate certificate that began taking students in the first semester of 2007, and a graduate diploma and Masters beginning in 2008) to provide a holistic approach to the understanding of the impact of all these areas on the management of business information.

The University of Adelaide

The CPA accreditation means that major changes of content are rare and have to be approved by the CPA. Nevertheless, minor changes are made each semester to reflect technological developments and any variance in practice, with the proviso that there must be sufficient available literature to support these changes. This focus meant that IS staff believed firmly that IS belonged in the School of Commerce, rather than in the computing area. Although IS is also offered as part of a computing degree at the University of Adelaide (and there is sufficient overlap in content to award credit should a student wish to study in the School of Commerce), IS is perceived as relating primarily to management and the use of systems to meet business needs, rather than being focused on technical elements, which staff associate with computing. They do not regard IS as having its own terminology, seeing this as a 'bridge' between business and computing.

Distinctive features of IS in research

There is a paucity of local funding for research in any area of computing within South Australia, although the three universities work fairly well together and have created some highly successful technical joint ventures (for example, the SACITT group and the SABREnet initiative; see http://www.sabrenet.edu.au/ for details). With IS playing such a minor role in the state, obtaining funding for any research activities has proven extremely difficult (although, as noted a little later in this chapter, individual academic staff members have been able to build up highly successful one-to-one relationships at various levels of state and local government and therefore obtain focused funding for specific projects).

The 'branch office' status of Adelaide means that developing strategic relationships with private-sector companies is also very difficult. Most university partner companies must refer all decisions to their head offices—usually located in Sydney or Melbourne. Research partnerships with industry therefore tend to be focused on innovative small to medium-sized enterprises, rather than on the larger companies, which generally form the bulk of the partners for universities in other states.

Given the current lack of funding at the state and federal levels (with NICTA absorbing almost all the federal ICT funding, it is increasingly difficult to obtain government funding for IS within Australia at all), other avenues of research funding clearly need to be found. Industry support has been the logical place to look, together with less obvious sources of government funding (targeted funding of one sort or another).

The University of South Australia

The School of CIS has a very large PhD student population of approximately 60 students, 20 of whom are specifically IS students. As is the case in so many

Australian IS schools/departments, lack of sufficient numbers of PhD supervisors is a limiting factor. Qualified supervisors therefore tend to take on the maximum number of PhD students permitted by university regulations. This lack is, however, slowly becoming less critical, with a number of PhD graduates obtaining teaching positions within the school and taking on supervisory roles themselves. This has been especially beneficial within individual research laboratories, as newly qualified staff members expand the supervisory capacity and the laboratories' ability to develop grant applications.

The school has one major research 'centre', which is funded by the university to support research activities, the Advanced Computing Research Centre (ACRC), which, in turn, supports a number of research 'laboratories' (the term is taken from MIT's approach to grouping researchers). Inevitably, there is some overlap between the activities of many of these laboratories, but two of them are primarily IS focused: the Information Systems Laboratory (InSyL), a solely IS-focused 'broad church' group; and the Strategic Information Management Laboratory (SIML), which has a strong interest in IS. There are two further laboratories—Health Informatics and Enterprise Security—which have at least a partial IS focus, as well as some interaction with the IS discipline group. Table 7.4 summarises the research foci of the two major IS research groups.

Table 7.4 Research group foci within the School of CIS at the University of South Australia

School of CIS Information Systems Research Laboratory foci	
InSyL	SIML
Socio-organisational systems	Data acquisition
Business information management	Data quality
Education	Interoperability standards
E-business/e-commerce	Knowledge management
Decision support and knowledge management	Data warehousing and data mining
IS methodology	Data security

InSyL (Information Systems Laboratory). The Information Systems Laboratory focuses on the impact of IS within organisations and society more broadly. Established in 2005, InSyL investigates the implications of ICT innovations and the ways in which organisations and individuals might capitalise on them. Some of the issues being researched include the digital divide, e-business innovations and business models, requirements engineering, evaluation methods, e-learning, creativity, nomadic computing and e-health.

SIML (Strategic Information Management Laboratory). SIML researches areas relating to information management in contemporary business. Major areas of research currently under investigation centre on data-quality issues and asset management. Industry partners include SA Water, the Defence Science and Technology Organisation (DSTO), the Centre for Integrated Engineering Asset Management and cooperative research centres.

The University of Adelaide

Staff are aware of the marginal status of IS within the School of Commerce, yet do not feel its effects personally. Their perception is that they are able to pursue their own areas of research interest without funding pressures influencing the direction of that research. Like most academic staff in any institution, however, there is a constant pressure for research output, with one member describing his daily duties as a constant 'juggling act' between research, teaching and administrative work. This pressure, combined with his relative inexperience, might explain his lack of appreciation of the status of IS within the university and across the theoretical debates within the IS discipline more broadly.

Key figures in IS education within South Australia

A number of industry players have had an influence on the IS curriculum in past decades and, of course, past and present heads of school have also had an impact; Terry Robbins-Jones, who founded the School of Information Systems at the UniSA, was particularly influential during the 1990s.

Vignette—Terry Robbins-Jones

The words mentioned most often by those who contributed to this vignette of Robbins-Jones are 'inspiring' and 'visionary'. He headed the first and only School of Information Systems in South Australia when the UniSA was established in 1991. Originally from England, Robbins-Jones held an MBA from Cranfield University. He worked at the South Australian Institute of Technology and the University of New England before his appointment to the UniSA School of Information Systems. Robbins-Jones had a background in small business and was passionate about IS, insisting that people and process were more important than the technology itself. He brought this perspective to his teaching and research as well as authoring a number of publications for small business. In addition, Robbins-Jones served on a number of committees, including the executive of the Australian Computer Society (ACS).

With an eye for innovation, Robbins-Jones earnestly championed the school within the university, the community and internationally. He strongly maintained that academic programs should meet the needs of business so he formed close links with industry, meeting with them every three months to keep the school's curriculum relevant. He believed that students needed a combination of business and technical skills, and to that end he established a number of postgraduate courses incorporating both aspects. A doctoral research centre was created within the school, marrying the approaches of doctoral education from the United Kingdom and the United States to provide a foundation for research and a supportive group environment.

Robbins-Jones always encouraged and supported new ideas, as exemplified when the School of Information Systems won an award in 1994 for the best new IT installation for its Enterprise Process Improvement (EPI) Centre. The EPI Centre consisted of an electronic meeting room—one of only three in Australia and New Zealand at the time—and an Oracle laboratory. It was a focus for research, consultancy and knowledge development within the university and fostered business and industry links. In fact, the business community donated most of the hardware and was its most frequent clientele. Seizing opportunities to promote IS, Robbins-Jones ensured that the school became a university alliance partner with SAP. He also introduced the teaching of Oracle and Visual Basic to the curriculum.

Perhaps his most important quality was the way he inspired and encouraged his staff to combine their research with their academic aspirations. Robbins-Jones believed his people were his greatest asset and promoted a philosophy of self-actualisation. He thought staff performed at their best if they were supported in following their passions and expertise. Once convinced of the validity of a proposition, Robbins-Jones would give his unequivocal support to realise its fruition. His ability to inspire staff contributed to the successful amalgamation of three diverse cultures of people when forming the School of Information Systems. Fundamentally, the school incorporated academics from management, business computing and administrative systems and they all had their own way of doing things. Under Robbins-Jones' leadership, these disparate groups cooperated and united to create an IS school that boasted high standards and academic integrity.

In sum, Robbins-Jones is remembered as a very affable and dynamic man who was evangelical about IS. His contribution to IS in this state remains indelible.

Review of findings

It has been quite difficult to collect reliable data about the state of IS in South Australia and impossible to make any intrastate comparisons among the three local universities in the state. Only the UniSA has a significant IS discipline operating across the breadth of academic activity: IS teaching, scholarship and research.

The IS discipline at the UniSA has quite a long history in relative terms, as it was created at the time of the university's own formation from its antecedent institutions in 1991. Although the IS discipline within the UniSA has been subject to organisational changes, it has remained an influencing discipline and, notwithstanding the cyclical oscillations of student demand for IT programs in general, it appears to have remained strong and to have held a high professional profile within the state throughout its history.

Although there is not sufficient evidence to support the contention that the IS discipline in South Australia is fully mature in the sense of Ridley's (2006) framework, it clearly meets a number of her level-two criteria. There is strong evidence that a clear 'core body of knowledge' exists, albeit in the only university that claims an IS discipline; and academics in the discipline share a 'unique symbol system'—another criterion of Ridley's framework identifying the discipline as mature. Furthermore, the 'key research and teaching of IS topics' suggest a well-established discipline, with a recognised international profile.

Clearly, then, the IS discipline in South Australia meets some (but not all) of the criteria in Ridley's framework, providing some evidence of the maturity of the IS discipline in South Australia, but raising a number of fascinating questions. The interviews with active IS discipline members have suggested that the state's unique qualities—the focus on resource, agriculture and defence sectors; the lack of large companies to provide substantial graduate employment possibilities and to drive research in certain directions; and the lack of a single state minister responsible for ICT—have played a large part in South Australia's unusually low level of academic interest in IS. The only other state similar to South Australia in terms of population and climate—Western Australia—has a significantly greater academic focus on the IS discipline, with four universities all offering directly competing IS degrees.

Although there is considerable debate about what constitutes, or what should constitute, the core content of IS, it is generally accepted that IS draws on a range of disciplines for its methods and research practices (Avison and Elliot 2006). While some see this as a weakness in the identity of IS, others view it as a strength in uniquely qualifying IS to 'offer essential insights and perspectives' into the 'complex and fragmented emergence of IT artifacts' and 'their computational capabilities and cultural meanings' (Orlikowski and Iacono 2001). It could well be that South Australia's limited range of core foci for ICT provides the major explanation for this state's unusual IS profile.

Limitations and future research

Clearly, this study suffers from a lack of sufficient data from which to draw meaningful conclusions. It is clear that only one of the three universities in the state has a distinct IS discipline and, while enough data have been gathered from the UniSA to draw some interesting and thought-provoking conclusions, this study has formed something of an exception to the rule, rather than contributing to the overall picture of the IS discipline in Australia. At the very least, however, IS academics at the UniSA have the ability to make a significant contribution to the further development of the discipline.

Further work in the form of a longitudinal study of this development would provide far richer insights into the trajectory of IS' ability to reach maturity as a discipline.

References

Avison, D. and Elliot, S. 2006, 'Scoping the discipline of information systems', in J. L. King and K. Lyytinen (eds), *Information Systems: The State of the Field*, John Wiley & Sons, Chichester, England, pp. 3–18.

Dixon-Woods, M., Agarwal, S., Jones, D., Young, B. and Sutton, A. 2005, 'Synthesising qualitative and quantitative evidence: a review of possible methods', *Journal of Health Services Research & Policy*, vol. 10, no. 1, pp. 45–53.

Galliers, B. 2006, 'Change as crisis or growth? Toward a trans-disciplinary view of information systems as a field of study: a response to Benbasat and Zmud's call for returning to the IT artifact', in J. L. King and K. Lyytinen (eds), *Information Systems: The State of the Field*, John Wiley & Sons, Chichester, England, pp. 147–62.

Hirschheim, R. and Klein, H. 2006, 'Crisis in the IS field? A critical reflection on the state of the discipline', in J. L. King and K. Lyytinen (eds), *Information Systems: The State of the Field*, John Wiley & Sons, Chichester, England, pp. 71–146.

Lyytinen, K. and King, J. L. 2006, 'Nothing at the center?: academic legitimacy in the information systems field', *Information Systems: The State of the Field*, John Wiley & Sons, Chichester, England, pp. 233–66.

Markus, M. L. 1999, 'Thinking the unthinkable: what happens if the IS field as we know it goes away?', in W. L. Currie and B. Galliers (eds), *Rethinking Management Information Systems*, Oxford University Press, Oxford, pp. 175–203.

Orlikowski, W. J. and Iacono, S. 2001, 'Desperately seeking the "IT" in IT research: a call to theorizing the IT artifact', *Information Systems Research*, vol. 12, no. 2, pp. 121–34.

Ridley, G. 2006, 'Characterising information systems in Australia: a theoretical framework', *Australasian Journal of Information Systems*, vol. 14, no. 1, pp. 141–62.

Robey, D. 2006, 'Identity, legitimacy and the dominant research paradigm: an alternative prescription for the IS discipline', in J. L. King and K. Lyytinen (eds), *Information Systems: The State of the Field*, John Wiley & Sons, Chichester, England, pp. 183–90.

Whitley, R. 1984, *The Intellectual and Social Organization of the Sciences*, Clarendon Press, Oxford, UK.

Yin, R. K. 2003, *Case Study Research: Design and Methods*, 3rd Edn, Sage Publications, Thousand Oaks.

8. The information systems discipline in Tasmania

Gail Ridley
School of Accounting and Corporate Governance
University of Tasmania

Abstract

This chapter reports on a study that examined the information systems (IS) discipline in Tasmania. The study draws on a theoretical framework reported earlier in this volume. The study aimed to characterise IS at the University of Tasmania, as well as to investigate the relationship between the impact of local contingencies on the IS discipline and its degree of professionalism, within the Tasmanian context. Data were collected through a qualitative survey with seven influential academics associated with the discipline at the university, and from statistical sources. The findings suggest that an inverse relationship exists between the impact of local factors and the degree of professionalism in this setting. A surprising finding was that the relationship found varied for research and teaching issues. As the structural location of the School of Information Systems changed from 2008, two different perspectives on the relationship between IS and computing at the University of Tasmania are presented, and vignettes are provided of two academics who have had an influence on IS in the past. The forthcoming structural relocation of IS at the university is a demonstration of the degree of change experienced in the discipline.

Figure 8.1 Location of Tasmania within Australia

Introduction

The current chapter reports on a study of the state of the IS discipline in the only university in Tasmania, and draws on a theoretical framework outlined in an earlier chapter in this volume. The theoretical construct that guides this investigation will not be restated. This study is one of a series of similar studies undertaken in each Australian state and the Australian Capital Territory, and reported on elsewhere in this volume. This chapter extends on an earlier publication, published in the *Australian Journal of Information Systems* (Ridley 2006).

Tasmania is a unique state in Australia as it has only a single university, which is one of the oldest universities in the country. The University of Tasmania (UTAS) was established in 1890 in Hobart. In 1991, the university merged with the Tasmanian State Institute of Technology in Launceston, forming a second campus, in the north of the state. Then in 1995, the North-West Centre was opened in Burnie, which was renamed the Cradle Coast Campus in 2005. In 2008, the integration of the UTAS and the Australian Maritime College took place. Although the UTAS has just more than 12 000 students, it offers one of the widest selections of courses in Australia (University of Tasmania 2007), including 15 within the discipline of IS.

Aims of the study

This study aims to characterise the state of the IS academic discipline in the UTAS, and also contribute to a better understanding of the same discipline in universities throughout Australia. Consequently, the data gathered for the study will be analysed at three levels. Table 8.1 sets out the three levels.

Table 8.1 Three levels of analysis discussed in the study

Covered in this paper	Level	Scope
	1	Descriptive analysis using quantitative and qualitative sources
	2	Examines whether an inverse relationship exists between the impact of local contingencies on the discipline and the degree of professionalism
	3	Cross-case analysis drawing on theoretical framework

The first level of analysis will be reported in this current chapter and provides a descriptive examination of IS at the UTAS from qualitative and quantitative sources. The second level of analysis will also be reported in this chapter, and aims to examine in the Tasmanian IS academic context the postulation contained within the theoretical framework that an inverse relationship exists between the impact of local contingencies on a discipline and its degree of professionalism.

At the third level of analysis, some of the data gathered for the current study will be utilised for a cross-case analysis, and reported elsewhere. The cross-case analysis will draw on the remainder of the theoretical framework, which contends that a discipline will establish over time with the development of mechanisms of control and a core body of knowledge. This component of the theoretical framework cannot be investigated in a single case, as cross-regional analysis is required on such issues as key IS research and teaching topics, and whether a unique symbol set exists for the discipline. Moreover, some Australian longitudinal data will be needed at this third level.

Consistent with the content of the other state reports, the following issues have been examined within Tasmanian IS academia:

- the extent to which IS is/was impacted on by local contingencies
- the extent to which IS is/was identified as a separate field at the university
- the distinctive features of the IS curriculum at the university
- the distinctive features of IS research at the university
- the perception of the key people in the region who have had an impact on IS at the UTAS.

Changes to the structural placement of the School of Information Systems at the UTAS were first proposed in 2006—for implementation in 2008—and involved a closer relationship between the IS and computing disciplines. Consequently, another aim of this chapter was to consider different perspectives of the relationship between the two disciplines, as provided by a senior academic from each discipline at the UTAS. A further aim of the chapter was to present vignettes of two academics who were influential on the IS discipline at the university in past years.

Background

The reader is referred to an extensive review of the literature on the development of disciplines that has been provided in the earlier framework chapter of this volume. The methodology used for the current study is presented next.

Methodology

The Tasmanian case study was based on a detailed case-study protocol developed by the Queensland study team members.

Before the two schools merged, an open-ended questionnaire was e-mailed as an attachment to the participants after piloting. Where a response had not arrived within the time frame indicated for the return of the questionnaire, contact was again made with the academic, either in person or by e-mail, to encourage them to respond.

Eight academics who were currently closely involved with IS at the UTAS, or who had been in the past, were approached to participate in the survey. Of these, five were currently involved in either IS teaching or research, or both, at the university in Information Systems. Of the remaining three academics, two were working as IS academics outside Tasmania, while the third was employed in an allied discipline elsewhere at the UTAS at the time the data were collected. Of the participants, four had been employed as a head of school or in a more senior position. The three participants no longer working with IS academics at the UTAS were known internationally in IS or an allied discipline. Although the author of this chapter was also a former member of the School of Information Systems at the UTAS, her views were not included in the data collection and care was taken to try to exclude them from the analysis. This was done by having another person trained in IS research methods categorise the data after they had been stripped of identifying characteristics, and, where the classification differed, agreement was reached after discussion.

The survey method was used as some of the participants were located in other states or nations. An interview was, however, conducted with one of the participants. Some of the responses took participants up to two hours to complete. Consequently, the survey and interview captured broad perceptions of the state of IS at the UTAS, as well as points of differentiation and distinctive characteristics of IS at that university. Existing statistical and archival material were also collated to supplement the data obtained from the participants, and to facilitate some degree of triangulation. After the chapter was written, the original participants were invited to comment on it. Five participants took up this invitation.

A thematic analysis process was followed, allowing the integration of the qualitative data collected from participants and the quantitative data collated from other sources (Dixon-Woods et al. 2005). Although thematic analysis can be data driven, in this study the themes were driven by those in the theoretical framework referred to earlier. The discussion reported in the findings section below was 'weighted towards themes that appear to have a high level of explanatory value', rather than reflecting how frequently the themes were reported (Dixon-Woods et al. 2005:47).

The text relating to each question was examined for themes arising from the framework. The themes, and issues arising from the themes, have been presented below, grouped into the five major categories set out earlier. Statistical and archival data have been incorporated into the discussion relating to the themes, where relevant. The discussion of the themes in the section below presents the findings of the descriptive examination of IS at the UTAS from qualitative and quantitative sources, and forms the first level of analysis for this study.

After discussion of the themes, two tables were prepared to analyse the data at the second level. The second-level analysis examines whether an inverse relationship exists between the impact of local contingencies on a discipline and its degree of professionalism, in the Tasmanian IS academic context. In order to do this, the impact of local contingencies on IS teaching and research at the UTAS, and its degree of professionalism, were each independently categorised by two researchers as high, medium or low. Consistent with the previous framework chapter, professionalism was regarded as having high task certainty, routinisation of activities and a clear division of labour. Where a discipline was not highly professionalised, however, the control of work process would be decentralised, with limited routinisation of tasks (Whitley 1984).

In addition to the data collected in the manner described above, a senior academic from the School of Information Systems at UTAS provided updated information in mid-2007 on the school's research and teaching directions. Also, two senior academics were approached to comment on the merger of the schools of IS and Computing, and its implications, from their perspective. Two vignettes on senior academics, linked to IS at the UTAS in the past, were also solicited and included in this chapter.

Analysis and findings: level one

This section first presents demographic characteristics of the respondents, as well as a discussion of the administrative placement of the School of Information Systems and the size of the IS presence at the UTAS. The findings and discussion follow, relating to the five common themes listed earlier.

Respondent characteristics and IS administrative placement and size

Responses were received from all but one of the people contacted. The replies were far from cursory and enabled personalised, reflective and deep responses, beyond what was likely to be obtained if all the data had been collected via interview. The demographic characteristics of respondents appear in Table 8.2.

Table 8.2 Demographic details of survey participants

Gender	Male	Female		
	5	2		
PhD held	Yes	No		
	5	2		
Discipline of PhD	IS	CS[a]		
	3	2		
Age (estimated)	40–50	51–60	61–70	
	2	3	2	
Current position	Professor	Associate professor	Senior lecturer	Lecturer
	3	2	1	1

[a] CS = computer science

Although the UTAS introduced a major in information technology (IT) about 1987, it was only about 1992 that a recognisable IS program was introduced. Before January 1997, the academic discipline of IS was co-located with computing in the Department of Computer Science, in the Faculty of Science and Engineering. The School of Information Systems was formed in January 1997, and was located administratively within the Faculty of Commerce (from 2006, the Faculty of Business). The School of Information Systems is one of four schools located within the faculty, the others being Management, Accounting and Corporate Governance, and Economics and Finance. In 2005, the school delivered IS units at six locations: Hobart, Launceston and the Cradle Coast Campus in Tasmania, Shanghai and Fuzhou in China and Jakarta in Indonesia.

In 2005, 17 staff members were employed either full-time or part-time, and based in the School of Information Systems. Of these, 13 were academic (one part-time), while two undertook research positions. All but 11 academic staff members were based in Hobart, two were located in Launceston and no staff member was based permanently at the Cradle Coast Campus, or in Shanghai, Fuzhou or Jakarta. Table 8.3 sets out the staff and teaching locations.

In semester two 2005, the school had 1010 students based in the six locations, which represented about 800 equivalent full-time student units (EFTSU) in total. Eight undergraduate programs existed at that time, four graduate course-work programs and a PhD program. Further course-work graduate programs were introduced in 2006. The programs on offer at the School of Information Systems as of the end of 2005, and as of mid-2007, have been set out in Appendix 1.

Table 8.3 Summary of staffing and teaching centres in 2005

UTAS teaching locations	Hobart	Launceston	Cradle Coast	Shanghai, Fuzhou, Jakarta
Academic staff	11	2	0	0
General staff	4	0	0	0

It was first proposed in 2006 that the School of Information Systems should merge with the School of Computing from the Faculty of Science, Engineering and Technology. Planning for the merger started in 2007, with the new merged school operating from the start of 2008.

Impact of local contingencies

The next section sets out the extent to which IS was believed by the survey participants to be impacted on by local contingencies at the UTAS.

Curriculum and teaching issues

The multi-campus operation of the university within Tasmania, and the associated delivery of IS in those three centres, was seen to have come about, at least in part, by the influence of Tasmanian politicians. A participant referred to the difficulty in adjusting the staff profile to student demand, which varied by campus, and balancing this issue and others due to funding pressures.

Course advisory committees were another way that local perspectives had impacted on the courses in the past. These committees, which met irregularly, were established for the IS programs when the School of Information Systems began in 1997. Although course advisory committees had provided feedback on the curriculum of the Bachelor of Information Systems and Honours programs, they did not influence their design or development significantly. The Master of Information Systems (MIS) program was, however, designed and introduced as a response to demand for graduate professional development in IS from the Tasmanian state government. The MIS Course Advisory Committee played a significant role in the curriculum and delivery modes for that program between 1997 and 1999. In contrast, the Bachelor of Information Systems degree curriculum was influenced strongly by the broader issues of national published curricula, which included IS'95 (Longnecker et al. 1995) and the Information Resources Management Association (IRMA 1996).

Another study participant commented on a need for greater involvement of course advisory committees in more recent years to update the curriculum, but noted the introduction of logistics to the undergraduate curriculum in the past few years as a response to external demand. Two other respondents saw little evidence of the school's curriculum responding to local external factors. One of these participants noted, however, that the school had responded to international demands in a considerable way, making reference to how the curriculum had changed to accommodate Department of Immigration and Multicultural and Indigenous Affairs (DIMIA) requirements and those of the international market.

The nature of the IS programs varied considerably, depending on location. Traditionally, the majority of the school's students were located in Hobart, while Launceston had the second-largest proportion of students. Few students were based in Burnie, and it has not been possible to complete an undergraduate IS degree there. Since the school started to deliver IS into Shanghai, however, the distribution of students by campus changed dramatically. For example, as of November 2005, 75 per cent of the total EFTSU of 800 (1010 students) of the School of Information Systems were international students. Although some of the international students studied onshore at Tasmanian campuses, 61 per cent of the school's total EFTSU were enrolled offshore in China. A total of 59 per cent of the school's EFTSU were enrolled in a Bachelor of Information Systems degree in Shanghai, while 38 per cent were enrolled in a range of programs in Hobart, which are listed in Appendix 8.1. All graduate programs were delivered onshore, although for the first time in 2006 students from the first cohort to graduate with a UTAS undergraduate degree from Shanghai undertook an IS course-work Masters degree based in Hobart.

In recent years, the teaching has become more centralised into the Hobart campus. A limited number of units were offered at Launceston, and fewer were available at the Cradle Coast Campus. Increased use has been made of video-conferencing and other electronic means of delivery into Launceston and the Cradle Coast Campus. The teaching focus within an individual unit did not, however, vary by campus. No Honours or Masters programs were offered in centres outside Hobart, although they had been offered in Launceston in past years.

Since the School of Information Systems was first established, emphasis had been placed on consistent teaching across the campuses, and moderation of assessment across the multiple campuses in Tasmania. This aim was achieved by using a single point of course development for each unit, while employing teaching teams that operated across all campuses. Moreover, either single points of assessment were utilised for each unit or team marking was used that spanned the centres. Although some divergence in delivery modes and assessment occurred in Shanghai and Fuzhou since the IS programs were introduced there in 2003, very similar content had been retained in all units across all centres.

Research issues

The research program has not been controlled centrally within the school, resulting in some variation in the nature of the research conducted within Tasmania. For example, there were few common topics between researchers in recent years other than an interest in e-commerce. This interest was seen by one participant to be related to the era rather than a consciously adopted focus. Another participant made reference to an early emphasis on e-commerce in the School of Information Systems, from a curriculum and a research perspective. The same participant identified the establishment of the Tasmanian Electronic Commerce Centre, originally located within the School of Information Systems in Hobart, as a driver for this emphasis. A comment was made about a perceived need to focus on fewer research areas.

A decision to emphasise qualitative research methods taken in the past was still apparent in 2005, with most Honours and PhD projects using qualitative techniques. In the same year, however, the school in the centres outside Tasmania undertook no research. One participant commented that the UTAS did not have a distinct research identity, while several references were made to the need for a greater research culture in the school. This influence and others were seen to act against the development of research collegiality, which also hindered research. Many staff members were early career researchers who were still working towards completing their PhD or gaining expertise and recognition within their research area. Other participants referred to the lack of qualified supervisors available in the school, and the situation in which one or two staff members supervised relatively large numbers of PhD students—in particular, Dr Paul Turner. The appointment of staff members who had studied within the school led to an emphasis on one research method, which was seen as problematic by one participant.

Another local contingency to act on research undertaken by the School of Information Systems was the funding obtained by Senator Brian Harradine and used in part to set up the Telstra Broadband Laboratory. The laboratory became the focus of some of the school's research for a period. One participant referred to the proposal to amalgamate all faculty research in a single school, while another participant pointed to the role of the Faculty of Business in identifying research areas. The appointment of the Woolworths Chair in Information Systems in 2004 was described as a consequence of political pressure on the state government to relax shop trading hours.

Other evidence was provided for the way the nature of research conducted in the school had been influenced by local contingencies. One participant pointed to the advantages of researching in a state capital with a small population. Several references were made to the range of local industry contacts that the school drew on, with many student projects based within the community. The small size of Tasmania had resulted in federal and state government agencies being relatively easy to access. In the past, both tiers of government were supportive of research that used their organisations for data collection. As a consequence, the School of Information Systems focused on applied projects with relevance to the industry and government bodies that participated in such research. As another example, the limited number of large private-sector organisations in Tasmania had directed research efforts to the small to medium-sized enterprises (SMEs) and public-sector environments. The minimal extent of manufacturing carried out in the state had also acted to limit research undertaken through the school in this setting.

Finally, it was claimed that IT was more likely to be dealt with by accountants in the state rather than by senior IT staff, while greater use of consultants and outsourcing in Tasmania was reported. All three of the last characteristics were seen to impact on research undertaken in the School of Information Systems.

Comparison with other disciplines

A degree of divergence was seen in the views of participants on whether IS was affected by local factors to a greater or lesser degree than for other disciplines at the UTAS. Several participants saw IS being affected by local factors to a similar extent as the other disciplines within the university, while another commented that little attention was paid to all computing-related disciplines.

Two participants commented that in comparison with other disciplines at the UTAS, the volatility of the IS discipline meant that there was a greater need to maintain the currency of the curriculum and to give students access to current technology, which had resource implications.

IS as a separate field

This section considers the extent to which IS has been identified as a separate field at the UTAS.

The extent to which IS has a separate identity

The introduction of IS within the Department of Computer Science at the UTAS was an initiative of Dr Michael Rees. After his departure, Dr (later Professor) Chris Keen took over the role of IS advocate. Since then IS has had a separate identity in the Faculty of Business, and communication with Computing has been reduced, which, according to one participant, has been to the loss of both schools.

Although IS at the UTAS was seen by the participants to have a separate identity, this characteristic had taken more than 10 years to achieve. Information systems has been acknowledged formally as a single field of study and research within the university since January 1997, with the formation of the School of Information Systems. From about 1994, IS was associated mainly with a group operating within the Department of Computer Science at the Hobart campus. Towards the end of that year, IS was identified formally as a distinct teaching field within the Department of Computer Science. There was, however, also a smaller IS teaching and research group within the Department of Applied Computing at Launceston. Referring to the time in which IS was establishing itself at the UTAS, a participant who had been associated with the school for many years commented that most discipline areas at the university were unclear about the nature of the field. Another participant now employed outside Tasmania saw relevance as the key for survival where confusion existed about the nature of the discipline, and where opportunities and the professional community were small.

Distinguishing IS from business and computer science

In 1996, extensive discussion occurred between the staff of the proposed School of Information Systems and what were at that time the departments of Computer Science and Applied Computing. A participant reported that teaching and research topics were readily grouped into those suggested at that time by the Australian Computer Society (ACS). The topics were divided into the technical aspects of computer programming, software engineering, networking, computer systems engineering and computer science, and for IS, the business and social aspects of the application of information and communications technology (ICT). The same distinction largely continued until 2008.

In general, until recently, the participants saw computing and IS as having different perspectives, with limited communication between the two disciplines; however, they saw less to distinguish IS from business, with IS being concerned with the management of IT and not as broadly based as business. The IS units offered limited technical content, which was found in the School of Computing. One participant saw pressure on computing schools to shift towards IS teaching areas, in response to falling student enrolments. As evidence of this claim, database management has been introduced by the School of Computing in some units in recent years, delivered by their own staff members. One participant saw the demise of service teaching to be partly responsible for this last development.

One participant pointed to current pressures that act against IS groups continuing as independent schools at the UTAS and elsewhere, foreshadowing the amalgamation of IS with computing at the UTAS in early 2008.

Comparative status of IS academics

Four participants believed that IS academics had a similar status to business and computing academics at the UTAS. A comment was made that while IS and business academics had the same status, academics from schools situated within the Faculty of Science and Technology had higher status, due to the better research profile in that faculty at the university—the School of Computing was located in the Faculty of Science and Technology at the UTAS. Another participant, however, compared the size of the Schools of Computing and Information Systems when considering the status of each. The Schools of Computing and Information Systems had similar EFTSU numbers as of late 2005, with the former being the third-largest school and the latter the fourth-largest school in the university at that time. Finally, another participant considered IS academics to have a lower status than their colleagues in computing or management at the UTAS.

Comparative use of terminology

Most of the participants who responded to this question considered that IS terminology used at the UTAS would be broadly familiar to their business and computing colleagues. One person, however, believed that there was relatively little understanding of the conceptual base of IS among many staff in business. Another noted the limited contact between IS and computing staff before 2008, which, it was assumed, would make it difficult to assess the commonality in the terminology used by each group.

Features of IS curriculum and teaching

In the next section, the IS curriculum and teaching at the UTAS will be characterised.

The role of IS service teaching

As the School of Information Systems did not differentiate strongly between service and core teaching, there was less service teaching undertaken than in some other universities. For example, the same undergraduate IS units are offered within the Bachelor of Information Systems degree and its associated combined degrees as are available across all other degrees offered by the university. A number of students undertake IS units within business, economics, science, computing, arts and geomatics degrees. Information systems degrees accounted for approximately 80 per cent of the teaching load while other degrees account for approximately 20 per cent. What is regarded commonly as service teaching occurs only with the provision of two IS units within the geomatics degree.

A pressure that acts against service teaching occurring is the motivation of other disciplines to retain funding and, according to one participant, the limited value placed on the philosophies of other schools. There was no core IS unit in the university's MBA program, which was seen as worthy of note.

Distinctive themes and teaching styles

A focus on management and strategy was identified in the IS teaching at the UTAS, with less emphasis on technical issues. This focus incorporated the major themes of project management, data modelling, data management and electronic commerce. Oracle database management is taught to Oracle-certification level. Oracle is taught because of its use in the Tasmanian government—a major employer of IS graduates. At the undergraduate level there are three majors: systems development, e-business and management of IS. The approach taken in earlier years at the school, when professional development was integrated into the undergraduate teaching program, was seen as distinctive. This focus had, however, waned more recently. The business logistics unit taught at undergraduate level was also identified as distinctive. One participant commented that the IS teaching program at the UTAS was not significantly different from the range of topics taught elsewhere in Australia.

Relatively few suggestions were made regarding distinctive features of IS teaching at the UTAS, while one participant stated that no features of the teaching program were distinctive. Mention was made, however, of the significant use of discussion workshops and case studies in the school. Reference was made also to the individual attention provided to students, which was perceived to foster their confidence and encourage them to continue on to higher degrees. Another participant commented on the high quality of the flexible online support that was provided to support the teaching program.

Distinctive tools, techniques and technologies

Although one participant commented that there were no tools, techniques or technologies that were distinctive in the IS teaching at the UTAS, some techniques associated with teaching delivery were identified as distinctive, including what was perceived as an effective combination of face-to-face and online delivery. Reference was made to the sequential delivery style for units from Year One to Three, designed to facilitate the progression of student responsibility for their own learning. For example, in the later semesters of a degree many units de-emphasised lectures to communicate knowledge, and placed more reliance on online resources with consolidation of the knowledge in workshops.

Other teaching issues

A range of teaching-related issues was raised by the academics as important. Declining local enrolments was one such issue, and the associated very high international load was another. One participant linked declining enrolments to a perceived falling interest from young people in IT, and a negative image for the discipline. Reference was made also to the associated unbalanced distribution of the teaching program across six centres, particularly as the majority of the school's students were located in China as of late 2005.

Several participants commented on the need to monitor whether the programs delivered by the School of Information Systems remained relevant to current needs and trends. In particular, several participants remarked on the need to ensure that the school's IS graduates had access to the technical skills expected from employers. It was noted that in past years the school's staff had included people with expertise in advanced databases and networking, but more management-oriented staff had been appointed since that time. More recently, an attempt had been made to correct this perceived imbalance through recruitment of staff with specialist technical skills. One participant no longer working in the discipline suggested the school should consider a greater degree of reintegration with computer science—which later took place.

Changes planned for teaching and curriculum in the next three years

Finally, few changes to the nature of the IS teaching or the curriculum in the coming three years were identified; however, the new Masters programs introduced from 2006 were raised: ME-Business, ME-Business with a Specialisation and M-Logistics.

One participant foreshadowed a move for the school in future years away from IT and systems development to operations management and a business process focus that would require greater coverage of business-analysis methodologies. This change was regarded as a necessary response to falling enrolments.

Features of IS research

The features of IS research at the UTAS are discussed below.

Research output and funding

Although there was general recognition that the research output of school staff was relatively low, several participants identified that the contribution was skewed. The majority of publications were in national and international refereed conferences, with a limited number of quality journal publications. One participant no longer working at the UTAS saw an opportunity for researchers to target high-quality conferences and journals in order to obtain quality feedback. For this to happen it was identified that broadly accepted academic leadership and a unifying research culture would be required, enabling the development of research groups and the emergence of research strengths for the school.

One participant believed that in the late 1990s the school's research focused on rigorous interpretive research methodologies. At that time, it produced a series of quality PhD theses, evidenced by comments from staff from other schools in Australia and the later success of some of those PhD graduates.

The school did not have a strong history of attracting Australian Research Council (ARC) Discovery funding. The majority of the research funding obtained by IS in recent years has come from external, national competitive grants from the Smart Internet and Sustainable Tourism collaborative research centres and ARC Linkage grants. A limited number of the school's staff was involved in attracting these research funds. More recently, one staff member in particular had attracted considerable industry funding to the school, particularly in the area of e-health.

Small internal research grants have been made available by the Faculty of Business, while the university-wide Institutional Research Grants Scheme is designed to prepare staff for the future submission of ARC grants.

Balance between research and teaching and incentives for each

As teaching loads were high, participants perceived that pressure existed to push the balance away from research towards teaching. Some staff had a teaching and administrative load only, while several staff members had a 75–85 per cent research load. The majority of staff members were, however, expected to undertake teaching, research and administration.

Some participants perceived greater recognition was given for good teaching than for research at the university through processes such as teaching merit certificates, teaching development grants and evaluation of teaching and learning. At a faculty level, however, there has been a recent attempt to redress this through the introduction of research awards. Faculty funding is available to assist staff to travel to conferences, which needs to be combined with school professional development funding. A faculty scheme of seed funding to encourage a range of different forms of research was introduced several years ago. A comment was made that incentives for the conduct of quality research could be defined and implemented better. For example, the same participant perceived that highly productive research staff did not receive recognition or incentives through the distribution of research quantum income. The same participant considered that the Department of Education, Science and Training (DEST) point system was ineffective in challenging staff to undertake better research. The new approach of the federal government to research outcomes in Australian universities could, however, redress this situation.

Research and teaching targets for individual staff are set within the compulsory performance management scheme implemented at the UTAS. Promotion is linked to good research outcomes and, more recently, an alternative route to promotion has been introduced through the demonstration of quality teaching.

Conference attendance

It was believed that active researchers in the school would attend on average one to two conferences a year. In the past, the Australasian Conference of Information Systems (ACIS) has been popular with staff and research students because it provides researchers with opportunities to network. One participant, however, commented that attendance at ACIS by school staff had declined in recent years. ICIS, ECIS, HICSS, GITMA, IRMA and other topic-specific national or regional conferences have been attended occasionally by at least one staff member, while health care and security conferences have been popular.

Changes planned for IS research in the next three years

Finally, few comments were made on changes planned for research in the School of Information Systems in coming years. Associated with the relatively recent appointment of a Woolworths Chair in Information Systems at the school, several participants referred to a new focus on IT governance and business process management. This move was seen as having potential to benefit the school, and several comments related to a desire for the emergence of a collegial research culture. While a senior participant foreshadowed a limited research group culture for the future, based on the belief that it was not possible to 'bureaucratise IS research', another saw progress of the IS discipline at the UTAS as being linked to the future research performance of the school.

Key people who have had an impact on IS

The last section in the analysis and findings for level one (descriptive analysis, as outlined earlier) considers key people who have had an impact on IS at the UTAS. While a range of individuals was identified as having had an impact on IS at the UTAS, only two were mentioned by more than one participant. Professor Chris Keen was the individual mentioned most frequently. He was seen to be responsible for the inception of the School of Information Systems, and acknowledgement was made of his considerable entrepreneurial skills and vision. Reference was also made to his influence on some of the current staff members as their supervisor while they completed their PhD. The role of Professor Arthur Sale was also acknowledged for recognising the need to introduce a more applied course in ICT at the UTAS when he was Head of the Department of Computer

Science. Vignettes that set out the background and achievements of Professors Keen and Sale are provided below, as representative of those who have made a major contribution to IS in the state.

Vignette—Chris Keen

Chris Keen had a formative impact on the development of the IS discipline in Tasmania. Keen was with the UTAS for 29 years from 1978 to the end of 2006. He spent much of that time in the Department of Information Science, later Computer Science. In 1996, he became head of that department and was instrumental in the formation of the new School of Information Systems on 1 January 1997. He continued as the head of that school until 2004, and was appointed Professor of Information Systems in 1999.

Keen gained his PhD in the area of analytical modelling of database systems in 1979, and pursued a teaching and research career that focused on applications of IT in the areas of database systems, simulation, management of IS, business logistics and strategic alignment of ICT. From 1991, he actively developed teaching and research programs in IS.

A key aspect of Keen's career has been a continuing, strong involvement with industry and government agencies and the conscious need to represent and advance the ICT industry in Tasmania. This has taken the form of numerous consultancies, appointments to boards and a range of other joint developments with industry partners. As an example, in 1996 Keen was instrumental in conceptualising, gaining funding for and establishing the Tasmanian Electronic Commerce Centre (TECC). As a joint venture between the UTAS and the Tasmanian government, the TECC provided an ideal portal through which researchers in IS could interact meaningfully with SMEs—albeit on quite different time scales, and always to the mutual benefit of all parties. More recently, Keen has pursued a similar approach through active involvement with the regional development authority, Northern Tasmania Development, especially in support of the tourism industry.

Keen has been active on a number of government and professional boards, including the Information Resource Management Task Force (1992–93), the Intelligent Island Board (2000–03), the Tasmanian IT Industry Council (2001–02) and the Tasmanian Branch of the ACS.

A key aspect of Keen's approach to scholarship has been the need to inform teaching and research through professional activities. His belief is that relevance must always be maintained, together with the pursuit of quality of teaching and learning and rigour in the application of research methodologies.

His main research interests are in the modelling of IS, business logistics and IS. A key objective in the early 1990s was the rapid recruitment of a large number of postgraduate research students to develop a pool of expertise and provide a vibrant research culture. One career highlight has been the opportunity to work with highly gifted graduate research students as they complete their candidatures. Keen has successfully co-supervised 15 postgraduate research students.

Between 1990 and 1994, Keen was a member of the executive of the Computer Science Association. This involvement highlighted the need for a peak body to represent IS academia in Australia. Between 1995 and 1999, Keen was active in the establishment of the Australian Council of Professors and Heads of Information Systems (ACPHIS). He saw the need for such a group to work towards binding the IS community in Australia, and to provide a national voice for the discipline.

In late 2006, Keen left academia to undertaken full-time consultancy with industry and, paradoxically, to be free to engage more actively in IS research and development.

Vignette—Arthur Sale

Arthur Sale started working in the ICT field in 1963 as one of the hardest of hard computer scientists: an electronics engineer designing a new computer system at Philips NV in the Netherlands. He later worked at the University of Natal in South Africa before emigrating to Australia to become a senior lecturer at the University of Sydney. He later took up the Foundation Chair of Information Science at the University of Tasmania, where he has been ever since—apart from study leave and international research travel.

In 1988–90, he was elected chair of the University's Professorial Board. From 1993–99, he held the position of Pro-Vice-Chancellor (Information Systems) and was a member of the Vice-Chancellor's Executive, including spells as Acting Vice-Chancellor.

At the time of writing, Sale holds a position as Professor of Computing (Research) and is an Emeritus Professor of the UTAS. He holds the unusual record of having given nine graduation addresses. Until March 2007, he was the School of Computing's Graduate Research Coordinator, responsible for all PhD candidates.

The Department of Information Science that he founded in 1974 diversified over time, and with his encouragement began teaching IS topics under the initial leadership of Mike Rees, and later Chris Keen. After Sale left to become Pro-Vice-Chancellor, the department divided into two computer science and IS schools.

Sale graduated with a bachelor degree in electronics engineering *cum laude* in 1961, followed by a very early PhD in computer science in 1969. His thesis title was 'Accelerating the arithmetic of binary digital computers' and dealt mainly with problems of fast binary divisions. He has been known to describe himself as a 'living dinosaur' because he wrote several programs for his research on a vacuum-tube computer.

In his research, Sale has spanned the range of ICT activities, writing and researching on topics from silicon-chip designs through to the impact of new technology on society, the importance of open-access repositories to universities globally and scientometric measures of research impact.

On his arrival in Australia, Sale joined the ACS and was quickly drafted into the NSW Branch Executive. When he moved to Tasmania, he acted to initiate the Tasmanian branch and was its first vice-chair. He has continued to be active in the ACS, serving as Tasmanian Chair, member of the National Council and National Vice-President. Sale holds all three ACS badges for service to the society. He was Tasmania's first Fellow of the ACS and is also a Fellow of Engineers Australia.

His main research interests at present include bioinformatics and algorithms for carrying out operations on DNA and proteins, open access and the measurement of quality in research, and mobile computing and human interface technology, particularly in usability and impact. Sale presently supervises four PhD candidates, spanning these issues as well as visualisation of fish schools using sonar, and parallelisation optimisations.

His awards include the Australian National Committee on Computation and Automatic Control (ANCCAC) Prize for the best paper published on ICT in Australia in 2001—on the impact of wireless networking on broadband access—and the Vice-Chancellor's Award for Outstanding Community Achievement (Tasmania, 2006).

Others

Other individuals were mentioned by participants. Jeremy Firth and Stephen Haynes from the Tasmanian public sector were described as strong advocates for an IS program at the UTAS in the 1990s. Reference was also made to the contribution made by Cathy Urquhart and her role in the development of the first IS course at the UTAS, and John Lamp for his development of a web-based service for the Australasian and international IS community. Bob Godfrey's role within the ACS and his involvement with the development of IS curricula were also acknowledged. More recent contributions that were recognised included Paul Turner's strong engagement with industry, Peter Marshall's focus on research and Roy Barkas's role within Logica CMG in hiring IS graduates and providing assistance with research.

This section has presented the findings for level one, providing a descriptive examination of IS at the UTAS, drawing on qualitative and quantitative sources. The next section sets out the analysis and findings for level two of this study, and examines whether an inverse relationship could be identified between the impact of local contingencies on the IS discipline and the degree of professionalism within the UTAS setting.

Analysis and findings: level two

Figure 3.2 of the theoretical framework guiding the study—and presented in an earlier chapter—postulated an inverse relationship between the impact of local contingencies on the IS discipline and its degree of professionalism.

The impact of local contingencies at the School of Information Systems at the UTAS was evaluated by categorising the level-one data relating to research and teaching issues, including the variation in both by centre, into high, medium or low impact. Non-local factors were omitted. Where the categorisation by the second researcher differed, discussion took place until agreement was reached. Qualitative and quantitative data were considered, where relevant. This analysis is presented in Table 8.4.

Overall, it can be seen from Table 8.4 that local contingencies had a low to medium impact on curriculum and teaching issues, while they had a high to medium impact on research issues. Research was influenced particularly by local factors, with no issues recorded in the low range and few in the medium range. An analysis of the extent of professionalism of the IS discipline at the UTAS follows.

The degree of professionalism for research and teaching issues at the School of Information Systems in Hobart was also evaluated using the level-one data, employing the same method used for the evaluation of the impact of local contingencies. Professionalism requires high task certainty, routinisation of activities and a clear division of labour. The analysis is set out in Table 8.5.

Table 8.4 Classification of the impact of local contingencies on research and curriculum/teaching

Area	High	Medium	Low
IS curriculum and teaching issues	Three-campus delivery of IS in Tasmania influenced by politicians; Oracle taught because of its use in the Tasmanian government, the major employer of IS graduates	Funding pressures make adjusting staff profile to student demand difficult; Role of course advisory committees, particularly for MIS degree; Increased use of video-conferencing, WebCT for teaching at non-Hobart campuses; Some variation in delivery to Shanghai and Fuzhou.	Teaching focus does not vary by campus; Moderation undertaken across multiple campuses; Team marking across campuses; Single points of course development for each unit; Very similar unit content across all centres; Teaching fairly centralised in Hobart.
IS research issues	Research not controlled centrally; Few common topics; Early emphasis on electronic commerce (EC), influenced by Tasmanian EC Centre; Some research involvement in Telstra Broadband Lab, enabled through funding from Senator Harradine; IT sometimes dealt with locally by accountants; greater use of consultants and outsourcing; Small size of state means easy access to supportive government agencies; Limited large private sector and manufacturing organisations has emphasised SME and government research; Limited research culture; Appointment of Woolworths Chair in IS associated with political pressure on state government; Limited PhD supervisors; No research conducted in school centres outside Tasmania.	Common interest in electronic commerce in previous years; diverging justification for this provided; Emphasis on interpretive methods, but positivist approaches used and taught; Faculty influence on research topics and structure.	

Table 8.5 suggests that IS curriculum and teaching activities had a high to medium level of professionalism at the UTAS, while research activities had a low to medium degree of professionalism.

Table 8.5 Classification of features of IS research and curriculum and teaching at the UTAS by degree of professionalism

Area	High	Medium	Low
IS curriculum and teaching issues	Relatively centralised location of staff in Hobart aids task certainty through opportunities for communication; Moderation of teaching across campuses; Similar teaching content across campuses; High-quality flexible online support is an example of clear division of labour in this area; Widespread use of workshops and case studies in teaching; Range of mechanisms exists to promote good teaching; Sequential delivery style used to develop student responsibility from Years 1–3; Focus on management and strategy in teaching; Four major teaching themes identified.	Staff performance management scheme sets teaching targets; Little emphasis on service teaching means greater routinisation across degrees; Oracle certification is an example of high task certainty.	
IS research issues		Some emphasis on qualitative research methods; Perceived fewer incentives for research than for teaching; Some incentives provided by faculty/university to do research. Some emphasis on SME and government research; New focus on IT governance, business process management; Majority of staff expected to undertake research.	Research program not controlled centrally; Few common topics; Research culture hard to sustain, detracting from routinisation of research; Perceived lack of recognition for productive research staff; Limited history of attracting ARC funds; Less attendance at conferences than in past; Perceived need to focus on fewer research areas; Limited quality journal publications reduces task certainty for publishing in these journals; High teaching loads leave little time to routinise research.

An examination of IS at the UTAS in 2007 and beyond will be presented next, before the conclusions of this study are considered.

IS at the UTAS in 2007 and beyond

In the past, the discipline of IS needed to be flexible in the face of change. This characteristic, as applied to the UTAS, is considered in this section. The position of teaching and research for the School of Information Systems is reviewed in the first subsection, as of mid-2007, as provided by a senior academic from the school. As indicated earlier, the structural position of the school changed from the beginning of 2008, when it merged with the School of Computing and transferred from the Faculty of Business to the Faculty of Science, Technology and Engineering. In a subsection that follows, two senior academics from the UTAS reflect on the future structural position of IS, from different perspectives.

IS research and teaching at the UTAS in mid-2007

Acknowledgement is made to Professor Peter Marshall, who provided the following updated information on research and teaching at the School of Information Systems in June 2007.

Due in large part to a number of research grants, the school had more than 20 PhD students as of June 2007. The PhD students have been welcomed to play a strong and inclusive role in the school, contributing to a vibrant research ambience. Regular research seminars have been held, as well as visits by eminent researchers from interstate and outside Australia. The vigorous research activity and research culture in the school has been due largely to the efforts of Associate Professor Paul Turner, as much of the research in the school has been directed and led by him. Since 2001, he has been involved directly in raising more than $4.3 million in research grants and consultancies. In working with his PhD students, Turner published more than 90 peer-reviewed journal articles, book chapters and conference papers.

There were three key research foci in the School of Information Systems at the UTAS as of 2007. First, there was a group led by Professor Marshall that focused on IS strategy and business process analysis, modelling and improvement in SMEs. Since 2005, this group, consisting of three academic staff members including Marshall, has carried out two action-research projects into IS strategy formulation in local SMEs. Two business-process experts from the Queensland University of Technology (QUT) have helped the group with this research.

Second, there was the e-health group led by Associate Professor Paul Turner. This group conducted research at basic, applied and strategic levels across acute, primary and aged and community care. The group had eight active researchers engaged in more than 10 funded research projects that had a combined value of more than $3 million. Since 2004, the group has published more than 44 peer-reviewed papers, as well as producing a number of reports, advisories and commentaries. The group also engaged in consultancy to government and industry.

Finally, there was the e-Forensics, Security and Business Logistics Group, also led by Turner. This group also had eight active researchers engaged in applied and strategic-level research covering the following areas:

- e-forensics (digital evidence acquisition related to criminal, illegal or inappropriate online behaviour)
- computer security (including investigations of cyber-terrorism and threats to critical infrastructure)
- Internet fraud
- organisational protection methods
- business logistics (tracking and traceability across entire cold-chain supply chains deploying radio frequency identification technologies (RFIDs) and other technologies with a focus on the perishable seafood export industry).

The e-Forensics, Security and Business Logistics Group has produced more than 27 peer-reviewed publications in recent years and has been involved in research collaborations with a value of more than $450,000.

The teaching program in the School of Information Systems at the UTAS continued to be similar to a number of IS programs across Australia and covered systems analysis, system development methodologies, project management, information management and IS strategic planning.

From information provided on the school's web site, by mid-2007, 15 staff members were employed either full-time or part-time, and based in the School of Information Systems. Of these, nine were academic staff members, while another two undertook research positions. The school continued to have three administrative officers, including those who worked part-time, and one technical officer was employed under a service-level agreement with the university. Of these staff members, all were based in Hobart except for two academic staff members, who were based in Launceston.

In the next section, two senior academics who have been associated with IS at the UTAS at different times reflect on changes to the structural placement of IS, from different perspectives.

The structural placement of IS with computing: perspective 1

Arthur Sale, Emeritus Professor of Computer Science, former Pro-Vice-Chancellor

This short statement expresses a personal view of the structural placement of IS (and computer science) in the UTAS. The views might be of relevance to other universities. This contributor has had no input to university decisions since 1999.

Context

The context is that IS and computer science have been taught by two 'schools' (or departments) in the UTAS. Both schools have been under financial stress from loss of undergraduate student numbers, especially of Australian students, and low research output. The stress was perhaps higher for IS than for computer science, since the latter was somewhat larger, had attracted a large international intake and was perhaps slightly more research active. The two schools are named (eponymously) Information Systems in the Faculty of Business and Computing in the Faculty of Science, Engineering and Technology. Both had their genesis in a single school. Senior executives do not believe that there are any distinguishing differences between the disciplines.

In March 2007, the vice-chancellor and the senior executive consisting of all the deputy and pro-vice-chancellors and the deans invited the two schools to come up with a plan for 'marriage' before the 2008 budget was drawn up. This gave urgency to the question of where the discipline of IS fits in the UTAS.

The background to this 'request' was that both schools were in trouble with funding related to outputs; neither school had been able to satisfactorily differentiate its offerings from the other to Tasmanian school-leavers despite enormous effort, marketing had been unsuccessful in leading to growth and the university was unconvinced that the 'corner had been turned'. The two schools were not seen as worth saving as separate entities for their research output or for their community contribution. These are all arguable assessments, but were nevertheless persuasive arguments to university management.

Views

Personally, I view IS as having established itself completely as a sub-discipline within the field of ICT. There are, however, many other sub-disciplines within this field, such as computer architecture, networking technologies, software engineering, theoretical computer science, mobile computing, Internet technologies, robotics, and so on. They form an overlapping and continuous spectrum of ICT application.

None have any existence without the pervasive impact of computer artefacts. As a former chair of a unified school but without influence, I regretted the break-up into two entities and I welcomed a possibility of reuniting them. This might not be so obvious to schools of IS that were founded independently, but I believe that the computer artefact is at the core of all these sub-disciplines, and unnecessary fragmentation serves no one.

In larger universities, the continued existence of IS and computer science schools might be retained, especially as IS often established itself in a separate faculty. If an amalgamated school would be too large for good management, independent existence is a good option.

Even then, however, IS is on difficult ground, as it is often moving out of its obsolescent business background into education, medicine, architecture and even science, as the discipline that deals with computer applications. This brings it into direct conflict with computer science, which has never given up this ground. The pressure will be on to bring the ICT disciplines closer together.

In smaller universities, such as the UTAS, the outcome is likely to be a single school, which has some advantages of greater coherence, though it might come with angst and turmoil in the short term.

In fact, when I look at the research output of the School of Computing at the UTAS, perhaps 50 per cent of the papers could be classified as 'information research' and are capable of being done in a large, competent IS school. The remainder consists of artificial intelligence, image processing, robotics and a few other theoretical computer science matters such as graph theory, bioinformatics and parallelism. In IS at the UTAS, its involvement in medical informatics and in ICT forensics could fit equally well in computer science.

Perhaps we all need to take a step back and decide what matters to us and to society, and whether the decades-old split between computer applications and infrastructure deserves to be mended. After all, the ACS has never ceased to encompass both.

The structural placement of IS with computing: perspective 2

Peter Marshall, Head of School of Information Systems and Woolworth's Chair of Information Technology and Systems

The following statement is written from my perspective as Woolworths Chair of Information Technology and Systems at the UTAS, having joined the School of Information Systems in June 2004. In December 2004, I became Head of School, and have continued in that role until the present day.

The research program in the School of Information Systems at the UTAS has had a strong emphasis on the identification, design, planning and management of IS in organisations. The context of the use of IT is taken to be critical to, and inseparable from, its effective utilisation. The teaching program is similar to other IS programs across Australia.

Skills and knowledge required by ICT professionals

The skills and knowledge taught in an IS program, particularly those related to the planning and management of IS, are, I believe, now the dominant skills and knowledge required by ICT professionals in Australia.

Courses that have a heavy emphasis on software engineering and computer science are now, I believe, suitable only for the few specialists who will be required in the technical domains of specialist software engineering, robotics, computer-game programming and similar areas. There have been some highly significant trends in ICT in the past 30 years that have apparently gone unnoticed by the more technically enthusiastic ICT academics. These include the considerable trend towards the use of ICT application packages including enterprise resource planning (ERP) systems, rather than the building of customised applications in every organisation, as was the case in the 1960s and 1970s. These trends also include the increasing use of outsourcing and offshoring, which has seen applications development focused in large multinationals, and in firms in India and other relatively low-wage countries. Another development that I believe will, again, reduce the need for technical ICT skills is the increasing availability and use of application service providers. These trends and developments, together with the obvious fact that ICT is now much more reliable than it was 20 to 30 years ago, means that, in my opinion, the disciplines of computer science and software engineering will decline in relevance and importance to the bulk of ICT students relative to that of IS. Of course, it will take some time for enrolments in computer science and software engineering to decline when compared with IS, since school students are less aware of the impact of these developments.

Merger of the Schools of Computing and Information Systems

Faced with declining enrolments in the Schools of Information Systems and Computing, the Vice-Chancellor of the UTAS urged both schools to merge. A working party on this issue formed from key individuals in both schools accepted the idea of a merged or joint school. The new combined school resides in the Faculty of Science, Engineering and Technology.

In the merger of the two schools, the problem of declining enrolments was considered. Generally, however, at present, the problem with declining enrolments in IS and computing throughout much of the world remains not well understood and awaiting resolution. Synergies in teaching and learning in the new merged school at the UTAS, and in new course design and implementation in particular, will be utilised to address declining enrolments. To assist with such endeavours, a market research study will be undertaken into the perceptions and opinions of potential students regarding ICT courses, and into the skills and knowledge needs of ICT professionals in contemporary business and government.

This background work will provide a firm basis on which to plan and design new courses that are attractive to potential students and relevant to the needs of business and government in Tasmania. This study will also provide a firm basis for planning marketing initiatives for ICT courses for the future at the UTAS.

After 11 years of operation as a separate school within the Faculty of Business, IS returned to the Faculty of Science, Engineering and Technology in 2008, in a combined structural relationship with computing. Although the IS research output in mid-2007 was reported as being healthy, the erosion in student numbers for IS and computing was pointed to as the driver behind the resumed co-location of the two disciplines at the UTAS. Two different perspectives on the relationship between computing and IS have been presented.

Conclusions

This final section reviews the findings, and presents the study's limitations and suggestions for future research.

In the descriptive analysis of the School of Information Systems at the UTAS, the extent to which IS was impacted on by local factors, whether it was perceived to be a separate field at the university, the distinctive characteristics of its curriculum and research and the key people who had an impact on IS at the UTAS were considered. An analysis was then undertaken of the perceived degree of impact of local contingencies and the degree of professionalism—for IS teaching and research at the UTAS.

The level-two analysis suggests that while local contingencies had a low to medium impact on curriculum and teaching, they had a high to medium impact on research issues. There were, however, indications that the reverse was the case for the degree of professionalism, in that curriculum and teaching issues had a high level of professionalism while research activities were assessed as low to medium. These findings for research issues are consistent with the view of IS as a fragmented adhocracy, as explained in the framework chapter earlier in this volume. The different findings for curriculum and teaching issues have not, it is believed, been identified before for IS, and make a contribution to research on the development of this discipline.

The level-two findings are consistent with the postulation from the theoretical framework that an inverse relationship exists between the impact of local contingencies on a discipline and its degree of professionalism. As the findings were derived from a single case study, however, the inverse relationship found is best confirmed by case studies conducted in other areas of Australia and elsewhere. Moreover, if the findings are confirmed in different regions using different methods of analysis, this characteristic will act to strengthen the findings.

Additional planned future work is to examine the remainder of the theoretical framework developed for the study through a cross-case analysis of how the components of the IS discipline developed over time. It is possible that the framework might need modification as a result of its application to further cases. Once these level-three findings are known, comparison can be made with research conducted in Europe and North America to see if the common findings extend to Australia at least six years later.

The degree of change experienced in the IS discipline is demonstrated by this case study from Tasmania. This chapter has reported that teaching and research into IS at the single university in the state resumed in a science-based faculty, in conjunction with computing, after 11 years in a separate school in a business faculty. Opportunities exist for future research that examines the impact of co-location of IS with computing at the UTAS on student enrolments, teaching and research.

Acknowledgements

Professors Chris Keen, Peter Marshall and Arthur Sale are thanked for their generous contribution to this chapter.

Select bibliography

Avgerou, C., Siemer, J. and Bjørn-Andersen, N. 1999, 'The academic field of information systems in Europe', *European Journal of Information Systems*, vol. 8, no. 2, pp. 136–53.

Dixon-Woods, M., Agarwal, S., Jones, D., Young, B. and Sutton, A. 2005, 'Synthesising qualitative and quantitative evidence: a review of possible methods', *Journal of Health Services Research & Policy*, vol. 10, no. 1, pp. 45–53.

Information Resources Management Association (IRMA) 1996, *The Information Resources Management Curriculum Model: An international curriculum model for a 4 year undergraduate program in IRM*, A joint activity of IRMA and DAMA, IRMA, Harrisburg, Pa.

Longnecker, H., Clark, J., Couger, D., Feinstein, D. and Clark, J. 1995, *IS'95: Model curriculum and guidelines for undergraduate degree programs in information*, A joint activity of DPMA, ACM, ICIS and AIS, School of CIS, University of South Alabama, Mobile, Ala.

Ridley, G. 2006, 'Characterising information systems in Australia: a theoretical framework', *Australasian Journal of Information Systems*, vol. 14, no. 1, pp. 141–62.

University of Tasmania 2007, *Welcome by the Vice-Chancellor*, University of Tasmania, viewed 15 June 2007, <http://www.utas.edu.au/uni/welcome.html>

Watson, H. J., Taylor, K. P., Higgins, G., Kadlec, C. and Meeks, M. 1999, 'Leaders assess the current state of the IS academic discipline', *Communications of the AIS*, vol. 2, no. 2.

Whitley, R. 1984, *The Intellectual and Social Organization of the Sciences*, Clarendon Press, Oxford, UK.

Appendix 8.1

Table A8.1 Programs offered at the School of Information Systems, University of Tasmania, as of the end of 2005 and of mid-2007

2005	2007
Undergraduate	Undergraduate
BIS	BIS[a]
BIS/BBus	BIS/BBus
BIS (Hons)	BIS (Hons)
BIS/BMusic	BIS/BMusic
BIS/BTeaching	BIS/BTeaching
BIS/BLaws	BIS/BLaws
BFA/BIS	BFA/BIS
BIS/DipIT[c]	BIS/DipIT[c]
Postgraduate course-work	Postgraduate course-work
MIS	MIS
	MEB[d]
	MEB (Specialisation)[d]
GDIS	GDIS
GDInfoMgt[b]	GDInfoMgt[b]
GCIS	GCIS
RHD	RHD
PhD	PhD

[a] three specialisations: management of IS, electronic business, systems development
[b] three specialisations: general librarianship, teaching–librarianship, information management
[c] DipIT component is delivered by TAFE
[d] two specialisations: IS and business

9. The information systems discipline in Victoria

Carol E. Pollard
Appalachian State University
Boone, North Carolina, USA

Elsie S. K. Chan
Australian Catholic University
Victoria, Australia

Abstract

This chapter describes the current state of the Information Systems (IS) discipline within the state of Victoria, Australia. It reports on the ways in which Victorian universities are addressing the challenges associated with reducing local and international student demand, and hence enrolments, at a time when IS in particular and information and communications technology (ICT) in general are seen by the business sector as necessary components contributing to organisational success. Transcripts of interviews with 14 academics at nine universities throughout Victoria are analysed to give a current profile of IS programs and identify the trends in their development over time. First, a profile of the state of Victoria, its education system and its ICT industry is provided to place this work in context. Next, the interview sample is described and a number of relevant topics of interest are identified and discussed, comparing and contrasting the various programs. Third, a summary of the findings is provided in light of the framework used to guide the larger study of the Australian IS programs, which includes an assessment of the impact of mechanisms of control and the core body of knowledge on research and teaching methods and standards, key research and teaching IS topics and laws, and rules and guidelines used within the IS programs. Finally, the relationship between the impact of local contingencies and the degree of professionalism is examined.

Introduction

Information systems is a fascinating and pervasive discipline that has struggled in the past three decades to establish itself as a distinct scientific discipline. This has proved somewhat difficult and elusive, possibly due in part to the fact that

IS is not confined only to business activities but profoundly affects our social activities (see, for example, Buckingham et al. 1987; DeSouza et al. 2006; Lee 2001; Lo 1989; Fielden 1990; Ang 1992; Ang and Lo 1991; Avison 1993; ACM et al. 1997; Clarke 1999; Tatnall 1999).

> [T]he information systems field examines more than just the technological system, or just the social system, or even the two side by side; in addition, it investigates the phenomena that emerge when the two interact. (Lee 2001:iii–vii)

In a recent communication to an international Listserv from Sid Huff, Chair of Information Systems at the University of Auckland, he referenced a recent Information Technology (IT) Governance Institute report that noted the view that IS was an important and integral component of the business value of organisations.

Given this, it follows that as the importance of IS has grown in business and government and has become more pervasive in our social lives, the educational and research programs that support IS have needed to evolve and stay abreast of business and social needs locally and globally and remain an attractive option for students. Unfortunately, in the past several years there has been an unprecedented decline in student enrolment in IS programs world-wide because of a perceived reduction in IS job opportunities. More recently, some Australian university administrations have been responding by drastically reducing the number of IS academics on staff.

This chapter reports on a study within a larger study of IS in Australia that investigates the evolution of IS teaching and research programs throughout Australia. The focus of this chapter is on the IS discipline within the state of Victoria and reports on how universities have taken on the teaching and research challenges associated with the dichotomy of reduced enrolments and the increasing importance of IS/IT to business, and explores the extent to which they have succeeded.

First, a profile of the state of Victoria, its education system and its ICT industry is provided to put the work in context. Next, the interview sample is described and a number of relevant topics of interest are discussed, comparing and contrasting the various programs. Finally, a summary of the findings is provided in light of the framework used to guide all of the state studies of the Australian IS discipline included in this book.

Figure 9.1 Location of Victoria within Australia

Purpose of the Victorian study

The state of Victoria is located in the south-eastern corner of the mainland of Australia. It is the smallest mainland state in area—representing only 3 per cent of the Australian land mass—but it is the most densely populated and urbanised state. Victoria began as a farming community in the 1800s. The discovery of gold at Anderson's Creek near Melbourne, in 1851, transformed it into a leading industrial and commercial centre and, in 1901, Victoria was designated officially as an Australian state. In September 2005, Victoria's population reached an estimated 5 087 300—making it the second-most populous Australian state, after New South Wales (Wikipedia, The Free Encyclopedia 2007).

Victoria is home to a vibrant and sophisticated ICT industry, which boasts a strong component of locally grown companies. Australian-owned firms account for approximately 69 per cent of the industry in Victoria. It is a centre for research and development, which is leading the Australian (and often global) research and development programs across a broad range of industry sectors.

In 2001–02, Victoria's globally focused ICT industry had a turnover of A$19.8 billion (US$15.3 billion) and a skilled and creative workforce of 60 000. With export revenue of A$615 million (US$476.4 million) and research and development expenditure of A$303 million (US$235 million), the ICT industry is at the heart of the modern Victorian economy. Although Victoria accounts for less than 25 per cent of Australia's population, it is home to 31 per cent of all Australian ICT jobs. These make up 48 per cent of all jobs in hardware manufacturing, 41 per cent of jobs in software engineering and 35 per cent of all ICT consulting jobs (Government of Victoria 2005). For example, leading Israeli IT services and solutions provider Ness Technologies Inc opened its Australia–New Zealand headquarters in Melbourne in April 2006, creating up to 50 new jobs (Government of Victoria 2006).

High Internet usage rates and world-class infrastructure make Victoria a test bed for e-commerce companies and, as a result, Victoria has emerged as Australia's leader in business-to-business and business-to-consumer e-commerce. Recently, it was reported that Melbourne in particular had a critical mass of creativity and skills to develop a competitive ICT hotspot (Newcomersnetwork.com 2006). These statistics provide a natural conduit for a discussion of the evolution of the many strong ICT programs that exist within Victorian universities.

The research method

The Victorian study utilises the case-study method. Walsham (1993, 1995) recommends case studies for interpretivist research, although this is by no means the only way in which case studies can be used, as clarified by Yin (2003). Hence a qualitative, interpretivist approach was chosen to conduct the research on which this chapter is based. Within and between this, case analysis was performed to offer a rich description and comparison of IS programs at the nine universities represented, as indicated in Table 9.1.

Face-to-face interviews were conducted with 14 senior academics in 2005. The number of interviews conducted at each university ranged from one to three, depending on the availability of participants, and included one key person from each university as the primary source of data. The semi-structured face-to-face interviews were based primarily on the standardised interview protocol developed for use in the larger IS-in-Australia study. In the interest of obtaining rich data, however, and within the constraints of collecting equivalent data systematically from each participant, interviewees were not discouraged from varying the order of the interview format during the interview.

At the outset of each interview, the researcher opened the session with a set of standard introductory remarks designed to: 1) indicate the importance and purpose of the interview; 2) give assurance of anonymity and confidentiality to the participant; and 3) establish rapport. Each interview began with elicitation of demographic information (name, title, department) and then sought information on the following topics of interest:

- the relative size and administrative placement of the IS presence at their university
- the extent to which IS at the university was impacted on by local contingencies
- the extent to which IS was identified as a separate field at their university
- distinctive features of the IS curriculum at their university
- distinctive features of IS research at their university
- the key people who has had an impact on IS in universities in Victoria.

Available documentation and archival material was also collected and analysed to provide some triangulation of data (Denzin and Lincoln 1998).

Theoretical framework guiding the study

Two frameworks were used to guide this study and evaluate its findings. The first was Whitley's theory of scientific change (1984b), which proposed that three conditions were needed for the establishment of a distinct scientific field. These three conditions are:

1. scientific reputations to become socially prestigious and to 'control critical rewards'
2. establishing standards of research competence and skills
3. a unique symbol system to allow exclusion of outsiders and unambiguous communication between initiates within the field.

Second, an updated framework proposed by Ridley (2006) was applied to the data collected. This more recent framework extends the Whitley set of conditions to include two additional conditions necessary to establish a distinct scientific field. Ridley's two additional conditions are:

1. laws, rules and evidenced guidelines
2. research and teaching key topics.

Ridley (2006) categorises the various criteria into two main components: mechanisms of control and a core body of knowledge (research and teaching methods and standards, the existence of a unique symbol set, key research and teaching topics and laws, rules and evidenced guidelines). She also proposes that it is important to add two other components—that is, the impact of local contingencies and the degree of professionalism—to evaluate the variation in IS programs in Australian universities and to track progress and compare programs in a given state.

More detail of the framework and its derivation are provided in Chapter 3 of this volume.

The universities in this study

Currently, Victoria has nine public universities, as shown in Table 9.1. Data were gathered from all nine universities. The oldest, the University of Melbourne, enrolled its first student in 1855. The largest, Monash University, has an enrolment of nearly 56 000 students—more than any other Australian university in 2004. Two of Victoria's universities—the University of Melbourne and Monash University—are members of the Group of Eight (Go8), an organisation that represents Australia's leading universities (www.go8.edu.au/). The total number of students enrolled in Victorian universities was 241 755 in 2004—an increase of 2 per cent from 2003. The largest number of enrolments was recorded in the fields of business, administration and economics, with nearly one-third of all students, followed by arts, humanities and social science, with 20 per cent of enrolments.[1] International students in Victoria make up 30 per cent of all enrolments.

Relative size of the IS presence in Victorian universities

The number of IS tertiary students in Victoria is approximately 7000. A comparison of the size of the IS presence ranges from 76 students at the Australian Catholic University (ACU; Melbourne campus) to approximately 1000 at the Universities of Ballarat and Monash, as shown in Table 9.1. Full-time IS academic staff number from three at the ACU (nationally) to 92 at the Royal Melbourne Institute of Technology (RMIT). It was noted, however, by those interviewed at Monash that their faculty size had been culled significantly since 2004 due to falling student numbers in the previous few years. Also in 2006, the School of Information Systems at Victoria University reduced its IS staff by nearly 54 per cent (from 26 to 14) as a first measure in staff reduction.

Table 9.1 IS presence in universities in Victoria

University	No. of full-time IS academic staff	No. of IS students
ACU (national)	3	76
Deakin	68	3 305
La Trobe	16	252
Monash	150	1000
RMIT	92	622
Swinburne	52	500
Melbourne	45	400
University of Ballarat	54	1 010
Victoria University	61	800

The administrative placement of IS in Victorian universities

While all nine universities in Victoria represented in the study offer IS programs, the location of the programs within the university structure differs by institution. Table 9.2 shows that IS programs in universities in Victoria can be categorised between business and science/technical/engineering faculties. Six departments are located within faculties of science/technical/engineering, whereas Deakin, RMIT and Victoria University offer IT programs through the business and the science/technical/engineering faculties.

The home faculties in which IS in Victorian universities was situated indicated a diverse mix. The two main faculties, shown in Table 9.2, are business and science; however, IS is also situated in an interesting mix of arts, law, engineering, communication and health science faculties. The demarcation between a science and/or a business focus in IS departments is quite clear. This

---

[1] Australian Bureau of Statistics, Department of Education and Training (Victoria), Department of Education, Science and Training (Commonwealth 2005) and National Centre for Vocational Education Research cited in Wikipedia, The Free Encyclopedia (2007).

diversity of home faculties seems to indicate that, on the whole, IS has not matured in Victoria as a stand-alone discipline.

Table 9.2 Placement of IS in Victorian universities

University	Department, school or group	Home faculty	Demarcation
ACU (national)	Business and Informatics	Arts and Sciences	Science
Deakin	Information Systems	Business and Law	Business
	Information Technology	Science and Technology	Science
La Trobe	Computer Science and Computer Engineering	Science, Technology and Engineering	Science
Monash	Berwick School, Caulfield School, Clayton School, Gippsland School	Information Technology	IT
RMIT	Business Information Technology	Business	Business
	Computer Science and Information Technology	Science, Engineering and Technology	Science
Swinburne	Astrophysics and Supercomputing	Information and Communication Technologies	IT
	Computer Science and Software Engineering		
	Information Systems		
	Telecommunications		
Melbourne	Information Systems	Science	Science
	Software Engineering	Engineering	
University of Ballarat	Information Technology and Mathematical Sciences	Information Technology and Mathematical Sciences	IT
Victoria University	Information Systems	Business and Law	Business
	Computer Science and Mathematics	Health, Engineering and Science	Science

Despite the placement of six of the nine IS departments within a non-IS home faculty, data revealed a move in an overwhelming majority of universities in Victoria to recognise IS as a separate entity. Table 9.3 shows that only three of the nine Victorian universities represented have not attained a separate identity for IS. In universities where there was a separate IS identity, this was expressed as:

- a clear demarcation between IS subjects and others in the faculty (RMIT, Victoria University)
- a strong reputation in industry (Swinburne)
- IS had long had a strong separate identity (Monash).

A specific example might serve to explain this better. For many years in the 1970s and 1980s, Caulfield and then Chisholm Institute of Technology pioneered IS education in Victoria. An early activity was the Commonwealth government's Programmer-in-Training (PIT) scheme. Some people also raised the issue of 'competing' with business, IT and computer science departments in connection with the existence of a separate identity.

Overall, the existence of a separate identity for IS was viewed positively, although at Melbourne it was indicated that while IS had a separate identity as a department, 'not many people know about our department'. Of the three universities (ACU National, University of Ballarat and La Trobe) that do not afford IS a separate identity, La Trobe has experienced some problems with this status, including the lack of representation of IS journals and conferences in a recent journal and conference ranking exercise undertaken to improve the department's (Computer Science and Computer Engineering) research profile. At the University of Ballarat, IS does not have separate administrative status and IS lecturers teach into other areas of the School of Information Technology and Mathematical Science. This is also true for ACU National, as one of the three IS lecturers teaches the business units and IS does not have separate administrative status.

Despite the generally positive perception of having a separate identity, senior academics in Victoria were relatively evenly divided between 'same' and 'less' in their views on status as shown in Table 9.3. Only one senior academic at Monash felt that IS academics were viewed more highly than their colleagues in other departments. At the four universities in Victoria where it was perceived that IS academics saw themselves as having a lesser status than their colleagues a number of reasons were given.

- In some cases it appeared to be due to the relatively new and evolving nature of IS departments in Australia (Melbourne, RMIT, Victoria University).
- A respondent representing Swinburne felt that the perception of the IS faculty was that they were 'less prominent in research than their colleagues'.
- At those universities where the perception was that there was no difference between the status of IS academics and their colleagues no elaboration for this perception was forthcoming.

Interestingly, Table 9.3 also shows that status and separate identity are not necessarily correlated. For example, academics at the University of Ballarat considered their status 'no more or less' and those at La Trobe were said to have mixed perceptions of status. In contrast, at those universities that had a separate identity, many viewed themselves as having less status for the reasons described above.

Table 9.3 IS identity and status in universities in Victoria

University	Separate identity	Status
ACU National	No	Same
Deakin	Yes	Same
La Trobe	No	Same/less
Monash	Yes	Same/higher
RMIT	Yes	Less
Swinburne	Yes	Less
Melbourne	Yes	Less
University of Ballarat	No	Same
Victoria University	Yes	Less

Distinctive features of the IS curriculum

Universities in Victoria offer a wide range of undergraduate and postgraduate IS courses and programs. Table 9.4 summarises the programs offered at the various institutions.

While the majority of the nine institutions represented offer the standard suite of BIS and BIS (Hons), Graduate Certificate, Graduate Diploma and Masters-level programs, Table 9.4 shows a wide range of innovative IS programs. Within Victoria, all universities offered PhD-level IS programs, although not all universities currently had PhD students enrolled (University of Ballarat) or they reported very small enrolments (ACU National, La Trobe and Swinburne).

Table 9.4 Diversity of IS programs offered

University	Undergraduate courses/program	Postgraduate courses/program
ACU National	BIS BIS (Hons) Bachelor of Business/BIS	PhD
Deakin	BIT (IT Security) BIS/BIT BIS BIS (Hons) BEng/BIT BIT (Multimedia Technology) BIT (CS and Software Development) BIT (Games Design and Development) BIT (Web and Mobile Technologies)	MArts (Professional Communication)/MIT MIT MIT (Professional) MIT/MCom MIT/MIS MAcct'g IS MCom/MIS PhD
La Trobe	BIT (Computer Networks) BIT/IS BIT (Software Development) BIS/BBus	MIT (Computer Networks) MIT (Intelligent Systems and Internet Computing) PhD
Monash	BIS BIT/BIS BArts/BIM and IS BCom/BIS	MApplied IT MBA/MIM and IS MIM and IS MIM and IS (Professional) MIS MIT MIT (Minor thesis) PhD
RMIT	BBus (BusIS) BAppSc (Computing and Internet Technology) BAppSc (IT) BAppSc (Honours—Computing and Internet Technology)	MBus (BusIT) MAppSc (Information Security) MAppSc (IS) MAppSc (IT) MEng (IT) MTech (IT) MTech (Internet and Web Computing) PhD

Table 9.4 Diversity of IS programs offered

University	Undergraduate courses/program	Postgraduate courses/program
Swinburne	BIT (Honours) BSc (IT) BIS (Honours) BIT BBus (IS)/BBus BBusIS	MIS Mgmt/MAcct'g MIS Mgmt MIS Mgmt/MBA MTech (IT) MIT PhD
Melbourne	BIS BIS (Honours)	MBus/IT MIS MIT MIT in Education PhD
University of Ballarat	BIS BIT BIT (Professional Practice)	MBusIS MIS MIT MIT Studies MIT Studies/MBA MICT PhD
Victoria University	BBus (Acct/IS) BBus (IS) BBus (Tourism Management/IS) BA/BBus (Information Systems) BBus (IS) (Honours) BSc in IT	Master of Business in Information Systems Master of Business in Information Systems and Enterprise Resource Planning Systems PhD

In addition to the traditional Bachelor of Information Systems or Information Technology, Bachelor of Business Information Systems and the Masters of Information Systems, a few institutions offer cross-disciplinary courses, such as the Bachelor of Computing with Applied Science and BComp with Visual Arts at La Trobe and the Bachelor of Computing/Information Systems offered at Swinburne. Victoria University offers joint degrees with arts and science and engineering faculties and a Masters in Enterprise Resource Planning and Marketing/E-Commerce. The ACU National offers double degrees in IS and business majoring in accounting, marketing and human resource management. It was observed that in 2002 students tended to study a single degree, Bachelor of Information Systems. Starting from 2004, students preferred to study a double degree. The reason for this change could be due to the perceptions of graduates, who believe those with double degrees will find jobs more easily than those with a single degree. Many of the universities have a large population of international students, the majority of whom are from Asia, with only a small representation from Europe. The offshore IS programs that are offered overseas include campuses in Hong Kong, Thailand, Singapore, China and Malaysia. Generally speaking, the courses taught in IS programs are less technical than would be found in a department of computer science or IT.

The distinctive themes taught within many of these programs varied considerably and included decision analysis and information management (Monash), global IS (University of Ballarat), electronic commerce (Deakin), enterprise resource planning (ERP), security and privacy (Victoria), design and support of business processes (Swinburne), educational theory and practice (La Trobe), ERP (Victoria University) and security, decision support, usability and interface design, business intelligence and ERP (RMIT).

It is also interesting to observe that universities offer many IS/IT-related Masters programs now compared with a decade ago. As mentioned in Keen (1996:129–32), there were only three universities offering IS/IT-related Masters programs by course-work. They were Master of Information Systems at Monash, Master of Business (IT) at RMIT and Master of Business in Computing at Victoria University of Technology (now renamed Victoria University).

The current diversity of IS curricula and degrees offered at all levels in Victorian universities is inconsistent with the Ridley framework requirement that a maturing discipline must have a readily identifiable core body of knowledge.

Distinctive features of IS research

Turning from the teaching profile and diversity of programs to that of research, an interesting and similar picture emerges. Table 9.5 demonstrates the diversity of research streams under way in universities in Victoria and recognises two successful formal research centres. Those universities that have active PhD programs have been successful in varying degrees in attracting and maintaining PhD students to support, in part, their research programs.

Table 9.5 Research streams in universities in Victoria

University	Areas of research	Formal research groups	No. of PhD students
ACU National	IS education E-commerce education		1
Deakin	Requirement engineering IT security Knowledge management Supply-chain management Software engineering E-commerce	Supply-Chain Management (SCM) and Business-to-Business (B2B) e-Commerce	20
La Trobe	Computational intelligence IS education Equity issues of women in IT IT adoption and impact		2

Table 9.5 Research streams in universities in Victoria

University	Areas of research	Formal research groups	No. of PhD students
Monash	Knowledge management Systems development Decision support systems Information management IT management E-business Conceptual modelling	Centre for Decision Support and Business Intelligence Research	60
RMIT	Strategic IS E-learning E-commerce	Knowledge management E-business	30
Swinburne	IS governance Process modelling IS project management Health informatics	Centre for Information Technology Research	1
Melbourne	E-commerce Technology adoption Usability design Security	Knowledge discovery	40
University of Ballarat	IT education Data mining and informatics Mathematics and statistical analysis Distributed simulation	Centre for Informatics and Optimisation (CIAO)	0
Victoria University	Semantic webs Business process modelling Negotiation support Legal systems in IS Ethics, privacy and censorship Portals for medical and aged-care support ERP	Electronic commerce research	16

Overall, IS research output in universities in Victoria was seen as being lower than in other departments. It should be noted, however, that for the most part IS research output appears to have been increasing in the past three to five years. Efforts are under way to bolster research output. Comments indicative of this include one at Monash to the effect that '[a]ll IS academics will be expected to be "research active" by 2008' and, one from the University of Ballarat, where it is a current requirement that 'all academics in the school are expected to undertake research'.

The mode of IS research in universities in Victoria is predominantly interpretive. Only the University of Ballarat reported using 'multi-method, with an emphasis on quantitative techniques'.

Although research is considered a high priority at almost all universities in Victoria, available funding appears to have a negative correlation with the avowed importance of research. Perceptions of 'very little funding', 'dwindling funding' and 'having trouble attracting ARC [Australian Research Council] and other external funding' were evident in the data. Where funding has been obtained, it is primarily in the form of competitive grants from internal university sources or associated with established research centres, with some funding forthcoming from industry. Relatively few IS departments have been successful in securing external grants from agencies such as the ARC, although there appears to be a trend towards encouraging external grants rather than relying on internal funding, which in almost all cases was seen to be increasingly difficult to secure.

Respondents stressed that rewards, when available, were being awarded increasingly for research that resulted in journal publications rather than conference chapters.

Key people who have had an impact on IS in universities in Victoria

A number of key individuals were recognised for their contributions to IS in Victorian universities. Predominantly, these individuals were long-standing academic leaders.

Examples included Tony Adams at RMIT, who was named as the champion for the establishment and direction of the IS department, along with Marianne Broadbent, head of the former Information Management School in arts, who worked with Professor Adams to establish the RMIT IS research and course-work frameworks. Robert Johnson was identified as an influential force at Melbourne University, as was Gerald Murphy at Swinburne and Angela Scollary for her tireless work to establish the IS school at Victoria University. The respondent from the University of Ballarat recognised Professor Sid Morris, their head of school, as one who 'has had a huge amount to do with the success we are having', and acknowledged the important contributions of Professor Wayne Robinson, University of Ballarat's Deputy Vice-Chancellor (Academic and Research), together with that of Professor Alex Rubinov, Director of the CIAO.

A long list of influential individuals was forthcoming from respondents at Monash. These included Gerry Maynard for his leadership in establishing the IS department; Jack Greig, current head of IS and the person responsible for the introduction of systems analysis units; Phil Steele, David Arnott, Graeme Shanks, Frada Burstein, Julie Fisher, Ron Weber and Ian Martin, an academic involved in industry-based learning at the Clayton campus. Less frequently mentioned, but no less important, were those non-academics who were seen to have influenced course design and skill requirements, such as the representatives at Bendigo Bank who were supportive and influential at La Trobe.

Vignettes of two of the many influential figures in the IS discipline in Victoria are presented next.

Vignette 1 — Graeme Shanks

Graeme Shanks has had a major impact on IS in Victoria during his 25 years as an academic. Currently, he is a Professorial Fellow in the Department of Information Systems at the University of Melbourne. Until recently, he was Associate Dean of Research and Professor in the School of Business Systems in the Faculty of Information Technology at Monash University. Before becoming an academic, Shanks worked for a number of years as programmer, programmer-analyst and project leader in several large organisations. Shanks has a number of research and teaching interests, including conceptual modelling, data quality, identity management and the implementation and impact of enterprise systems and inter-organisational systems.

Shanks began his academic career in 1982 at the Chisholm Institute of Technology in Melbourne. He was course leader for graduate programs in IT and helped to develop the first Australian course-work degree in IT in the mid-1980s. Many years later, he led the restructuring of the Master of Information Systems program at the University of Melbourne. Over many years, Shanks has developed subjects in the areas of data management, systems analysis, conceptual modelling, enterprise systems and data warehousing. He has published several papers on curriculum development in these areas. Shanks has successfully supervised eight PhD students to completion.

Shanks has been involved actively with the Australian Conference on Information Systems (ACIS), having presented a paper at the first ACIS in 1990; he was Program Chair of ACIS1994 at Monash University, and presented many papers and panel sessions in the years since. At the 1994 conference, together with others including David Arnott, Graham Pervan, Bernie Glasson and Rudi Hirschheim, he helped to devise the 'evolving charter' for ACIS, which defines the governance and operation of the conference series. He was executive officer of ACIS for several years, helping to ensure the successful operation of the ACIS series. Shanks has been an active member of the Australian Computer Society (ACS) for many years and was elected a Fellow in 1999. He also served on the committee of the Data Management Association. Shanks has been a member of the Australian Council of Professors and Heads of Information Systems (ACPHIS) for many years.

Shanks completed a PhD in IS in 1997 and has since focused strongly on research. He is a member of several editorial boards, including *Asia Pacific Management Review* (Regional Editor), *Journal of Knowledge Management Theory and Practice*, *Data Warehousing Journal*, *International Journal of Data Warehousing and Mining*, *Journal of Database Management* and the *New Zealand Journal of Applied Computing and Information Technology*. He has published the outcomes of his research in more than 100 refereed journal and conference papers in outlets including *Information Systems Journal*, *Journal of Information Technology*, *Journal of Strategic Information Systems*, *Communications of the ACM* and the International Conference on Information Systems (ICIS).

During his career, Shanks has received more than $1 million in research funding from the ARC, including Discovery grants and industry linkage grants. He was a member of the ARC College of Experts from 2004 to 2005, representing the IS community. He has presented seminars on ARC grant schemes throughout Australia and at the annual ACPHIS workshops.

Vignette 2 — Gerald Murphy

Gerald Murphy is one of the founding fathers of Australia's IT education sector, having completed a commerce degree at the University of Melbourne in 1960, when computers received only a passing mention in one subject.

After nine years in the IT industry, Murphy moved to Swinburne University of Technology (now Swinburne University), where the challenge had become producing graduates who were *not* too IT focused. There he was instrumental in establishing the Bachelor of Information Technology (BIT) in 1998. The BIT was part of a national pilot program initiated by the Business Council of Australia and currently generates approximately $1 million in scholarships annually.

During his career at Swinburne, Murphy made a distinguished contribution to ICT through his pioneering work in cooperative education in IT, introducing other innovative courses, and gaining recognition for IT management as an independent course. Murphy's important contributions were recognised in 1997, when he was awarded the World Association's MacLaren Prize for his contribution internationally to work-integrated learning.

As a result of his further contributions to the IS field, Murphy was installed as a Fellow of the ACS in 2005.

Since retiring from Swinburne University, Murphy has continued his work in a number of innovative industry programs. He is currently the Certification Program Manager of the ACS and Chair of the Australian Cooperative Education Society. In this role, Murphy writes regularly for *Computerworld* and other industry publications to further promote the IT profession.

In his role as Chair of the Australian Cooperative Education Society, and his former role as manager of an employer-sponsored degree course at Swinburne University, he has developed an excellent understanding of how to integrate subject content with work experience and how to encourage employer support for those undertaking such study.

The status of IS as a distinct discipline in Victoria

In the short term, relating the Victorian data to the underlying framework that guides the IS-in-Australia study as proposed by Whitley (1984b) and refined by

Ridley (2006), it would appear that the Victorian data do not support IS as a distinct scientific discipline under the conditions for acceptance as an academic discipline. Each of the framework's criteria will be addressed separately in light of the Victorian data to demonstrate the conclusions reached.

The first of Whitley's three conditions that must be met in order for an area of study to be considered a 'distinct scientific field' is a social process that results in scientific reputations becoming socially prestigious and controlling critical rewards. Mingers and Stowell (1997) suggest this can be evidenced through publications and success in attracting research funding. Clearly, Victorian researchers view themselves as being somewhat less respected than their counterparts in other disciplines, with only one respondent feeling that IS researchers were of higher status than those in other departments. On the other hand, documentary evidence shows that a number of senior IS academics in Victoria have attained status as full professors and are recognised as being as qualified as their peers in other more mature disciplines. The deficiency in meeting this criterion is perhaps more telling in regard to 'attracting research funding', where the data demonstrate clearly that external funding support for IS research continues to be elusive and IS researchers appear to be losing ground as they struggle with dwindling internal funding.

The second of Whitley's criteria is the need to establish standards of research competence and skills. Here, the Victorian data add to the long-standing discussion about whether IS is a discipline (Dickson et al. 1982; Benbasat and Weber 1996; Boudreau et al. 2001) and the current perception that IS continues to align itself more closely with a 'fragmented adhocracy', as suggested by Checkland and Holwell (1998) and Kanungo (2004), than a distinct discipline. For example, while there were pockets of successful grant applications and a limited number of research centres throughout the state, the data revealed an overall lack of success in attracting research funding. This could be construed as a negative reflection on research competence and skills that appeared to be limited to interpretivism and lacking the application of the more diverse, blended approach usually evident in more mature disciplines.

The third and final Whitley criterion is one that requires the existence of a unique symbol system to allow exclusion of outsiders and unambiguous communication between initiates within the field. There are a few IS departments that have achieved autonomy (Monash, Swinburne, University of Ballarat), but for the most part the IS programs are situated within business, arts or science faculties. Similarly, only two-thirds of Victorian IS programs are recognised as separate entities and the diversity of research topics under scrutiny would clearly demonstrate a heavy reliance on reference disciplines with little or no discussion of the use of an IS theory. This would suggest that this criterion has not been met.

Applying Ridley's (2006) two additional criteria—theory or laws, rules and evidenced guidelines and research and teaching key topics—led to mixed conclusions. As to theory, there appears to be a strong focus on interpretivist research methods, which could lead to the conclusion that in IS programs in Victoria there is an agreed set of laws, rules and evidenced guidelines. This is not the case with respect to teaching. The distinctive themes taught within many of the IS programs vary considerably, and it is difficult to see any key teaching topics across programs and institutions in Victoria. Similarly, little evidence points to a coherent set of key research topics. Table 9.5 lists no less than 33 different areas of research across the nine Victorian universities. This indicates that even within a single program there is no homogeneous set of key research topics, with the exception of the ACU National, where its research focuses almost exclusively on IS/e-commerce education.

Finally, we assess the data with respect to the relationships between the degree of professionalism and impacts of local contingencies. Whitley (1984a, 1984b) suggests that to be professional a discipline will not be highly influenced by local contingencies. From the data collected in Victoria, it would appear that while universities in Victoria are currently seeking increased collaboration with the local community and industry as part of their strategic vision—as in the strong industry-based learning degree programs at Swinburne and Monash Universities, established about 1990 as an initiative of the Business Council of Australia—the majority of universities felt the influence of local industries was negligible in terms of having an impact on their curriculum. Efforts to increase interaction with external partners are, however, under way and, in some cases, are being promoted by top university officials. In the case of Victoria University, it is the vice-chancellor who is spearheading these initiatives. Victoria University was one of the earliest universities to link the program to systems in the market. The Faculty of Business and Law and SAP signed an agreement in March 1998 to enable the university to develop courses and conduct research based on SAP's Enterprise Resource Planning System, referred to as SAP R/3. In the case of Monash, the Dean of Information Systems and full professors were primarily instrumental in this area. At Swinburne, the faculty as a whole was attempting to increase ties to industry to be 'alert to any possible "competitive advantage" in responding to special local needs'. Where local influences were present, the most influential industries named were manufacturing and consulting services. At the ACU National, IS curricula are not affected by local factors but are affected more by the ethical influence in the Catholic mission as well as ethical and social responsibilities, which will influence the curricula to a certain extent.

National influences, on the other hand, are affecting IS curricula across Victoria. For example, Monash appears to be affected more strongly by national rather than local community and industry influences, or by individual influences within the university attributed to staffing changes over the years. Likewise, Swinburne saw national influences as being most influential. Overall, these findings suggest that IS programs in Victorian universities have achieved a certain degree of professionalism.

Review of findings

Despite declining enrolments and dwindling research support, from a teaching perspective, IS programs in the universities in Victoria appear to be well placed to provide top-calibre IS graduates at the undergraduate and postgraduate levels to meet the projected increased demand from industry and IS programs projected for the next five years. Programs at all tertiary education levels are varied and carefully crafted, influenced by national rather than local impacts.

It is encouraging to see that the research output and quality of the IS community in Victoria have improved greatly in the past few years. A large number of IS academics have gained PhDs, published in leading IS journals, joined editorial boards of prestigious journals and some have obtained ARC Linkage and Discovery grants. While research topics are diverse within the state, methods are not. Information systems academics in Victoria appear to align themselves more closely with interpretivist European research traditions than with the quantitative, positivist approaches found more commonly in North America. Despite the increased importance that research appears to have in measuring performance, funding is dwindling and success in securing external competitive grants such as those offered by the ARC appears to continue to elude the majority of IS researchers in Victoria.

It is encouraging to see that the Victorian government is acting to combat the declining number of IS students. For example, in 2005, Multimedia Victoria initiated a project—the Industry and Universities Collaboration Pilot Program—to encourage more students to enrol in IS courses in Victorian universities. The program provides funds to universities in Victoria to promote and improve IS courses and is designed to benefit all universities in Victoria.

In addition, Marsha Thomson, the state Minister for Information, Communication and Technology, convened a meeting on 26 May 2006 to discuss matters relating to an apparent shortage of ICT skills in Australia, and notably in Victoria.

The cyclical nature of demand for IS courses was seen, in most cases, to be the factor that influenced IS enrolment most. Some respondents emphasised it was not always factors 'local' to their Australian location that affected their IS curriculum. For example, RMIT's IS program was impacted on by factors at its offshore Hong Kong location. This is not surprising since many of the universities indicated that international students accounted for a large percentage of their enrolments at graduate and postgraduate levels.

In conclusion, IS programs in Victoria appear to be evolving to meet the demands of industry from a teaching perspective, but are somewhat lacking in the area of research output *vis-à-vis* their counterparts in other departments. While some universities have, however, yet to establish IS as a separate entity, research output is increasing along with efforts to win external competitive grants. It would appear that the main challenges being faced include the significant drop in students studying IS and the expected drop in full-fee overseas students, coupled with the foreshadowed replacement of the Research Quality Framework (RQF), which will focus attention on the quality of IS research. Opportunities include building on recent successes in IS research in Victoria, which should lead to a stronger IS research base in the future.

Assessing the data along the dimensions of professionalisation and conditions for acceptance as an academic discipline indicate that while the IS discipline in Victoria has worked hard to achieve a certain degree of professionalisation, it has a long way to go before it can be considered a mature academic discipline.

Limitations and future research

The Victorian study draws on interview data from all nine Victorian universities, however, it does not represent all campuses or a majority of viewpoints within the IS departments. At some universities, only one point of view is represented and, at best, the data is compiled from only three viewpoints. Historical data were even more limited across all universities and this should be taken into account when considering the conclusions reached.

By the nature of the data-collection process, this research provides a snapshot in time of what would appear to be a rapidly changing environment. In particular, the recent increase in demand for IS/IT skills would suggest the need to take a longitudinal approach to data collection to replicate the study at set periods over time. This approach would reveal trends in teaching and research and track the maturation of the IS discipline in Victoria.

General findings from the Victorian study

Two main lessons were learned from conducting the Victorian study.

1. Interviews take time and scheduling is difficult. Given the large time commitment required for interviews and the difficulties associated with coordinating schedules to conduct an interview, it is envisioned that in future studies it might be more appropriate to use a survey approach and, with this in mind, a survey has been developed to replace the interview protocol used in this study. To improve the richness of the data collected via the survey, many open-ended questions are included.

2. A guiding theoretical framework is essential. The Ridley framework proved invaluable in developing the interview protocol (and subsequent survey) that enabled the researchers to focus their questions and assess their findings. Without it, it would have been impossible to conduct a valid

comparison of the Victorian data with those of all other states in Australia. Given that other countries where this type of data-collection effort might prove useful have considerably more universities than Australia, it is anticipated that the Ridley framework will prove even more valuable in assisting researchers to collect, analyse and assess their findings.

Acknowledgements

The authors would like to express their gratitude to Angela Scollary for her valuable contribution to the data-collection phase of this research project.

References

ACM, AIS and AITP 1997, *IS'97 Model Curriculum and Guidelines for Undergraduate Degree Programs in Information Systems*, viewed 30 May 2006, <http://webfoot.csom.umn.edu/faculty/gdavis/curcomre.pdf>

Ang, A. Y. 1992, 'Australian information systems curricula: a comparison between the views of universities and TAFE colleges', *Proceedings of Third Australian Conference on Information Systems*, Wollongong, Australia, 5–8 October, pp. 747–58.

Ang, A. Y. and Lo, B. W. N. 1991, 'Changing emphasis in information systems curricula: an Australian industrial perception', *Proceedings ACC'91 MOSAIC*, Adelaide, 6–10 October, pp. 11–28.

Avison, D. E. 1993, 'Research in information systems development and the discipline of information systems', *Proceedings of 4th Australasian Conference on Information Systems*, Queensland, Australia, 1–27 September, pp. 28–30.

Benbasat, I. and Weber, R. 1996, 'Research commentary: rethinking "diversity" in information systems research', *Information Systems Research*, vol. 7, no. 4, pp. 389–99.

Boudreau, M., Gefen, D. and Straub, D. 2001, 'Validation in information systems research', *MIS Quarterly*, vol. 25, no. 1, pp. 1–16.

Buckingham, R. A., Hirschheim, R. A., Land, F. F. and Tully, C. J. 1987, 'Information systems curriculum: a basis for course design', in Buckingham et al. (eds), *Information Systems Education: Recommendations and Implementation*, Cambridge University Press, Cambridge, Great Britain, pp. 114–33.

Checkland, P. and Holwell, S. 1998, *Information, Systems and Information Systems—Making Sense of the Field*, University of Illinois Press, Urbana, Illinois.

Clarke, R. 1999, *Comments on Information Systems Curriculum*, viewed 26 March 2007, <http://www.anu.edu.au/people/Roger.Clarke/SOS/ISCurric.html>

Denzin, N. K. and Lincoln, Y. S. 1998, *The Landscape of Qualitative Research*, Sage, Thousand Oaks, Calif.

DeSouza, K. C., El Sawy, O. A., Galliers, R. D., Loebbecke, C. and Watson, R. 2006, 'Beyond rigor and relevance towards responsibility and reverberation: information systems research that really matters', *Communications of the AIS*, vol. 17, pp. 341–53.

Dickson, G. W., Benbasat, I. and King, W. R. 1982, 'The MIS area: problems, challenges and opportunities', *DataBase*, vol. 14, no. 1, pp. 7–12.

Fielden, K. 1990, 'Facts, skills and creativity: an innovative approach to learning in information systems', *Proceedings of First Annual Conference on Information Systems*, Monash University, Melbourne, Australia, 6 February, pp. 2–14.

Government of Victoria 2005, *Key Facts*, viewed 26 March 2007, <http://invest.vic.gov.au/Archive/Industry+Sectors/It+and+Communications/Key+Facts.htm>

Government of Victoria 2006, *Melbourne Home to New Headquarters for Leading Israeli IT Company*, 27 April, viewed 26 March 2007, <http://invest.vic.gov.au/News/News+Archive/ness+technologies.htm>

Kanungo, S. 2004, 'On the emancipatory role of rural information systems', *Information and People*, vol. 17, no. 4, pp. 407–22.

Keen, C. 1996, 'A survey of course work Masters in information systems in Australia', in D. Arnott, K. Dampney and A. Scollary (eds), *The Australian Debate on Information Systems Curriculum, Proceedings of the Australian Information Systems Curriculum Working Conference*, Monash University, Australia, 24–25 September, pp. 119–32.

Lee, A. 2001, 'Editor's comments', *MIS Quarterly*, vol. 25, no. 1, pp. iii–vii.

Lo, B. W. N. 1989, 'A survey of information systems educational programmes in Australian tertiary institutions', *Working Chapter Series No. 1*, Department of Information Systems, The University of Wollongong.

Mingers, J. and Stowell, F. (eds) 1997, *Information Systems: An Emerging Discipline?*, Maidenhead, McGraw-Hill, Maidenhead, UK.

Newcomersnetwork.com 2006, *Business in Melbourne, Victoria, Australia—Facts, figures, information, statistics, industries, manufacturing, biotechnology, ICT, innovation and more*, viewed 26 March 2007, <http://www.newcomersnetwork.com/mel/oursay/expertadvice/bimv.php>

Ridley, G. 2006, 'Characterising information systems in Australia: a theoretical framework', *Australasian Journal of Information Systems*, vol. 14, no. 1, pp. 141–62.

Tatnall, A. 1999, Innovation and change in the information systems curriculum of an Australian university: a socio-technical perspective, PhD thesis, Central Queensland University.

Walsham, G. 1993, *Interpreting Information Systems in Organization*, Wiley, Chichester.

Walsham, G. 1995, 'Interpretive case studies in IS research: nature and method', *European Journal of Information Systems*, vol. 4, pp. 74–81.

Whitley, R. 1984a, 'The development of management studies as a fragmented adhocracy', *Social Science Information*, vol. 23, no. 4–5, pp. 775–818.

Whitley, R. 1984b, *The Intellectual and Social Organization of the Sciences*, Clarendon Press, Oxford, UK.

Wikipedia, The Free Encyclopedia 2007, *Victoria (Australia)*, viewed 26 March 2007 <http://en.wikipedia.org/wiki/Victoria_(Australia)>

Yin, R. K. 2003, *Case Study Research: Design and Methods*, 3rd edn, Sage, Thousand Oaks.

10. Information systems teaching and research in West Australian universities

Janice Burn
School of Management Information Systems
Edith Cowan University

Craig Standing
School of Management Information Systems
Edith Cowan University

Chad Lin
Division of Health Sciences
Curtin University of Technology

Abstract

The authors of this chapter examine the current state of the development of information systems (IS) teaching and research within Western Australia (WA). A brief overview of the WA environment is followed by an exploration of teaching and research in the four main universities. This is examined against the framework for the study and, in particular, the impact of social processes (Ariav et al. 1987; Klein et al. 1991) and local contingencies (Culnan et al. 1993; Checkland and Holwell 1998), which are found to be of relevance to historical developments.

The West Australian scene

Western Australia is the largest state in Australia, spanning 2400 km from north to south and encompassing more than 2.5 million square kilometres. The state is fairly isolated from the rest of Australia and still maintains something of a 'frontier' mentality. This is compounded by the low population, with only two million inhabitants, approximately 73 per cent of whom live in the capital city of Perth, which has a current population of 1.5 million. The rest of Western Australia is populated by small country towns, which are typically remote from other centres and many of which lack basic infrastructure such as health and education services. In particular, broadband access is variable and information and communication technology (ICT) services can be poor.

Figure 10.1 Location of Western Australia within Australia

The capital city of Perth has the dubious reputation of being the most remote city in the world, being as close to Singapore as it is to Sydney and a five-hour flight from either. This has compensations since Perth is on the same time zone as the Asian centres of Hong Kong and Singapore and hence is attractive for international collaboration in business and, indeed, in education. The remoteness of the state has, however, meant that few businesses headquarter in Western Australia and, as such, collaboration with local industry becomes a problem since they tend to favour states where they are headquartered. The state also derives most of its revenue from the minerals and oil industries, with the majority of large companies associated with mining in some form.

These location factors have impacted on the development of WA universities, since, while all four public universities are based in Perth, they all have a remit to service the whole state and so typically have remote campuses across Western Australia. Additionally, all universities have substantial external offerings, which initially targeted the distant WA population but now recruit from a global community. The WA population has remained fairly stable but is now forecast to grow; however, the growth in university students has come largely from out-of-state enrolments and, specifically, from Asia.

Overview of WA universities

The five universities in Western Australia (ordered by number of enrolments from largest) are:

- Curtin University of Technology
- Edith Cowan University (ECU)
- the University of Western Australia (UWA)
- Murdoch University
- Notre Dame University.

Table 10.1 Overall enrolment figures for 2004 and comparative statistics

University	Total	% overseas	% postgraduate	% research	% school-leavers
Curtin	36 064	39.7	22.2	4.3	43.1
ECU	23 887	17.8	19.6	2.6	33.1
UWA	16 806	17.7	25.8	11.3	75.0
Murdoch	12 655	17.5	17.8	6.5	34.9
Notre Dame	3 000 +	N/A	N/A	N/A	N/A[a]

[a] Notre Dame University is a private Catholic university
Source: Department of Education, Science and Training Selected Higher Education Statistics.

A brief historical overview of these five universities helps to explain the particular unique focus of each institution and the positioning of IS within the universities.

University of Western Australia

The UWA was the state's first university, established in 1911, and is a member of the Group of Eight—the eight most prominent research-oriented universities in Australia, often referred to as the 'Sandstone universities'. The UWA has proportionately the highest intake of school-leavers nationally (national average, 44.3 per cent) and consistently recruits more than 80 per cent of the state's top 5 per cent of school-leavers. The *Good Universities Guide* says that the 'UWA has more young, bright full-timers than any other University in the country—it is at the top of the WA academic totem pole'. Typically, all undergraduate students are full-time. With this profile of students, the most popular disciplines are the traditional ones and IS plays only a supporting role. Originally, IS was part of the Department of Information Management and Marketing (DIMM), founded in 1993. A full major of IS units was first offered in 1998. The information management (IM) discipline group is now embedded within the School of Economics and Commerce—itself one of two schools in the UWA Business School.

Curtin University of Technology

Curtin University of Technology is Western Australia's largest university and evolved from the Western Australian Institute of Technology (WAIT) in 1986. The WAIT was itself created in 1966 from the Perth Technical College, which in 1969 merged with the WA School of Mines, the Muresk Agricultural College and the Schools of Physiotherapy and Occupational Therapy. Between 1966 and 1976, student enrolments expanded from 2000 to more than 10 000 and the WAIT consolidated around three large schools of Health Sciences, Business and Administration and Arts and Architecture.

The WAIT's Business School was the largest in Australia and, in 1975, the School of Computing and Quantitative Studies was formed, with a prime focus on IS. In 1986, when Curtin University was formed, the school was renamed the School of Information Systems and remains within the Business Faculty. There is a separate School of Computer Science in a different faculty.

Curtin has a main campus and two additional metropolitan campuses in Perth, as well as regional campuses in Kalgoorlie and Northam. In addition, it has an offshore campus in Sarawak, Malaysia, and a new campus in Sydney's central business district. Curtin has 13 education centres within Western Australia and 15 overseas education centres.

Curtin has the largest international student population in the state, with about 40 per cent—which is high by national standards. These students will typically be full-time and their Australian counterparts a mix of full-time and part-time.

Edith Cowan University

Edith Cowan University (ECU) was granted university status in 1991 and evolved from a number of education colleges formed as early as 1902. ECU remains the state's major provider of teacher education. While it is the state's second-largest university, it has the largest enrolment of WA students. ECU focuses on the service professions and defines its particular strengths as:

- education
- nursing
- business
- computing
- communications
- creative and performing arts.

Information systems was part of the School of Information Systems and Management Science in the 1980s and became the Department of Management Information Systems in 1988 within the Faculty of Business. A separate School of Computer Science is in a different faculty.

ECU had many campuses but has recently consolidated and now has its main campus 28 km north of the city centre in Joondalup—one of the fastest growth areas in Australia. It has a second city campus and a regional campus at Bunbury in the south.

More than 50 per cent of the students at ECU are 'mature' entrants and are typically part-time students. With this profile, IS students would normally come from within the IT industry. As IT suffered a decline in 2004 and 2005, so the student population declined in this period.

Murdoch University

Murdoch University was formally constituted as Western Australia's second university in 1973 and, while a research-based university, it has a strong emphasis on good teaching. Information systems has had a chequered history as part of an IT group. Originally, the Department of Information Technology was part of the School of Mathematics, Business and Sciences, but, in 1997, IT was moved to Business Information Technology and Law. In 2003, the School of Information Technology was moved into the Division of Arts.

Murdoch University has three campuses—two regional campuses and one city campus.

Notre Dame University

The University of Notre Dame was founded in 1990 and is a private Catholic university. Despite its small size, it has eight colleges and the School of Information Technology resides within the College of Science and Technology. Interestingly, all the courses offered in IT are offered in online mode and the university spawned a separate company to promote the development of such online material. There is no IS group as such and the IT school has only two permanent staff members.

For the purposes of this study, only the public universities are considered in depth. Notre Dame does not have an IS department.

Table 10.2 An overview of the approximate numbers of IS staff and student numbers within the four public universities.

University	Unit	IS staff	IS undergraduate students	IS postgraduate students
Curtin	School of IS	24	~ 160	~ 200
ECU	School of MIS	18	~ 150	~ 110
UWA	School of IT	7	~ 100	~ 25
Murdoch	School E and C	8	~ 70	~ 10

Within these staffing numbers, Curtin University has three IS professors, Edith Cowan has three IS professors and the UWA and Murdoch have no IS professors.

The study

Interviews were conducted with senior academics at the four public universities. The data summarised below represent the picture at that time. It should be noted, however, that in all cases, numbers were falling at the time of the interviews, with a severe decline in student enrolments and commensurate reduction in staff numbers. The dramatic upswings and down-swings in student numbers in the IS discipline over the years suggest that the 'discipline' is aligned very tightly with the perceived industry needs of the moment rather than being viewed as a substantive 'professionalised' academic discipline in its own right (Ruscio 1987).

Courses

Curtin University covers the whole spectrum of IT, electronic commerce (EC) and IS, with a recent emphasis towards some of the more technical IS subjects;

ECU focuses on the business applications of IS, EC and IM with a specialisation in enterprise resource planning (ERP) at postgraduate level; the UWA clearly identifies IM as its specialisation, with a focus on support for other discipline majors such as accounting and marketing; and Murdoch focuses on the more technical aspects of IS such as IS development and the use of multimedia. ECU is also targeting a new market, with a Masters Degree in Strategic Project Management, which it hopes will appeal to a broader market base.

Table 10.3 The wide variety of courses offered across all four universities.

University	Undergraduate courses	Postgraduate courses
Curtin	Bachelor of Commerce (IS) Bachelor of Commerce (IT) Bachelor of Commerce (EC)	Grad Dip/Certificates Postgrad Dip/Certificates Master (IS) Master of Commerce PhD
ECU	Bachelor of Business (IS) Bachelor of Business (EC) Bachelor of Business (IM) Bachelor of IS	Grad Dip/Certificates (IS, EC, ERP) Master (IS) Master Strategic Project Management DBA (IS) PhD
UWA	Bachelor of Commerce (IS)	Master of Information Management Master of Commerce (IM) PhD
Murdoch	Bachelor of Science (IS Dev) Bachelor of Science (BIS) Bachelor Science (Multimedia) Bachelor of Science in IS	Grad Dip Masters IS PhD

Despite some low enrolments in the undergraduate and postgraduate programs, PhD programs continue to thrive in all four IS groups, with a total of about 60 doctoral students by research. In addition, ECU offers a unique DBA program in IS. This is a partially taught program with a shorter thesis component and has a further 20 doctoral students, drawn mainly from senior managers in the WA community. In general, enrolments in general degrees such as the Bachelor of Business with IS specialisations remain fairly steady, but enrolments in specialist IS degrees are dropping radically. Interest in multimedia has declined significantly and electronic commerce no longer holds the appeal it once did. There has been a substantial decline in international recruitment, impacting on the postgraduate market.

Research

Research focus within the four universities also varies widely and this could be one of the reasons why all interviewees identified a low level of collaboration between WA universities. Indeed, at the time of writing, there were no joint projects and staff in each university seemed unfamiliar with research being conducted in other WA institutions. Funding was variable, with the onus on staff to generate funding through successful grant applications, internally or externally, or through collaborative partnerships with industry. Curtin has an industry-sponsored professor, which comes with considerable prestige in addition to research funds.

Research output also varied considerably. At the UWA, the research activity of staff was largely interdisciplinary and had a relatively low proportion contributing to strictly IS-related research, compared with a high output overall at ECU, with about 90 per cent of staff research active. Curtin followed the more typical path, with 20 per cent of staff providing 80 per cent of output. It was stated that Curtin had shifted emphasis towards teaching over research in recent years, but this could be changing as Curtin has made a strategic move to be a research-intensive university. Identified themes for continuing research are shown in Table 10.4.

Table 10.4 Research themes

University	Themes	Groups	Funding
Curtin	Technology adoption Information technology Management Health informatics Relational ontology World-wide databases Grid supercomputing Electronic commerce Soft-systems methodology	Individuals + PhD groupings around professors	Grant-based + Research Performance Index funding system
ECU	Electronic markets Collaborative commerce in small and medium-sized enterprises (SMEs) IS evaluation IS in the construction industry IS education and IS in education	Five formal research groups led by the professors/associate professors + individual	Grant-based + Research Activity Index funding system
UWA	Knowledge management Virtual communities E-government Transport modelling Compliance-monitoring systems	Individuals and interdisciplinary and inter-faculty collaborations	Grant-based and individual research support from school funds
Murdoch	Human factors in IS Knowledge management E-learning Decision support Business strategy alignment	Individuals	Grant-based + individual allocation from school

Curtin and ECU operate a research performance-monitoring scheme, which is linked directly to research funding (Curtin University—Research Performance Index; ECU—Research Activity Index). In this way, staff members are rewarded with a dollar value applied to the number of points they have generated towards the research assessment quantum. This scheme provides considerable incentive for staff to become productive but can favour quantity over quality. At ECU, however, the recent trend has been to decrease the funding per point being allocated to staff and to the use the money to provide competitive internal research grants.

All four universities support qualitative and quantitative research and employ multiple methods. Case studies and interpretive research were commonly applied. The overall research picture in Western Australia fits closely with the view of a 'fragmented adhocracy' (Whitley 1984; Culnan et al. 1993; Checkland and Holwell 1998), with low researcher mutual dependency and very different contributions from each of the four universities, reflecting local political pressures from within their different institutions but also from within the state—where all four compete for highly limited funding.

IS leadership

The particular environment of Western Australia has strongly influenced IS leadership since West Australians are often loath to leave the state because of the rather laidback life-style and Mediterranean climate, with core academic staff remaining fairly static over the long term. In addition, Western Australia is seen as a desirable location for international immigrants and, hence, the state attracts a fair share of international academics. It is rare to see Australian academics from the eastern states choose to relocate to the west. This has had two consequences: WA academics have had to strive for excellence within the Australian arena; and Western Australia has gained an international profile through its international academics. Richard Watson (originally from Western Australia), Bob Galliers and Janice Burn have all contributed to the development of IS within the state, coming from an international perspective, and West Australians Graham Pervan and Bernie Glasson have had significant input nationally and internationally. All six current professors at Curtin and ECU are well-known researchers with national and international reputations.

Interviewees stressed the real need for IS leadership and active involvement in IS research by the professoriate. Information systems groups without a professor tended to have a significantly lower profile in their home university.

Key academics in the development of IS in Western Australia

Richard Watson

Richard Watson led the development of the School of Information Systems at the Western Australian College of Advanced Education in the 1980s before it was granted university status. During this period, he undertook a PhD in the United States and, after returning to Perth for a period, decided to relocate to Athens, Georgia, in 1989. He has retained links with universities in Western Australia and is a frequent visitor. He is currently J. Rex Fuqua Distinguished

Chair for Internet Strategy in the Department of MIS at the University of Georgia's Terry College of Business.

Graham Pervan

Graham Pervan is Professor of Information Systems at Curtin University. He has been involved in the development of the discipline for more than 25 years, has been head of school and is currently President of the Australian Council of Professors and Heads of Information Systems (ACPHIS).

Janice Burn

Janice Burn has had a 30-year career in IS and was Foundation Professor and Head of School of Management Information Systems at Edith Cowan University from 1997 to 2005. She previously held senior academic posts in Hong Kong (Associate Professor and Associate Head of School, Hong Kong Polytechnic) and the United Kingdom (Principal Lecturer, Coventry Polytechnic). She was a member of the Australian Research Council (ARC) and an adviser to the Australian government on IT and national research priorities. Burn was instrumental in developing the School of Management Information Systems into a research-intensive school during her time at ECU. She was also highly innovative in leading course development, with many successful courses launched.

Conclusions

The main IS strength in Western Australia lies in Curtin and ECU, where separate IS schools have been in existence for more than 30 years. In 2007, the IS school at ECU merged with the School of Management to form a new school, but it still retains its identity as a discipline. Information systems is recognised as a discipline at the UWA and Murdoch, but as a subset of other disciplines, and it has a somewhat lower status in these two institutions. Different value systems and funding models inhibit collaboration between the four institutions. In 1998, Curtin took the lead to organise the WA workshop in IS research (WAWISR) and this was repeated each year, hosted by each university in turn until 2001, when enthusiasm to organise it was exhausted. Sadly, one of the reasons for this could be the increased emphasis on recognised research output, lessening the motivation for activities that would be regarded solely as community building. Similarly, in 1999, ECU ran the first Working for e-Business (WeB) conference based in Perth and continued to organise this until 2004. This conference attracted some local attendees but many more came from across Australia to forge national collaborative links.

With respect to the development of IS as a discipline, social processes and local contingencies seem to have had considerable impact. Western Australia is the most distant state in Australia and hence looks inward to local industry for direction, but also outwards from Australia to forge international reputations.

Mechanisms of control are very much still in a developmental mode although this applies to the country as a whole, with IS representation on the national research funding body, the ARC, being achieved only in 2000 with the appointment of Professor Janice Burn as the IS discipline representative on the ARC research panel for Mathematics, Information and Computer Sciences. The core body of knowledge taught at each of the four universities tends to reflect local allegiances with industry, services and professions and varies in line with local developments and needs rather than necessarily responding directly to demands from within the discipline itself.

All interviewees commented on the decrease in numbers in IS and diminishing staff numbers, which suggests that the picture painted in this study could change significantly in the next few years. It was also interesting to note that IS was seen to be a discipline grouping that could be transposed easily from within one discipline grouping to another, with residual homes having been found in business, science, mathematics and even engineering at one time or another across the four institutions. From the WA perspective, it would appear that IS is still 'a perspective' (Fitzgerald 2003) rather than a discipline—and a perpetually shifting perspective at that.

Acknowledgements

Thanks are due to the following interviewees: Professor Janice Burn, ECU; Dr Nick Letch, the UWA; Professor Graham Pervan, Curtin; Professor Craig Standing, ECU; Dr Fay Sudweeks, Murdoch; and Danny Toohey, Murdoch.

References

Ariav, G., de Sanctis, G. and Moore, J. 1987, 'Competing reference disciplines for MIS research', *Proceedings of the Eighth International Conference on Information Systems*, Pittsburgh, pp. 455–8.

Checkland, P. and Holwell, S. 1998, *Information, Systems and Information Systems—Making Sense of the Field*, Wiley & Sons, Chichester.

Culnan, M. J., Swanson, E. B. and Keller, M. T. 1993, 'MIS research in the 1980s: shifting points of work and reference', *Proceedings of the 26th Hawaii International Conference on Systems Sciences*, vol. 3, pp. 597–606.

Fitzgerald, G. 2003, 'Information systems: a subject with particular perspective, no more, no less', *European Journal of Information Systems*, vol. 12, no. 3, pp. 225–9.

Klein, H. K., Hirshheim, R. and Nissen, H. 1991, 'A pluralist perspective of the information systems research arena', in H. E. Nissen, H. K. Klein and R. Hirshheim (eds), *Information Systems Research: Contemporary Approaches and Emergent Traditions*, Elsevier, Amsterdam.

Ruscio, K. 1987, 'Many sectors, many professionals', in B. Clarke (ed.), *The Academic Profession*, University of California Press.

Whitley, R. 1984, 'The development of management studies as a fragmented adhocracy', *Social Science Information*, vol. 23, no. 4–5, pp. 775–818.

AUSTRALIA-WIDE

11. A longitudinal study of information systems research in Australia

Graham Pervan
School of Information Systems
Curtin University of Technology

Graeme Shanks
Department of Information Systems
University of Melbourne

Abstract

This chapter reports a longitudinal study that explores the state of information systems (IS) research in Australia. A series of surveys was distributed to the heads of all IS discipline groups in Australian universities in 2004, 2005 and 2006. The study highlights the current state of IS research in Australia from the 2006 survey and analyses the trends in IS research in the past few years. The study revealed a wide range of topics researched (with rapid growth in electronic commerce and knowledge management), a range of foci, a balance between positivist and interpretive research, surveys as the most frequently used research method and the fact that most research was directed at informing IS professionals. A SWOT (strengths, weaknesses, opportunities, threats) analysis identified the growing importance of industry relevance and collaboration. Research performance, measured by publication output and research grant income, is shown to be improving, but is dominated by universities from the 'Sandstone/Redbrick' and 'Unitech' sectors, and overall does not compare favourably with other disciplines.

Introduction

The first academic programs in IS appeared in Australia in the late 1960s and have grown steadily to be available in almost all Australian universities. While the teaching of IS has grown, the growth of IS research has been slower and few studies have examined its progress. Ridley et al. (1998) studied publication performance over a seven-year period, but there has been no longitudinal study of the research profile of IS in Australian universities.

This chapter explores the Australian IS research field along lines similar to part of the study conducted by Avgerou et al. (1999) in Europe, except that it focuses only on research, and is based on an earlier study by Pervan and Cecez-Kecmanovic (2001). The study targeted the views of the heads of discipline from Australian IS groups and was conducted on behalf of the Australian Council of Professors and Heads of Information Systems (ACPHIS).

Research approach

In order to investigate the state of IS research in Australia, a series of surveys was distributed to the heads of all IS discipline groups in Australian universities in 2004, 2005 and 2006. We focused on the 'school' level (where 'school' represents a group of people focused primarily on teaching and researching IS). The group of target respondents expected to represent these schools was the head of discipline for each of the groups identified by the Information Systems Heads of Department (ISHoDs) mailing list. Based on the previous study by Avgerou et al. (1999) and aspects of paradigm and method from Neuman (2006), a number of dimensions of the schools' research activities were identified and incorporated into the original questionnaire. The survey has been refined progressively to the current instrument, although the broad focus remains consistent. The survey contained questions on:

- *people*—number, level and research activity of staff, number of enrolled and completing PhD students
- *structures*—school structural titles, real names and super-organisations
- *foci*—topics of research interest, unit of analysis, human–technology spectrum, beneficiaries of the research
- *paradigm*—positivist, interpretivist or critical
- *methods*—survey, case study, action research, laboratory experiment, and so on
- *performance*—publication output, research funds obtained, collaboration.

In addition, a brief SWOT analysis of Australian IS research was added to the questionnaire.

As indicated, the target group was the groups on the ISHoDs mailing list (one response required from the head of discipline of each group) and the survey was distributed and returned via e-mail.

Results

The questionnaires were distributed electronically and, after some follow-up, 24 responses were received in 2006, 24 responses were received in 2005 and 25 responses were received in 2004. This represents a response from about 60 per cent of the universities. A number of universities, however, have no IS discipline group, so the effective response rate is more than 80 per cent (of the 30 or so IS groups) and can therefore be claimed to be representative of the population of IS groups as a whole. There is a mix of titles (most commonly schools, but also departments and other titles), but hereafter the groupings will be referred to as schools. The discipline titles of these schools of the 24 respondents in 2006 were 50 per cent (12 respondents) IS, 25 per cent information technology (IT) and 25 per cent other titles. Furthermore, 14 of these schools were in a business/commerce faculty, seven in an IT faculty and three in a mix of others.

Academic staff levels are shown in Table 11.1 and indicate a 2006 mean of 16.3 total academic staff in IS schools, with a reduction in size evident from 2004 and 2005. This is consistent with the reduction in IS student numbers during this period. Table 11.2 shows a breakdown into staff categories and highlights the low number of senior staff (levels D and E) and research-only staff (research fellows) in each school.

Table 11.1 Academic staff levels

	Mean 2004	Range 2004	Mean 2005	Range 2005	Mean 2006	Range 2006
Continuing	17.8	2–40	17.2	1–41	14.4	3–30
Contract	2.5	0–12	2.0	0–7	1.9	0–7
Total academic staff	20.3		19.2		16.3	

The overall view is that there is a mix of names and locations for IS schools, but the majority are medium-sized groups with IS in the name and reside in a business/commerce faculty where they can maintain a close association with the areas of application of IS.

Table 11.2 Academic staff categories

	Mean 2004	Range 2004	Mean 2005	Range 2005	Mean 2006	Range 2006
Research fellows	0.9	0–5	0.7	0–4	0.7	0–4
Level Es (professors)	1.3	0–3	1.4	0–3	1.3	0–3
Level Ds (associate professors)	2.0	0–11	1.7	0–4	1.6	0–5
Level Cs (senior lecturers)	4.8	0–13	5.3	0–14	4.0	0–11
Level Bs (lecturer Bs)	8.7	0–23	7.9	1–22	7.3	1–18
Level As (lecturer As)	2.8	0–11	2.1	0–10	1.6	0–8
Total	20.5		19.1		16.5	

Staff research activity levels are shown in Table 11.3 and indicate that in 2006 the majority (mean 83.7 per cent) of staff were doing some research although only about half of these were research active according to the strict Department of Education, Science and Training (DEST) definition (mean 41 per cent). Just more than half (mean 57.5 per cent) have PhDs and a further quarter are doing PhDs (mean 23.6 per cent). Just more than one-third (mean 37.6 per cent) are supervising PhDs and one-quarter (mean 25 per cent) have supervised a PhD to completion. It can be seen that although the proportions of staff doing some research and those considered DEST research-active have remained about the same, there has been an increase in the number of staff with PhDs and in supervision in the period 2004–06.

Table 11.3 Staff research activity

	Mean 2004	Range 2004	% 2004	Mean 2005	Range 2005	% 2005	Mean 2006	Range 2006	% 2006
Doing some research	-	-	-	15.3	1–37	80.1	13.4	4–30	83.7
Research active (DEST)	7.9	0–21	43.9	6.3	0–18	37.5	6.0	0–18	41.9
Doing PhDs	-	-	-	5.2	1–16	28.7	3.8	0–11	23.6
Have PhDs	8.7	2–24	43.5	9.3	1–24	51.3	8.6	3–22	57.5
Supervising PhDs	6.1	1–15	31.6	6.2	1–16	36.0	5.7	1–16	37.6
Supervised ≥1 PhD to completion	3.1	0–8	17.0	3.3	0–8	19.8	3.5	0–9	25.0

Doctoral student numbers are shown in Table 11.4 and it can be seen that the mean number of doctoral students and the mean number of PhD completions per school have remained much the same since 2004. The results indicate that in 2006 the mean number of full-time equivalent (FTE) PhD students in each school was 11.5 (7.8 full-time and half of 7.4 part-time), while the mean number of PhD graduations per school in the previous year was 1.4. With that many PhD students, there would be an expectation of three to four graduates per annum (based on a target of 3.5 FTE years for completion of a PhD), but the real completion rate is less than half that. This signals a throughput problem, which might exist because of variable-quality supervision practices (within schools and across the sector) and a lack of adequate resources, which needs to be addressed.

Table 11.4 Doctoral student numbers

	Mean	Range
Enrolled full-time 2004	8.0	0–25
Enrolled part-time 2004	7.9	0–23
Enrolled full-time 2005	8.2	0–21
Enrolled part-time 2005	8.4	0–23
Enrolled full-time 2006	7.8	0–26
Enrolled part-time 2006	7.4	0–25
2002 graduates	0.6	0–2
2003 graduates	1.3	0–6
2004 graduates	1.6	0–5
2005 graduates	1.4	0–3
2006 graduates (half-year)	1.0	0–4

Respondents were asked to indicate the topics of research interest in the past, present and future, and responses for the 2006 survey are summarised in Table 11.5 below, sorted by future topic of interest. The results demonstrate the substantial interest in research on IS management and strategy and the organisational implications of IS and IT, IS adoption/diffusion, electronic commerce and knowledge management, with almost all groups indicating an interest in these areas. In addition, interest is strong in topics such as IS development and business modelling, mobile commerce and the theoretical underpinnings of IS. On the other hand, specific topics and technical issues such as computer and network applications and computer-supported cooperative work (CSCW)/groupware are relatively less popular. It should be pointed out, however, that the table reveals how many groups are interested in these topics and does not show how large these groups are. So, further research is needed at the individual researcher level.

The respondents were asked also to indicate the usual unit of analysis of their research. In the 2006 survey this was the organisation (22 responses), groups/teams (19), clusters of organisations (19), industry (16), processes/tasks (15), individuals (14), national economy/society (eight) and world economy/society (three). Clearly, researchers focused most on organisations and the people within them, and significantly less on studying IS at the national or global levels. This could represent an opportunity to collaborate with other researchers (for example, economists) to investigate the impact of IS and information technologies on Australia's economy and its links with the region and globally. In terms of a research paradigm, responses revealed dominance of the positivist paradigm (in 71 per cent of schools), but the interpretivist paradigm was also used often (54 per cent). The survey data confirmed a growing recognition that IS researchers in Australia did conduct research based on non-positivist research paradigms. Few mentioned any significant emphasis on research using a critical paradigm, which was also the case at the international level (Mingers 2001).

Table 11.5 IS research topics (2006 survey data)

Topic	Past	Present	Future	Topic	Past	Present	Future
Organisational implications of IS&T	19	21	20	Human–computer interaction	11	11	10
IS management/strategy	17	17	16	Systems development	13	10	9
Electronic commerce	19	18	16	Knowledge-based/expert systems	11	12	9
IS adoption/diffusion	16	16	15	Economic effects of IS&T	5	8	8
Knowledge management	13	17	14	Databases	9	9	8
Theoretical underpinnings of IS	15	14	13	DSS/EIS/data warehousing	9	9	7
IS development methods	12	12	13	IS outsourcing/offshoring	5	7	7
Mobile commerce	7	13	13	Legal/ethical aspects of IS&T	8	8	7
Business modelling	10	13	13	Computer and network applications	3	3	3
Societal effects of IS&T	10	12	11	CSCW/groupware	6	3	3
IS security	8	9	10				

When asked to indicate the specific research methods used, the responses revealed that the full range of research methods were being applied by IS researchers (see Table 11.6 below, sorted by the research method used most often). The most popular method is the survey, but also popular are positivist and interpretive case studies, and design science. This balanced application of paradigm and method is perhaps an indicator that Australian IS researchers are more like their European than their North American counterparts. Arnott and Pervan (2005) found that, in published research in decision support systems, North American journals were overwhelmingly positivist whereas European journals were more balanced on paradigm and method. Again, these data are at a school level, so a study of individual researchers is needed to reveal the true extent of usage of the different methods.

Table 11.6 Research methods used (2006 survey data)

	Never	Sometimes	Often	Always
Survey	0	7	16	1
Interpretivist case study	2	7	15	0
Positivist case study	3	10	11	0
Design science	0	13	10	1
Literature meta-analysis	5	13	2	4
Business modelling/simulation	7	11	4	2
Secondary data analysis	5	13	5	1
IS development	6	12	6	0
Action research	6	13	5	0
Conceptual study	4	16	3	1
Ethnography	10	11	3	0
Longitudinal case study	5	17	2	0
Laboratory experiment	11	11	2	0

Respondents in the 2006 survey indicated clearly that the primary beneficiaries of their research were other IS academics (20), managers (17) and IS professionals (15 responses), followed distantly by end users/workers (seven), policymakers (six) and people in general (zero). This might again show that we (IS researchers) are not taking up the opportunity to influence governments and society, and it could be a major reason for the apparent lack of recognition of IS as a discipline by some government agencies. Respondents indicated that, where it occurred, most research collaboration occurred with IS colleagues within that particular academic group. Clearly, there is a need to widen the collaboration net nationally and internationally, which could help to increase quality, and with practitioners, which increases relevance and provides opportunities for funding—for example, the Australian Research Council (ARC) Linkage grants. It could also serve to enhance the impact of IS research, which might be an advantage in the research quality-assurance mechanism that will replace the proposed Research Quality Framework (RQF), once developed. The planned RQF was abandoned in December 2007 by the new Labor government.

School research output is shown in Table 11.7 and indicates that in 2006 schools generated a mean of about 52 publications, 34 of which were conference papers, 11 journal papers and a small number of other types. It can be seen that there has been a substantial increase in the mean number of publications in the period 2002–05. The largest increase has been in conference papers, although the number of journal papers has also increased.

Table 11.7 Publications per school

	2002 mean	2003 mean	2004 mean	2005 mean
Refereed journal papers	6.3	10.0	9.8	11.0
Refereed conference papers	21.1	29.2	29.1	33.8
Chapters in books	4.3	3.7	3.4	5.3
Authored books	0.4	0.9	0.4	0.6
Edited books/proceedings	0.6	0.8	0.5	1.7
Total publications	32.7	44.6	43.2	52.4

Research performance per staff member is shown in Table 11.8 and indicates that in 2005 the mean output per academic staff member was 2.6 publications per annum and the mean grant income per academic staff member was about $17 800 per annum. It can be seen that there has been a substantial increase in publications and grant income since 2002, although the rate of increase has decreased substantially and the differences between 2004 means and 2005 means are very small. Further, Tables 11.7 and 11.8 reveal that the mean number of journal papers (of any type—there was no assessment of journal quality) per IS academic is much less than one per annum. Follow-up investigation would be required to determine publication rates in tier-one and tier-two journals, but it is certain to be even lower. This would have severely limited the chances of IS research groups achieving a high rating in the proposed RQF process—thus constraining IS research funding.

Table 11.8 Research performance (per staff member)

	Mean	Median	Range
2002 publications	1.6	1.3	0.0–4.4
2003 publications	2.3	2.1	0.0–6.7
2004 publications	2.3	2.4	0.4–3.9
2005 publications	2.6	2.2	0.3–8.5
2002 grant $K	8.9	2.8	0.0–45.6
2003 grant $K	15.5	9.7	0.0–48.9
2004 grant $K	17.0	14.8	0.0–63.6
2005 grant $K	17.8	15.0	0.0–53.3

Research grant income per school is shown in Table 11.9 and indicates that in 2005 the mean grant income was more than $300 000 per annum. The amount of research grant income varied considerably between the groups, with a few groups doing very well in gaining funds from external sources, but most having to depend on internal university resources. The main source of research grant income in 2006 was from the ARC (Linkage and Discovery grants), although substantial research income was also generated from collaborative research centres (CRCs), industry contracts and internal university resources. It can be seen that although the total research income increased significantly after 2002, it has remained much the same throughout 2003–05. Generally, these figures compare poorly with other disciplines, including computer science and computer engineering.

Table 11.9 Research grant income ($K) (per school)

	2002 mean	2002 median	2003 mean	2003 median	2004 mean	2004 median	2005 mean	2005 median
ARC Linkage	68.9	0.0	107.8	0.0	90.2	6.0	98.8	20.0
ARC Discovery	32.4	0.0	58.4	0.0	64.8	0.0	33.7	0.0
Internal university	32.5	20.0	58.5	45.0	47.6	15.6	58.6	20.0
CRC	-	-	-	-	46.5	0.0	60.0	0.0
Industry contract	10.5	0.0	32.8	0.0	46.3	0.0	41.2	0.0
Consulting	4.4	0.0	12.3	0.0	9.6	0.0	11.4	0.0
International	8.0	0.0	3.1	0.0	4.8	0.0	1.1	0.0
Other (various)	22.8	0.0	28.8	0.0	3.3	0.0	0.0	0.0
National Health and Medical Research Council (NHMRC)	-	-	-	-	0.0	0.0	2.0	0.0
Total	179.5		301.7		313.1		306.8	

Table 11.10 shows a comparison of several research variables with significantly different means across university categories. The university categories are based on those of Marginson and Considine (2000) and provide a useful means of comparing research performance. The categories are defined as follows (Marginson and Considine 2000:15–16):

- Sandstone/Redbricks: established before World War I (Sandstones) or in the 1940s–1950s (Redbricks)
- Unitechs: the former institutes of technology
- Gumtrees: founded between the early 1960s and mid-1970s
- New: founded after 1986.

It is clear from Table 11.10 that the mean size of IS schools in each of the categories is very similar. The Sandstone/Redbrick and Unitech categories have, however, significantly greater mean numbers of professors, mean numbers of DEST research-active staff, mean numbers of doctoral students, mean numbers of papers in refereed journals and refereed conferences, mean numbers of publications per staff member, mean total amounts of grant income and mean grant incomes per staff member. This is consistent with the research-intensive nature of universities in the Sandstone/Redbrick category and the historical location of IS schools within the Unitech universities.

Table 11.10 2006 significant means across university categories

	Sandstone/ Redbricks	Unitechs	Gumtrees	New
Total academic staff	15.5	17.0	17.8	16.1
Number of professors	1.4	2.3	0.3	0.9
Number of DEST research active	8.5	6.3	3.3	4.2
Number of doctoral students (EFT)	16.0	12.7	6.7	7.4
Papers in refereed journals	14.0	13.2	7.3	7.8
Papers in refereed conferences	39.5	51.2	17.3	21.2
Publications per staff member	3.0	3.5	1.2	2.0
Total grants ($,000)	397.1	500.8	26.0	179.1
Grant $ per staff member ($,000)	23.6	29.1	0.9	10.0

The final part of the survey allowed each respondent to suggest the three main strengths, weaknesses, opportunities and threats (SWOT) for the IS discipline research; a summary of the most frequently cited issues in the 2006 survey is provided in Table 11.11. In total, more than 150 ideas were generated in the SWOT and the top five in each category are presented here.

Table 11.11 Results from the SWOT analysis

Strengths	Weaknesses
Industry relevance and links (10)	Lack of industry relevance (8)
Diversity of method (6)	Lack of identity of IS as a discipline (6)
Diversity of research undertaken (5)	Poor funding and recognition by funding bodies (6)
Feeling of community (ACIS, ACPHIS) (4)	Poor/variable research training (5)
Critical mass of quality IS researchers (3)	Conflicts of research focus (5)
Opportunities	**Threats**
Industry collaboration/linkage grants (13)	Falling student numbers/staffing (9)
Raising profile in industry and government (6)	Other fields claiming IS as their own (8)
Cooperative doctoral research training (4)	Lack of research funding (6)
Collaboration generally (3)	Nelson Higher Education Policy/Research Quality Framework (6)
Improved quality and success (2)	Lack of industry relevance/recognition (4)

The respondents clearly believe there is strength in our diversity and relevance. Diversity was indicated in types of research undertaken, the research approaches taken (and the underlying epistemology) and in the breadth of experience most IS researchers brought with them from their background in IS practice and their grounding in practitioner activity. These strengths in diversity and relevance need to be nurtured and exploited.

Key weaknesses are the lack of relevance and identity and poor funding (relative to computer science/computer engineering), which is associated with other weaknesses such as the lack of a research culture in Australian business and lack of recognition from funding agencies such as the ARC. These and other research focus and training issues need to be overcome.

The respondents clearly recognise that there are numerous opportunities of which we should attempt to take advantage. In this, collaboration (with industry, international colleagues and other Australian universities) is the key. In addition and as indicated earlier, the opportunity exists for IS to increase its profile and recognition by conducting research on societal and economic issues, which might influence government policy.

While industry collaboration was seen as an opportunity, it could also be a threat if proper linkages were not built. Research impact will be critical in any research quality-assurance mechanism. Perhaps the greatest threats to IS research in Australian universities lie in the lack of recognition of IS as a discipline and its location in the academic structure, the falling numbers and excessive teaching loads in most schools and the career and financial opportunities outside academia.

Conclusions and future work

In this chapter, we have presented a longitudinal analysis of an annual survey of Australian IS 'heads of discipline', which shows something of the current state of IS research in Australia from the 2006 survey and analyses the trends in IS research in the past few years. The study has revealed that, in terms of research, IS schools in Australian universities seek and demonstrate diversity in topic, paradigm and method. Publication and research grant performance is steadily improving, particularly in Sandstone/Redbrick and Unitech universities, but it varies significantly across the sector and within schools and even the better performers do not compare particularly well with other, more established, academic disciplines.

It should be noted that the data collected and presented do not necessarily represent the views of individual IS researchers. Future work is needed to obtain those views. The chapter can, however, and should be used to initiate discussion within the IS academic community on where we are, where we want to be in the future and how we aim to get there.

References

Arnott, D. and Pervan, G. 2005, 'A critical analysis of decision support systems research', *Journal of Information Technology*, vol. 20, no. 2, pp. 67–87.

Avgerou, C., Siemer, J. and Bjørn-Andersen, N. 1999, 'The academic field of information systems in Europe', *European Journal of Information Systems*, vol. 8, pp. 136–53.

Marginson, S. and Considine, M. 2000, *The Enterprise University: Power, Governance and Reinvention in Australia*, Cambridge University Press, Cambridge, UK.

Mingers, J. 2001, 'Combining IS research methods: towards a pluralist methodology', *Information Systems Research*, vol. 12, no. 3, pp. 240–59.

Neuman, W. L. 2006, *Social Research Methods: Qualitative and Quantitative Approaches*, 6th edn, Allyn and Bacon, Needham Heights, Massachusetts, USA.

Pervan, G. P. and Cecez-Kecmanovic, D. 2001, 'The status of information systems research in Australia: stage 1—the HODs view', *Proceedings of the 12th Australasian Conference on Information Systems*, Coffs Harbour, NSW, Australia, 5–7 December, pp. 503–6.

Ridley, G., Goulding, P., Lowry, G. and Pervan, G. P. 1998, 'The Australian information systems research community: an analysis of mainstream publication outlets', *Australian Journal of Information Systems*, vol. 5, no. 2, pp. 69–80.

12. The information systems academic discipline in Australian universities: a meta-analysis

Gail Ridley
IT Control Research Group
School of Accounting and Corporate Governance
University of Tasmania

Guy Gable
Faculty of Information Technology
Queensland University of Technology

Bob Smyth
Faculty of Information Technology
Queensland University of Technology

Shirley Gregor
School of Accounting and Business Information Systems
The Australian National University

Roger Clarke
Xamax Consultancy Pty Ltd
Canberra, Australia

Abstract

The meta-analysis chapter integrates and interprets data from earlier chapters in this monograph, drawing on the theoretical framework developed for the study. Mixed results were seen in the development of mechanisms of control and a core body of knowledge when analysis was made of information systems (IS) in Australian universities in the most recent years. The limitations on progress were related mainly to reduced IS enrolments and the associated decline in staff numbers and the autonomy of IS groups, along with the restructuring and relocation of many IS groups within universities. It appears, however, that the introduction of the Research Quality Framework (RQF) was intended to increase the quantity and quality of Australian IS research publications. While great diversity was reported regarding some components of the body of knowledge, the existence of key IS research topics was demonstrated from a national analysis, which was not evident from analysis at a local level. Little IS theory was reported, but recognition was given to the kind of theory that was appropriate for IS. When the development of Australian IS is considered over a longer period, significant progress has been made in some mechanisms of control, including steady growth in professorial appointments. Although local contingencies were found to have had an impact on the degree of professionalism, the study was not able to confirm that these two components of the framework—responsiveness to local contingencies and degree of professionalism—were inversely related. Information systems in Australia is not likely to be unique in its development relative to other parts of the world. The study concluded that, based on IS in Australian universities, IS might be regarded as a field rather than as a discipline.

Introduction

This chapter sets out a consolidation and interpretation of data from previous chapters in this volume. By doing so it aims, in part, to present an overview of the IS academic discipline in Australian universities through the lens of the theoretical framework developed for the study by Ridley, which appears in Chapter 3 of this volume. The framework was derived from Whitley's theory of scientific change (1984a, 1984b).

An assumption behind the framework is that the development of IS in Australian universities is a response to the pressures that act on the discipline. The framework provides a common means of analysing the data collected across a range of dimensions from different regions in Australia, and presented in this monograph. As outlined in the state chapters, individual states varied in the extent of their application of and reliance on this framework.

According to the framework, the maturity of the IS discipline in Australia can be evaluated on the basis of two constructs. The first construct is the extent to which mechanisms of control have been established. Key among these are means of reputation building and a core body of knowledge. The second construct is the extent to which professionalism is able to overcome the impact of local contingencies.

This chapter applies the two framework constructs to guide analysis of data presented in previous chapters of this volume, in particular in the case studies from each state and the Australian Capital Territory (ACT). Beyond the assessment of observed data against the proposed framework, this meta-analysis seeks to draw from the Australian data some observations on observed trends and tensions, with an emphasis on national and international factors impacting on the status of IS in Australian universities.

Approach adopted

The first construct of the framework relates to *mechanisms of control* and the IS knowledge base or *core body of knowledge*. It is to be expected that these will increase over time with the development of the discipline. With regard to *mechanisms of control*, the development of a discipline depends on reputations being established and critical rewards being obtained through a range of social processes. These mechanisms of control include attracting research funding, the introduction of publication outlets and the administrative location of IS groups in universities.

A particularly important mechanism involved in the development of a discipline is the emergence of a *core body of knowledge*. This has four components. The first is the establishment of *research and teaching methods and standards*, which refers to knowledge gain and transfer. The second component, a *unique symbol set*, enables unambiguous communication between initiates in the discipline and, in the process, prevents other disciplines trying to subsume the area into their own. The third component, *key research and teaching of IS topics*, sets out the knowledge domain, while the fourth component, *laws, rules and evidenced guidelines*, refers to the knowledge types required in the discipline.

The second framework construct concerns the *degree of professionalism* of the discipline, or accepted ways of undertaking IS research and teaching, and the extent to which it enables the community to withstand the *impact of local contingencies*. It is postulated that where a discipline is not highly professionalised, local contingencies such as political pressures have high impact. Consequently, the degree of professionalism of IS is suggested by the extent of variation in the nature of its research and teaching across the 'states' of Australia and over time.

It is argued that an examination of progress in the constructs and their components will reveal the nature and development of the IS academic discipline in Australia. This chapter reports on that examination, through a meta-analysis of the data collected and reported elsewhere in this volume. This analysis draws initially on points of similarity and difference from the 'state' case studies, and their relationship to the framework.

The framework constructs and their components guided the development of a protocol for the state reports in this volume (Gable 2006). The analysis presented below utilised data gathered in seven broad topic areas embodied in the common case-study protocol. The broad topic questions were:

- What is the relative size of the IS presence at the university?

- What is the administrative placement of IS (including changes over time)?
- To what extent has IS at the university been impacted on by local contingencies?
- To what extent is IS identified as a separate field at the university?
- What are the distinctive features of the IS curriculum at the university?
- What are the distinctive features of IS research at the university?
- Who are the key people who have had an impact on IS in universities in the state?

The middle five topics were designed to gather data for evaluation of the framework, while the first and the last topics listed provided complementary information. The key people who have had an impact on IS in the states are not addressed in this chapter, as this has been presented in detail in the previous chapters through vignettes—and these data do not lend themselves to aggregation.

Thematic analysis was undertaken of the state reports presented in this volume (Dixon-Woods et al. 2005). Beyond reporting on the similarities and differences across the states from the perspective of the framework, the meta-analysis also aggregates the findings to provide an Australian perspective. This meta-analysis chapter comments further on several significant issues that lie outside the guiding framework.

Size of the IS presence in Australian universities

The starting point in the meta-analysis is an examination of the size of the IS presence in Australian universities. It is hypothesised that the size of the IS presence can be related to the mechanisms of control for IS in Australian universities. For example, where there are few staff, or where the student/staff ratio is high, it is likely to be more difficult for staff to demonstrate mechanisms of control, such as engagement in research that is able to attract research funding, or involvement in the introduction or management of IS publication outlets.

Table 12.1 lists the 39 universities in Australia—37 public and two private (Bond and Notre Dame). Marginson and Considine (2000) characterised the public universities as 'Sandstones', 'Redbricks', 'Gumtrees', 'Unitechs' and 'New Universities'. The six Sandstones were founded in Australia before World War I. The three Redbricks were founded in the 1940s and 1950s. The 10 Gumtrees are postwar and pre-Dawkins general universities founded between the early 1960s and mid-1970s. The five Unitechs are former large institutes of technology formed post-Dawkins. The 13 New Universities are other post-Dawkins universities, often formed out of colleges of advanced education; several New Universities are specialist regional and/or distance-education providers.

Table12.1 Australian universities by state within era

Era/university		State	Unitechs (former institutes of technology)	
Sandstones (pre-World War I)			20	University of Technology, Sydney (UTS)	NSW
1	University of Sydney	NSW	21	Queensland University of Technology (QUT)	Qld
2	University of Queensland (UQ)	Qld	22	University of South Australia (UniSA)	SA
3	University of Adelaide	SA	23	RMIT University	Vic
4	University of Tasmania (UTAS)	Tas	24	Curtin University of Technology	WA
5	University of Melbourne	Vic	**New Universities (post-1987)**		
6	University of Western Australia (UWA)	WA	25	University of Canberra	ACT
Redbricks (1940–50s)			26	Australian Catholic University (ACU)	multi
7	The Australian National University (ANU)	ACT	27	Charles Sturt University (CSU)	NSW
8	University of New South Wales (UNSW)	NSW	28	Southern Cross University (SCU)	NSW
9	Monash University	Vic	29	University of Western Sydney (UWS)	NSW
Gumtrees (1960s to mid-1970s)			30	Charles Darwin University (CDU)	NT
10	Macquarie University	NSW	31	Central Queensland University (CQU)	Qld
11	University of New England (UNE)	NSW	32	University of Southern Queensland (USQ)	Qld
12	University of Newcastle	NSW	33	University of the Sunshine Coast (USC)	Qld
13	University of Wollongong (UoW)	NSW	34	University of Ballarat	VIC
14	Griffith University	QLD	35	Swinburne University of Technology	VIC
15	James Cook University (JCU)	QLD	36	Victoria University (VU)	VIC
16	Flinders University	SA	37	Edith Cowan University (ECU)	WA
17	Deakin University	VIC	**Private**		
18	La Trobe University	VIC	38	Bond University	QLD
19	Murdoch University	WA	39	Notre Dame University	WA

The number of universities identified in the seven regions varied from a single university in Tasmania to 10 in the most populous state, New South Wales (NSW). Although Tasmania has the smallest population of the six Australian states, the Australian Capital Territory has a smaller population again. Three campuses of the one university service Tasmania, while the Australian Capital Territory has three universities. The number of IS groups in universities in the regions (more than one IS group was reported in several universities) ranged from one in Tasmania to 10 in New South Wales. From Table 12.2, it can be seen that the size of the IS presence in each university (staff and students) varied considerably. It is important to note that the numbers in Table 12.2 are very much in flux, representing a consolidation of indicative data gathered over a period when IS was in the process of major change. The NSW figures are also notably incomplete. Hence, the values in the table should not be regarded as precise. In spite of the acknowledged limitations in precision of the figures, it is felt that some meaningful differences and broad trends can be discerned from the numbers in Table 12.2.

Table 12.2 Size of IS presence in Australian universities

Attribute	WA	SA	Tas	Vic	ACT	NSW	Qld
Approx. population (million) [Total 20.3]	2.0	1.5	0.5	5.0	0.3	7.0	4.0
No. IS groups/ universities	4/5	2/3 [?]	1/1	9/9	3/3	10/13 or 14	11/9
Total approx. IS staff [Total 751]	57	15	11	391	25	Not provided	135
IS staff per 100 000 of population [Mean 3.7]	2.9	1.0	2.2	7.8	8.3	1.7	3.4
Total approx. IS students [Total c. 18 500]	480 UG 345 PG	>2 000	>1 000 (800 EFTSU)	7 000	450	Not provided	5 400
IS students per 100 000 of population [Mean 125, excl. NSW]	24 UG 17 PG	>133	200 (160 EFTSU)	140	150	Not provided	135
Raw ratio student/staff	14.5	>133 [?]	90 [?]	17.9	18	Not provided	40 [?]
Enrolment trend	Severe decline	?	Decline		ADFA growth in PhD, course-work Masters		Downturn in course demand
Staff no. trend	Staff reductions	?	Some attrition	Staff cuts Monash, Victoria Uni			Staff reductions
Other aspects relating to size of IS presence	Strong in post-1987 unis; limited in others	Significant presence only in post-Dawkins uni	Fourth-largest school at UTAS in 2005	Strong staff and student nos across 9 unis	Strong IS staff numbers relative to uni sizes	Strong at UNSW and UTS; small–medium at other unis	Strong at QUT, Griffith and UQ; particularly strong relative to uni size at CQU and USQ

Although a few universities had no IS presence, some universities had multiple IS groups. As expected, larger universities were those most likely to have multiple IS groups. Although the data are incomplete, it can be seen that all universities in some states had an IS presence, while this was not the case in Western Australia and South Australia, and most noticeably not the case in New South Wales.

From the number of IS staff and students reported, it appears that a considerable variation in both exist across the universities. Some inconsistencies, however, in the way that the figures for both were reported across the regions could affect the extent to which conclusions can be drawn. For example, whether the staff members reported were full-time or part-time, and included support staff, might not be consistent from one region to another. Similarly, student numbers reported from the states might not be reported on a consistent basis, as some could relate to student numbers studying IS, student numbers undertaking an IS major, or equivalent full-time student units (EFTSU). To allow for possible inconsistencies, only broad patterns will be discussed.

The authors of the Queensland case study suggested that the number of IS academics was a better guide to the size of the IS presence than other characteristics. If this is the case—and even if the count is normalised against population—it is apparent that Victoria is the Australian region with the greatest IS presence. Victoria had about three times the number of IS academic staff reported in the region with the next highest number, which was Queensland, although in New South Wales not all universities were canvassed. A large variation was seen in the number of staff in different IS groups. The Australian Catholic University was reported to have just three IS staff, while a total of 92 staff was reported at the Royal Melbourne Institute of Technology (RMIT) University.

The number of IS students also varied considerably within and across the states. The Australian Catholic University reported just 76 IS students, while there were up to 1000 IS students each at Monash University and the University of Ballarat.

Considerable variation was also seen in the ratio between the number of IS staff and the number of IS students. This characteristic is very likely to impact on teaching loads and therefore research outputs and other aspects relevant to mechanisms of control. Some states appeared to have an over-representation of IS staff for the student numbers reported—for example, in Western Australia, Victoria and the Australian Capital Territory—while the reverse was indicated in other states—for example, South Australia and Tasmania. Some of the differences could be accounted for by different approaches to delivery of courses to offshore students. For example, the majority of the IS students reported for Tasmania were offshore. Although Australian staff are involved in delivery to offshore IS students, there are, however, also offshore staff not employed by the University of Tasmania who are excluded from the figures.

The study was undertaken in the aftermath of the 'dotcom implosion' about 2000. It was therefore unsurprising that many states reported declines in student and staff numbers in recent years. All interviewees in Western Australia reported both declines. The authors of the Tasmanian and Queensland chapters referred to reduced enrolments, while Victoria reported IS staff cuts at two of its large universities. South Australia commented in particular on a decline in local student enrolments. Western Australia reported declining enrolments in specialist IS programs, local students and postgraduate students. Queensland predicted that the demand for IS places in universities in that state would lag behind the demand for IS practitioner skills. Reference was made to the difficulty of attracting research students to one university that was not located in a state capital. The Australian Defence Force Academy (ADFA), however, had experienced growth in PhD and graduate course-work enrolments. It is too early to know whether the declines in student and staff counts have been a lengthy lull or a shift to a new and considerably lower plateau.

The raw student/staff ratios calculated from the data provided in several of the state reports are anomalous. This presumably arises from distinctly different definitions of student counts adopted (enrolled count versus EFTSUs). Comments arising from Table 12.2, however, provide some assistance in explaining some of the variation in the ratio between student and staff numbers in the different regions. In particular, a strong IS presence was reported in some universities in Queensland relative to the size of the university (Central Queensland University and the University of Southern Queensland), although in general in that state the IS presence was consistent with the size of the university. The West Australian case reported that the post-Dawkins (post-1987) institutions in that state had a strong IS presence, while it was more limited at the other universities. Like Western Australia, New South Wales reported a strong IS presence at some universities (the UNSW and the UTS), with a smaller presence at the others. The ACT report commented on the generally strong IS staff numbers relative to the size of the universities, as did Victoria. The ACT report highlighted the strong staff numbers relative to student enrolments, which was apparent in the comparison made against the other states, and was seen also in Western Australia and Victoria. Although Tasmania reported that the School of Information Systems was the fourth-largest school at the University of Tasmania in 2005, by 2007, its presence had declined and it merged with the School of Computing at the start of 2008.

Summary

Analysis in this section indicates that the majority of universities in Australia contained at least one IS group, suggesting that IS has broad acceptance in Australia as an area that needs representation in university teaching and/or research programs. As not all universities contain an IS group, however, IS is not considered universally throughout Australia to be an essential teaching and/or research area. The number of students and IS staff varied a great deal within Australian universities with an IS group. While this characteristic might be accounted for in part by variations in university size, large variations in the staff/student ratio suggest that other forces are also at play, as the regions could be categorised largely into those with a high and those with a low staff/student ratio. Cross-state analysis also revealed a general decline in IS student enrolment in Australian universities in recent years, particularly for domestic students, with consequent reductions in staff numbers.

Mechanisms of control

The theoretical framework's first construct includes mechanisms of control. Control of resources, curriculum and research is seen to derive from the increasing autonomy of IS groups. The autonomy of IS academic groups and, therefore, their structural location in universities can also be used to evaluate the extent to which IS academic groups are able to control critical rewards.

This construct also reflects the dependence of academics on the development of prestigious reputations for individuals and groups, leading to the control of critical rewards (Whitley 1984a). Reputation building and critical rewards are attained through publication records and attracting research funding (Mingers and Stowell 1997), the development and management of publication outlets and similar processes.

Publication records

In comparison with some other disciplines, the research output of IS was seen as being generally lower. One possible explanation offered is that many IS academics have entered academia from a practitioner background rather than a researcher background.

Research output was, however, considered to have increased in recent years in Victoria and the Australian Capital Territory, reflecting increased effort and productivity. Although Tasmania reported a focus on conference proceedings, in Victoria incentives for publications were linked increasingly to journal rather than conference publications. Queensland also reported a growing preference for journal publications, even when compared with prestigious conferences, which could relate to the planned introduction of the RQF, which is discussed later. Some universities, including those in Western Australia, reported considerable numbers of PhD students, including 20 at the UniSA, which could be expected to bolster the publication records of those schools.

Different factors, however, were reported in some universities. Researchers at Charles Sturt University identified little with IS. In some IS groups in New South Wales, the Australasian Conference on Information Systems (ACIS) and the International Conference on Information Systems (ICIS) were not universally considered central conferences for the discipline. Also in New South Wales, some interviewees found it difficult to agree on a definition of IS.

The *Australasian Journal of Information Systems* (*AJIS*) is a core local IS journal; however, no reference was made in any state report to the development of any additional Australian IS publication outlets.

Attracting research funding

Analysis indicated that IS academics have found it difficult to gain research funding, particularly funding from the prestigious Australian Research Council

(ARC). As reported in the retrospective chapter, the ARC coding scheme for many years omitted IS, forcing bids to be made within either business or computer science codes—with the result that they were evaluated by assessors who were often unfamiliar with IS.

Academics in Victoria reported that research funding was 'dwindling'. The limited success reported for IS in attaining ARC funding contrasts with the greater success of the computing discipline. More emphasis on research funding from industry, internal university sources or from research centres was noted by ADFA, the U Tasmania and in Victoria. The low proportion of IS staff holding a PhD at some Australian universities, such as at the UTS, or completing one, would act to limit opportunity to apply and gain research funding, particularly from the ARC, where track record is of major importance

Structural location and independence of IS groups

Information systems was seen to have little autonomy in some universities, such as at the UTS, where IS courses were integrated with computing courses.

Many examples were provided where IS groups were dependent on the outcomes from other disciplines. Several states, including Victoria, reported IS groups that delivered teaching within non-IS programs. As an example of common delivery arrangements found in Australian IS, the IS group at the University of Sydney delivers an introductory IS unit to 1000 students in the Bachelor of Commerce degree, while at the UniSA an even greater number of students studied an IS unit within a Bachelor of Commerce. The IS groups at all universities in New South Wales, other than at the UNSW, were dependent on enrolments in other programs and on the number of compulsory IS units in those programs. To counter the disadvantages of such dependence on other disciplines, the substantial financial rewards from teaching large service classes have been seen as a means for IS groups to 'subsidise' the running of small specialist IS classes.

It was suggested in the Queensland chapter that IS groups had a greater level of academic control and prestige where they had a separate identity in the university structure. The findings from Western Australia were consistent with this perspective, as the IS groups that were considered to be a subset of other disciplines in their structural location in the university had lower status. In Victoria, however, no correlation was seen between having a separate structural identity in a university and the perception by IS academics of having greater status.

Information systems groups are located in a diversity of faculties. In Victorian universities, although most IS groups were based in science or business, others were located in arts, law, engineering, communication and health science faculties. Variability was noted similarly in the home faculty for IS groups in

Queensland. The Queensland report commented that often the IS groups that had moved out from business faculties were highly autonomous

The Queensland chapter commented on a remarkable variation in the location of IS staff in the university structure. In New South Wales, fragmentation of IS staff was reported across different departments and faculties, particularly in science and computing, where most IS groups were *ad hoc* or informal groups within larger departments, with little interaction among the IS groups. As an example of this characteristic, at Macquarie University there was an *ad hoc* IS group in computing, while other IS groups existed also in accounting and management, and information management was taught in statistics. Other examples were given in which IS was one component of a school that represented a different discipline, such as at the UniSA.

A range of consequences was identified arising from IS not being seen as having a separate identity in the university structure. It was reported that the wider university communities in New South Wales did not see IS as a separate field. Some IS groups might not have identified themselves in this way either. For example, at the University of Adelaide, where there were only three IS staff and IS degrees were not offered, the staff were not aware of current issues for IS groups at other institutions. In three of the nine universities in Victoria, IS was not seen as having attained a separate identity. In some states, it was reported that there were few strongly identified IS programs; for example, in New South Wales, only the UNSW was seen as having a strongly identified IS program. In one Victorian university, IS staff perceived that IS journals and conferences had not been included in the ranking exercise of their department. Variety in the nomenclature adopted for IS courses was seen, while IS was not offered as a degree at some universities, including at Flinders University.

Queensland reported that many IS groups had restructured or planned to do so during 2004–06, as a result of reduced demand from students for IT courses. The same state reported two different trends regarding changes to the structural placement of IS groups in that state. Information systems groups at Central Queensland University, Griffith University and the Queensland University of Technology had, before this study, moved to separate IS schools, while the IS groups from the University of Southern Queensland and Bond University at the time of the study were relocating to business. The IS school at Edith Cowan University merged with management in 2007, while at the University of Tasmania, the School of Information Systems in the Faculty of Business merged with the School of Computing into a Faculty of Science, Engineering and Technology in 2008. Queensland noted that reduced autonomy of IS groups was associated with the more recent decline in student demand for IS programs, as seen also in Tasmania.

The NSW report noted that of the 10 universities with IS groups in New South Wales, the main IS group at only three included IS in their name. Not being identified with IS by name would also act to reduce the identity of these IS groups.

In New South Wales, a perception was reported that regional universities were less threatened by the decline in IS student demand reported elsewhere, and felt less need to conform with research trends. Certainly, a subset of regional universities reported a disproportionately strong IS presence, associated with positioning of the institution to emphasise external studies and the development of multiple campuses away from the home campus. Two Queensland regional universities, Central Queensland University and the University of Southern Queensland, showed these characteristics.

After the initial state case studies, further data were gathered to assess the extent to which 'business' or 'technology' predominated in the administrative placement of IS groups in Australian universities. In addition, an analysis was made of the administrative placement of IS groups in relation to the era in which each university was established. The concept of categories of university types associated with different eras is discussed earlier in this chapter, in relation to Table 12.1.

Table 12.3 summarises the placement of IS at Australian universities. 'Business' includes faculties that are called business, economics or commerce. 'Technology' includes faculties that are called science, IT or engineering. 'Both' refers to universities that have an IS group in the 'business' and the 'technology' faculty types. 'Combined' is where the university has a combined faculty called something like 'business and technology'. 'Other' indicates that IS is situated in some other type of faculty, such as arts.

From Table 12.3, we note that IS is located within business at 17 universities, in technology at 11 and in 'other' at two. At five universities, IS exists in business and technology, and in four universities IS resides in a combined business–technology area. Information systems is located solely in business in 44 per cent of universities (17), solely in technical in 28 per cent of universities (11), in business or business and technical (17 plus five) in 56 per cent of universities, in technical or technical and business (11 plus five) in 41 per cent of universities. Broadly, we observe an approximately 60/40 ratio of business versus technical.

Table 12.3 IS placement relative to university era/type

Era	Business	Tech	Both	Combined	Other	Total
Gumtree	4	3	2		1	10
Unitech	2	3				5
Sandstone	3	1	2			6
Redbrick	2	1				3
New	5	3	1	3	1	13
Private	1			1		2
Count:	17	11	5	4	2	39

Note: Several universities have more than one IS group in the same faculty type—for example, Deakin has IS groups in the School of Information Systems and the Deakin Business School, both of which are within the Faculty of Business and Law. ADFA was not included in the count.

We note further that IS is located within business relatively more often for all but one of the six 'eras', with IS located more often in technical only at the Unitech universities. Information systems at the Sandstones is generally associated with the Faculty of Commerce/Business/Economics. In two of the three Redbrick universities (the ANU and the UNSW), the main concentration of IS seems to be in the Faculty of Economics/Commerce. The other Redbrick, Monash, has a Faculty of Information Technology in which IS is sited. Although ADFA is a college of the UNSW, IS there is located within a school of technology. Three of the five Unitechs (the QUT, UTS, UniSA) have faculties/divisions of IT in which IS is concentrated. At the other two 'Unitechs' (Curtin and RMIT), IS is associated with business.

There is little pattern to the placement of IS at the Gumtrees universities; four have IS situated in business-type faculties, three in technology faculties and two (Macquarie and Griffith) have IS groups in both types of faculty. Information systems groups are associated most often with business at the New universities. There seems, however, to be a trend towards the creation of a faculty that combines business and informatics/computing at some of these universities. Three of the New universities have this type of combined faculty.

Other ways of attaining prestigious reputations

In Queensland and elsewhere, numbers of IS academics had achieved increased status in their universities, with the professorial staff total having increased considerably in the past two decades. These staff had similar levels of influence as did professorial staff in other disciplines.

The achievement of IS professorial staff was seen as a crucial step in the enhancement of the reputation of an associated IS group in a university, while IS groups without professorial staff were seen to have a lower profile in their university.

An industry-based Chair in Business Information Systems was appointed at the UniSA in 2006. In addition to local professors, the UniSA also appointed two IS adjunct professors from Europe, which contributed to the reputation of the IS group at that university. It was seen that some professorial appointments had taken place only relatively recently. At the ANU, the first IS professor was appointed only in 2000, which suggests a restricted profile for IS at that university until that year. Also noteworthy is the late emergence of departments and chairs at the University of Melbourne, in 1996, and at the University of Sydney, in 2002. There are no professors in IS at two Sandstone universities—Adelaide University and the UWA.

Appendix 2.4 in the 'retrospective' chapter, Chapter 2, identified a total of 69 individuals who had been identified as having held chairs in IS during the period 1974–2007, in 31 of a total of approximately 42 institutions. When people who have held multiple successive professorships are counted, the total is 82. In early 2007, there appeared to be 52 IS professors in 28 institutions. The period 1974–2007 was examined. Building on the steady progress made from 1990 to 1997, considerable growth took place between 1998 and 2004 inclusive, during which time more than 60 per cent of the IS professorial appointments occurred.

A number of senior IS academics had taken on other significant and prestigious roles with recognition beyond IS, particularly since about 2000. In the 1990s, IS researchers had little input into ARC panels; however, in more recent years, a number of senior IS academics had become expert assessors for the ARC, while one had acted as an advisor to the Australian government on IT and national research priorities. In the past five or six years, there has been a concerted effort by the Australasian Chapter of the Association for Information Systems (AAIS) and the Australian Council of Professors and Heads of Information Systems (ACPHIS) to have IS representation on the ARC MICS Panel (the panel that is likely to assess the majority of IS ARC grant applications). Janice Burn, Graeme Shanks and Michael Rosemann have been IS representatives on the MICS Panel; however, Rosemann's term ends in December 2007, and the AAIS/ACPHIS nomination for 2008–09 was unsuccessful.

As a further example of Australian IS academics gaining national and international status, while at the University of Queensland, Ron Weber was named as the first president from Region 3 of the Association for Information Systems (AIS), and was also the 2001 Co-Chair of ICIS and the 2001 Chair of the ICIS Executive Committee. Weber also received the Prime Minister's Award for University Teacher of the Year in 2000, and was the first non-US resident to hold the position of editor-in-chief of *MIS Quarterly*. Shirley Gregor from the ANU was awarded an Order for Australia in 2005 and became the Director of the Professional Standards Board for the Australian Computer Society (ACS) in 2007. Alan Underwood developed the core body of knowledge used by the ACS when accrediting IT courses in Australian institutions. In 2007, Ed Lewis from the

Australian Capital Territory chaired the IT-030 Committee for Standards Australia. All these roles enhance the reputation of IS groups, and the IS field.

Summary

This section considered the autonomy of IS academic groups from their structural location in universities, and the associated extent to which IS academic groups controlled critical rewards. Although the research output of IS schools was perceived as low in comparison with other disciplines, effort was being made in many IS groups recently to increase research output and to publish in journals rather than in conference proceedings. Although research funding within IS was seen as difficult to obtain—particularly ARC grants—at least one IS group reported increasing success. The independence of IS groups in Australian universities varied considerably, with some being dependent on the enrolment and structure of programs in other disciplines. While most IS groups were found in science or business faculties, many other structures were reported. Although some IS groups had strongly identified programs, and delivered IS degrees, often IS groups were fragmented across departments and faculties, which reduced opportunities for those groups to control critical rewards. Although the number of professorial appointments and the attainment of other prestigious roles for senior IS academics that had an impact outside IS had increased significantly since about 2000, it was hard to generalise about the achievement of mechanisms of control for IS in Australia. This is because the diversity in arrangements is considerable, with significant autonomy experienced by some IS groups, but with little in others. Reduced student numbers have, however, placed pressure for restructuring on IS groups in recent years, which, in turn, has eroded autonomy for IS in Australian universities.

Core body of knowledge

In the theoretical framework that guides this meta-analysis, the first construct proposed included a core body of knowledge, comprising the four components: research and teaching methods and standards; a unique symbol set; key research and teaching IS topics; and laws, rules and evidenced guidelines. Each component will be considered in turn below, by reviewing the data derived from the case studies presented in this monograph.

Research and teaching methods and standards

The theoretical framework underpinning this study suggests that a discipline will show consensus in research and teaching methods and standards. The degree to which this holds for IS groups in Australian universities will be examined next, using data from the case studies from each of the seven regions.

Research

Diversity of research methods was reported in many of the regions, including in Western Australia and Queensland. The reason for research diversity was accounted for in a range of ways, including being driven by staff research interests, by the nature and requirements of grant funding sought or obtained and appointing new staff who had existing research interests. Other IS staff saw the diversity in research methods as a response to the RQF, a proposed Australian government approach that linked the allocation of research funding to Australian universities with an assessment of research quality. A shortage of supervisory capacity was reported at the University of Canberra, which intended to restrict the future number of IS PhD students at that university. This characteristic was expected to impact on that university's capacity to attract government funding for research, as the RQF proposed to link the allocation of some research funds to PhD completions. An IS group's publication output would also be affected by limited PhD numbers.

In Victoria, IS research was seen to be predominantly interpretivist, and aligned more to European approaches than to those from North America. Consequently, diverse blended approaches to research were not reported as common in IS research in Victoria, which was interpreted by the authors of the case study from that state as inconsistent with practice in mature disciplines.

Diversity of research administration was also reported. For example, in Queensland universities, no consistent patterns were seen in the organisational approaches taken to promote IS research. Strategies that were evident ranged from the formation of formal research groups and research centres to voluntary collaboration initiated by researchers. Research undertaken in Queensland universities varied from those having a tight IS focus to others where broad interdisciplinary collaboration was evident. NSW universities commented that there were few large IS research projects, and research activity was fragmented and diverse.

In contrast, the ANU reported an increased quantity and quality of IS research in recent years, and recognised plurality in research methods. Universities from several Australian regions referred to research seminars that were held regularly, and the ANU reported that it hosted a biennial workshop on 'IS foundations'.

Teaching

Relatively few comments on teaching methods and standards were made in the reports from the seven regions. WA universities reported much variety in teaching methods and standards, while in the Australian Capital Territory, lectures, seminars, tutorials, group projects, case studies, presentations, use of online learning management systems (WebCT) and laboratory sessions were used for IS delivery.

As suggested earlier, where an IS group teaches IS within another degree or discipline, it is likely to have limited control over delivery. A number of IS groups referred to delivering an introductory IS unit to large numbers of students in a commerce or business degree. As an example of the restrictions such an arrangement could impose, at the UniSA, where IS is taught in association with an accounting program, CPA accreditation determines not only the content, but the standards of the teaching.

Distance-education methods are used in some universities for the delivery of IS, including at the NSW regional university, Charles Sturt, and at the University of Southern Queensland. At ADFA, most postgraduate course-work programs are taught through distance education, using WebCT until 2007, and then ILIVE from that year. Other IS groups referred to the delivery of their programs using WebCT.

The applied nature of IS is reflected in some of the IS delivery styles and requirements for teaching. For example, at the University of Canberra, tutors and guest lecturers are often appointed from industry, while ADFA uses 'problem-based learning'. At the UTS, all IS students were required to undertake work experience before graduation, until 2002, which resulted in the students either studying part-time or in a 'sandwich' mode that interwove study and professional work experience. A different approach to ensuring that graduates of IS programs were equipped to apply their learning in the workplace was referred to by the University of Canberra and the University of Tasmania; both taught interpersonal and group skills through group projects, role-plays, case studies and similar methods.

Several universities reported high numbers of international students, including those located offshore. Such arrangements necessitate changes to delivery arrangements. For example, the University of Tasmania used local staff and visiting staff from Australia to deliver its IS programs in Shanghai.

Summary

Diversity of research methods and standards was seen in IS groups across Australian universities. Approaches to administering IS research were also varied, with a lack of consensus on research methods and standards. Many regions regarded the lack of consensus on research approaches as an indicator of restricted progress in the development of IS. At least one region, however, considered that having a single predominant research approach suggested a lack of maturity for IS. Limited data on teaching methods and standards hamper the interpretation that can be made in this area. Some evidence was seen of matching delivery methods to the applied nature of IS; however, other teaching methods and delivery styles appeared to be in part an outcome of mechanisms adopted for pragmatic reasons to compensate for declining IS enrolments and staff reductions.

Arrangements made for offshore delivery, distance education, use of online learning management systems and IS delivery in non-IS programs or disciplines might be examples of this characteristic.

Unique symbol set

Although relatively few comments were made by the authors of each state report regarding whether a unique symbol set existed for IS in their universities, the comments made were remarkably consistent.

In Western Australia, IS was seen as an area that could be transposed readily from one discipline grouping to another, while at the University of Canberra there was a history of integration of IS with other information and communication technologies (ICTs). Both characteristics suggest that IS does not have a unique symbol set. At the University of Adelaide, the placement of IS in a school of commerce acted to dissipate shared assumptions and language. Information systems staff of the University of Adelaide did not believe that IS had its own terminology, as IS was seen as a bridge between business and computing. Staff at the University of Tasmania also believed that IS terminology was broadly familiar to business and computing academics, while some ACT IS groups accepted the commonalities with allied fields such as software engineering and computing. The Queensland report found no evidence of a unique symbol set, attributing this to the diversity in the content of the curriculum and research topics.

The ACT report noted with concern that much of the symbol system of IS was used also by application areas when using IS and IT as tools. Consequently, people from outside IS feel able to teach IS within their own areas, as there is little barrier to doing so posed by a unique symbol set. The problem is compounded further by a poor understanding from outside IS of the meaning of information systems, and continuing debate within IS about how to define the discipline.

Summary

Australian IS staff members believe that IS has no unique symbol set. Information systems terms are used by related disciplines such as business and computing, and also for teaching in application areas by those not associated with IS. Consequently, IS is not able to exclude outsiders from its domain through use of an IS symbol set as a barrier, or to clearly delineate its boundaries. Both characteristics suggest that IS will experience continued incursions on its borders.

Key IS topics in research and teaching

The theoretical framework for this study suggests that key research and teaching topics will become more consistent as the IS discipline develops. This section evaluates the degree to which consensus exists on the key IS research and teaching topics in Australian universities, using the considerable evidence provided in the state reports.

Key IS teaching topics

Circumstances surrounding IS teaching that impacts on the topics taught are considered first. It is acknowledged that the structural placement within which the IS teaching is undertaken affects the teaching topics. For example, the NSW authors commented that the least distinctive IS curriculum was found in IS support classes in commerce, and some IS groups were required to conform to CPA accreditation requirements when delivering IS within accounting programs. The integration of IS with other areas for teaching at the University of Canberra affected the topics taught. To illustrate, the co-location of IS with computing at that university resulted in the integration of the two fields, which meant that IS curriculum was not presented in a theoretical way, but in an applied way. In South Australia, relocating IS within the university brought about a re-examination of how IS courses related to IT and computing.

The nature of the degree programs and the organisational location of the IS staff influence the IS topics taught. Victoria identified the trend that from about 2004 students preferred to enrol in a double degree, one of which was IS, while before this time there was greater preference for a single IS degree, such as a Bachelor of Information Systems. Victoria also commented on a big increase in IS and IT course-work Masters degrees in the past decade. A wide range of IS programs was noted in Queensland. Other influences on IS teaching topics were also identified. For example, at the University of Canberra, many of the students were Australian government employees.

Numerous IS groups, including those at the UniSA and in Queensland universities, pointed to broad and diverse teaching topics. Victoria reported a diversity in IS degrees and their curricula, which made it challenging to identify an IS core body of knowledge. Consequently, few key teaching topics could be identified across programs or units in Victoria. The Queensland report suggested a reason for the variety in IS teaching topics in its universities. The Queensland authors identified a lack of consistency regarding the boundary for curriculum content between IS and related areas, and therefore the core body of knowledge. For example, databases and web-related topics are sometimes considered to be included within IS, while elsewhere they are seen as falling outside of IS.

Some states and universities were able to identify principles that guided the development of IS teaching topics. In Tasmania, the IS curriculum included little technical content, but focused on IS management and strategy. As mentioned above, at the Universities of Tasmania and Canberra, the IS curriculum included a focus on professional development, including interpersonal and group skills. At ADFA, a systems approach was adopted for the IS curriculum. In Western

Australia, the IS body of knowledge of the four universities with an IS presence reflected local needs and developments, and their links with local industry and professions.

Several state reports referred to use of the ACS accreditation guidelines in the development of IS curricula. Although the ACS guidelines allow considerable flexibility in development of the curriculum, there is a common understanding of topics usually covered. Examples are systems analysis and design, database design and management, project management, managerial and organisational issues, ethical and social implications, professional practice and interpersonal communications. Two of the three ACT universities with an IS program use the ACS guidelines, in combination with specialist knowledge that reflects staff interests and expertise. Programming and software construction was included in the IS curriculum of one university in the Australian Capital Territory, but not in the other two.

South Australian universities indicated that software engineering, computer-supported cooperative work (CSCW), electronic commerce and business information management were key IS teaching topics. The major IS teaching themes in Tasmania were project management, data modelling, data management and electronic commerce, most of which appeared in the ACS guidelines.

The ACT case reported an inconsistency between the topics in the core body of knowledge and IS research methods. Although the core body of knowledge involved construction of artefacts, graduate research students were not exposed to design theory, apart from at the University of Canberra.

Key IS research topics

Several IS groups identified that their research was applied—for example, ADFA works in the nexus between consultancy and research. The applied nature of much IS research could be seen from the research topics listed for each region.

There was great breadth in the IS research topics studied in Australian universities. To illustrate, the two primary IS research groups at the UniSA had 12 main research foci, while 33 separate research areas were identified at the nine Queensland universities. Six research themes were pinpointed by the IS group at the University of Tasmania.

Despite some differences in the terminology used by different research groups, considerable commonality was found in many of the research topics after analysis. For example, seven of the research foci from the UniSA could be matched to research interests from Queensland universities. Five of the six research themes from the Tasmanian IS were also common to the Queensland research topics. Appendix 12.1 lists the collated research topics identified from all seven regions, showing the common topics. Note, however, that the NSW report identified only a few research topics.

Summary

As expected from the diversity in the organisational location of IS teachers, the extent of autonomy of IS groups and the degree programs within which IS teaching took place, IS teaching topics in Australian universities varied enormously. While many of the regions pointed out the difficulty in identifying key IS teaching topics, a number of IS groups taught programs that were consistent with the ACS guidelines. Even though the ACS guidelines allow considerable discretion for curriculum development, many IS groups have a common view of key IS teaching topics from the ACS guidelines.

The topics researched by IS groups were found to be broad and diverse; however, some frequently recurring research topics could be identified that appeared in many of the Australian regions. It is clear that key IS research and teaching topics are influenced by a variety of factors that will vary from one IS group to another, including staff interests and expertise. These factors help account for the breadth of the teaching and research topics seen. Despite the diversity in teaching and research topics, some consensus in key IS topics for both appears possible.

Laws, rules and evidenced guidelines

Laws, rules and evidenced guidelines is the last component of the core body of knowledge from the first framework construct. Laws or rules are similar to those found in the natural sciences, while evidenced guidelines arise from practice. Little reference was made to laws, rules and evidenced guidelines in the state case studies. The Victorian authors remarked that limited reference to use of an IS theory was made, although the emphasis on interpretive research methods could suggest that agreement exists on a set of evidenced guidelines for research. The Queensland authors reported that no evidence of a theory base was found. The ANU recognised plurality in theory types, while the ACT chapter indicated that little core knowledge from IS could be classified as laws or rules in the way that the natural sciences regarded these theory types. Instead, the authors from the Australian Capital Territory consider that evidenced guidelines are used in IS, which are derived from practice. An example provided was software cost-estimation practices. An additional kind of 'theory' or 'knowledge type', called normative guidelines, was also identified by the same writers. Design theory was seen to be a normative guideline, such as Codd's relational database theory.

Summary

Although only one region made significant mention of laws, rules and evidenced guidelines for IS, the omission by the others could confirm the view from the ACT authors that laws and rules, as developed in the natural sciences, are largely irrelevant for IS. Instead, the 'more well-grounded, participative style' of knowledge type, such as evidenced (and normative) guidelines, is more appropriate in a field that is at the junction of 'science, technology and human and organisational behaviour' (Gregor et al. 2006:190).

Impact of local contingencies versus degree of professionalism

The second construct in the theoretical framework involves the impact of local contingencies on the IS discipline and its degree of professionalism. Professionalism can be regarded as ways of undertaking IS research and teaching so that there is high task certainty, centralised control of work processes and routinisation of tasks (Whitley 1984b). In such an environment, IS academics will be mutually dependent on each other, and the division of labour for teaching and research sub-tasks might be expected. If IS is not highly professionalised, local contingencies will have a high impact, leading to a considerable variation in the nature of IS research and teaching undertaken in different regions of Australia.

If IS is professionalised, less variation will be seen when comparing the approaches in the regions at one point in time. The degree of professionalism in IS teaching and research will be considered first below, followed by the impact of local contingencies.

Degree of professionalism

Although few of the reports from the seven Australian regions explicitly considered the degree of professionalism of their IS groups, information could be inferred from other data provided. The professionalism of research and teaching activities will be considered separately, as the circumstances for each differ.

Research

The authors of the ACT report saw some commonality in the research content undertaken by the IS groups in that region, regardless of whether the research was applied or not. All ACT IS researchers investigated areas that were recognisable as falling within the boundaries of IS, and their fellow researchers had a common understanding of their research.

On the other hand, many IS groups were not able to recognise any commonality in IS research topics. The University of Canberra concluded that the degree of professionalism in research was low, as the IS research of their IS group was largely individual and eclectic. In New South Wales and Tasmania too, the fragmentation and diversity of IS research were seen to limit its professionalism.

While diversity of research topics was certainly seen at the IS group and university level, it is only when the topics were aggregated across the nation, and to a lesser extent, across states, that the existence of key research topics could be recognised—as displayed in Appendix 12.1. The many overlapping research topics uncovered in the earlier analysis of research areas from IS groups around Australia suggest that the existence of core research topics that are familiar to other researchers is not unique to ACT universities. It is unsurprising that IS groups and universities considered that there was limited commonality in research topics, given that they had access largely to local evidence only. The issue of whether identifiable core research topics exist in Australian IS is, however, relevant when evaluating whether professionalism occurs in IS research.

Even the ACT authors argued that the wide variation in the research methods used in IS groups in that region acted against the development of professionalism in research, as the routinisation of tasks was not supported. Similarly, the West Australian chapter commented that, because all local universities used many approaches (qualitative and quantitative methods, multiple methods and case studies), the diversity of research methods acted against achieving professionalism in IS research in that state. A number of other universities shared the view that the professionalism of IS research was limited. Limited cooperation in IS research was reported across institutions, particularly in New South Wales. The dispersal of IS groups in 'silos' across universities, particularly within settings in which the researchers are not identifiable as belonging to IS, restricts opportunities for cooperation, and the professionalism of research and teaching.

A further test is the extent to which ACIS committees, reviewers and participants, and *AJIS* editorial board members, reviewers and readers, mutually recognise one another, one another's topics and one another's research methods, or perceive strangers and strangeness. *AJIS* has been healthy and, subject to current perturbations associated with the RQF, and discussed shortly, ACIS has also continued to attract healthy attendances. These characteristics are consistent with at least a moderate level of commonality being perceived among community members.

Professionalism requires a common research culture. It is difficult to develop a common culture in research in which groups are fragmented, dispersed, hidden behind non-IS nomenclatures, immersed in the cultures of other disciplines, use a great variety of methods or examine disconnected research topics. Analysis of IS in Australia shows some, but limited, evidence of it being a professionalised discipline from a research perspective.

Teaching

Those universities that teach research methods in discrete units in postgraduate programs, such as ADFA, help promote the development of professionalism in research through promulgating standard approaches and a common understanding. The operation of IS doctoral programs appears to be another mechanism that contributes to increasing professionalism, and links the professionalism of IS teaching to achieving more professionalism in IS research.

Inconsistencies, however, between the research methods taught to students in the Australian Capital Territory and the core knowledge of the undergraduate IS curricula delivered in the same region point to a low degree of professionalism. At the time that the ACT chapter was written, research students in two of the three IS groups in the Australian Capital Territory did not have exposure to 'design theory', as they studied research methods with business students; yet the common IS undergraduate curricula in those universities included artefact construction. It seems likely that other Australian IS graduate programs experience the same inconsistency between their undergraduate and research training.

At least for one ACT university, undergraduate IS programs were not designed to prepare students to be IS professionals, but instead aimed to produce 'well-informed users', with an expectation that on-the-job training would develop more uniform work processes within organisations.

The professional skills training offered in some IS programs, however—and referred to earlier—is expected to increase professionalism in the graduates of those programs. Use of the ACS accreditation guidelines for IS curriculum development will also increase professionalism, where adopted.

Within one specific institution, the University of Tasmania, a high to medium level of professionalism was found for IS curriculum and teaching issues, when task certainty, routinisation of activities and division of labour were assessed.

Summary

Many IS groups commented on the disparity and fragmentation of IS research topics at their university, along with limited collaboration with other IS researchers—attributes that were interpreted as reducing the professionalism of Australian IS research. When, however, the research topics were aggregated across the nation in particular, considerable commonality was displayed, which suggests that core topics exist for Australian IS research. Research methods were also recognised as diverse. The collation of Australian IS research methods across the nation might, however, also reveal a greater uniformity than has been suggested by authors of the individual state chapters.

Mechanisms to increase communication with other IS groups, such as research collaborations across IS groups, joint seminars and appointing staff who are PhD graduates of another university, will help promote professionalism in research by breaking down silos. Increased communication will also increase the awareness of IS researchers that many of their colleagues in other institutions are researching related issues.

One university reported a high to medium degree of professionalism for its IS teaching, and a low to medium degree of professionalism in its IS research. As reported earlier, the same university IS group has recently merged with a school of computing. This and other recent and future restructuring of IS groups in Australian universities could reduce the professionalism of IS research and teaching. A range of pressures were identified that acted to promote or reduce the professionalism of teaching, which operated at the undergraduate or graduate level. Given the limitations of the data in the state reports, however, the professionalism of Australian IS teaching was difficult to determine.

Impact of local contingencies

The following discussion sets out the impact of local contingencies reported by the regions in three sections: on research, on teaching and on both.

Research

A range of local issues were considered to influence IS research. Few joint research projects were conducted in Western Australia, as a result of little interaction and collaboration among the universities there. In South Australia and Tasmania, the development of strategic relationships with large corporations was difficult as few large companies were present in those states or, where they were present, the head office was located elsewhere. One result of this characteristic has been that research in both states has investigated phenomena in small and medium-sized enterprises. Another characteristic mentioned by several universities, including the UniSA, was that PhD numbers were restricted by the availability of supervisors.

In Queensland, the nature of research conducted in IS groups was seen to be influenced by the competencies and interests of academic research leaders more than geography. There was, however, some evidence of a deliberate policy to focus on global issues in IS in that state rather than on those that were more local.

Teaching

The nature of local contingencies that affected IS teaching issues was found to be highly variable.

One local contingency pointed to in South Australia was a perceived limited interest in IS. This was accounted for in two ways. The first was the state's interest in resources, agriculture and defence. The second reason given was that there was no single state minister with responsibility for ICT; it was shared among six ministers. A comparison was made of South Australia's interest in IS with that in Western Australia, a neighbouring state. Despite some similarities between the two states, all four of the West Australian universities that offered

IS also offered an IS degree, contrasting with South Australia, where only one of its three universities offered an IS degree.

In South Australia, the relationship between the IS and computing curricula in one university was described as being 'finely focused' as a consequence of the recent amalgamation of the two disciplinary groups. In South Australia as well, the content of IS teaching was influenced by local and interstate industries, and by the fact that defence was the major ICT industry in Adelaide. At ADFA in the Australian Capital Territory, the defence services encouraged study in IS and computing to at least second year in a degree, which helped increase enrolments.

In Tasmania, local contingencies were found to have a low to medium impact on curriculum and teaching.

It was reported in the Victorian chapter that local industry had little impact on IS curricula. National influences were seen to have had a greater role than the local community and industry in the development of Victorian IS curricula. The Victorian chapter identified that a cyclical demand for IS courses had influenced IS enrolment most. For example, in the late 1990s, IS had strong enrolments in Australian universities, but this trend had reversed by 2004. Declining IS enrolment was identified by many state reports including that from New South Wales, and also by the international commentators in the theoretical framework chapter. This pressure then is a global one, and not local.

Impact on research and teaching

A number of local contingencies influenced IS research and teaching. Geography was referred to by the more remote states as a contingency that was able to act on teaching and research. The remote location of West Australian IS groups resulted in reliance on local industry and international connections, rather than on those in the eastern states of Australia. Western Australia also referred to local and state political pressures, which could have an impact either on teaching or research. The Tasmanian interviewees also mentioned political pressures. The South Australian government outsourced all ICT to interstate or offshore locations, which was seen to impact on the IS groups within the state, with ramifications for teaching and research.

Local contingencies had an impact on IS in the three universities in the Australian Capital Territory to a moderate degree. The position of the IS groups in the university structure influenced the units taught and the nature of the research. The business orientation of the IS group in one ACT university influenced teaching and research differently than that for the IS group in another university with a primary role to educate defence force personnel.

The NSW case concluded that local contingencies were restricted in their application, and were not state wide. Examples given were variable and included organisational politics, the nature of nearby employers and competitors, support from a large local industrial organisation in Wollongong and faculty rules at the University of Sydney.

In Queensland, the IS leader was sometimes seen to determine the nature of the curriculum and research, rather than both being determined by local community characteristics. An example was provided of an IS group at a Queensland university where the curriculum and research direction changed from a focus on soft systems to technical issues when the IS leader changed. The Queensland case commented that local contingencies had high impact.

At Charles Sturt, a regional university in New South Wales, the visibility of IS has been linked to the cross-campus structure of that university, and to university politics.

Summary

Local, and therefore different, contingencies had acted on research and teaching. Some local contingencies had impacted on the nature of IS research and teaching in Australia, including geography, political pressures and organisational structure.

Linking the degree of professionalism and the impact of local contingencies

The Tasmanian chapter reported that local contingencies appeared to have a low to medium impact on curriculum and teaching, while also having a high to medium impact on research issues. The reverse, however, appeared to be the case for the degree of professionalism, in that curriculum and teaching issues were seen as having a high level of professionalism while research activities were assessed as low to medium. As IS curricula in Victoria have been influenced more by national forces than by local ones, this characteristic suggests that Victorian universities have achieved a degree of professionalism in teaching.

Australian responses to reduced ICT enrolments

Since the 'dotcom implosion' of about 2000, enrolments in IS courses have decreased substantially. This section consolidates information about the patterns following that phenomenon that are evident in the various state reports.

Changes to organisational arrangements

Across universities in all states there was evidence that IS groups had restructured, or were planning to do so. In Queensland, for example, this was the case with every one of the 11 universities surveyed.

In some instances, IS groups that had achieved administrative independence from business faculties were subsumed back within business after the decline in IS enrolments. In other instances, administratively separate IS groups lost their independent status, instead being recognised less formally as IS groups within a more generic ICT school or faculty. The state report on Tasmania also refers to pressure on computing to take over IS teaching areas. Almost without exception, the planned restructuring in Australian universities involved a reduction in staffing levels within IS groups.

Changes to IS curriculum

This downsizing was accompanied invariably by a rationalisation of ICT curriculum offerings. It is clear, however, that the consequent planned reduction in IS subjects is far from uniform across Australia. In one reported Victorian university, for example, the process of rationalising the ICT curriculum led to a strengthening of the relative position of IS. In such cases, senior ICT academics have taken the strategic view that, in an Australian context, future job opportunities will favour ICT graduates with a good grasp of the organisational and application context, as well as the technology—that is, IS graduates. A similar positive view for IS is proposed by David Wilson in his response to the Underwood and Jordan report on IS in New South Wales. The latter NSW authors had commented that, because IS was fragmented, a continued decline in undergraduate enrolments would weaken the position further.

Changes in IS research

The decline in the range of subjects in the IS curriculum does not appear to have been matched by a comparable decline in IS research. While the impending reduction in the number of IS academics could be expected to lead to a reduction in IS research output from Australian universities, a more recent focus on research quality has been reported. This latter development was driven by the proposed introduction of the RQF in the Australian university sector. The planned RQF and its potential wider impact on IS in Australian universities are discussed more fully in the next section of this chapter.

Summary

The recent reduced student enrolments led to changes in the organisational location of IS groups in many universities, reduced staffing and rationalisation of the ICT curriculum. In some IS groups, these changes were used strategically to strengthen the position of IS in comparison with related disciplines. Reduced student enrolments appeared not to have impacted on the quality of Australian IS research.

The RQF and its impact

The RQF was a federal Liberal government initiative planned for implementation in Australian universities in 2008. It can be viewed as an attempt to increase the quantity and, in particular, the quality and impact of research in Australian universities.

A more cynical view of the RQF was that its purpose was to further concentrate funding in those institutions, and in those disciplines and multi-disciplinary centres, that had achieved maturity and already had substantial research resources.

Under the provisions of the RQF, an assessment was to be made of the research produced by research groups within each Australian university. Based on this assessment, the Australian government was to distribute research funding to the universities. It seemed likely that the RQF would have more than just a financial influence; there was a likelihood that the RQF rating of individual Australian universities would be viewed as a significant indicator of the relative status of each university. The state reports each touch on various aspects of the proposed RQF and its impact on IS in Australian universities. The incoming Labor government announced, in December 2007, the abandonment of the RQF; however, an alternative mechanism for evaluating Australian university research output was foreshadowed.

Impact on the long-term viability of IS conferences

A feature of the RQF was that researchers would receive little weight for publications in conference proceedings; much greater recognition was to be given for publication in research journals.

On the basis of the planned RQF, there is evidence that the low recognition accorded by the framework for publishing research in conference proceedings was leading to a change in the choice of publication outlets by Australian IS researchers. Since the RQF was to assess research publications from the previous three years as evidence of research productivity, IS researchers were seeking outlets for their research results in journals rather than via conferences. It could be supposed that the characteristics of any replacement for the RQF will result in some new reactive behaviour by Australian IS academics.

Summary

Researchers considered that the RQF would have an important influence on IS in Australian universities. One anticipated consequence was reduced participation in IS conferences by Australian IS researchers. In light of the observed impact of the proposed RQF, it is predicted that its foreshadowed replacement will also have the effect of changing aspects of the IS discipline in Australian universities.

Limitations and future research

A feature of the study, commented on by researchers in the individual Australian states, was that the evidence presented represented no more than a snapshot of the situation during a period of major perturbation in the IS academic discipline in Australia. Although analysis of the aggregated data has sought to detect some significant trends, there is a clear need to replicate the study over time. At a time of major change, threats and opportunities multiply; the success of responses to these will become apparent in future studies.

Conclusions

The meta-analysis chapter consolidated and interpreted the data from earlier chapters in this monograph, to set out an overview of the IS academic discipline in Australian universities, using the theoretical framework developed for the investigation.

Although IS has broad (but not universal) acceptance in Australian universities as a teaching and research program, considerable variation was noted in staff and student numbers from one IS group to another, and in the staff/student ratio. The organisational location and independence of the IS groups also varied, sometimes being fragmented across departments and faculties, although most were located in science or business. This fragmentation, and the pressure for restructuring placed on IS groups more recently as student enrolments have declined, has eroded autonomy for IS in Australian universities. Despite the rapid growth in IS professorial appointments in Australian universities between 1998 and 2004, and the strongly identified IS programs in some universities, reduced opportunities for control of critical rewards have been seen since that time. Diversity of research methods and standards, and of teaching methods and standards, was reported.

Australian IS staff considered that the discipline did not have a unique symbol set, which could help to explain the diversity in the organisational location of IS groups. Without a recognised unique symbol set, there are few limitations on other disciplines to deliver IS teaching programs or undertake IS research. Teaching topics varied broadly, although many IS groups delivered programs that were consistent with the ACS guidelines. Although IS research topics were viewed as being very diverse across the universities, analysis of topics across the states and, in particular, across Australia, revealed considerable commonality. The consensus reached about IS teaching, and in particular research topics, could offer some potential for the future development of an IS symbol set. One barrier that would need to be overcome is the perception from Australian IS university academics that IS topics studied by one group have little in common with those examined by another. Increased mechanisms for communication among Australian IS researchers and lecturers might reduce this obstacle and limit silos. Having core topics for Australian IS research and increasing focus on high-quality journal publications brought about through the RQF process could act to increase the professionalism of Australian IS research. Conversely, recent restructuring of

IS groups in Australia could work to reduce the professionalism of IS research and teaching.

The study findings suggest that laws and rules, as understood by the natural sciences, are not appropriate for the IS discipline. Evidenced guidelines and normative guidelines are more suitable. This recognition of the most relevant theory types for the discipline could signal increasing maturity for the IS discipline in Australia, rather than having IS apply less suitable theory types to emulate high-status disciplines.

Although a range of local pressures acted on research and teaching, there were some signs of increasing professionalism, including Victorian IS curricula responding to global influences, as well as the responses of Australian IS researchers to the proposed RQF process. Reduced student enrolments in recent times resulted in some organisational relocation of IS groups, changes to the ICT curriculum and reduced IS staff numbers, but these outcomes had not hampered the quantity or quality of IS research.

Just as the diversity found in different aspects of IS in Australian universities implied that some groups were more successful than others across a range of criteria, including publication output, success in gaining external funding, reduced staff/student ratios and group autonomy, some IS groups were able to strengthen their position in comparison with other ICT disciplines during recent organisational restructuring. The ANU and some Victorian IS groups stood out on several criteria, as reported in the study. Although beyond the scope of this current volume, it is interesting to conjecture on possible reasons for these differences. The historical origins of some of the universities in which the IS groups appear might offer some explanation, as might the nature of the leadership of IS groups. Certainly, the achievements of key Australian IS leaders, as reported in this monograph, have helped some groups gain greater access to resources and status.

With the reduced student enrolment in IS programs in universities around the world in recent years, it would be easy to dwell on this phenomenon, as data collection and analysis took place at one time during this period. Yet this study also examined indirectly the achievements to date of Australian IS as a discipline, in addition to the relative change to that position in recent times.

The framework's first construct referred to mechanisms of control and the core body of knowledge. Although achievements for mechanisms of control were mixed, considerable progress had been made towards this component in the past decades in IS, including the number of professorial appointments, the inclusion of IS representation on ARC panels and the establishment and recognition of a national IS journal, a national conference and ACPHIS. Of the four components that make up the core body of knowledge, acknowledgement needs to be made that key research topics have been established, and ACS teaching topics have been developed and are recognised. The framework's second construct referred to the impact of local contingencies versus the degree of professionalism. Local contingencies were found to have impacted on the degree of professionalism; however, the study was not able to confirm that the two components were inversely related.

One broad aim of this current investigation was to consider whether IS in the Australian context should be labelled a discipline or a field, using the definitions of both reported in Chapter 3 and restated below for the reader's convenience. The contributions of significant international IS researchers to this study suggest that the answer to this question will be one that is common to IS groups outside Australia.

If a discipline is defined as

> a body of knowledge, definitions, and concepts built up over a long period and receiving consensus recognition by scholars; theories which interrelate the concepts and provide explanations of observed phenomena and permit predictions from them; and well established research methodologies (Tardif 1989)

the findings of the current investigation from IS academics in Australian universities demonstrate that IS cannot satisfy this definition of a discipline. Although the types of theory that are appropriate for IS have been distinguished (see Gregor et al. 2006), few of the theories so developed interrelate the concepts, provide explanations of observed phenomena and permit predictions from them. Further, using this definition of a discipline and the nature of IS theory discussed in this study, as distinct from the laws and rules found in some other disciplines, it appears that IS has some way to go to become a discipline. Analysis on a national scale revealed that core IS research topics existed in Australia; however, this characteristic did not yet have consensus recognition by individual researchers or groups. Also, since the first Australian IS professor was appointed only just more than two decades ago, such a period is insufficient to have allowed IS to have developed into a discipline. If IS is not then a discipline, can it be considered as a field, where a field is

> an area of knowledge and learning which is not yet accepted as a discipline. Fields of study tend to be more recent areas of scholarship with somewhat fuzzy boundaries; significant numbers of concepts within them are open to debate; and researchers and scholars in the area tend to draw heavily on old-established disciplines for their methodologies and conceptualisations. (Tardif 1989)

Certainly, it appears that IS cannot be accepted as a discipline as yet and it is a recent area of scholarship. This study indicates that the boundaries of IS are fuzzy, and its concepts are debated; for example, there is no accepted symbol set that would enable common terms to be used to represent concepts. Although IS has a history of borrowing from its reference disciplines for its methodologies and 'conceptualisations', this study has revealed some signs that IS is starting to reflect on both that are of particular relevance, as is seen in the recent focus on 'design science' (see Hevner et al. 2004; Gregor and Jones 2007). Overall, this study of IS in Australian universities provided evidence that IS is more like a field than a discipline.

Select bibliography

Bryant A. 2006, *Thinking 'Informatically': A New Understanding of Information Technology, Communications and Technology*, Edwin Mellon Press, Lewiston, New York.

Dixon-Woods, M., Agarwal, S., Jones, D., Young, B. and Sutton, A. 2005, 'Synthesising qualitative and quantitative evidence: a review of possible methods', *Journal of Health Services Research & Policy*, vol. 10, no. 1, pp. 45–53.

Gable, G. 2006, 'The information systems discipline in Australian universities: a contextual framework', *Australasian Journal of Information Systems*, vol. 14, no. 1, pp. 103–22.

Gregor, S. and Jones, D. 2007, 'The anatomy of a design theory', *Journal of the Association of Information Systems*, vol. 8, no. 5, pp. 312–35.

Gregor, S., Lewis, E. and McDonald, C. 2006, 'Case study: the state of information systems in Australian Capital Territory universities', *Australasian Journal of Information Systems*, vol. 14, no. 1, pp. 177–92.

Hevner, A. R., March, S. T., Park, J. and Ram, S. 2004, 'Design science in information systems research', *MIS Quarterly*, vol. 28, no. 1, p. 75.

Marginson, S. and Considine, M. 2000, *The Enterprise University: Power, Governance, and Reinvention in Australia*, Cambridge University Press, Cambridge, UK.

Mingers, J. and Stowell, F. (eds) 1997, *IS: An Emerging Discipline*, McGraw-Hill, London.

Tardif, R. (ed.) 1989, *The Penguin Macquarie Dictionary of Australian Education*, Penguin, Ringwood, Victoria, Australia.

Whitley, R. 1984a, 'The development of management studies as a fragmented adhocracy', *Social Science Information*, vol. 23, no. 4–5, pp. 775–818.

Whitley, R. 1984b, *The Intellectual and Social Organization of the Sciences*, Clarendon Press, Oxford, UK.

Appendix 12.1: analysis of IS research topics by state

Table A12.1 Collated IS research topics reported, by state

Topic	States							Total
Anti-terrorist management			ACT					1
Business intelligence						Qld		1
Business logistics/transport modelling				Tas	WA			2
Business process modelling	Vic			Tas		Qld		3
Compliance monitoring systems					WA			1
Computational intelligence	Vic							1
Conceptual modelling/ontology/relational ontology	Vic		ACT		WA	Qld		4
Data acquisition		SA						1
Data quality		SA				Qld		2
Data warehousing/data mining and informatics	Vic	SA				Qld		3
Databases					WA	Qld		2
Decision support systems/intelligent and collaborative systems	Vic	SA	ACT		WA	Qld	NSW	6
Distributed simulation	Vic							1
E-commerce education	Vic							1
E-commerce/e-business/electronic markets	Vic	SA			WA	Qld		4
E-forensics				Tas		Qld		2
E-government/e-law/legal systems in IS	Vic		ACT		WA			3
E-research			ACT					1
Enterprise resource planning/enterprise systems	Vic					Qld		2
Ethics, privacy and censorship	Vic		ACT					2
Gender and IT	Vic					Qld		2
Grid supercomputing					WA			1
Health informatics	Vic		ACT	Tas	WA	Qld		5
Information management	Vic	SA						2
Interoperability standards		SA						1
IS evaluation					WA			1
IS in the construction industry					WA			1
IS methodologies		SA			WA	Qld		3
IS/IT education/e-learning	Vic	SA	ACT		WA	Qld		5
IS/IT governance	Vic		ACT			Qld		3
IT professional services/consulting						Qld		1
IT sourcing						Qld		1
IT/IS management	Vic				WA	Qld		3
Knowledge management	Vic	SA			WA	Qld		4
Mathematics and statistical analysis	Vic							1
Multimedia						Qld		1
Packaged software						Qld		1
Programming methodology						Qld		1
Project management	Vic		ACT					2
Requirements engineering	Vic					Qld		2
Risk management			ACT					1
Rural IS						Qld		1

Table A12.1 Collated IS research topics reported, by state

Topic	States							Total
Security	Vic	SA		Tas		Qld		4
Semantic webs	Vic							1
Socio-organisational systems/human factors in IS		SA			WA	Qld		3
Soft systems					WA			1
Software engineering/software quality and assurance	Vic					Qld	NSW	3
Strategic IS	Vic		ACT	Tas	WA	Qld		5
Supply-chain management	Vic							1
Systems development	Vic					Qld		2
Systems modelling/simulation						Qld		1
Technology adoption and impact	Vic		ACT		WA			3
Theoretical foundations			ACT					1
Tools for human thinking			ACT				NSW	2
Usability design/human–computer interaction/end-user issues	Vic		ACT			Qld		3
Virtual communities/virtual behaviour			ACT		WA			2
Web services						Qld		1
Workflow						Qld		1

Note: Occurrence recorded for each state, not frequency.

Table A12.2: Frequency and proportion of common IS research topics reported, by state

Proportion of common IS research topics	Count	%
Topics researched in 1 state	27	47
Topics researched in 2 states	13	22
Topics researched in 3 states	10	17
Topics researched in 4 states	4	7
Topics researched in 5 states	3	5
Topics researched in 6 states	1	2
Total topics	**58**	**100**

Table A12.3: Most-popular IS research topics reported in Australian states

Topic	No. of states
Decision support systems/intelligent and collaborative systems	6
Strategic IS	5
IS/IT education/e-learning	5
Health informatics	5
Security	4
Knowledge management	4
E-commerce/e-business/electronic markets	4
Conceptual modelling/ontology/relational ontology	4
Business process modelling	3
Data warehousing/data mining and informatics	3
E-government/e-law/legal systems in IS	3
IS methodologies	3
IS/IT governance	3
IT/IS management	3
Socio-organisational systems/human factors in IS	3
Software engineering/software quality and assurance	3
Technology adoption and impact	3
Usability design/human–computer interaction/end-user issues	3

Note: Occurrence recorded for each state, not frequency.

Glossary of terms

This glossary includes definitions of terms, expressions and acronyms used by chapter authors but warranting explanation for readers from outside Australian information systems (IS) academia. We hope that these definitions will make the chapters more accessible to non-IS readers, and readers outside the region.

It is also recognised that there is a lack of consistency in the terminology employed by universities in Australia (and around the world). For example, the terms 'unit', 'subject' and 'course' can apply to the same entity at different universities. The glossary below also includes brief descriptions for those terms.

Term	Meaning
AAIS	See 'Australasian Chapter of the Association for Information Systems'
ACIS	See 'Australasian Conference on Information Systems'
ACPHIS	See 'Australian Council of Professors and Heads of Information Systems'
ACS	See 'Australian Computer Society'
ACT	The Australian Capital Territory (ACT) is the capital territory of the Commonwealth of Australia. It is home to Australia's national capital, Canberra.
AIS	See 'Association for Information Systems'
AJIS	See '*Australasian Journal of Information Systems*'
ANCCAC	See 'Australian National Committee on Computation and Automatic Control'
ARC	See 'Australian Research Council'
ARC Discovery grant	External competitive funding for research activities obtained by university staff, and awarded by the prestigious Australian Research Council (ARC).
ARC Linkage grant	External competitive funding for research activities undertaken with industry partners, awarded by the prestigious ARC.
Association for Information Systems	The Association for Information Systems (AIS) founded in 1994, is a professional organisation whose purpose is to serve as the premier global organisation for academics specialising in information systems (http://home.aisnet.org/displaycommon.cfm?an=3).
Australasia	In this study, the term Australasia is used to refer to the combination of Australia and New Zealand (though in more common usage, it also includes New Guinea and the islands of the South Pacific Ocean, and sometimes extends to include all of Oceania).
Australasian Chapter of the Association for Information Systems	AAIS is a regional chapter of the Association for Information Systems (AIS). The AIS was founded in 1994 as a world-wide professional organisation for academics in information systems (IS). AAIS began in 2001 to support AIS members working in or with an interest in the Australasian IS community.
Australasian Conference on Information Systems	The Australasian Conference on Information Systems (ACIS) is the premier Australasian conference for information systems academics, covering technical, organisational, industry and social issues in the application of IT to real-world problems. Conferences have been held since 1990.
Australasian Journal of Information Systems	*AJIS* is an international-quality, peer-reviewed journal that publishes articles contributing to information systems theory and practice. It was founded in 1993 and is the academic organ of the Australasian Association for Information Systems (http://dl.acs.org.au/index.php/ajis).
Australian National Committee on Computation and Automatic Control	The Australian National Committee on Computation and Automatic Control (ANCCAC) was formed in 1958. It ran a series of successful computing conferences and represented Australia internationally. In 1969, the ACS replaced ANCCAC as the Australian representative body within IFIP and ANCCAC was dissolved, handing over all its assets to the ACS (http://www.acs.org.au/media/docs/mcli/ACSfinal.pdf).

Term	Meaning
Australian Computer Society	ACS is the recognised association for information and communications technology (ICT) professionals in Australia, attracting a large and active membership from all levels of the ICT industry. A member of the Australian Council of Professions, the ACS is the public voice of the ICT profession and the guardian of professional ethics and standards in the ICT industry, with a commitment to the wider community to ensure the beneficial use of ICT (http://www.acs.org.au/index.cfm?action = show&conID = aboutacs).
Australian Council of Professors and Heads of Information Systems	ACPHIS is the peak body established to represent Australian information systems academics in matters of national and international importance (http://www.acphis.org.au/).
Australian Research Council	The Australian Research Council (ARC) is the main advisor to the government on research policy and the allocation of funding to support research. Its core responsibility is to develop and maintain a broad foundation of high-quality, internationally competitive research across a range of disciplines (http://www.dest.gov.au/archive/highered/otherpub/greenpaper/chapt8.htm).
CAIS	See 'Communications of the Association for Information Systems'
College of Experts	The College of Experts members assess and rank ARC grant applications submitted under the National Competitive Grants Program, make funding recommendations to the ARC and provide strategic advice to the ARC on emerging disciplines and cross-disciplinary developments. Its members are experts of international standing drawn from the Australian research community: from higher education, industry and public-sector research organisations. College of Experts members are approved by the minister for appointment of periods of between one and three years (http://www.arc.gov.au/about_arc/expert.htm).
Communications of the Association for Information Systems	The primary role of a professional society is to facilitate communications among its members. The journal Communications of the Association for Information Systems carries out this role for the AIS by publishing articles on a wide range of subjects of interest to the membership (http://cais.isworld.org/).
Core body of knowledge	The core body of knowledge or the knowledge base for information systems covers research and teaching methods and standards, a unique symbol set, key research and teaching topics (knowledge topics) and laws, rules and evidenced guidelines (knowledge types).
Course	The term 'course' varies in meaning from place to place (for example, in many places this term is used to refer to a subject, while in other places it refers to a degree program). Within this book, the term refers to a complete body of prescribed studies. It is a coherent set of units that leads to the granting of an award registered by the university—for example, BA (Bachelor of Arts) is a course; PYB205 Social Psychology is a unit within that course.
Dawkins reforms	A series of Australian tertiary education reforms instituted by John Dawkins, the Education Minister (1987–92). The reforms were aimed at improving the efficiency and international competitiveness of Australian universities. These reforms included the introduction of the Higher Education Contribution Scheme (HECS), the conversion of all colleges of advanced education (CAEs) into universities and a series of provisions for universities to provide plans, profiles, statistics and so on to justify courses and research (http://en.wikipedia.org/wiki/Dawkins_Revolution).
Degree of professionalism	In professionalised disciplines, activities are routinised and there is high task certainty and division of labour. Disciplines that are not highly professionalised, however, have high task uncertainty, decentralised control of work process and limited routinisation of tasks; derived from Whitley (1984b).
DIMIA requirements	The requirements of the Department of Immigration and Multicultural and Indigenous Affairs (DIMIA), as they impact on the entry and stay of information systems students.
ECIS	European Conference on Information Systems
EFTSU	An abbreviation used in Australia to denote equivalent full-time student unit.
GITMA	Global Information Technology Association World Conference
HECS	The Higher Education Contribution Scheme (HECS) is a charge that eligible domestic students are liable to pay towards the cost of their university tuition. Contributions are deferrable and can be made through the taxation system once income rises above a certain threshold.
HICSS	Hawaii International Conference on Information Systems
Impact of local contingencies	The effect of local events and conditions.

Term	Meaning
Information systems	Note that wherever we refer to 'IS', unless a more specific explanation is provided, we mean the 'information systems academic discipline' inclusive of research and teaching.
Information Systems Board	A board of the Australian Computer Society (http://www.acs.org.au/index.cfm?action = show&conID = acsis).
Institutional Research Grants Scheme	A research funding grant scheme awarded internally within a university that offers modest amounts of money for research projects, designed to train researchers to obtain ARC funding.
IRMA	Information Resources Management Association conference
IS	See 'Information systems'
IS'95	Guidelines for information systems (IS) undergraduate IS curriculum published in *MIS Quarterly* September 1995.
IS-in-Oz	An abbreviation for 'IS in Australia'
IS-in-PA	An abbreviation for 'IS in the Pacific Asia Region'.
Key research and teaching topics	The information systems (IS) knowledge domain; these are the important knowledge topics for IS that cover teaching and research areas.
Laws, rules and evidenced guidelines	Different forms of theory that cover the spectrum from formal theory to guidelines used by practitioners.
Mechanisms of control	The social mechanisms that create a discipline, including journals, conferences and academic departments.
Meta-analysis	A closing article reflects analysis across all study evidence, including the multiple states case study, and any sub-studies.
Methodological action research	Methodological action research (MAR) refers to an action-research approach to studying the process of research; it is a reflexive process of progressive problem solving led by individual researchers, possibly working with others in a team, to improve the way they address research issues and solve research problems. MAR is conducted above and behind the main research activity, with the researcher, on this second level, observing themselves (and their team) and their experience of the research process, the intent being to better understand and improve that process and to document related methodological learning.
Nelson reforms	The reform package of then education minister Dr Brendan Nelson, which passed the Senate in 2003, introduced a series of radical changes to Australia's higher education system, simultaneously imposing more direct government control over the management of universities while allowing them to earn more revenue by charging higher fees to students. It permitted the introduction of Domestic Undergraduate Up-Front Fees (DUFF) by universities in addition to HECS places, and allowed universities to increase their HECS rates by 25 per cent (http://en.wikipedia.org/wiki/National_Union_of_Students_of_Australia).
Oracle certification	Credentials offered by the software company Oracle Corporation, which are recognised by industry.
PA	See 'Pacific Asia'
Pacific Asia	The AIS (see 'AIS') recognises in its governance structure three international regions, representing: 1) the Americas; 2) Europe, the Middle East and Africa; and 3) Asia and the Pacific. The third region is often referred to as Region 3 or Pacific Asia. Each region has two regional representatives on the council and a president of the association is chosen from a particular region on a rotating basis.
Pacific Asia Conference on Information Systems	PACIS is the conference recognised by the AIS as its Asia-Pacific regional conference (Region 3).
PACIS	See 'Pacific Asia Conference on Information Systems'
RFID	Radio Frequency Identification Technology
Region 3	See 'Pacific Asia'

Term	Meaning
Research Quality Framework	The Research Quality Framework (RQF) was a 2004 Australian government initiative intended to 'provide a consistent and comprehensive approach to assessing publicly funded research', which would 'encourage researchers and research organisations to focus on the quality and impact of their research' (http://www.dest.gov.au/sectors/research_sector/policies_issues_ reviews/key_issues/research_quality_framework/issues_paper.htm). In December 2007, the new Rudd government announced that it would cease implementation of the RQF and would implement a new approach to research quality assurance.
Research and teaching methods and standards	The methods and standards that are accepted in a discipline—for teaching and research (that is, knowledge gain plus knowledge transfer).
Research Fields, Courses and Disciplines (RFCD) classification	A classification scheme of the ARC that is intended to allow research and development activity and other activity within the higher education sector to be categorised. The categories in the classification include recognised academic disciplines and related major sub-fields taught at universities or tertiary institutions, major fields of research investigated by national research institutions and organisations and emerging areas of study (http://www.arc.gov.au/applicants/codes.htm#RFCD).
RFCD	See 'Research Fields, Courses and Disciplines classification'
Service teaching	Delivering information systems (IS) teaching at a university to students enrolled in a non-IS program.
SMEs	Small and medium-sized enterprises
State report	The main report produced from the state case study.
Subject	See 'Unit'
Sub-study	Refers to each of the component studies of the IS-in-Oz (or IS-in-PA) studies, including the retrospective, the framework, the information systems research survey and each of the state case studies.
Thematic analysis	Analysis of themes that emerge from textual data.
Unique symbol set	The existence of a dedicated and accepted symbol system for a discipline.
Unit	A unit is a coherent set of learning activities (including lectures, tutorials and workshops), which is assigned a unit code. A unit is usually taught across a semester. Many universities adopt the term 'subject' rather than 'unit'.
Vignette	In this context, a short biography of an academic who is significant to the information systems discipline in a particular region.
Intrastate reviewer	An individual with special knowledge of the information systems (IS) academic discipline in a given state, who offers critical comment on draft reports of the IS discipline in that state.

www.ingramcontent.com/pod-product-compliance
Lightning Source LLC
LaVergne TN
LVHW071357070326
832902LV00028B/4628